Leadership

Second Edition

Leadership
A Critical Text

by Simon Western

Los Angeles | London | New Delhi
Singapore | Washington DC

Dedication

I dedicate this book to Fynn, who continues to inspire me
and who I miss so much.

Also to Agata, with big love and huge thanks for the joy shared,
encouragement and support during the writing of this book. This book will
always evoke such happy memories of writing and walking in the woods
and hillsides around Krynica, Poland, summer 2012.

To all friends and colleagues who share my journey.

To all I work with. My consulting and coaching work gives me privileged
access to engage with people at all levels in organizations, who share with
me their strengths, vulnerabilities and struggles. I work in diverse spaces
and places, where I observe, listen and intervene, learning and feeding my
insatiable curiosity, and putting theory into practice, and practice into
theory. This book could not be written without their full engagement.
Thank you all.

Finally, to distributed leaders everywhere, often unrecognized and
unacknowledged, who share the ethos of this book; striving for emancipation
and to create a better world.

SAGE

Los Angeles | London | New Delhi
Singapore | Washington DC

SAGE Publications Ltd
1 Oliver's Yard
55 City Road
London EC1Y 1SP

SAGE Publications Inc.
2455 Teller Road
Thousand Oaks, California 91320

SAGE Publications India Pvt Ltd
B 1/I 1 Mohan Cooperative Industrial Area
Mathura Road
New Delhi 110 044

SAGE Publications Asia-Pacific Pte Ltd
3 Church Street
#10-04 Samsung Hub
Singapore 049483

Editor: Kirsty Smy
Editorial assistant: Nina Smith
Production editor: Sarah Cooke
Copyeditor: Elaine Leek
Proofreader: Audrey Scriven
Indexer: Judith Lavender
Marketing manager: Alison Borg
Cover design: Lisa Harper
Typeset by: C&M Digitals (P) Ltd, Chennai, India
Printed and bound by
CPI Group (UK) Ltd, Croydon, CR0 4YY

MIX
Paper from
responsible sources
FSC
www.fsc.org   FSC® C013604

All photographs by the author
Artwork at beginning of discourse chapters by Maia Kirchkheli
All other graphic design by Martyna Adamska

Library of Congress Control Number: 2012954157

British Library Cataloguing in Publication data

A catalogue record for this book is available from the British Library

ISBN 978-1-4462-6989-3
ISBN 978-1-4462-6990-9 (pbk)

Contents

List of Boxes

List of Figures

About the Author

Dr Simon Western
Director of Analytic-Network Coaching Ltd. (A-Nc Ltd)
Coaching leaders to act in 'Good faith' to build the 'Good society'
www.simonwestern.com
Simon@analyticnetwork.com

Simon formed A-Nc Ltd to address the organizational and leadership challenges outlined in this book. He works strategically with CEOs and leadership teams in complex environments, such as banks and hospital eco-systems to implement whole-system changes. A-Nc Ltd has developed accessible and effective OD change processes, delivered through distributed leadership networks, whilst working with strategic coaching to CEOs and senior teams. This dual approach recognizes the need for alignment and full engagement between senior leaders and employees throughout the organization, to create dynamic and sustainable change.

Recent Clients include London Business School, Global OD Team HSBC Bank, CEO of international bank, CEO and leadership teams in the NHS, Educational sector, not-for-profit organizations and SMEs.

Background

Simon draws on an unusually diverse and rich work experience, having previously worked in a factory, as a general and psychiatric nurse, psychotherapist and Family Therapist, a clinical NHS manager, organizational consultant, executive coach, academic and company director.

Academia and Teaching

Simon has a pedigree of international teaching, key note speaking and publishing on leadership and coaching (see *Coaching and Mentoring: A Critical*

Text, Sage, 2012). He has taught at leading business schools and led Masters programmes; previous roles include: Director of Coaching, Lancaster University Management School; Director of Masters in Organizational Consultancy, (psychoanalytic approaches) The Tavistock Clinic. He draws on cross-disciplinary theory i.e. psychoanalysis and family systems theory, leadership and organizational theory, social movement theory, religious studies and environmentalism. Simon takes a psychosocial, critical and emancipatory perspective to develop ideas such as Eco-leadership, that address ethical and business concerns in today's 'network society'.

Positions

- Honorary Teaching Fellow at Lancaster University Management School

- Honorary Associate Fellow Department of Psychosocial Studies, Birkbeck University

- Senior Fellow Birmingham University, Health Service Management Centre

- Associate Tavistock Institute

- Associate Tutor: Woodbrooke Quaker Study Centre

- Member: ISPSO

Introduction

Leadership is everywhere: it has a dominant and privileged place in our society; it is constantly in our news, politics, businesses, films, books and magazines. Leadership is part of our social narrative, predominantly as a mythological force of goodness and success.

A key aim of this book is to *deconstruct leadership*, to challenge over-simplified accounts of leadership that may be desirable and offer us the comfort of 'messiahs' who can save us, but that actually distort leadership in unhelpful ways. Another aim is to *reconstruct leadership*, to offer new accounts of leadership for new times.

This book provides an accessible critical perspective that is relevant both to those studying leadership and to practising leaders. Critical theory can be off-putting for practical implementation due to elitist academic language, and the gap between 'cloistered academia' and the world of work (Parker, 2002; Stookey, 2008). I am convinced that critical theory is vital to help leaders create more humane workplaces, a better society and an environmentally sustainable world. Emancipatory ethics are at the core of this book, with the hope that it contributes to help leaders develop the capability of rethinking organizational purpose and reimagining how work can be organized.

In recent years, leadership has challenged the dominance of managerialism in our business schools and organizations. We aspire to have creative and inspiring leaders who will bring success, rather than bureaucratic managers who cannot adapt to the brave new world of globalization and the networked society (Castells, 2000). Leadership is a contemporary holy grail: ambitious individuals want to be successful leaders, companies want to hire exceptional leaders and people want to be led by great leaders. Yet leadership is slippery, hard to get hold of, and what is usually 'sold' as leadership is very limited and partial. The paradox is this; whilst leadership is everywhere, the leadership espoused is unattainable to most, it is an elitist, individualized and idealized form of leadership that sits at the top of organizations, with CEOs, presidents and prime ministers. Recently, moves have been made to teach leadership to the masses, but it is usually reduced to become a set of trainable competencies and, unfortunately, when leadership is broken down into component parts, leadership itself is lost as it disappears into a mist of words, a set of behaviours that people mimic or learn, and this is not leadership.

I believe that leadership is everywhere, but that it mostly goes unrecognized, is misunderstood, and, worse, it is constrained and limited by social forces that reproduce power elites rather than help generate genuine leadership. The leadership we see is limited to a few celebrity or powerful individual leaders, and it is they who are seen everywhere, not leadership itself.

To face the growing social, economic and environmental challenges of our times, leadership needs to be rethought. The shape of leadership needs to change from a hierarchical pyramid, with leaders at the pinnacle and followers beneath, to a network where leadership and followership work fluidly, interchangeably, as a network of actors.

This book takes a critical stance to explore leadership, in order to promote ethical, and dynamic forms, fit for 21st century organizations. Drawing on diverse theory, leadership is examined from a psychosocial perspective to reveal the underlying dynamics that shape and constrain leadership practice. A critical perspective reveals hidden power dynamics that shape leadership and followership, and utilizing four different discourses, shows how different forms of leadership influence and control employees.

Common perceptions of leaders are of charismatic extroverts, great speakers, motivational characters, for example; however, as psychoanalysis reveals, overly confident leaders often live with dissonance, masking hidden insecurities (Kets de Vries, 2006). When coaching senior leaders, the 'coaching confessional' (Western, 2012) reveals how leaders who are seen by others as ultra confident, often reveal anxieties such as imposter syndromes, and other personal anxieties about their role and performance.

Messiah leaders (Chapter 11) offer a seductive mirage of power and influence, yet real influence and power are much more dispersed and complex. Leadership moves quietly and fluently, distributed amongst many, and often appears so discreetly that it is hardly noticed – yet this is how change takes place. Leadership is not boundaried, it accompanies, complements and merges with other relational interactions of followership, teamwork, collaboration and participation. The book explores how other dimensions of leadership appear when looking from different perspectives, for example, Chapter 4 describes 'autonomist leadership', a non-hierarchical form that is determined by *spontaneity*, *autonomy* and *mutuality*, often found in new social movements such as the Occupy movement, and Chapter 12 explores the relatively new form, Eco-Leadership Discourse, capturing contemporary forms of leadership emerging in our new zeitgeist.

Locating Ourselves

When coaching leaders I use an exercise called 'locating ourselves', based on the notion that all leadership is biographical, and here I offer a brief biographical account of my working life. I write as a practitioner–scholar drawing on an unusual breadth of workplace experience. My experiences of leadership and followership in a wide variety of settings (see Box 1) have informed this book, and the ideas presented here emerge from the messiness of real work, rather than from the tidiness of academic ideals. My recent work as an executive coach and organizational consultant using psychosocial methods has also given me unusual and privileged access to the psychological, social and emotional experiences of leaders.

Box 1 offers a brief summary of my work experiences, where I 'locate myself' to reveal how I formed my own leadership views and to provide a context for this book. Contextualizing leadership in the social world is a key theme throughout, and I hope my own reflections will stimulate readers and leaders to reflect on how their experiences have shaped their leadership approaches and views.

Box 1   What Authored the Author?

I left school with few qualifications and a very poor education, and began work at the age of 17 as an office boy in a factory, witnessing 'scientific management' techniques on production lines. Unionized labour, clocking in and out, women spending all day packing paper bags which tumbled off loud, clattering machines, men labouring to keep the machines going 24 hours a day, feeding them with heavy rolls of paper and ink, this mundane work (now exported to Asia) was brutalizing. I remember tough men and women, with a fierce humour to cope. Factory work was manual labour, the employer bought the labourer's time and body. Emotions and thinking were to be left at home.

Encouraged by a nursing friend, I left the factory at the age of 18 to train as a general nurse. Nurses work intimately with the physical body. Touching and cleaning, injecting, lifting and turning, administering drugs, dressing wounds, evacuating bowels, the nurse works with the inside and outside, and the living and dead body. Working with the injured, sick and dying made me acutely aware of the existential issues of mortality, and how important our emotions, thinking and identities are embodied. Later in my work in offices and universities, I reflected on how the body is largely ignored and marginalized. I worked

(Continued)

(Continued)

long nursing shifts experiencing the primitive human emotions of fear and anxiety when facing mortal threats. The leadership context was a rigid matriarchal nursing system that had echoes of the military, a commander in chief (the matron) with uniforms denoting rank, strict authority, no first names on the ward. The hospital-organization was structured as a social defence against facing the emotional pain of working with illness and death (Menzies Lyth, 1960). Nurses didn't talk about their feelings, and many patients were cared for physically but not emotionally. No counselling occurred after having worked with a traumatic death, just an early coffee break and gallows humour in the bar after work. I loved the work, made great friends, learnt huge amounts about life and myself, but struggled in this constraining institutional culture. Nursing leadership was predominantly female, from ward sister to hospital matron, in opposition to the medical leadership, which was predominantly male. This dual leadership created a symbolic structure replicating a 'hetero-normative' parental structure – father leading with technical expertise, mother being the carer.[1] This raised my awareness of gender issues, of power, responsibility, and of pay disparity. I was a male on the female team and often in life have found myself in the position of experiencing 'otherness' from a very close proximity.

Within this archetypal parental leadership model, Daddy Doctor and Mummy Nurse, the patients were symbolically childlike in their dependency. When a patient is facing major surgery or death, the contemporary rhetoric of individual choice, and the omnipotence of our desire to be in control, is confronted by Freud's 'reality principle'. For some patients the dependency culture was wholly appropriate, enabling them to give up their autonomy to enable the surgeon's knife to be wielded, and to be bed-bathed, toileted and cared for like an infant. For others in rehabilitation, the dependency culture was completely wrong and hindered their attempts to regain autonomy. Dependency cultures have a place in some organizations; in education for example, learning requires us to enter a state of 'not-knowing' (if we know already we cannot learn something new) and therefore a level of dependency is required in order to learn (Obholzer and Roberts, 1994; Western, 2005). In the hospital, this dependency culture unfortunately affected the staff as well as patients, and became very damaging, undermining innovation and autonomous decision-making. Since this time I have been alerted to issues of too much dependency and a lack of autonomy in the workplace.

During this period I was a skilled rugby player and captained my local club, experiencing leadership at an early age. Rugby provided me with the

---

[1] This is not to paint the stereotypical gendered picture of female nurses as caring angels, which draws on the essentialist rhetoric that women are naturally more humane and emotionally literate leaders than men (see Chapter 5). Scandals of cruel leadership in 'caring' institutions such as hospitals, monasteries and convents reveals that caring or harsh leadership behaviour is less gender specific, and more closely linked to perverse organizational cultures.

opportunity to learn motivational skills, experience teamwork, and it was probably the most honest and egalitarian community I ever participated in. Our club consisted of lawyers, entrepreneurs, business leaders, the unemployed, ex-convicts, and all were treated with respect. Anybody pulling ego or rank over another was teased mercilessly; it was a levelling experience. Teamwork, having the courage to have a go, and being able to laugh at myself were lessons I took from leading the rugby club.

Whilst doing general nursing I became fascinated by the human condition, and after running a geriatric ward I left to train as a psychiatric nurse. I found freedom in a more relaxed, uniform-free setting, and became totally engaged in the human psychology, discovering a life-long passion for psychotherapy and the 'talking cure'. I worked with the severely mentally ill: obsessive, neurotic, depressed, schizophrenic and psychotic patients in Victorian built asylums, which Goffman (1961) describes as Total Institutions. I witnessed electro-convulsive therapy and worked on some wards where 70 men slept in long dorms without curtains or any privacy. The system of 'token economy', a behaviour treatment, was used with the institutionalized patients. Patients received tokens which were exchanged for cigarettes to reinforce good behaviours, for example for getting out of bed, and they had tokens taken away for 'bad behaviour'. Institutionalization had an impact on both staff and patients (sometimes it was hard to tell the difference), and the concept of the asylum and the totalizing institution has stayed with me. The asylum had two aspects: while firstly it provided 'asylum', i.e. a container, a safe and caring space, a refuge from the terrors of the world, on the other hand it was an oppressive and totalizing space. When working in corporations and large public sector organizations I am often reminded of the asylum, seeing the token economy and the institutional culture control that I witnessed but in a more benign, hidden form.

When I see HR teams, managers and trainers using transactional leadership, 'carrot and stick' to change behaviour, I wonder about the humanity of their methods. When transformational leaders draw on culture control, and I see conformist employees, in their dark suited uniforms, sitting in rows upon rows in a open office, institutionally eating in the canteen together, I see a modern day asylum. I will never forget this formative experience, which alerts me to ethics and the power of institutionalization. Humanizing organizations is a passion, and I ask myself at work, 'Does this leadership stance enhance or diminish humanity?' Other important lessons were discovering how thin and blurred the line is between madness and sanity, and this has helped me work with some of the undiagnosed pathology that occurs in the workplace. I also learnt counselling skills, group facilitation skills and, most importantly, how to manage my own and others' anxiety when facing dangerous disturbance and distress.

At the age of 23 I became a Charge Nurse, leading a regional residential unit for emotionally disturbed adolescents. This was run as a therapeutic

(Continued)

(Continued)

community with the philosophy to devolve leadership to the young people themselves, empowering them to find their voices and to learn how to take responsibility for themselves and others, through experimenting in a safe environment. I was given a huge amount of responsibility at a very young age, working with young people who had serious problems such as anorexia, who were suicidal and who were abused. Working closely with the staff team, we radicalized the unit to make it fully self-catering, and the medical input was marginalized, removing the dependency culture and the stigma of being given a medical diagnosis and treated as a patient. This was the most thera-peutic environment I have experienced and I learnt two key lessons here. First, my idealism that if you remove leadership, power will be removed and pure democracy will flourish was crushed. Actually, chaos and fear flourish. Secondly, devolving power and decision-making responsibly, and enabling dispersed leadership within safe boundaries, works wonderfully. Our so-called 'disturbed' young people were able to run the unit, making important decisions together and working on their emotional selves at the same time. They helped us to interview and appoint new staff, took control over their own destinies and supported their peers with great skill and empathy. This experimental community, set in the NHS, marginalized the medical model and gave power back to the client group. I am indebted to this intense learning experience, and to Mike Broughton, who was an excellent leader and the first to help me realize my own leadership potential. The core of this work was family therapy, group and drama therapy.

In my mid-20s I spent three years as a single parent on welfare, and again found myself challenging gender stereotypes, wandering into mother and toddler groups and struggling with the responses I received. Sometimes I was mothered (which I rejected) and at other times I was considered a threat to the group norm, an external male body to be ejected. However, I loved the freedom of being a home-parent, each day being thrown back to my own resources to make ends meet and creating each day with my beautiful and delightful son, Fynn. Living on the margins in terms of money, and without the identity/respect work gives you, I was nevertheless immensely happy as a father, making fires, stories and pancakes – this was a time of adventures!

On returning to work I spent ten years training and working as a family therapist and psychotherapist with the urban underclass, in a deprived northern city. I was a clinical manager of a community-based, multi-professional health-care team. I loved family therapy, and took the opportunity to be immensely creative in therapy sessions. In family therapy you quickly discover (a) that power is not where you (or the family) think it is, (b) how systems impact on individuals and (c) how patterns of communication completely entrap us, even if we really want to change. This learning has hugely influenced my leadership work since.

In my 30s I decided to get educated and studied for a Master's in Counselling at Keele University, and felt exposed and overwhelmed by the academic language, rituals and culture which made me feel inadequate and an imposter (not having A-levels or a Bachelor's Degree). I adjusted and found great joy in learning and excelled in my studies.

Later I studied for another Master's degree, in Psychoanalytic Approaches to Organizational Consultancy, at the internationally renowned Tavistock Centre. My interest was to understand why change was so resisted and to promote collaborative working across health, education and social services in order to better serve families. Developing an understanding of the unconscious processes that underpin organizational culture was a huge learning experience for me, which I have applied in my work ever since.

I finally left the NHS, feeling 'burnt out' from the pressure of working with disturbed families and suicidal teenagers in an under-resourced provision. I was frustrated by a leadership dominated by the hegemony of medical power, which allowed little room for constructive dissent and change, particularly if it came from a nurse. The medical model provided the wrong leadership, wrong culture and wrong treatment for this client group. For the most part my clients were not ill but suffered from the emotional and social strains of living in poverty and unemployment. They required therapeutic and emotional support, more resources and structural-political change rather than a medical diagnosis, labels and medicines. My attempts to make changes were partly successful, and more collaborative work now takes place. However the NHS has an institutional leadership culture that allows little room for innovation or creativity, and it was time for me to break out of this institution.

In the past decade I also worked with real estate, working closely with the building trade observing how the leadership is transient, moving between trades on the same building job. The building trade is interesting as it is both highly competitive with a harsh culture and wholly dependent on collaboration. Designing and altering physical spaces is a passion of mine, which I apply to my consultancy work, helping leaders to think like organizational architects.

Another experience, which has informed my understanding of leadership and organizational culture, is my religious affiliation. I have been a Quaker (Religious Society of Friends) for fifteen years, which has an unusual organizational structure without a formal leadership. It does not appoint church ministers but believes in a 'priesthood of all believers' abolishing *not* the idea of priests but abolishing the laity. The business meetings are run (and have been for 350 years) by spiritual consensus, which can mean up to 1,000 Quakers at a yearly meeting deciding on Quaker 'policy' (www.quaker.org. uk). Quaker meetings are structured around the idea of equality. Sitting in a circle, in silence, anyone moved to speak can 'minister' to those present. The Quaker history was an important part of my PhD research, leading me to examine how their informal leadership and organization have changed over the centuries to accommodate social change, while still holding onto the central experience and structures. My experience of leadership has been

(Continued)

(Continued)

further informed by engaging with social movements; trade unions, feminist, anarchist, and green activist movements.

Frustrated by being a nurse, a clinical manager in the NHS, and a little burnt out by the intense therapeutic work, I decided to seek pastures new and wanted to experience corporate life and the private sector. I entered a university business school to study for a PhD in leadership and quickly found employment working in leadership development and executive education. Academia I found is underpinned by a dependency culture that replicates educational models of teacher–student dynamics, and tends towards a bureaucratic managerialism. However, it also has an adolescent rebellious nature, maybe due to very bright individuals, expert in their own fields, resisting external control, and maybe because it employs adults, many of whom just never left school!

At Lancaster University's management school I suddenly found myself working with very senior corporate leaders internationally designing and offering coaching and experiential learning. The cultural difference and the language of the corporate world was a huge learning curve for me. A big adjustment took place from working with the poor, disempowered and disturbed, to working with the rich, successful and powerful. My saving grace was the capacity I had developed to 'think in the face of anxiety' and draw on my past experience to work in depth with these executives.

I was later appointed Director of Coaching at Lancaster, where I established a critical approach to coaching drawing heavily on psychoanalytic and systems thinking. I also designed and ran a new postgraduate coaching course (see *Coaching and Mentoring: A Critical Text*, Sage, 2012). After ten years of executive education, I left to work as an organizational consultant and direct a Master's Degree in Organizational Consultancy at the Tavistock Clinic, and later chose to work independently setting up a new coaching and consulting company specializing in leadership.

As a practitioner–scholar, I continue to write and deliver training and keynotes at universities and conferences, coaching and consulting a delightfully interesting and diverse client group. I deliver Eco-leadership interventions, and coach chief executives and senior leadership teams from global banks and top business schools. I also work with hospitals, hospices and small companies. Running a small business is interesting and extremely liberating, and I love the autonomy. I spend a lot of time developing my writing, and publishing. My journey highlights a movement from working with the body (in the factory and as a nurse) to working with the mind (as a psychiatric nurse and therapist), the individual and small group (as a family psychotherapist), then with organizational systems (as an organizational consultant), and finally with the social through engaging with academia, and taking political and philosophical positions.

Leadership crosses all of these dimensions, body, mind, individual, team, organization and social, and this book emanates from the culmination of my lived experience.

This introduction will now offer an overview of the book's structure before summarizing how practitioners, students and course leaders can use this book.

Structure of the Book

This second edition of the book has enabled me to restructure it in order to make the content more accessible, and to add new materials and new chapters on culture and Eco-leadership. I have divided the book into two parts.

Part One: Deconstructing Leadership

Part One undertakes the task of deconstructing leadership, offering a polemic critique of key issues. A deconstruction of normative assumptions is necessary to reveal the illusions and distortion of what leadership is and how it is portrayed, perceived and practised. The deconstruction of over-simple leadership formulations reveal nuanced and plural explanations, that enable a more realistic and useful reconstruction of leadership to take place.

Part Two: Reconstructing Leadership

Part Two reconstructs leadership, putting leadership back together using the learning from Part One. Critics of post-structuralism and deconstruction claim that it can lead to nihilism and extreme relativism, that it is easier to pull things apart than offer new theory and explanations to help understand and improve leadership practice. Part Two addresses this criticism by offering new theory and explanations of how four dominant discourses of leadership have emerged in the past century. These discourses are informed by historical, social and economic influences alongside changing work practices. The discourses help to explain what underpins leadership thinking, offering theory to explain how leadership is practised and why tensions and resistances occur when leaders try to implement organizational change. Finally, a chapter on leadership formation offers a different perspective on how leadership (as opposed to leaders) can be developed.

Using This Book

This book has been written to take the reader on a journey; beginning by establishing methodologies and theory to critique leadership, then setting out some of the key debates about leadership, before introducing a historical and social review that reveals how leadership is thought about and enacted today.

The book addresses three reader groups.

1. Practitioners

This book is an academic text written with practitioners in mind. Part One can be used as a reference point for practising leaders who wish to develop a deeper understanding of the complexities of leadership. Part Two is especially useful to managers and leaders, as it offers insights into their own leadership approach, and that of their organization, and can guide leadership development and leadership approaches. Chapter 13 provides a useful overview and summary of the discourses, and Chapter 14, Leadership Formation, will help practising leaders and managers to rethink leadership development in their organizations, and how to promote inexpensive yet effective ways to distribute leadership.

2. Students

This book offers a thoughtful counter-balance to the multitude of positivist and individualistic leadership approaches you will encounter when studying leadership. If you are being asked to critique leadership, or find yourself questioning the dominant approaches of leadership, then this book is for you.

3. Course leaders

This book can be used in three ways by course leaders:

(a) As a supplementary text for lectures/courses on leadership.

(b) To structure an entire leadership course.

(c) Part Two can be used as an heuristic tool for managers and leaders in executive education, to examine and guide their leadership practice (a web-based discourse analysis tool can support this process (www.simonwestern.com).

At the end of each chapter are Suggested Readings and Reflection Points, with a sample question that can be used for an essay/assignment or exam question. Box 2 offers a brief example of how to use this text for teaching and training.

Box 2 Using This Book for Teaching and Training

Part One

The content and structure of Part One provide the basis for a stand-alone course with the suggested title Understanding Leadership, or Critical Approaches to Leadership. Each chapter also provides separate lectures, as below.

Chapter 1 Why A Critical Approach to Leadership?

Individual Lecture: Setting out a clear and accessible methodology for critical approaches.

Chapter 2 What Is Leadership?

Individual Lecture: Offers a comprehensive review of the ideas and meanings of leadership.

Chapter 3 Asymmetric Leadership

Individual Lecture: Provides a short case study showing how multilayered and plural leadership is.

Chapter 4 Against Leadership: Autonomist Leadership

Individual Lecture: Questioning the accepted norms of leadership, discussing power and leadership, and leaderless groups, and offering new perspectives on autonomist leadership.

Chapter 5 Leadership and Diversity

Individual Lecture: Insights into diversity, difference and leadership.

Chapter 6 Leadership and Culture

Individual Lecture: Exploring organizational culture and how culture forms leaders, as much as leaders form cultures.

Chapter 7 Corporate Fundamentalism

Individual Lecture: To show how social phenomena impact on organizational cultures, and how leadership can create totalizing organizational cultures (this can be taught with Messiah leadership, Chapter 11).

(Continued)

(Continued)

Part Two

The content of Part Two can be offered as a stand-alone course with the suggested titles:

(a) Social Influences on Leadership

(b) The Four Discourses of Leadership

A course can be structured thus:

Social and historical influences on how leadership ideas have formed and been enacted over the past century

How leadership today is influenced by the four discourses

Eco-leadership – the future for leadership: systemic and networked approaches

Applications to practice: what discourses are working in you and your organization?

Three chapters from Part Two can be used for individual lectures:

Chapter 12 Eco-Leadership

Individual Lecture: A separate lecture on the future of leadership, and systemic and networked approaches.

Chapter 13 An Overview of the Leadership Discourses

Individual Lecture: A brief summary and overview of the leadership discourses that inform practice today.

Chapter 14 Leadership Formation: Creating Spaces for Leadership to Flourish

Individual Lecture: Offering a short critique of leadership development and proposing a more holistic approach aimed to develop and generate leadership rather than leaders.

Part One
Deconstructing Leadership

1   Why a Critical Theory Approach to Leadership?

> **Chapter Structure**
>
> - Introduction
> - Critical Thinking and Critical Theory (CT)
> - Why Critical Theory Is Marginalized
> - A Critical Framework: Four Frames of Critical Inquiry
> - Conclusion: Critical Theory and Leadership

Introduction

This book takes a critical theory (CT) approach to leadership for four core reasons:

1 To establish a critical theoretical framework, supporting an individual's process of inquiry into the theory and practice of leadership.

2 To contribute an accessible critical account of leadership, challenging 'taken-for-granted' (normative) assumptions and offering new insights into the underlying discourses and dynamics of leadership.

3 To contribute to the task of improving and rethinking leadership practice, taking into account contemporary social change, to benefit our organizations and institutions.

4 To situate leadership within an ethical and emancipatory framework, with the greater aim of creating the 'Good Society'.

Critical theoretical approaches work in two ways, the first being to scrutinize leadership, to offer an analysis of the deeper, less obvious ways in which leadership is theorized, practised and utilized to attain organizational aims. Secondly, CT has progressive intentions: it aims to create a better society by rethinking, rediscovering and reinventing leadership; bringing new theoretical resources to the challenges revealed through its critique. Critical theory can sometimes veer towards the first aspect, the scrutiny and deconstruction, with too little attention given to the reconstruction and rethinking of leadership. To be critical in popular terms has inferences of being negative, and in academia, where critical takes a different meaning, critiquing and applying critical theory can easily become focused on finding the flaws and revealing the oppressive forces within mainstream leadership. Adler et al. (2007: 14) write, 'As with most counter-movements, CMS[1] proponents have been more articulate about what they are against than what they are for'. Critical theory then becomes a pathologizing activity rather than an emancipatory theory. This book is firmly placed in the emancipatory camp of critical theory, believing that critique is important when used to promote a progressive agenda, or, as Cunliffe (2008: 937) writes, 'I believe the central thread is our interest in the *critique* of contemporary forms of knowledge, social and institutional processes and in generating *radical alternatives*'. To repeat Marx's famous quote in his 'Theses on Feuerbach': 'The philosophers have only interpreted the world, the point is to change it' (Marx, 1845/1978: 45).

CT is a diverse body, as I will explore later. Some believe that only a radical critique is worthwhile, and that attempting to improve the workplace through a reformist agenda is 'selling out' to a capitalist system that is inherently unfair. This polarization of views strikes me as dualistic thinking that critical scholars themselves condemn. The CT task is both a progressive *and* a radical agenda. A reformist engagement with contemporary managers and leaders achieves two things; firstly it can improve the situation on the ground (micro-emancipation); secondly it can work towards structural and radical change (macro-emancipation) by (a) educating and engaging practitioners in new possibilities beyond their current vision, thereby building a greater consensus for more radical possibilities of change, and (b) reformist engagement can also be used by critical theorists as action-research, to better understand the system in order to work out what a radical agenda might look like.

This chapter will initially discuss what it means to take a critical approach, and then offer a critical framework that informs this book and can be used by practitioners to support their own critical inquiry. Finally, it addresses applying critical theory to leadership itself, acknowledging some of the challenges that are encountered.

Critical Thinking and Critical Theory (CT)

Critical thinking and critical theory are overlapping terms that require differentiating and clarifying for the purpose of this book. Critical thinking

---

[1] CMS – Critical Management Studies – a grouping of academics using critical theory to study management, leadership and all aspects of organizations and work.

or a critical approach are generic terms which are often used loosely and at times indiscriminately and interchangeably with critical theory, but as Johnson and Duberley identify, there is more to critical theory than being reflective and critical:

> Whilst many researchers of management may consider themselves to be critical, in that they attempt to stand back from their work and interrogate their findings with a critical eye, this does not mean they are operating within a critical theory perspective. (2000: 124)

To be critical is to take a more radical, reflective and questioning stance that doesn't accept at face value, what is 'taken for granted' in a mainstream, positivistic or rationalistic perspectives. Fulop and Linstead (1999) write in the opening of their book *Management: A Critical Text*:

> This introduction outlines a critical approach to management that enables us to reflect on how we learn about management. It is designed to help us develop the intellectual rigour and knowledge to deal with the complex and multifaceted issues that arise in everyday work situations. (1999: 4)

Their approach focuses on being reflective and developing a rigor of inquiry, which is one element of a CT stance but there are more. Calhoun (1995: 35) offers his perspective on CT:

1 CT critiques the contemporary social world looking for new possibilities, and positive implications for social action.

2 CT gives a critical account of historical and cultural conditions.

3 CT gives a continuous critical re-examination of the conceptual frameworks used (including the historical construction of these frameworks).

4 CT confronts other works of social explanation, analyzing their strengths and weaknesses, as well as their blind spots, but then demonstrates the capacity to incorporate their insights for stronger foundations.

These examples illustrate a use of CT which brings into play critical thinking from a social, historical and cultural perspective, taking a social constructionist and a discursive approach, i.e. questioning how reality is constructed and made sense of through processes of socialization, the use of language and historical influences. Finally, there is another tradition in CT that aims to use its insights to take an explicitly ethical position.

Good Leadership and Ethical Leadership

Perhaps the greatest differentiating point is that mainstream approaches (rational/positivist) attempt to improve leadership with the aim of making organizations more effective and productive, without reference to broader social and ethical concerns. Good leadership in mainstream thinking means effective leadership, usually with a 'values perspective', as an additional extra. For example, Bass (1998) says transformational leadership is also about 'doing good', yet without looking at structural power issues, and the systemic violence (Žižek, 2008) that occurs through corporate activity, whilst they take an individualist morality, 'doing good' is nothing more than a hollow claim. For example, transformational leadership claims to empower followers, yet under the scrutiny of CT transformational leaders aiming to create strong 'cultures' can end up with 'cult-like cultures' as a new form of organizational control, aiming to maximize productivity from these employees (see Chapters 7 and 12).

Some mainstream scholars do take a more sceptical stance to leadership, but critical scholars Alvesson and Willmott (1996) claim that this sceptical approach has serious limitations because whilst it examines aspects such as power, it does so from an intraorganizational context, ignoring a broader social and political context.

Individualistic leadership theories focusing on special personal traits such as charisma inherently support the idea of 'special leaders' who can motivate 'followers', thereby increasing productivity, and these leaders are rewarded with 'special' remuneration packages. This idea of leadership has led to chief executives' pay rising in astronomical terms in the past 20 years. As Mintzberg (2012) points out, 'Any CEO who allows himself to be paid 400 or 500 times more than the workers is not a leader but an exploiter'. These 'super' leaders receive huge bonuses rewarding them for short-term success and growth, following the neo-liberal agenda of ever-increasing productivity within liberal markets, decreasing regulation, increasing financial and trade liberalization, and reducing protection for the labour force. Short-term profiteering ignores developing more sustainable business growth, or ethical concerns such as humanizing the workplace and taking responsibility for a sustainable natural environment. Is this good leadership?

There are many covert vested interests at stake in organizational life, such as power, identity and economic benefit, which is one reason why critical theory is marginalized. Bhaskar (2010: 107) explains:

> The oppressed have an interest in explanatory knowledge of the structures that oppress them. But their oppressors do not need to have that explanatory

knowledge and it might be better for them if they do not. The sort of knowledge they need to have is best not called knowledge, but rather information or even data, and that is about how to manipulate events and circumstances and discourses.

Good leadership in the workplace must mean more than increasing short-term share prices, and growth. Good leadership should also mean ethical leadership, and this is not just for altruistic reasons, it is also to promote sustainable success. One of the key points I wish to make is that critical theory is not an abstract construction useful only in academic circles, it is fundamental to successful organizational and social functioning, creating more humane institutions and a sustainable world.

Why Critical Theory Is Marginalized

To critique means to look at deeper, underlying questions, not just at the challenges raised by a particular problem.

Business Schools, Management Science and the Corporate Agenda

The basic assumptions behind much of leadership and organizational thinking emanate from business schools (Grey, 2004), which operate with two combined, underpinning biases:

1 **The purpose of business is to maximize productivity and profit:** Business schools take the position that is most likely to align with their key stakeholder, the corporate client, whose agenda is 'more productivity and growth, with ever-greater efficiency, to maximize profit'.

2 **Management science:** Business schools were founded on the premise of using scientific knowledge to improve productivity more efficiently, and this continues today, i.e. 'management science', dominated by technocratic values (Adler et al., 2007; MacIntyre, 1985).

Business schools produce knowledge about leadership and organizations, training leaders to use this knowledge. Privileging management science as the method, (positivism) works on the assumptions that this knowledge is value-neutral, free from bias, factual and scientific. Yet the knowledge they produce is heavily biased towards a single focus, 'instrumentalism'.

> In the instrumentalist approach to management and organization, the goal
> of profitability – or, in the not-for-profit sectors, performance targets – takes
> on a fetishized, naturalized quality. All action is then evaluated under the
> norms of instrumental means–ends rationality. Ethical and political
> questions concerning the value of such ends are excluded, suppressed, or
> assumed to be resolved. (Adler et al., 2007: 127)

The corporate agenda aligns itself with the management science agenda,
both aiming for the same results – greater efficiency and productivity –
without questioning the wider implications for stakeholders and wider
society.

CT challenges both of these underlying premises, claiming that an
organization has a social as well as a business purpose. Neither does it
accept the premise that science (positivism) is neutral and free from bias. It
questions political interests in any research being undertaken, it asks why
certain questions are being asked and others not, questioning the taken-for-
granted assumptions behind the research. Positivism claims to measure a
world that simply exists:

> ...people are taught to accept the world 'as it is', thus unthinkingly
> perpetuating it. CT thus sees positivism as pivotal in an ideology of
> adjustment, undermining our power to imagine a radically better world.
> (Adler et al., 2007: 138)

CT responds by saying that the world is socially constructed, and shaped by
discourse, and we must ask questions about what kind of world we are
perpetuating, and what kind of world we can create. The task of critical
theory is to study power and knowledge relations, to challenge dominating
structures, and also to prevent leadership becoming another instrumental
project, serving only to promote greater efficiency, productivity, profit, with
little reflection on its wider impact on society.

Critical theory has been successful in terms of theoretical influence, but
remains marginalized, and there are concerns about its lack of impact on
practice. Cooke (2008: 914) cites that only 1.7% of papers at the Academy of
Management meeting were in the Critical Management programme.

In a 2008 edition of the journal *Organization* the editors invited critical
scholars to reflect on the future of CMS (Critical Management Studies –
which includes organizational and leadership theory), and the results were
interesting. Three dominant challenges stood out that contributed to the
marginalization of critical theory.

1. An Elitist CMS

Stookey (2008: 922) summed up this view, writing that critical studies challenge elitism whilst paradoxically being part of an 'elitist enterprise' itself, i.e. academia. She notes with concern that 'a society dominated by elitism is fundamentally delusional and self-destructive'. The divide between critical theory and practice is a false dichotomy, perhaps one that is perversely enjoyed and perpetuated by critical scholars, making them an 'elite' group, who benefit from the status, comfort and salaries of the academy, whilst retaining an outsider 'maverick' status (Parker, 2002). CT scholars exclude practitioners with an (often unnecessary) post-structural and academic jargon, yet critical thinking is not in opposition to leadership but a prerequisite for competent leadership that promotes strategic, successful, sustainable and progressive change within organizations.

2. A Cloistered CMS: Theory before Practice

There was wide acknowledgement that CMS was also becoming a cloistered and self-referential entity that was consumed by theory at the expense of engaging with and having an impact on practice. Svensson (2010: 3) writes in *Ephemera*:

> Critical management scholars have been highly successful in publishing excellent articles, and many of them are amazingly productive ... The hyper-productivity of critical management scholars, targeted at excellent journals, has turned critical management into an excellent institution, and many critically oriented scholars are employed because of this mastery in publishing excellent papers.

This success in the academic and theoretical realm is contrasted with CMS's impact on what happens in practice:

> CMS has had little or no impact on what organizations actually do ... there are some serious and fascinating issues being discussed within CMS, but they tend to stay within the cloistered boundaries of academic work and find little echo outside those who are already converted. (Parker, 2002: 115-16)

Addressing the dissonance between theory and practice is a major concern for CMS scholars if they are serious about having emancipatory concerns, and contributing to social transformation as well as publication.

3. Diversity of Critical Studies

Scholars sometimes speak of CMS as a singular, homogeneous entity, speaking with one voice, when it is actually a very diverse body. Adler (2008: 925) challenges the idea that there is a singular body of theory for CMS:

> In reality, there is a buzzing confusion and profusion, running the gamut from post-structuralism to labour process theory, from Derrida to Marx, from radical postcolonial feminism to moderate social democratic liberalism, from positivism to critical realism to social constructivism.

This diversity needs to be recognized, in order to maximize the benefits of the potential breadth of theory and research that is available as a resource to understand leadership and organizational dynamics.

Reversing the Marginalization of CMS

These three factors add to the marginalization of critical theory. Critical studies therefore needs to find a new engagement with non-critical scholars and practitioners. Voronov (2008: 943) suggests four possibilities for critical scholars to increase their engagement with practitioners:

- **Focused critique** – issue-based critiques focused on specific issues that speak to managers and leaders because they relate to real challenges. This offers critical theorists the opportunity to shape new discourses.

- **Engaged scholarship** – creating knowledge that is both theoretically rich and practically useful, exemplified by participatory research.

- **Consulting** – although objectionable to some CMS scholars, consulting can be an excellent way to gain and deliver critical insights into leadership practice'.

- **Critical action learning** – 'introducing critical elements into the action learning tradition' (Reynolds and Vince, 2004).

I would add *business school executive education* to this list. University-led training and development programmes are currently the domain of mainstream scholars, yet they offer many opportunities for critical scholars to engage and disseminate critical theory to practitioners, and to utilize practitioner knowledge and insight to inform their theorizing. Having worked in executive education, I believe it offers the potential to work through normative assumptions, and some (though not all) executives will thrive and grow in such an atmosphere. Critical thinking and practice should not be alien bedfellows!

A Critical Framework: Four Frames of Critical Inquiry

These four frames of critical inquiry underpin the thinking in this book and offer a tangible framework to guide both practitioners and scholars:

- Emancipation

- Depth analysis

- Looking awry

- Network analysis

Emancipation
Ethics, Liberation, Autonomy, Sustainability, Equality and Justice

The lens of emancipation is concerned with promoting justice, equality, ethics, a sustainable environment, liberation and autonomy. Leadership has a mixed reception in emancipatory movements; traditional social movements herald heroic leaders such as Martin Luther King, Ghandi, Rosa Luxemburg, Trotsky and Lenin (following populist notions of leadership), whilst new social movements such as feminism and the green movement often treat leadership with suspicion. This is for two reasons: (1) because the word leadership infers hierarchy and elitism and challenges the idea of autonomy and equality, and (2) leadership past and present has often distorted and created unjust power relationships that marginalize some and benefit others. For example, patriarchal and class-based leadership are still very present; male networks perpetuate the male leadership that dominates corporate/ political life, and class opportunities offer resources and networks that keep an elite, wealthy class in leadership positions across society, thereby undermining meritocracy and social mobility. In the UK at the time of writing the political elite is dominated by males who went to expensive private schools:

> Cameron, Clegg and Osborne all went to private schools with fees now higher than the average annual wage. Half the cabinet went to fee-paying schools – versus only 7% of the country – as did a third of all MPs. (BBC News, 2011)

In the USA, leadership also reflects social inequality. There has never been a female president, and, according to Stille (2011), 'more than half the presidents over the past 110 years attended Harvard, Yale or Princeton and graduates of Harvard and Yale have had a lock on the White House for the last 23 years, across four presidencies'.

These biases are being better addressed in some countries. Norway, for example, has been described by the UN Committee on the Elimination of Discrimination against Women as 'a haven for gender equality', legislating to increase female representation in parliament and boardrooms.

Taking a critical emancipatory stance is to try to increase representation at senior political and business levels (a reformist perspective) and also to offer radical leadership ideas that will address the wider social issues. In utilizing new social movement and feminist theory for example, CT aims to expand distributed and grass-roots leadership, drawing on different readings of what traditional leadership means, and mobilizing leadership in unexpected places.

Theoretical Resources

The emancipatory approach taken in this book draws upon eclectic ideas from diverse sources, including new social movement theorists, post-Marxist thinkers, e.g. the Frankfurt School, Habermas and Adorno, Alain Badiou, Slavoj Žižek, and autonomous Marxists such as 'Biffo' Beradi. Post-structuralists, such as Michel Foucault and the feminist Judith Butler, have also developed emancipatory agendas through their work:

> Foucault … taught us to be wary of the institutions through which we are governed. We must always beware of the possibilities that our own institutional arrangements will encourage the rise of new destructive forces inimical to the possibilities of our being free. (Dumm, 1996: 153)

Post-structuralists help us understand that leadership, like power, is everywhere, not just residing at the top of a hierarchy. The CT task is not to condemn or remove leadership or power, but to scrutinize them, offering alternatives to autocratic and elitist leadership. Post-structuralist and discourse theory reveals how social conditions produce certain leadership approaches, and how leadership approaches reproduce social conditions.

For Habermas (1984), communication is a key tool of emancipation or oppression, and Foucault's body of work shows how discourses and language create a power–knowledge link (Foucault, 1980), revealing how our subjective selves are formed and governed by discourses which entrap us (Rose, 1990).

Judith Butler shows how gender and identity are not as fixed as modernity led us to believe (Butler, 1990), and relating this to leadership, we see how fluid the concepts of leadership are, with new links being developed between leadership and identity formation.

Habermas observed that increasingly the public sphere is administered remotely from individual citizens, diminishing their freedom and agency, and describing the 'colonisation of the lifeworld' (Habermas, 1984), where the individual subject is penetrated by bureaucracy, using the ideology of efficiency and rationality to justify this. Corporate leadership becomes part of this 'colonising force' and is most apparent when culture control is used rather than more obvious transactional or coercive controls (discussed in Chapter 11 on Messiah leadership). The Habermasian goal of critical theory is 'a form of life free from unnecessary domination in all of its forms' (McCarthy, 1978: 273).

To summarize the emancipatory lens of CT:

- Rationalism and knowledge must be linked to values and interest, if they are to be used as a force for emancipation.

- Emancipatory CT challenges relativism, the postmodern claim that all points of view are of equal value. Leaders from elitist groups reproduce their hold on power, making their views privileged whilst less privileged groups are silenced. These hidden power relations ensure that not all views are of equal value. CT links politics, values and interests to knowledge to undermine relativism.

- CT aims to reveal the power relations that exist within social structures, discourses and symbolic practices. It then focuses on how to change the practices that undermine liberty and how to find new ways to promote human agency and freedom.

Depth Analysis

Revealing Hidden Dynamics: Hermeneutics, Psychosocial Approaches, Discourse Analysis

Depth analysis is derived from the methods of psychoanalysis and discourse analysis that look beneath-the-surface to discover underlying patterns, structures and influences that are not immediately obvious or easy to discern. Depth analysis challenges the dominant rational assumptions of leadership and organizational studies, and clearly makes a case for including the irrational forces of the unconscious: the emotions, herd-behaviours, group-think and other hidden forces that influence social dynamics. These human factors are not accounted for in computer-generated data-banks, or scientific rationalist accounts of organizational behaviour; yet the 2007 financial collapse shows that we must account for human factors such as greed, mania and herd instincts (Sievers, 2011; Stein and Pinto, 2011).

Psychoanalytic Approaches

Johnson and Duberley claim that psychoanalysis is perhaps the earliest example of a critical theorist method:

> Perhaps the prototype for critical science is psychoanalysis because it involves 'depth-hermeneutics' [Habermas, 1972: 218] in which the distorted texts of the patient's behaviour become intelligible to them through self-reflection. In this fashion emancipation occurs as the patient becomes liberated from the terror of their own unconscious as previously suppressed and latent determinants of behaviour are revealed and thereby lose their power. (Johnson and Duberley, 2000: 120)

Depth analysis is clearly linked to an emancipatory agenda through making the unconscious conscious, and revealing other hidden knowledge and power sources such as how discourses are created and influence us. The aim of depth analysis is to gain insight in order to disempower hidden forces, and enable us to form strategies to create change.

This book draws on psychoanalytic theorists such as Sigmund Freud, Jacques Lacan, Melanie Klein, Wilfred Bion and Slavoj Žižek. There is also a long tradition of applying psychoanalytic thinking to organizations and leadership studies, emanating from the Tavistock Institute, utilizing object relations theory (Kleinian approaches), and now strongly represented by ISPSO (the International Society of Psychoanalytic Study of Organization). Scholars such as Manfred Kets de Vries, Larry Hirschhorn, Mark Stein, Burkard Sievers, Susan Long and Gabriel Yannis, amongst others, offer important contributions to the field. This work applies a clinical perspective to organizations/leadership; for example Schwartz (1990) and Stein (2003) apply a psychoanalytic understanding of narcissism to corporate culture, whilst Kets de Vries' book *The Leader on the Couch* (2006) uses clinical psychoanalytic insights to study leadership and is probably the best known work in this field.

However these authors do not always take a critical approach, and sometimes the work takes an intrapersonal and relational perspective at the expense of addressing wider social perspectives. The strong contribution they make is to reveal how depth perspectives of a leader's personality and interpersonal relationships inform their leadership approach. Leaders can become dysfunctionally grandiose and omnipotent when followers treat them unconsciously like a saviour. Psychoanalytic concepts such as projection help explain how followers can idealize (or denigrate) leaders, projecting their repressed desires onto them. Leaders represent authority figures and can replicate 'good mummy/daddy or bad mummy/daddy' in the minds of followers, and this has implications when followers can become dependent on the leader rather than autonomous, thinking employees (Miller, 1993).

To make interpretations from a psychoanalytic perspective means to draw upon our emotions and our subjectivity as researchers and observers. Drawing on the 'self' to make sense of one's feelings in relation to another, or to a social situation, is off limits for positivist and rational approaches. These psychosocial methodologies are under-used and under-developed, and offer a complementary lens to positivistic research. There is a small but growing interest in psychosocial research. Professor Sasha Roseneil writes of her psychosocial research:

> ...the psychosocial-analysis I carried out drew on principles from clinical psychoanalysis, in its concern to explore interviewees' psychic reality, the non-rational, unarticulated, unconscious dimensions of the experiences they narrated, as well as the emotions and affects that they were able to formulate expressly in discourse. (Roseneil, 2006: 864)

My training and background are in psychoanalytic theory and clinical practice. I spent many years as a psychotherapist and recently directed a Master's programme in Organizational Consultancy at the Tavistock Clinic, studying the unconscious and emotional dynamics in organizational life, and the insights gained through this experience strongly influence this book. Lacanian psychoanalysis has become a popular academic resource in critical theory, drawing on linguistic and post-structural readings of Freud. Using psychoanalytic theory without reference to practice or the clinical method is, however, problematic. Bhaskar claims that he could 'not use psychoanalysis as a potential science of emancipation without actually having experienced it' (2010: 94).

Freud's theories went beyond individual analysis and he considered his most important contribution was to deepen an understanding of society and culture. In his book *Civilisation and Its Discontents* (1930/2002) Freud identified the frustrations of being part of a social group:

noting that the human animal, with its insatiable needs, must always
remain an enemy to organized society, which exists largely to tamp down
sexual and aggressive desires. At best, civilized living is a compromise
between wishes and repression – not a comfortable doctrine. It ensures that
Freud, taken straight, will never become truly popular, even if today we all
speak Freud. (Gay, 1999)

Freud's work influences society today, Philip Rieff announced in *The
Triumph of the Therapeutic* (1966), and we find the 'talking cure' everywhere,
in mutated forms such as counselling, therapy, coaching, social work,
psychology. 'Therapeutic culture' (Furedi, 2003) has been pervasive in the
past 50 years and this culture has also infiltrated leadership theory and
practice (see Chapter 10 on the leader as therapist). Advertising and
marketing campaigns now have integrated Freudian concepts into their
thinking by relying on the unconscious to attract new customers through
linking their brands to individual identity (Klein, 2000). Subliminal
advertising is commonplace, drawing on Freud's links between sex and
power and his understanding of unconscious fantasy, hence the stereotypical
advert of fast cars being linked to glamorous women, to appeal to the male
desires and fantasies of having more phallic power. Turkle (2011) applies
psychoanalytic insights as part of her analysis of humans and technology
that provides rich data to try to understand social dynamics in hi-tech and
virtual surroundings.

Psychoanalysis, however, remains marginal within leadership,
management and organizational studies, partly due to the positivistic and
rationalist bias in management, which discounts complex understandings in
favour of measurable outcomes.

Discourse Approaches

Depth analysis draws upon other critical theory methods, which investigate
what happens beneath the surface in organizational life, e.g. discourse
analysis, narrative analysis. Religious hermeneutic interpretation offers
ancient methods of depth analysis, trying to uncover the meaning within
holy texts. Foucault (1980) teaches us that power and knowledge are closely
related, and that power is exerted through normative control: 'the way
things are done around here'. Rose (1990) draws on Foucault to show how
our intimate selves are governed by social discourses, and this has many
implications for leadership and workplace dynamics. To see beyond the
established 'natural order of things' means to 'unmask' what is hidden. For
example, many cultural assumptions are made about heterosexuality and

marriage, and whilst these seem normal to many, from gay or queer perspectives, they are oppressive. Power is performed through Westernized ideals of the hetero-normative nuclear family, and those outside this framework are disciplined by social rules, either explicitly or implicitly (Butler, 2004). In this book four discourses reveal how normative expectations of leadership have changed over the past century.

Discourse approaches to depth analysis are very popular in critical theory today; in leadership studies new insights through discourse analysis and discursive approaches come from scholars such as Fairclough (1995) and Collinson (2003).

In summary, psychoanalysis, discourse analysis and other depth analysis techniques are employed in this text as a core CT method to help reveal how social and unconscious processes become internalized, embodied and enacted by individuals, social groups and organizations, and how language shapes our world. Leadership raises issues of the individual and the group; leadership and followership, power and authority, manipulation and control, and therefore depth analysis is vital to understand the processes that help develop models of successful leadership.

Looking Awry

Reframing, Short-circuiting, Disrupting the Normative

Looking awry encourages leadership researchers and practitioners to disrupt the taken-for-granted, and look from a different place. To see something differently we have to look differently. If a critical approach is to offer a radical critique, and to find radical solutions, then looking awry is an essential frame from which to discover something new.

Žižek (1992, 2003) claims that a frontal view of an object or text offers a distorted and a limited perspective, rather than what is traditionally regarded as a clear view. To really see what is happening, he suggests the need to *look awry* and paradoxically take a 'distorted' view:

> The object assumes clear and distinctive features only if we look 'at an angle', i.e. with an interested view, supported permeated, and 'distorted' by *desire*. (Žižek, 1992: 12; emphasis added)

Žižek (1992) describes how a change in the angle of a camera during film making can give a whole different perspective on the scene, and claims the observer also needs to bring their *desire* and subjectivity to the viewing rather than to try to take an objective neutral stance. This challenges rational approaches, and the Cartesian dualism (the subject–object, observer–observed, knower–known dichotomy). We become over-familiar with the normative discourses which surround us; our individual and cultural scripts make the world familiar and recognizable, yet often we cannot 'see the wood for the trees'. When we are 'liberated' from a particular way of seeing, new options then become available. This is not only an intellectual exercise but can also be a powerful change agent. When working as a family therapist 'reframing' proved a useful way for individuals and families to find new options to change patterns of behaving that they found destructive:

> In Family Therapy, Reframing is a technique developed by the Palo Alto Group. The therapist offers a description that gives the client a different way to look at their actions, hoping that this will enable them to see their problem differently and develop new options for actions as a result. (Weakland et al., 1974)

Likewise within leadership training, reframing opens up new options for leaders so that they view their role and can see different options and ways to act or intervene.

Short-Circuiting

Žižek describes 'short-circuiting' as a process that brings new resources from different traditions, in order to see something new or hidden:

> Is not short-circuiting, therefore, one of the best metaphors for a critical reading? Is it not one of the most effective critical procedures to cross wires that do not usually touch: to take a major text and read it in a short-circuiting way, through the lens of a minor (marginalized) author, text or conceptual apparatus? ... such a procedure can lead to insights which completely shatter and undermine our common perceptions. ... The aim is to illuminate a standard text or ideological formation, making it readable in a totally new way. (Žižek, 2003: Foreword)

To see beyond the obvious requires both new resources and also the ability to look and observe in new ways. This dual process of *short-circuiting* and *looking awry* provides options to reveal what was previously concealed within a dominant discourse.

In this text I use theoretical, historical and experiential resources to short-circuit common perceptions; for example, drawing on theological resources and exploring religious fundamentalism as a lens to look awry at leadership (Chapter 7). Bringing my own subjectivity and desire to my work with leaders, as a coach and consultant, also provides me with rich data that I have used in this text. I make 'disruptive interventions' in my leadership development work; for example, asking leaders to undertake unusual observation exercises at airports or busy streets; to stop and observe the outside world like a video camera, recording everything they have seen, then to be like a mirror, observing their bodies, feelings, emotions and thoughts as they observe the outer world. I then coach and debrief them (sometimes individually or in groups) and offer interpretations about what they saw and also what they didn't see, what their focus was. This exercise reveals feelings and insights, and tells them something different about their leadership and followership experiences, often something profound. For example, one leader observed pairs all the time: couples in love, couples arguing, two children, and on exploration he realized that he avoided teamwork, and needed to develop his team leadership capability if he was to develop his career. Another leader observed the technical apparatus of an airport flight announcing system, and reflected on how his focus at work was technical rather than on people; yet when we discussed his feelings, he revealed deep feelings of loss and sadness at the amount of time he spent away from family, on work assignments, and how he had to change roles to rebalance a dysfunctional life–work balance. These interventions help leaders look awry at their work, put them sharply in touch with something that is not immediately obvious, and can have a powerful impact on their working lives.

In this text I have also drawn from New Social Movement (NSM) theorists such as Alberto Melucci and Alain Touraine and other anthropologists, ethnographers and sociologists, who theorize how NSMs form and how they differ from traditional social movements. NSM theory provides new ways to look at leadership, as in these movements traditional leadership is not accepted, and de-centralized movements focus on 'identity' rather than on fighting for material gains. NSMs offer new ways to understand leadership in new organizational forms, such as developing networked and dispersed leadership or organizational matrix structures, for example. Leadership theorists have largely neglected this particular sociological and anthropological literature.

Looking awry is to draw on new resources, to short-circuit them, and to place oneself as a reader/researcher or practitioner in a different place so that something new can perhaps be discovered.

Network Analysis

Actor-Networks, Ecosystems, Systems Thinking

Manuel Castells (2000) describes the 'Information Age' and the 'Network Society', addressing how technology has impacted on contemporary society. Network analysis accounts for the 'network society' in which we live and work, and ensures that critical theory takes a systemic view of activity and leadership.

Leadership is fundamentally an influencing activity, and to understand leadership we have to try also to understand what we are influencing. Many mainstream leadership perspectives are firmly rooted in modernity's vision of the world, one of structures, hierarchies, clear divisions and boundaries. Yet in the postmodern/post-industrial world there is instability, fluidity and fast change, so that organizations are no longer clearly boundaried and ordered, if they ever were (Latour, 2005).

Manual labour has largely migrated, and is surpassed in the West by cognitive or digital labour (Beradi, 2009). Global networks produce new forms of organizing and new organizational forms. Global flows create virtual worlds which are no longer peripheral but run our finance systems and global brands. The real and the virtual entwine in hybrid networks, and the contemporary workplace is interconnected and interdependent; Actor Network scholars (Latour, 2005; Law, 1993) inform us how organizations and the social world are better understood as networks of actors that are fluid and always changing. Actor Network scholars make the radical claim that both human and non-humans actors have agency in our networks, that we cannot understand the social world from a purely human-centric position. To understand leadership we must first try to understand how change takes place in organizations, and we achieve this only if we take a network and a systems perspective.

Systems theory takes a holistic perspective and ecological view (Bateson, 1972; Churchman, 1968, 1979; Maturana and Varela, 1980, 1987; Naess, 1989; Von Bertalanffy, 1968). In the contemporary leadership and management literature Peter Senge (1994) is best known for his use of systems thinking and influential texts have also come from complexity theorists and integrative theorists such as Wilber (2000). Wheately (2006) wrote an informative account of 'leadership and these new science' incorporating these concepts and taking a network perspective:

> Our zeitgeist is a new (and ancient) awareness that we participate in a world of exquisite interconnectedness. We are learning to see systems

rather than isolated parts and players. ... We can see the webs of inter-connections that weave the world together. (Wheatley, 2006: 158)

One challenge to systemic, ecological, holistic and integrative theorists is that they often lack a power critique, and see systems thinking in terms of communication feedback loops without accounting for the real and discursive power issues that impact on any system (see Chapter 12, Eco-Leadership).

Critical theorists refer to context as being hugely important, and argue that we must take account of power in networks, yet the bridge between theory and practice is very problematic. I draw upon my experience as a family therapist and systemically informed consultant to apply systems thinking to the practice of leadership. The professional expertise developed through 'clinical practice' by family therapists offers a transferable and adaptable knowledge base to further develop the bridge between systemic theory and leadership practice.[2]

Leadership theory must develop a greater vigilance of the wider impact of leadership interventions taken. Network analysis attempts to address the complex social, political, economic and environmental challenges which are present in our organizations. Chapter 12 on Eco-leadership helps us to rethink organizations as 'ecosystems within ecosystems' and describes the new forms of leadership developing for 21st century organizations.

Workplace networks are fluid, and employees are increasingly nomadic, moving between roles, project teams and virtual and real working spaces and places. The global and networked world offers new challenges and new opportunities; I coach and consult leaders using network analysis as a frame to help them think more strategically and more emergently. To be strategic, to think about the big picture, to understand change and the resistance to change, and to decipher how to influence organizations, leaders must first locate themselves in their own networks.

Frames Summary

These four frames, *Emancipation*, *Depth Analysis*, *Looking Awry* and *Network Analysis*, provide the basis for a critical approach to leadership and they also provide the four critical lenses from which leadership is viewed within this book.

---

[2] Western (2008) offers an account of a systemic consultation to an organization, utilizing family therapy and other systemic techniques with the aim to distribute leadership and 'democratize strategy'.

Box 3   Summary of Critical Frames

Emancipation Analysis

Ethics, liberation, autonomy and justice

Applying CT to leadership aims to help create the conditions that diminish coercion and oppression and maximize the potential for well-being and a sustainable environment. Thus allowing leaders to maximize their creativity and agency in order to generate leadership in others, and pursue the greater good for all, within an organizational and social context.

CT invites leaders to reflect on:

1 Are they leading in 'good faith'

2 Does their leadership work towards the 'good society' and a sustainable world?

3 Are their organizational aims ethical and just?

Depth Analysis

Revealing hidden dynamics

Depth analysis draws upon psychoanalysis and discourse analysis. Much of human relations and organizational dynamics happens 'beneath the surface', in our individual and collective unconscious processes, and in the texts and language we use. To understand the relations between, power, knowledge emotions and change, is to undertake depth analysis.

Leaders are encouraged to mirror the reflexivity of the psychoanalytic approach, to become aware of the emotional and unconscious cultures in organizational settings.

Looking Awry

Reframing, short-circuiting, disrupting the normative

Looking Awry is to disrupt the normative, to look differently in order to discover something new. To 'think outside the box' has become a tired cliché that no longer suffices. To see things differently means to bring desire and subjectivity to the looking and to try to find radical alternatives. This means looking from different

Network Analysis

Actor-networks, ecosystems, interdependence, systems thinking

Network analysis accounts for the changes we face through globalization, technological advances and environmental threats, creating a networked interdependent world that requires new leadership approaches.

angles and from a different place from within ourselves. By bringing desire to observation, and cross-wiring diverse theoretical resources, new insights are revealed and hidden power relations are 'unmasked'. Disrupting, engaging, rethinking and reframing: looking awry means to begin from a different beginning.

The world of work is changing dramatically, yet many leaders and leadership developers work on 20th century assumptions, when what is required in today's organizations are more adaptive forms of distributed leadership, described in Chapter 12 as 'Eco-leadership'.

Conclusion: Critical Theory and Leadership

Applying critical theory to leadership demands that we identify some of the undercurrents, the historical and social trends that inform how leadership is thought about and practised. To achieve this we must look beyond the management and organizational leadership literature that draws too heavily on an 'insider view' and is saturated with rationalistic and individualist 'heroic' accounts of leadership. Box 4 offers some working assumptions on a critical approach to leadership.

Box 4   Critical Theory and Leadership: Working Assumptions

1 Leadership exists within all forms of organization, whether this is overtly or covertly recognized. It is therefore important to understand how leadership works in practice. The task is to look beyond and beneath the norms and assumptions espoused about leadership in popular culture and the mainstream organizational literature.

2 Mainstream leadership assumptions and discourses reproduce the organizational power structures that already exist. Critical theorists pay particular attention to the discursive, systemic and structural aspects of leadership that privilege some and marginalize others. There is a tendency for organizations to drift blindly and unknowingly towards seductive but dangerous

(Continued)

(Continued)

totalizing cultures. Revealing the role leadership plays within these pro-cesses and then to transform negative power-relations is the task.

3 There is no leadership without followership and no leadership without power, influence and authority. Individual and communal autonomy and liberty therefore rely on organizations with non-authoritarian leadership approaches. It is possible to take up leadership authority without being authoritarian. It is a utopian error to try to eliminate power relations. Critical theory attempts to make transparent and address (rather than eradicate) the relations between leadership and followership, authority and power.

4 Contemporary workplaces are increasingly important sites of social activity and community, replacing traditional communal structures such as the church. What happens in the workplace has a reflexive relationship with the wider environment. Understanding and improving the dynamics of leadership in the workplace is therefore essential to society in general. Reflexive learning between workplace leadership and socio-political leader-ship will have a systemic impact on governance and leadership across all social structures.

5 Critical theory, as well as offering a critique, strives to offer reformist and radical options that can create more humane workplaces, and contribute to building the good society.

It is the task of this book to create theoretical frames to identify ways in which 'leadership in practice' can minimize power-relations that rely on control and coercion, and maximize the potential for emancipatory workplaces. Leadership is not inherently good or bad, it is potentially both. Ricoeur claims that Ethical Selfhood means 'aiming for the good life with and for others in just institutions' (Marsh, 2002: 224). Ricoeur's statement guides us: leadership from a critical theory perspective is underpinned by an ethical stance. Leadership is to aim for the good life, to work with and for others to create the good society, and to lead and co-create just institutions. I will add a further ethical aim: leadership should also work towards protecting the natural environment.

Suggested Readings

- Alvesson, M. and Wilmott, H. (1992) *Critical Management Studies*. London: Sage.

- Bhaskar, R. (2010) *The Formation of Critical Realism: A Personal Perspective*. Oxford/New York: Routledge.

Reflection Points

- What does it mean to be entrapped by 'normative assumptions'?

- Why is it important to take an emancipatory position when adopting a critical stance?

- Reflect on the key challenges critical theory faces when influencing leadership practice.

Sample Assignment Question

Briefly describe the four frames of critical inquiry, and choose one or more of these to explore an example of leadership practice you have encountered (this may be in the workplace, a social setting, or political leadership).

2　What Is Leadership?

Chapter Structure

- Introduction
- The Idea of Leadership
- The Meaning of Leadership
- Conclusion: The Experience of Leadership

Introduction

Leadership is a contested term with multiple meanings and diverse practical applications. This chapter offers a brief overview, initially exploring 'the idea of leadership', and then explores the meanings we attribute to leadership, briefly scoping the main themes in leadership studies. There are many excellent resources that offer overviews of leadership but this book is particularly interested in placing leadership in its broader context, so I 'begin at the beginning', which is to explore our individual and collective ambivalent feelings towards leadership. Exploring the idea of leadership from a psychosocial perspective reflects on our individual and collective emotional experience of leadership, showing how our feelings shape, how we theorize, perceive and enact leadership and followership.

There is a deep longing and desire for leadership, symbolically played out in popular culture. Hollywood films and best-selling books mythologize leaders and are forever finding new leadership characters to feed our insatiable desire for heroic figures. The popularity of leadership is based on a desire to be led, to be saved, to be looked after, to be given meaning, and with the attractive subtext that seduces our egos:'you too could be like them'. We have deep attachments to the idea of leadership, yet so often we also feel let down, overpowered, anxious, envious, distrustful, or even afraid of our leaders. We interpret and create leaders and leadership, depending on our ambivalent feelings towards the 'object' inside ourselves that relates to leadership. To 'begin at the beginning' is to acknowledge these strong emotional and ambivalent responses within ourselves as individuals, and collectively as social groups. Leadership cannot escape these emotional and unconscious responses, however rational we try to make it, because leadership sits at the heart of human desire and fear. From our infancy to our deathbeds, there is ambivalence: we desire to be led and also to be leaders. This ambivalence is expressed by Jacques Lacan in a story of psychoanalysis with a patient.

- The psychoanalyst asks the patient on the couch: 'What do you desire?'

- Patient replies: 'I desire a master.'

- Psychoanalyst asks: 'What kind of master?'

- Patient responds: 'A master I can dominate.'

We desire to be looked after, cared for, and guided and nourished (to be loved and cherished, to find the perfect parent), and we fear losing our individuality and autonomy, or worse we fear being mistreated or coerced by others with power and influence. Our parents, teachers, bosses, religious and political leaders, all signify forms of leadership that carry these real hopes, dangers and emotional anxieties. History and personal experience teach us that leadership can be uplifting, benevolent and tyrannical; sometimes all three together.

This chapter begins with psychosocial insights, exploring our conscious and unconscious 'ideas of leadership', because only with this understanding can we begin to make sense of the key meanings attributed to leadership in contemporary society.

The Idea of Leadership

Psychosocial Insights

Leadership is created in our minds (individually and collectively), converted into social roles and positions, and internalized into identities. Leadership is a constant flux of psychosocial dynamics, enacted on the stage of life; power dynamics, individual feelings, collective identifications, herd behaviours, autonomy and dependency issues, courage and fear, unconscious fantasies, virtual communications, kindness and love, abuse and terror, politics and negotiations, the use and control of resources, manipulation and the strategic use of communications, influencing language and discourse, creating symbolic events, all and much more underpin the psychosocial dynamics of leadership. A mistake is to reduce leadership to the property of a heroic individual, to a set of skills or competencies or to a particular way of being.

Leadership begins with an idea in our minds, and even when it becomes a social role, a reality so to speak, it remains essentially an idea that we are constantly and dynamically reworking, acting out and performing. Leadership is an idea we are constantly at work with, and play with.

The Splitting of Leadership

Leadership is often constructed as an 'idealized' form of human endeavour, in a tone that suggests a heroic beauty. The popular idea of leaders in the workplace is represented by key words such as strategic, future, change, passion, charisma, courage, integrity, authenticity and vision (this contrasts with a more mundane idea about management).

Alvesson and Svenginsson (2003: 4) sum up the leadership literature:

> Contemporary writings usually frame leadership in terms of the visionary and heroic aspects, it is the leader's abilities to address [by talking and persuading] the many through the use of charisma, symbols and other strongly emotional devices, the ambition being to arouse and encourage people to embark upon organizational projects.

Hirschhorn (1999: 146) writes:

> A leader's major role is to give us a dream. Without the dream there is no basis for us to mobilise the extra effort, attention and skill we need to achieve a goal fraught with risks. Many of us, perhaps most of us, would rather sit on the sidelines, do our daily work and hope that we can participate in the gains that others have sweated for. The dream, by contrast, excites us all.

Leadership is often portrayed as a golden chalice, a most sought after object, yet on the other hand we take pleasure in decrying and bemoaning our leaders too. This idea of leadership as a 'good object' also has a shadow side, leadership as a 'bad object' that creates a splitting of leadership, reflecting our ambivalent feelings about leaders. Freud presented us with our conflicted selves, with the ambivalence that's sits within us, revealing that we can have conscious feelings: 'I love my Mother' conflicted with unconscious feelings of 'I hate my Mother', and the latter is often repressed into our unconscious, as it is socially and personally unacceptable.

The Return of the Repressed

Psychoanalysis reveals that repressed unconscious material returns to haunt us. Leaders who are idealized beyond their capacity for goodness, with their shadow side being repressed, can end up self-destructing, either through becoming narcissistic and grandiose and behaving irrationally, or by simply making bad judgements based on their feelings of omnipotence and invincibility.

Repression means that we experience our feelings, yet we are not fully aware of them and act on them in distorted ways. For example, if I repress feelings of envy and anger towards a 'good leader' I may unconsciously sabotage her at important meetings; alternatively, these feelings may make me over-compensate and become overly compliant, and super-positive about her, ignoring misjudgements and unable to offer constructive criticism. This latter state of being 'super-positive' is commonplace in leadership studies, where the 'good object' transformational leader is desired and acclaimed, yet the shadow side of leadership is either hidden or exported to others such as 'boring managers' (explored later on in the chapter). This splitting is not always obvious.

Bass offers an example:

> Leaders are authentically transformational when they increase awareness of what is right, good, important and beautiful, when they help to elevate followers' needs for achievement and self-actualization, when they foster in followers higher moral maturity and when they move followers to go beyond their self interests for the good of their group, organization or society. (Bass, 1990b: 171)

This statement at face value seems uplifting and helpful, yet it reproduces the classic split between 'idealized leader' and 'disempowered followers'. The leader has the charisma and influence to elevate followers, to move them beyond themselves, to foster in them a higher morality. The follower is the passive recipient, awaiting the charismatic leader to spark them into becoming a higher being (like the leader themselves). As a colleague whispered to me recently during a keynote speech by such a transformational leader, 'It's like being at church!'

Leadership splitting occurs between leaders and followers, managers and leaders, and between good and bad leaders. When leadership is spilt, we are either powerful leaders with agency or disempowered followers. Our leaders become saviours or villains (sometimes this is modified to become less polemic: 'She's a really good leader' or 'He's hopeless but a nice guy'). Splitting leadership between good and bad can focus on a single leader who carries both parts of the split in our minds, or two characters can be involved; all the good projected into one leader, and all the bad into another.

I observed Tony Blair's leadership with great interest over a number of years, and noticed how he always had an alter-ego, a 'disliked' shadow, who took many of the negative projections leaving him to take the positive ones (Alistair Campbell, Gordon Brown, and Peter Mandelson all fulfilled this role for him).

In a 2012 banking mis-selling scandal at Barclays bank, the reaction was a classic case of splitting: (a) demonize bad leaders, (b) call for new saviour leaders. Simon Walker, head of the Institute of Directors, was infuriated by the abusive treatment of small business in the banking scandal, saying 'There is a serious failure of leadership of many banks and there should be a clearout of the leaders who created this mess', while Sir Mervin King, Governor of the Bank of England, said 'What I hope is that everyone – everyone – under-stands that something went very wrong with the UK banking industry and we have to put it right'; he then called for 'leadership of an unusually high order' (Pratley, 2012).

In this case the CEO of Barclays, Bob Diamond, was pushed to resign only to be replaced by another senior insider from the bank, who self-evidently must have been part of the culture that caused the problem in the first place. A leader becomes a 'bad object' overnight, and is replaced by a 'good object' who immediately claims he will clean up the culture of the bank. The good sheriff rides into town as his corrupt predecessor is chased by the posse into the distant hills … our leadership narratives from Hollywood get played out in our corporations far too often!

Leadership is written about objectively in rational, and scholarly, terms yet leadership stimulates primal emotions that are both conscious and unconscious, individual and collective.

Cultural Leadership Scripts

Each of us has personal conscious and unconscious reactions to individual leaders and we also have cultural scripts that we embody and act out col-lectively. In the USA the cultural script has strong resonance with the heroic, individual leader, striving to better themselves, to strive for a 'free' society, to fulfil the American Dream. This cultural script is seen in social move-ments (Martin Luther King), in media stars (Oprah Winfrey), in corporate settings (Steve Jobs), and it is also reflected in leadership scholarship. Trans-formational and charismatic exceptional leadership rhetoric emanates from and dominates the American market. In Europe a greater scepticism and ambivalence exists about leadership, perhaps due to recent catastrophes linked to despotic leaders such as Hitler, Stalin, Mussolini and Franco; and this also may be due to cultural experiences: strong historical social and egalitarian inspired movements, such as socialism, the French revolution with its legacy of 'liberty, fraternity, equality', the trade union movement, social religious movements, and strong social democratic politics pursuing ideals such as the welfare state and public health provision.

My personal observations are of a healthy scepticism about leadership in Europe (critical theorists are much more prevalent in Europe than in the USA), but also a less generous attitude and more envy of individual success in the UK/Europe than in the USA. The pop star Morrissey from Manchester captures this in a song entitled 'We hate it when our friends become successful', containing the line 'if we can destroy them, you bet your life we will destroy them', and the UK press certainly relishes destroying leaders, whether political figures or football managers. Beyond Europe and the USA, leadership has many diverse cultural and historical narratives that inform how it is socially enacted, though with too much diversity to address here.

Box 5   Power Corrupts but Projections Corrupt More

Leadership and projective identification

Psychoanalytic insights refer to regressed childhood experiences being acted out on the stage of adult life, as one explanation for this splitting. It suggests we seek the idealized parent figures in our leaders: we desire 'a good mummy or daddy' or conversely we transfer angry feelings onto leaders if we perceive ill-treatment from parents or authority figures from our past. Melanie Klein (1959) explains the notion of splitting and projection, how we take unwanted feelings and project them onto others. Our leaders are excellent receptacles for these projected feelings due to their roles as authority figures. We see in our leaders the aspects of ourselves we have projected into them, and we can feel very let down if a leader fails to live up to our idealized desires. The leader themselves becomes shaped by these projections, identifying with them, and so can feel persecuted by negative projections, by envious followers, or can become grandiose and omnipotent if they identify with idealized projections about how wonderful they are.

It is often said that 'power corrupts', which I am sure is a truism for some leaders, but in my experience of working with leaders 'projections corrupt' more than power. How else can we explain the number of leaders who reach high office, and then lose the plot, acting in ways that are beyond rational understanding, and self-destruct. Bill Clinton in the White House, taking ridiculous sexual risks for example: this was not just abusing his power, it was

(Continued)

(Continued)

beyond rational explanation for such an intelligent man to take such risks after all he had worked for. The only explanation is the unconscious one. My hypothesis is that Clinton over-identified with the positive projections from his admiring followers, internalizing these idealized projections, and became grandiose and omnipotent. Unconsciously believing he was beyond 'normal' scrutiny, beyond normal codes of behaviour, he regressed to a childlike and narcissistic state that led an inner voice to tell him, 'I can do anything I want to and nobody can stop me.'

A leader can often receive good and bad projections: 'She's such a big head and she thinks she knows it all' … 'She's fantastic, what she has achieved is amazing.'

Leaders attract and react to these projections, and one of the tasks of leaders is to try to take a mature position, not to be seduced by good projections, becoming grandiose and omnipotent, or not to be destroyed or dysfunctionally hurt by bad projections. To be a leader is to walk a tightrope, between two poles created by social and unconscious forces.

'Leadership as an Attractor and Container of Projections'

Most leadership texts, coaches and developmental processes focus on leadership behaviours and how a leader projects their image outward, and less on how they attract and manage conscious and unconscious projections from followers. One of the leadership development activities I work with as coach is 'Leadership as an Attractor and Container of Projections'. Exploring these processes is deep work, but vitally important for leaders and leadership teams.

Individual leaders have an advantage over group or collective leadership due to the capacity for individual personalities to attract 'good' projections, where a 'faceless' collective body, for example a boardroom or political party, find it much more difficult. This explains how even though collective leadership may be taking place, a figurehead is chosen or is seen to be leading. Individual figureheads, even when they are not the most gifted leaders, are sometimes selected as they can galvanize positive projections and identifications that lead to a loyal followership (some claim that Ronald Regan was a classic example). This also explains how individuals can falsely believe they are, and be experienced by others as, the sole 'heroic' change agent when co-leaders are involved.

An individual leader's role and personality will attract projections from individual and collective followers, and it is these projections onto the leader that they then identify with. If they project ideas of intelligence onto the leader for example, they may give up their own intelligent thoughts and wait for the 'wise' intelligent leader to come up with the answers. I have often facilitated boardroom meetings where this occurs. The leader also projects unwanted parts of themselves onto others in order to protect and sustain their identity, exporting negative elements onto others (Petriglieri and Stein, 2012).

A leader's ability to stimulate the positive projections of followers, to contain the negative ones, and not to be seduced or overwhelmed by either, is an exceptional leadership quality.

Management vs Leadership

I will now explore both the split and the overlaps between management and leadership. The terms 'management' and 'leadership' are often used interchangeably and both evoke multiple meanings. Managers demonstrate leadership and likewise leaders usually have managerial skills. Traditionally leadership is a concept largely used in social and political settings yet in recent years is has become very prominent in the workplace, taking an elevated status above management, as Bennis and Nanus (1985: 218) point out:

> Management typically constitutes a set of contractual exchanges ... What gets exchanged is not trivial: jobs, security, and money. The result, at best, is compliance; at worst you get a spiteful obedience. The end result of leadership is completely different: it is empowerment. Not just higher profits and wages ... but an organizational culture that helps employees generate a sense of meaning in their work and a desire to challenge themselves to experience success.

Leaders and leadership have become a very sought-after commodity. Bennis (1986: 45) states that many American companies are 'over-managed and under-led', saying, 'I tend to think of the differences between leaders and managers as those who master the context and those who surrender to it'. Leadership has been rediscovered in an attempt to address the contemporary social and economic conditions faced by organizations. Leaders are thought to possess more of the qualities to address the contemporary organizational challenges than managers. There are many articles discussing the managers versus leadership debate (Barker, 1997; Kotter, 1990; Zaleznik, 1992), but the general tone is similar: managers are more rational and controlling, and they relate to structure, stability and bureaucracy, whereas leadership is about passion, vision, inspiration, creativity and cooperation rather than control. Alvesson and Sveningsson (2003: 1436) note:

> Leadership is often defined as being about 'voluntary' obedience. There are assumptions of harmony and convergence of interest, and the leader seldom uses formal authority or reward/punishment in order to accomplish compliance [Barker, 2001; Nicholls, 1987; Zaleznik, 1977].

Levy says 'in each individual you need to have the mind of a manager and the soul of a leader' (2004: 3; cited in Jackson and Parry, 2011); management then becomes the earthly, material, rational aspect of organizing, whereas leadership becomes the heartfelt, soulful, spiritual aspect. Zaleznik (1992) separates leadership and management neatly, perhaps too neatly:

> A managerial culture emphasizes rationality and control. Whether his or her energies are directed toward goals, resources, organization structures, or people, a manager is a problem solver ... It takes neither genius nor heroism to be a manager, but rather persistence, tough-mindedness, hard work, intelligence, analytical ability and perhaps most important, tolerance and goodwill. (1992: 126)

Whereas leaders:

> Leaders work from high-risk positions; indeed, they are often temperamentally disposed to seek out risk and danger, especially where the chance of opportunity and reward appears promising. (p. 126)

Others see the leaders as network builders, integrators and communicators, wedded to the ideas of cooperation (Alvesson, 2002). Bryman (1996) says that leaders have an integrative role: creating change and organizational culture through the transmission of cultural values. Much of the literature idealizes contemporary leaders, claiming they seldom use formal authority or means of rewards/punishment to accomplish compliance (Zaleznik, 1992). Yet in practice I observe that leaders use formal authority alongside influencing skills, demonstrating the blurring between leadership and management.

Management as the 'Other' to Leadership

Management has assumed the derogatory 'other' to leadership. The manager has been relegated to an outdated, functionalist and mechanistic mode of operating more suited to the industrial age than the post-industrial workplace.

Yet there is a fight-back, and Dubrin points to the need for management as well as leadership: 'Without being led as well as managed, organizations face the threat of extinction' (2000: 4).

Mintzberg writes:

> Leadership is supposed to be something bigger, more important. I reject this distinction, simply because managers have to lead and leaders have to manage. Management without leadership is sterile; leadership without management is disconnected and encourages hubris. (2004: 6)

Paul du Gay's (2000) *In Praise of Bureaucracy* and Elliot Jaques' (1990) article 'In praise of hierarchy' also challenge this general trend, which puts leadership in front of management in contemporary organizational life. Dubrin (2000) offers the following leader/manager dualisms: visionary as opposed to rational, passionate vs consulting, creative vs persistent, inspiring vs tough-minded, innovative vs analytical, courageous vs structured. Yukl critiques two-factor leadership examples – Task versus Relations, Autocratic versus Participative, Leadership versus Management, and Transformational versus Transactional leadership – and finds 'These dichotomies provide some insights, but they also over-simplify a complex phenomenon and encourage stereotyping of individual leaders' (Yukl, 1999: 34).

Management is clearly the 'other' to leadership and helps define leadership by showing what it is not. Leadership is very clearly in vogue and 'sexy', and the hopes are that it will provide answers to the new era rather than manage the present.

A.K. Rice is very clear that a manager must also be a leader because 'any institution whose managers do not give leadership … is obviously in difficulty' (Rice, 1965: 20). Rice, however, sees management as essentially rational and conscious, whereas leadership can also be exercised unconsciously. Rice identifies two tasks of leadership: a conscious task and an unconscious task. He is suggesting that leaders need to develop an awareness of their own conscious and unconscious roles. This implies that the leader has a conscious and manifest role relating to the work environment and task performance and an unconscious role to contain the emotions and expectations they have placed on them by the group. In this book I will not attempt to separate the manager and leader with surgical precision. I work on the assumption that managers will have some leadership qualities and responsibilities and vice versa. The idea of leadership in our conscious and unconscious minds underpins how we perceive and enact leadership.

The Meaning of Leadership

The next part of this chapter explores the different meanings we give to leadership. When listening to discussions about leadership in workplaces, people rarely explore what they mean by the term, yet Dubrin (2000) estimates there are 35,000 definitions of leadership in academic literature (Pye, 2005: 32). Kets de Vries notes a rapid increase in articles in the leadership bible *Stogdills Handbook of Leadership*, yet describes the contents as 'plodding and detached, often far removed from the reality of day-to-day life' (2006: 251).

Yet in spite of so much interest and research, leadership always seems just beyond our reach. Leadership selection remains ad hoc and leadership development is subject to arbitrary methods and with 'remarkable little evidence of the impact of leadership or leadership development on organizational performance' (Bolden et al., 2011: 5). Annie Pye suggests:

> The continuing search for the Holy Grail, which seems to characterize interest in leadership, implies that research efforts are perhaps being directed at 'solving the wrong problem'. (Pye, 2005: 31)

Definitions of Leadership

Barnard (1938/1991: 81) identified that 'lead' is both a noun and a verb and therefore has a double meaning. The noun could mean 'to be a guide to others, to be the head of an organization', whilst the verb could mean 'to excel and to be in advance'. Likewise, 'leadership' is used to describe social interaction between people and the term 'leader' is used to denote a person (or sometimes a group/company) who has influence over others (Northouse, 2004; Yukl, 2002). The term 'leadership' is also used to describe personality traits and behaviours and to denote the roles of individuals and collectives.

Box 6 sets out the definition that has emerged from researching this book.

Box 6　Definition of Leadership

Leadership is a psychosocial influencing dynamic

Leadership is not solely the property of individuals or groups, nor a set of competencies or skills, it more accurately described as *a psychosocial influencing dynamic*.

- *Psycho* refers to the psychodynamics of leadership, referencing that it occurs both *within and between* people. Leadership (and followership) stimulate intrapsychic, unconscious and emotional responses within us, and inter-relational dynamics between us.

- *Social* refers to the social construction and social dynamics of leadership. Leadership is more than a relational phenomena, it also references power and authority, control of material and symbolic resources, use of knowledge and technology. Discourses, history, culture and politics, i.e. the social field, must be accounted for in our understanding of leadership.

- *Influencing:* leadership signifies a specific agency, which is to influence others. Influencing is a wide-ranging term, and leadership draws on a vast array of resources, from personality to coercive power to influence others.

- *Dynamic* refers to the dynamic movement of leadership. It is never one thing, it is fluid not static, and cannot be reduced to skills, competencies, or a way of being. Leadership cannot be fixed; it moves between people as a dynamic social process.

Organizing Leadership

Different scholars have ordered leadership to try to help us organize it into categories. Northouse (2004: 3), reviewing leadership theory, identified four common themes:

- Leadership is a process

- Leadership involves influence

- Leadership occurs in a group context

- Leadership involves goal attainment

Keith Grint (2005) identifies a similar four-fold leadership typology of leadership:

- Person: who leads – traits and personality approaches

- Results: what leaders achieve

- Position: where they lead from – in front, alongside etc.

- Process: how leadership works

Jackson and Parry (2011) use five perspectives:

- Leader-centred

- Follower-centred

- Cultural perspectives

- Critical/distributed perspectives

- Leadership as a higher purpose

Leadership is framed in different ways and there are a multitude of leadership styles/approaches currently in circulation. Box 7 offers a few of the approaches available.

Box 7   Leadership Approaches

Autonomist	Patriarchal
Action-centred	Post-modern
Adaptive	Post-heroic
Authoritarian	Primal emotional
Charismatic	Principle-centred
Collective	Process
Consensual	Relational
Connected	Servant–leader
Contingency	Sense-making
Controller	Situated
Democratic	Spiritual
Distributive	Spontaneous
Dictatorial	Strategic
Discursive	Systemic
Eco-leadership	Technical
Expert	Therapist
Emergent	Thought leaders
Feminized	Transactional
Invisible	Transformational
Matriarchal	Transitional
Messiah	Values-based
Networked	
Participative	

In this chapter I order leadership into the following perspectives and take a critical view of each:

- Individual

- Collective

- Contextual

- Followers

- New leadership

Individual Leadership

Traits Competencies and Transformational Leadership

The main body of leadership literature focuses on leaders as individuals, taking behaviours, traits and competencies approaches. These use a positivist theoretical framework and are critiqued as oversimplistic, reductionist and offering unrealistic solutions to complex problems (Barley and Kunda, 1992; Calas and Smircich, 1995; Casey, 1995; Tourish and Pinnington, 2002). Grint (2005: 14) claims we need to move beyond individualistic approaches and 'put the –ship back in leadership'.

Today the multi-million dollar business of leadership development tends to focus on developing leadership traits and competencies. There has been a long search to try to define which aspects of the personality (i.e. traits) make a good leader. Observations and studies of exceptional leaders try to identify which aspects of their personality enabled them to be 'great leaders', and examples such as courage, charisma, vision, fortitude were identified as traits to be exemplified. Another approach derived from cognitive behavioural psychology attempts to identify what leaders do, rather than what their personalities consist of. This functionalist approach aims to modify and develop a potential leader's behaviour, in order to improve their leadership. Having identified the traits and competencies that good leaders have, individuals are trained and tested against this list to improve these behaviours or competencies. Manfred Kets de Vries finds the literature on leadership traits overwhelming and confusing but identifies some commonality in the findings: 'conscientiousness, extroversion, dominance, self-confidence, energy, agreeableness, intelligence, openness to experience and emotional stability' (Kets de Vries, 1994). As Kets de Vries points out, these traits are very open-ended and, when discussed, they open up a heated polemic as to the nature of what they really mean. The most common criticism of the trait/competency approach is that they offer 'one-size-fits-all' approaches, defining universal competencies or traits, which all individuals must have if they are to be successful leaders. For example, a National Health Service Quality framework for leadership provided a competency framework for its leaders (see www.nhsleadershipqualities.nhs.uk). Bolden and Gosling (2006) critique this competency approach, pointing out that vast resources were spent on NHS quality and leadership competency frameworks. Sadly the competencies leaders across the whole of the NHS were expected to attain had very little research validity or linkage to practice as the competencies were derived from a small number of self-reported interviews from chief executives. How these competencies can universally be relevant to clinical leaders in surgery, nurse leaders, finance leaders and a multitude of others is a mystery. The most popular current individual leadership approach is transformational leadership.

Transformational Leadership: 'The Charisma Trait'

Gemmil and Oakley (1992) pointed to a resurgence in the 1990s of the 'traitist' approach, identifying charisma as an embodiment of this approach: 'Charisma is the leadership trait most often examined by members of the "leadership mafia"' (in Grint, 1997: 277). Gemmil and Oakley's anti-leadership polemic names Bennis and Nanus (1985), Zaleznik (1989) and Tichy and Devanna (1986) as part of the new wave of leadership theorists drawing on the trait approach. Transactional leadership is often juxtaposed with transformational leadership, yet it still fits within the individualistic approach, but focuses on how leadership takes place through transactional behaviours rather than influencing skills.

Collective Leadership

Collective leadership can refer to team leadership, leadership as a process, or distributed leadership. Senior teams, project teams, and boards of directors work together in offering 'collective leadership'; the process of leadership occurs between collective groups of people; and finally distributed leadership disperses leadership throughout organizations, creating a collective leadership approach. Pearce and Conger (2003: 1) describe 'shared leadership' as a dynamic interaction whereby the 'objective is to lead one another to the achievement of group or organizational goals'. Some claim that leadership is essentially collective and not individual. Senge (1990) has defined leadership as 'the collective capacity to create useful things', and Collinson states, 'In effect, leadership is the property and consequence of a community rather than the property and consequence of an individual leader' (2006: 183). The word 'Ubuntu' crops up in leadership studies (Hickman, 2012); emanating from Africa, it relates to the interdependencies of the group and fits with the ideas of collective leadership.

Team Leadership

Collective team leadership provides a different level of containment and confidence than an individual leader, who is more likely to stimulate dependency responses from followers. Team leadership also provides more balance and working well optimizes the diverse capabilities of the group.

Leadership as a Process

Critical theorists claim that leadership is a relational and social process, rather than being the property of an individual or team (Collinson, 2006; Grint, 2005). This perspective shifts the emphasis away from elitism and hierarchy, but doesn't yet offer many practical insights as to how leadership as a process can be worked with beyond a conceptual idea.

Distributed Leadership

Distributive or dispersed leadership are popular concepts and relate to the changing post-industrial work conditions that cannot be managed in a top-down, expert, command and control structure. Chapter 12, Eco-Leadership, offers an in-depth view of distributed leadership for post-industrial organizations. Raelin (2003) argues that leaders should create environments that develop 'leaderful' organizations, where all are expected to be leaders in a collective endeavour. Daniel Goleman describes this distributive leadership as 'every person at entry level who in one way or another, acts as a leader' (2002: 14). Elmore agrees: '[in] knowledge intensive enterprises like teaching and learning there is no way to perform these complex tasks without widely distributing the responsibility for leadership among roles in the organization' (2000: 14).

Collective leadership distributed across an organization requires democratization, connectivity and collaboration. The advantages are a more alive, adaptive and energized organization; the disadvantages are that many leadership voices compete for airtime, and if power and leadership are really distributed, it can create a more conflictual organization than with a 'dependent' group of conformist followers. This latter point is not often aired in the literature yet it needs addressing. A healthy democracy cannot operate without opposition voices to those governing, and in organizations dissenting voices are vital for healthy and creative organizations.

In my experience the gap between the rhetoric of distributed leadership and the actual practice of distributing leadership is wide. Distributing leadership means distributing power and control from the centre to the edges, and this creates huge anxiety, and real challenges at the top of organizational structures. Senior leaders face a paradox: they can no longer control from the centre, yet to distribute influence and power can feel highly risky, when they are accountable to the board and shareholders. Those companies and organizations that achieve distributed leadership operate with higher levels of trust and with a general belief in their shared goals than companies who wish to distribute leadership simply to gain market share or increase productivity.

Another paradox exists. Sometimes it requires a 'Messiah leader', a charismatic and visionary individual or team, to drive change and create new collaborative cultures with distributed leadership. The challenge here is for the Messiah leader to initiate, provoke and stimulate change and be prepared to let go of power when successful: a difficult task!

Contextual Leadership

The Social Context of an Organization

The essence of contextual leadership approaches is the acknowledgement that it is foolish to try to apply universal leadership approaches to non-universal, diverse contexts. Organizations have diverse structures and cultures, depending on the wider environmental, social, cultural and political contexts, as well as their product/outputs, client base etc. All have to be taken into account when reflecting on what leadership fits the context.

Fred Fiedler's Contingency approach (1967, 1974) attempted to rescue leadership theory from the simplistic notion of the 'one-best-fit' leader for all situations. Fiedler proposed that the leadership style would need to be different to fit different situations, i.e. it had to be situational and contingent. He attempted to find the optimal match between leadership style and situation. Critics challenge his research claims of success on the grounds that there has been a failure to replicate results and some of the results conflict with subordinates' accounts of leaders (Bryman, 1986). Contingency approaches challenge the notion of the one-best-style leader for different situations yet they focus on the two-factor model of *relationship- or task-centred* leader. Task-centred leaders focus on the task rather than people and are more directive. This approach suits certain situations, for example, in hierarchical organizations with unstructured tasks, whereas relationship-centred leaders are favoured in the majority of situations as they focus on people and participation. Unfortunately this offers yet another dualistic model, 'relational or task', that does not account for the complexity of understanding relationships, power and leadership from multiple perspectives. Contingency leadership is also critiqued for still treating followers passively, in spite of recognizing that different leadership approaches are required for different follower situations. The contingency approach attempts to address some of the social context issues faced by leaders but tries to package it into oversimplistic assumptions. Much more work is required in this area as a one-best-fit leadership style or an over-simplified contingency approach to leadership is still common practice. There are many factors to consider, such as *functions and outputs*. Within organizations there is a diversity of outputs and functions depending on the department; as different skills, training and cultures are required in different departments, so also are different leadership styles, structures and processes. Other factors are *product and meaning*. The product or output of the organization is very underestimated in the leadership literature, as it impacts on the leadership requirements and needs of that organization. For example, leadership of a public sector hospital differs from leading McDonald's food chain or a global weapons manufacturer. Multinationals have found to their cost through the failure rate of mergers and acquisitions that underestimating diverse cultures can have a huge impact on success and failure. The output of the organization impacts on the technical and structural aspects of organizational life and also on the psychosocial dynamics of the organization. Hospitals produce different outputs to supermarkets, and also different meanings for workers, and user groups/customers: leaders must also address the question of meaning in an organization.

Size Matters: Individuals, Teams and Mass Leadership

Can we talk about a single leadership approach and refer to a small start-up company and a global institution? One leader requires an entrepreneurial mindset and the other, symbolic leadership skills, communicating to mass employees, and their market and stakeholder groups. The leadership task of a national president is different from that of a team leader. Showing leadership in a one-to-one mentoring session can be very effective and influential, but differs from leading a virtual project team. Some leaders excel when utilizing symbolic leadership to a mass audience, whilst their interpersonal leadership skills at a team level can be very poor. When selecting and developing leaders context matters, and leadership must always be 'local and specific'. Certainly common features exist, and generic skills are useful, but leadership has to be considered adaptable to its environment, otherwise it feels like an imposition.

Followers

Without followership leadership doesn't exist. Followership is symbiotic with leadership, and to understand leadership is to recognize how leaders and followers co-produce and sustain each other (Ladkin, 2006). Leaders and followers have tended to be seen as dualist opposites, with the main focus being on the leader. Through this dualistic lens followers have been presented both individually and collectively as passive objects, to be moulded, coerced and influenced by the leader. However, due to the rise in interest of dispersed leadership and autonomous teams, with post-structuralists deconstructing leadership, followership has gained importance and the dualistic approach is being challenged. Collinson (2006: Intro) cites a widening literature that insists that followers are integral to the leadership process:

> rejecting the common stereotype of followers as timid, docile sheep, these writers argue that in the contemporary context of greater team working, 'empowered, knowledge workers', and 'distributed' and 'shared' leadership, 'good followership skills' have never been more important.

There is a growing 'follower literature' that attempts to diminish the agency of the leader and assert the agency of the follower, who, if anything, 'raises up the leader' (Meindl, 1995). Grint claims 'the power of leaders is a consequence of the actions of the followers rather than the cause of it' (Grint, 2005: 38). The terms 'follower' and 'leader' are problematic; perhaps the notion of followers should be replaced by a term such as 'participators', describing the reality that 'followers participate in the leadership process', sometimes by following, other times by taking a leadership role, at other times producing leadership, and at other times neither following nor leading but partaking. Servant leadership (Greenleaf, 1977) was an early adopter of refocusing leadership as a service to followers, therefore raising their status, and the relationship between the two. How much influence followers have on leaders is a debated point; the Arab Spring uprisings demonstrated that when followers find their voice and power they can have an ultimate influence on deposing leaders; and conversely where leaders attempt to lead without consent, their timeline is limited. Followership can be passive or active, compliant or aggressive; it has many forms. Leadership and followership are entwined and the recent research and deeper exploration of this entanglement have been welcome.

New Leadership

Mutton Dressed as Lamb?

Much of what is regarded as new leadership literature is critiqued because it recycles previous leadership theories; for example, Calas and Smircich critiqued Peters and Waterman's so-called innovative text of the 1990s *In Search of Excellence* and their celebrated transcendent leader: 'Under the guise of "newness" the authors do no more than articulate some empty discourses from the 1980s' (Calas and Smircich, 1991: 589). Yukl claims this also applies to leadership research:

> Despite all the hype about a 'new paradigm' for studying leadership, most of the research uses the same superficial methods that have been prevalent for decades. (Yukl, 1999: 42)

However, new trends in leadership are emerging. Petriglieri and Stein (2012) cite three current leadership trends that point towards reframing the problem and changing the way we think about leadership:

- The first is the resurgence of a perspective less preoccupied with leaders' impact on organizational performance and more with their function as sources and symbols of the values and meaning-making of organizational members (Podolny et al., 2005; Smircich and Morgan, 1982).

- The second is a move beyond the study of traits, behaviors, and contingencies that allow leaders to exert their influence over followers (Reicher et al., 2005).

- The third is a transcendence of traditional views of leadership as the preserve of individuals in positions of formal authority (DeRue and Ashford, 2010).

I would add three more trends:

- The fourth is the move towards systems, *networked and distributed* approaches to leadership, recognizing the impact that technology, the network society and globalization are having on organizational life, which demands new leadership approaches.

- The fifth is the ever-greater calls for *ethical leadership*, with a particular focus on values, diversity, corporate social responsibility and sustainable environmental practices.

- The sixth is *leadership spirit*: this reflects a trend from logos to mythos, an attempt in postmodernism to reclaim deeper personal and collective experiences, that became marginalized in the instrumentalism of the 20th century workplace. In the 21st century a trend is to turn 'human resources' into 'soul workers'.

These final three trends in particular inform the emergent Eco-leadership discourse (Chapter 12). I will now look at three examples of new leadership: *post-heroic approaches, postmodern approaches* and *spiritual leadership*.

Post-heroic Leadership

As a reaction to the hubris (and perhaps the failure to deliver) of transformational leadership, the term 'post-heroic leadership' signifies a change of emphasis (Huey, 1994). Binney et al. (2004) write about leaders as ordinary heroes whilst Badarraco (2001), in his article 'We don't need another hero', makes the case for quiet moral leadership: 'modesty and restraint are in large measure responsible for their extraordinary achievement'. The post-heroic leader is a reaction to the noise and bells of the 'tub-thumping' evangelic style of the transformational leader. The leader is toned down and forceful, but with humility and a quiet but focused influence. Examples of this approach are Badarraco's (2001) 'quiet leader', and Jim Collins' (2001) 'Level 5 leader', 'who blends extreme personal humility with intense professional will'. Binney et al. summarize the effective post-heroic leader:

> If leaders are to connect with others and understand the context, they need to bring themselves to the job of leading. Leaders can do this in the following ways:

- They come across to others as genuinely human, and don't wear any kind of mask.

- They draw on all their humanity, their intelligence, their emotions and their intuition. They don't stay in their heads and draw solely on their rational selves. They make use of all their senses and intelligence.

- They remember what they know from their life experiences and make use of them in the world of work (Binney et al., 2004).

As can be seen, the leader needs to be authentic, emotionally intelligent, sensitive and less rational, privileging the emotional and internal self. The post-heroic leadership literature also includes the recent idea of 'leader–coaches', advocating that leaders should be coaches to their followers and should create 'coaching cultures' in the workplace.

Much of this literature re-presents ideas from the democratic and human relations movement, and is particularly close to Greenleaf's (1977) 'servant leader', which pioneered post-heroic leadership under a different name more than thirty years ago. Post-heroic leadership resonates with a therapist discourse (Chapter 10). The digital and cognitive labourer, working in a knowledge economy, does not require coercion but 'therapeutic' leadership to support and motivate them. As Rose says: 'The management of subjectivity has become a central task for the modern organization' (Rose, 1990).

Humble Heroes

These leaders appear not so much post-heroic, but rather reflect the desire for a new breed of hero, just as effective and as charismatic, yet the charisma is not extravert but more intravert, it shines through the leader's authenticity, humility, generosity and ability to lead quietly. Jim Collins' Level 5 leader retains the heroism but inverts it. Rather than acting with machismo and visionary language the Level 5 leader advocates humility, focus and resilience as tools to achieve the same outcome:

> The most powerfully transformative executives possess a paradoxical mixture of personal humility and professional will. They are timid and ferocious. Shy and fearless, they are rare – and unstoppable. (Collins, 2001: 1)

The new post-heroic leader literature also leans towards spiritual leadership, which is sometimes explicit and also implicit in the tone of its claims about these very special leaders.

Postmodern Approaches: Discursive and Sense-Making Leadership

'Discursive leadership' (Fairhurst, 2007), drawing on post-structural theory and Foucault, focuses on how language and discourses shape our understanding and actions, and accounts for the historical, cultural and social influences that form our 'taken-for-granted' thinking about leadership (the discourses in this book emerge partly from this approach). Sense-making leadership (Pye, 2005; Weick, 1995) focuses on how leaders shape the way followers respond to challenges.

Postmodern leadership replaces modernity's focus on production and efficiency. The new conditions of today's global, post-industrial, knowledge-based workplaces mean that new insights into social processes and organizational dynamics are required. Critical scholars drawing on post-structural theories such as Lyotard (1979/1984) and Derrida (1982) also offer new insights, such as how power is much more dispersed and how identity is less fixed, and therefore how leadership itself becomes less fixed, and how power is enacted is much less hierarchal. Leadership from a post-modern perspective has always to be negotiated, is always partial, is socially constructed through language and focuses on the symbolic and virtual realms. Critics of postmodern approaches claim they are too distant from practice, too elitist in their academic language, and that they don't address material power imbalances, but focus too much on symbolism, identity and meaning.

Spiritual Leadership: Compassionate Corporate Bodhisattvas

A sharp rise in spiritual leadership literature reflects a new search for meaning and values at work. Spiritual leadership is entering mainstream university and corporate life. James LoRusso (2011) writes:

> Self-proclaimed 'corporate mystic' Lynne Sedgmore read this passage by Khalil Gibran during her keynote address at the International Faith and Spirit at Work Conference recently held at the University of Arkansas.
>
> 'Work is love made visible. And if you cannot work with love but only with distaste, it is better that you should leave your work and sit at the gate of the temple and take alms of those who work with joy.' – Khalil Gibran

Whilst some regard the idea of corporate spirituality an anathema and wacky (and there are many pitfalls that I address later), some use their spirituality to support their mission with great effect. I coached Lynne Sedgmore CBE and consulted to her organization for two years when she was CEO of a National Leadership Centre for Education in the UK, which she led with determination, skill and passion. Hendricks and Ludeman, in their book *The Corporate Mystic*, support this view; they claim that corporate mystics 'have a respect and even fondness for change ... At times they may have unpleasant feelings about the directions of change, but they are careful not to let those feelings limit their ability to respond.' Corporate mystics have a 'type of discipline that makes them flexible and adaptable rather than rigid' (Hendricks and Ludeman, 1997).

Others identifying themselves as 'corporate mystics' are clearly narcissistic and grandiose leaders, using spirituality as a prop to support their omnipotence. They use spirituality to reinforce their sense of being 'special leaders', called to perform on a higher esoteric level, led by a higher spirit. The Academy of Management has a Special Interest Group on Management, Spirituality and Religion at its conference, and academic and popular work journals are full of references to spirituality. Calas and Smircich write: 'For at least a decade the press has reported company leaders speaking about spirituality and business, while multiple publications have advocated links between corporate success and issues of the soul' (2003: 329). The strength of this movement has grown: Hendricks and Ludeman's (1997) book *The Corporate Mystic* and Neal's (2006) *Edgewalkers* join many others. Case and Gosling (2010: 277) list popular publications: Barrett, *Liberating the Corporate Soul* (1998); Conger, *The Spirit at Work*

(1994); Howard and Welbourn, *The Spirit at Work Phenomenon* (2004); Jones, *Jesus CEO* (1996); Klein and Izzo, *Awakening Corporate Soul* (1999); Lodahl and Powell, *Embodied Holiness: A Corporate Theology of Spiritual Growth* (1999); Mitroff and Denton, *A Spritual Audit of Corporate America* (1999).

The *Journal of Management, Spirituality & Religion* (Routledge) specifically addresses this issue. In the USA religion still has a strong hold; Conlon (1999) estimates that at least 10,000 Bible and prayer groups meet regularly in American workplaces. Historically, faith and leadership have long been associated, and religion and business have been strongly linked since the industrial revolution with many industrial social reforms coming through religious leadership such as the Quakers and other non-conformist religious groups (Walvin, 1997). In Europe, the religious influence in business and leadership has declined as secularization has increased, yet spirituality has recently emerged as its successor. The growing interest in spiritual leadership reflects the postmodern shift from institutions to individualism, from authority figures to self-authorization, and from religion to spirituality.

In 2009 I facilitated a conference entitled '(A Crisis of) Faith in Leadership',[1] spending two days in the company of leaders from business and the public sector, psychoanalysts, individuals from the army and academia, priests and monks, exploring the idea of a secular crisis of 'faith in leadership', and the relationship between spiritual and religious faith, and leadership. What emerged was a strong sense that faith in leadership is vitally important, and that 'faith in leaders' often depends on the 'faith of leaders', however they describe or understand the source of their faith.

A Thirst for Meaning, Calmness and Connection

Reflecting these social trends, there is a genuine desire by many leaders and employees who seek a deeper meaning from their work-life, and attempt to integrate a 'spiritual and work' identity (Bell and Taylor, 2004; Giacalone and Jurkiewicz, 2003). Mitroff and Denton in *A Spiritual Audit of Corporate America* write: 'If one word best captures the meaning of spirituality and the vital role it plays in people's lives, it is inter-connectedness' (1999: xvi). Their spiritual audit found these responses to how corporate employees define their personal spirituality:

- Highly individual and intensely personal.

- Belief that there is a supreme being that governs the universe and that there is a purpose for everybody and everything.

---

[1] Tavistock Clinic 2009

- We are all interconnected. Everything affects everything else.

- Being in touch with your interconnectedness.

- No matter how bad things are, they will always work out.

- We are here to serve others/mankind.

- Connected to caring, hope, kindness, love and optimism.

  (Mitroff and Denton, 1999: 23–5, cited in Katz, 2006)

Much of the spiritual literature merges with humanism, individualism and rationalism. For example, Zohar and Marshall use the term spiritual *intelligence* where spirituality paradoxically becomes linked to cognitive intelligence and rationality, and that makes it easier to sell to the management market. Zohar and Marshall describe spiritual intelligence (SQ) as 'the intelligence with which we access our deepest meanings, values, purposes and highest emotions' (2004: 3). They state:

> In understanding SQ and Spiritual Leadership it is important to list the twelve transformative processes of SQ (these are characteristics displayed in a person of high SQ):

> Self-awareness, Spontaneity, Vision and Value led, Holistic, Compassion, Celebration of diversity, Field-independence, Asking why?, Reframe, Positive use of adversity, Humility, Sense of vocation. (2004: 80)

This list raises the question of what separates the spiritual leader from an ethical 'good' leader, as all 12 points could also be listed under a humanist banner.

Spiritual Leadership: A Critique

The assumption that being religious or spiritual leads to ethical goodness and positive outcomes is false as many spiritual leaders will fail, often due to their immoral and unethical acts. The words 'spiritual' and 'leadership' both carry potent meanings and together are a powerful and dangerous combination, potentially creating over-zealous and dependent followers, and over-confident omnipotent leaders. As discussed previously, being a leader stimulates dependency feelings and projections of idealization, being a spiritual leader doubles this impact, and unless the leader is mature, self-aware and has reflective supervision, or critical friends to manage these projections, dangers await. Thomas Merton warned of the dangers of monastic novices idealizing him when he was their spiritual guide, with very damaging results, as they lost their autonomy in aiming only to please and mimic him, and he lost his bearings as their spiritual director for a while: 'Penitents (Novice Monks) seduce you into taking the role of omnipotence and omniscience and in this situation you are deluding yourself' (Merton, 1966: 55). Ackers and Preston (1992) claim that a new priestly cadre is being 'developed':

> ... [a]rguing that a new evangelical, revelatory form of management development is making its way from the margins to the mainstream, wherein managers are treated as a 'priestly cadre' whose spiritual needs must be satisfied through semi-monastic retreats to recharge their batteries. (1992: 697–8)

The dangers of a 'priestly cadre' leading businesses for profit are rarely discussed by those singing the praises of spiritual leadership.

Instrumentalizing Spirituality

Carrette and King's (2005) book *Selling Spirituality* warns how spirituality is instrumentalized and used as a 'tool' to increase both consumption and production.

Zen and Taoist leadership, Benedictine monks, Gaia holism, American Indian rituals, yoga and mindfulness are all part of today's leadership development approaches. Bringing your 'whole self to work', including your spiritual self, is an liberating ideal for some and a nightmare for others, whereby the corporation not only wants your body and mind for eight hours a day, but also your soul! Whilst according to May (2000), spirituality is the most important influence in leadership, Tourish and Pinnington point out that 'Ironically, this effort is often driven by a very non-spiritual concern – the desire to increase profits' (2002: 165).

What is surprising to me is how claims are made that spiritual-work cultures increase productivity (Altman, 2001; Becker, 1998), with very little if any sense that this may be problematic. It is often presented simply as a good thing. Žižek claims that New Age and Eastern spirituality are popular with global business, because the effects lead to passive workers and ultra-conformist cultures:

> The 'Western Buddhist' meditative stance is arguably the most efficient way for us to fully participate in the capitalist economy while retaining the appearance of sanity. If Max Weber were alive today, he would definitely write a second, supplementary volume to his Protestant Ethic, titled The Taoist Ethic and the Spirit of Global Capitalism. (Žižek, 2002)

Bell and Taylor (2004) agree that when an individual engages in the Westernized spiritual work of non-attachment it frees them from ethical engagement; they are able to use their private inward spirituality as a coping mechanism which supports them but does not encourage external engagement. These therapeutic/spiritual cultures can also lead to an increased sense of focus on one's self, further embellishing a leader's narcissistic ego. This approach undermines the solidarity of collective agency by increasing a detached inward attitude that ends up being in servitude to, rather than engaging with, the corporate machine. Spiritual leadership can help challenge the excesses of modernity; it can bring different values to the workplace that are welcome; and it can also be misused and misconstrued, sometimes intentionally and often unintentionally. For a fuller critique and exploration of spirituality and work/leadership see:

- Bell, E. and Taylor, S. (2004) 'From outward bound to inward bound: the prophetic voices and discursive practices of spiritual management development', *Human Relations*, 57 (4): 439–66.

- Carrette, J. and King, R. (2005) *Selling Spirituality: The Silent Takeover of Religion*. London: Routledge.

- Case, P. and Gosling, J. (2010) 'The spiritual organization: critical reflections on the instrumentality of workplace spirituality', *Journal of Management, Spirituality & Religion*, 7 (4): 257–82.

- Heelas, P. (2008) *Spiritualities of Life: New Age Romanticism and Consumptive Capitalism*. Oxford: Blackwell.

New leadership comes in many forms: post-structural, postmodern, new spirituality, and it always mirrors other social, political, economic and technological changes. Sometimes new leadership is the old dressed as new, but there are also new developments that inspire hope, and these can be further explored in Chapter 12, Eco-Leadership.

Conclusion: The Experience of Leadership

This chapter asked the question 'What is leadership?' and answered it with a definition; *leadership is a psychosocial influencing dynamic*.

We experience leadership as an idea, we give it meanings, names, structures and form, attributing formal and informal social roles to it, and to followers. Leadership is performed on us, within us, between us, and all around us. Leadership is not symmetrical and neat, but asymmetrical, dynamic and complex. How we experience leadership depends on our personal history, our collective socialization and the context. We perceive, enact and respond to leadership, individually and collectively, consciously and unconsciously. Our best chance of improving leadership is to improve our understanding of it. Understanding leadership begins with understanding our ambivalence to leadership. It is important for individuals to try to locate their own perceptions and emotions (personal and cultural) that are attached to leadership. Learning about leadership is as much about feeling as it is about thinking as these two are intimately connected.

Suggested Readings

- Bolden, R., Gosling, J., Hawkins, B. and Taylor, S. (2011) *Exploring Leadership: Individual, Organizational, and Societal Perspectives*. Oxford: Oxford University Press.

- Fairhurst, G. (2009) 'Considering context in discursive leadership research', *Human Relations*, 62 (11): 1607–35.

- Northouse, P. G. (2007) *Leadership: Theory and Practice*, 4th edn. Thousand Oaks, CA: Sage.

- Pearce, C. L. and Conger, J. A (eds) (2003) *Shared Leadership: Reframing the Hows and Whys of Leadership*. Thousand Oaks, CA: Sage.

- Tourish, D. and Tourish, N. (2010) 'Spirituality at work, and its implications for leadership and followership: a post-structuralist perspective', *Leadership*, 6 (2): 207–24.

Reflection Points

- Reflect on your own feelings and assumptions about leadership, and try and see patterns in your responses to leaders to discover your 'unconscious process' regarding leadership. Ask yourself: do you generally admire or criticize leaders? Do you expect a little or a lot from leaders? Do you usually assume leadership is in someone else more important than you? Are you in awe of important leaders?

- How can leadership be both an individual and collective phenomenon?

- What are the differences and overlaps between management and leadership?

Sample Assignment Question

Explain in your own words the definition 'leadership is a psychosocial influencing dynamic' and then draw upon leadership examples to highlight your explanation.

3 Asymmetric Leadership: A Brief Case Study

Figure 3.1   Women in mosque: Damascus, Syria 2009

> **Chapter Structure**
>
> - **Introduction**
> - **Case Study: Lenin's Leadership of the Communist Revolution**
> - **Conclusion: The Challenge of Asymmetric Leadership**

Introduction

This chapter highlights the asymmetric nature and plurality of leadership. I have taken a brief case study of a single social movement, a few pages of text written about the Communist Revolution by one of its leading figures, Leon Trosky. This case study offers insights into the multiple layers of leadership, identifying some of the key issues raised in the book so far. It identifies seven leadership themes from this single movement, and demonstrates how leadership emerges in asymmetrical forms to address different contexts.

The Case Study

This case study offers an analysis of a short piece of unpublished writing from Leon Trotsky on Vladimir Lenin's role in the Soviet Revolution. A traditional 'Great Man' theory of leadership would focus solely on the hero leader, i.e. Lenin. Post-structuralist writing and many critical theorists focus on the process of leadership and minimize the individual's role (Collinson, 2006; Grint, 1997). However, as this short text demonstrates, leadership is not solely situated in a single person, or a small group, and yet these are vital to leadership as well. This analysis reveals at least seven faces of leadership, including a 'heroic' individual leader. One of the key tasks of leadership research is to improve our understanding of how the individual leader and the collective process of leadership occurs in organizations. Trotsky's writing on Lenin's leadership offers an interesting narrative which gives a valuable account, in its content and in the subtext, that is revealed when it is analysed. This case helps illuminate the interdependency between solo actors and collective actors when understanding leadership. The relationship between individual leaders and followers, distributed leaders and collective leadership in groups, determines the relationship between a leader and the process of leadership. The text in italics is taken from Trotsky's unfinished work *The Class, The Party and the Leadership* (Trotsky, 1940).

Text Analysis

The analysis shows how Trotsky's text offers at least seven differing examples of leadership, which together make up a leadership process:

1 Intellectual leadership

2 Unconscious leadership

3 Group leadership

4 Distributed leadership

5 Individual leadership

6 Mass leadership

7 Symbolic leadership

The first four categories show how leadership emerges differently when people are in different groupings or patterns, i.e. individuals, groups/ teams, distributed networks and collective masses. The final three examples show how leadership is an experiential phenomena, leadership is experienced through symbolism, cognition and intellectual ideas, and through our emotions, often stimulated by unconscious processes such as projection.

   Note: I have highlighted Trotsky's words in italics, the text is in chronological order and I have selected relevant material from two pages of his writing. The bold headings are my own to clarify the analysis.

Case Study: Lenin's Leadership of the Communist Revolution

The Setting

The Bolshevik party in March 1917 was followed by an insignificant minority of the working class and furthermore there was discord within the party itself. An overwhelming majority of the workers supported the Mensheviks and the 'Socialist-Revolutionists', i.e. conservative social-patriots. The situation was even less favourable with regard to the army and the peasantry.

(1) Intellectual Leadership (Thought Leadership)

What was the 'active' of Bolshevism? A clear and thoroughly thought out revolutionary conception at the beginning of the revolution was held only by Lenin. The Russian cadres of the party were scattered and to a considerable degree bewildered.

But the party had authority among the advanced workers. Lenin had great author-
ity with the party cadres. These elements of the 'active' worked wonders in a
revolutionary situation, that is, in conditions of bitter class struggle. The party
quickly aligned its policy to correspond with Lenin's conception, to correspond
that is with the actual course of the revolution.

The Early Success

Thanks to this, the party met with firm support among tens of thousands of
advanced workers. Within a few months, by basing itself upon the development of
the revolution the party was able to convince the majority of the workers of the
correctness of its slogans. This majority organized into Soviets, was able in its
turn to attract the soldiers and peasants.

Trotsky's first point is that Lenin showed the intellectual leadership that
managed to appeal to the masses in a very short period of time. *'What was the*
"active" of Bolshevism? A clear and thoroughly thought out revolutionary conception
at the beginning of the revolution was held only by Lenin'. Trosky describes the
active in Bolshevism as Lenin's intellectual leadership. Interestingly Trosky
realizes that this intellectual clarity, this 'thought leadership', gave him *'great*
authority with the party cadres'. Authority is often equated with position,
power and resources, but clearly authority can also come from intellectual
leadership.

Intellectual leadership is a powerful and vital leadership form and is
increasingly being separated from other forms of leadership. Nowadays
leaders select specialist experts, strategic consultants, or think tanks
(collectivized thought leadership) to support them in this role. Intellectual
leadership has never been the sole property of an individual. Lenin's thinking
was obviously built upon Marx and Engels and was formulated amongst
other leading socialist thinkers of the time. Lenin, however, did manage to:

(a) bring original and creative thinking to this process;

(b) synthesize ideas into a coherent form;

(c) translate these ideas into action and strategies;

(d) communicate these to others.

(2) Unconscious Leadership: Leadership and Projective Identification

A colossal factor in the maturity of the Russian proletariat in February or March
1917 was Lenin. He did not fall from the skies. He personified the revolutionary
tradition of the working class.

Trotsky describes Lenin as *'personifying the revolutionary tradition of the working class'*. This means that 'the masses' were able to identify with Lenin, to project onto him the ideals of the revolution, their ideals of freedom. Lenin was able both to stimulate and contain these positive projections (as well as manage negative projections), which made him an extraordinary leader, able to lead the successful revolution.

Individuals and groups project onto a leader their own internal desires and anxieties, which means that leaders attract multiple projections, as Lilley and Platt's (1997: 319–37) research shows. They analysed 621 letters written to Martin Luther King and found that followers (activists in the civil rights movement) saw him as one of at least four identifiably different leaders; the division did not map naturally onto the background of the writer – for example, not all black writers regarded him as first and foremost a black leader:

- Black leader.

- Christian leader.

- Non-violent leader.

- Democratic leader.

King himself acknowledged these projections:

> I am aware of two Martin Luther Kings … the Martin Luther King people talk about seems foreign to me. (Oates, 1982: 283)

Ramor Ryan (2003) describes the masked 'Zapatistas' leader Sub-Commandante Marcos, who uses writing and intellect as his main leadership tools:

> Marcos' writing is beautiful and expansive enough to fit every revolutionary tradition. His great ruse is to make each tradition think of him as representing them – the indigenous say he is one of them, the guerrillas claim him as one of their own, the intellectuals include him in their pantheon, Mexican nationalists see him as a great Mexican nationalist, NGOs see him as an advocate for NGOs, Marxists see him as one of their sect, anarchists claim him as part of their tradition, even the base church sees him as an advocate of their preferential option of the poor. This potentially complex multiple personality disorder is of course symbolised by the ever-present mask. Would the real Sub Marcos, please stand up?! (Ryan, 2003)

The mask does not cover a multiple personality disorder but is a very astute leadership ploy aimed at attracting the projections of diverse and marginalized groups and their global supporters. The mask makes Marcos mysterious and enhances his enigma, his charisma, and therefore his influence (he smokes a pipe which comes out of the mask, making him immediately recognizable as an individual), but more importantly it allows others to project onto the mask whatever they wish. Behind the mask is the person they want to believe in and Marcos uses this device as part of his ploy to create solidarity across globally diverse and marginalized groups. This verse comes from a Zapatista international gathering 1997:

> Behind our black mask
>
> Behind our armed voice
>
> Behind our unnameable name
>
> Behind what you see of us
>
> Behind this, we are you
>
> (Ruggiero and Sahulka, 1998)

Leaders bear several meanings, projected onto them from their followers. Individual personalities and characters are, however, like magnets for particular projections, and some leaders manage to boost their capacity to attract positive projections and diminish their capacity to attract negative ones. Creating a leadership image, which attracts the desired projections, has become a huge business in its own right. Executive coaching, the makeover, the spin doctor and other 'image creators' all aim to help the leader give out the right image and signals, which in turn will determine the type of projections a leader attracts. Contemporary leaders regard this as just as important as getting the right message across. A leader is a receptacle for others' projections and also projects their own image outwards; it's a reciprocal process.

Lilley and Platt draw an important implication from their work on Martin Luther King:

> That a social movement need not be consensual to achieve successfully an effective solidarity. What King represented was not consensus and yet there did appear to be an effective solidarity within the civil rights movement. (Lilley and Platt, 1997: 319)

The solidarity described in the civil rights movement under Martin Luther King's leadership is also desired by corporate boards, who want employees to buy into their values and give loyalty to the company. A leader's ability to stimulate and to psychically contain and make sense of the projections of followers is an exceptional leadership quality. Some leaders do this knowingly, others instinctively, and often do both. Lenin clearly had this quality of 'Unconscious Leadership' that enabled supporters to project their aspirations onto him, so that he came to 'personify' their struggle.

(3) Group Leadership (The Party)

The vital mainspring in this process (the revolution) is the party, just as the vital mainspring in the mechanism of the party is its leadership. The role and the responsibility of the leadership in a revolutionary epoch are colossal.

Trotsky describes the collective group leadership shown by 'the party' as the vanguard of the revolution. Without this group leadership there would be no revolution; an individual is not enough. The party is the organization's inner corporate leadership body, a hierarchical decision-making body, and provides an institutional structure that offers containment to the whole organization and the movement beyond. When group leadership functions well, there is a powerful sense of corporate shared responsibility and discipline. This corporate sense of leadership can be seen in governments and boardrooms; in fact most 'traditional organizational forms have a leadership group. Any group, whether it is a formal organization or informal movement, requires organizing activities and some kind of discipline and boundaries, otherwise it would not be a recognizable entity, and this means some form and structure of leadership. The collective actors and individual actors within an organization are in a dynamic relationship, one that is reflexive. The leader needs to be confident in the party leadership and the party must have confidence in the individual leader. However, sometimes the individual is merely the face of the group to the world, and others in the group wield more power.

(4) Distributed Leadership (Empowering the Cadres)

For Lenin's slogans to find their way to the masses there had to exist cadres, even though numerically small at the beginning; there had to exist the confidence of the cadres in the leadership, a confidence based on the entire experience of the past …

Trotsky realized that without cadres (leading party activists), Lenin's message would not have had any impact. The individual leader (Lenin) and the group leadership (the party) needed to have confidence in the distributed leadership on the ground (the cadres) to make any impact on the masses. It is the dynamic relationship between the individual (Lenin), the group (the party leadership), the network (the cadres) and the masses, which makes up the process of leadership. In contemporary organizations it is recognized (as identified by Trotsky) that a dispersed leadership is the vital link between activity on the ground and organizing and persuading the masses to take up their followership and local leadership roles. Distributing leadership is vital not only to get the message across to the masses, but also to communicate what's happening on the ground back to the centre. If Lenin and the party are going to make strategic decisions they need the cadres to tell them what's happening, what the mood is, where the challenges and opportunities are. In contemporary global businesses distributed leadership is vital, to motivate and generate leadership throughout the organization, and to feed back knowledge from the edges to the centre.

(5) Individual Leadership (Personalities in History)

Hence the cheap jibes about the role of individuals, good and bad. History is a process of the class struggle. But classes do not bring their full weight to bear automatically and simultaneously. In the process of struggle the classes create various organs, which play an important and independent role and are subject to deformations. This also provides the basis for the role of personalities in history. There are naturally great objective causes, which created the autocratic rule of Hitler but only dull-witted pedants of 'determinism' could deny today the enormous historic role of Hitler.

The interplay and interdependence between the individual leader and the collective actors are paramount in Trotsky's account. Both are absolutely vital; a denial of either creates a myth about leadership. In this citation Trotsky states that history is about collective actors struggling (class struggle in Marxist terminology), and he acknowledges clearly that this does not occur automatically but that individual leaders, 'personalities' for good or bad, have an enormous role.

(6) Mass Leadership (Social Movement Leadership)

The October victory is a serious testimonial of the 'maturity' of the proletariat. But this maturity is relative. A few years later the very same proletariat permitted the revolution to be strangled by a bureaucracy, which rose from its ranks.

Trotsky also acknowledges the enormous responsibility and role of the collective actors who become more than simply followers (as in most leadership accounts), but a collective leadership actor in their own right. Mass leadership describes how a social movement activates itself, drawing on the principles of 'self-organization'.

The social movement itself acted as an inspiration and took on a momentum of its own, acting with 'maturity'. Non-violent revolutions in the ex-Soviet bloc and the Arab Spring uprisings are examples of mass leadership. The 1917 Russian Revolution inspired many in other countries to act, with collective actions empowering others and demonstrating leadership in a global sense. Trotsky also explicitly holds these collective actors, 'the masses', to account for the failings after the October Revolution, when the proletariat *'permitted the revolution to be strangled by a bureaucracy, which rose from its ranks'*. Collective actors can become more than disparate individuals and passive followers given the right conditions. It is not always conscious organized actions in which collective actors take leadership; spontaneous mass demonstrations or consumer boycotts are other examples of mass leadership. There are also other less tangible ways in which the 'masses' collectively act without any formal organization, and find ways to resist tyrannies, through small yet multiple acts of defiance and resistance. Conversely the masses can take leadership during elections, by overturning media and political directives to create change, or simply by withholding their votes and refusing to partake in 'corrupt' politics. The term 'active followership' doesn't do justice to the role a 'collective actor' can take in the leadership process. Mass leadership rarely if ever acts without individual and group leaders (sometimes these are informal and temporary) but the energy they act with is not always determined by these leaders; inversing the process the 'leaders' can become followers of the masses, and social movements can cause leaders to U-turn and respond in different ways. The collective actor differs from 'the crowd' when it acts to bring about a change. The solidarity and activity of the collective actor is driven by conscious and unconscious group processes, which are unpredictable. One of the tasks of individual and corporate leaders is to read and understand these collective processes and then to acknowledge, respond and try to influence them appropriately. This is achieved through reflexivity, feedback loops of communication between complex networks and the leadership, and also through symbolic leadership actions (see below). The Arab Spring revolutions and the Occupy movements in Western cities show us that new social movements are now using new communication technologies and virtual spaces alongside physical spaces to expand how social movements can effect social change. Mass leadership is becoming a phenomena many companies fear; mass boycotts following viral internet campaigns against unethical behaviour for example can destroy or dent brands very quickly.

(7) Symbolic Leadership

The arrival of Lenin in Petrograd, on April 3, 1917, turned the Bolshevik party in time and enabled the party to lead the revolution to victory. Our sages might say that had Lenin died abroad at the beginning of 1917, the October revolution would have taken place 'just the same'. But that is not so. Lenin represented one of the living elements of the historical process. He personified the experience and the perspicacity of the most active section of the proletariat. His timely appearance on the arena of the revolution was necessary in order to mobilise the vanguard and provide it with an opportunity to rally the working class and the peasant masses. Political leadership in the crucial moments of historical turns can become just as decisive a factor as is the role of the chief command during the critical moments of war. History is not an automatic process. Otherwise, why leaders? Why parties? Why programmes? Why theoretical struggles?

Lenin's arrival in Petrograd mobilized the vanguard, which in turn mobilized the masses: 'His timely appearance on the arena of the revolution was necessary in order to mobilise the vanguard and provide it with an opportunity to rally the working class and the peasant masses.'

Trotsky identifies that an individual leader who personifies for followers their ideals can have a huge social impact through symbolic actions, such as Lenin's arrival at Petrograd. These actions are signifiers to followers and can be catalysts providing the inspiration for social movements or organizations to take risks and create change. Symbolic leadership can happen through many mediums, timely appearances, speeches, media messages and images, and sometimes many small actions – perhaps a CEO unexpectedly offering support at factory floor levels to show the need for solidarity during lean periods, though sometimes a big 'performative act' can create a dynamic change in a situation. Martin Luther King and his leadership cadres understood symbolic leadership and the performative act well. Many of his actions were planned and calculated to maximize the symbolic value of his personifying leadership. By getting imprisoned he symbolized the resistance and highlighted the 'repressive machinery'. Mahatma Ghandi was perhaps the master; his famous walk to the sea to produce salt was a typical symbolic action. Britain had a monopoly on salt production in India and Gandhi's decision to produce salt by the sea would have no big real/material impact but symbolically represented two things: (1) the need for India to become self-reliant; to produce its own salt, which was a fundamental product used by all, and a natural product in India; (2) to resist British rule by not paying the salt tax. Symbolic leadership is in many ways the most potent form of leadership, especially in the contemporary age of media saturation and global communications, whereby leaders have to communicate to many whom they cannot influence directly. But 'being a leader' and getting the message across has always been about symbolic action; for example, these word are attributed to St. Francis of Assisi:

'Preach the Gospel at all times; if necessary, use words.'

Unfortunately despots and dictators have often excelled at symbolic leadership. Hitler's Nuremburg rally in 1934 was a powerful example of the Nazi leadership turning a political rally into a symbolic event that was a living enactment of their future vision of Nazi Germany. Terrorist groups such as al-Qaeda have become media masters of using symbolic leadership to devastating effect.

Reflections

This short excerpt from Trotsky's work highlights key aspects of leadership, and the relationship between leadership and followership. Trotsky's final sentence in the paragraph brings together some of the key elements of leadership: *'History is not an automatic process. Otherwise, why leaders? Why parties? Why programmes? Why theoretical struggles?'*

In this case study it is the combined impact of individual leaders, group leadership and mass leadership that forms an asymmetric but effective leadership process. These leadership processes also involve intellect, unconscious dynamics, and the symbolic realm. This provides a parallel to the dynamics of leadership operating in the contemporary organizational and business world. The collapse of communism in the late 20th century revealed the fragility of empires, nation states and organizations built on fear and coercion. One could argue that a key factor in the downfall was the limitation of leadership, the attempt to stifle mass leadership and distribute leadership and to locate power and leadership solely in the realm of individuals (Stalin) and the group (the Communist Party). Perhaps the sign of a healthy organization, or socially functioning movement or nation, is its capacity through whatever governance form or mechanism to ensure that asymmetric leadership doesn't get reduced to symmetrical leadership, i.e. power and influence in the hands of the few.

Successful leadership reveals how leaders generate more leaders, followers empower leaders, and leaders also empower followers. Followership then becomes an active and participatory role, and there is an asymmetric fluidity; leadership resides not in one person or place but in multiple places that are not always obvious.

The leader (and those close to him/her) provides intellectual leadership, personifying leadership, and is a symbolic figurehead. Distributed leaders interact with the 'masses' and communicate theoretical ideas, values and strategies/programmes to the wider followership, also symbolizing spirit, commitment and vigour in small actions and engagements. In turn they act as communication networks between the masses (of employees) and those taking strategic decisions, and between each other. This study shows the diversity and active ingredients of what we call leadership. Yes Lenin was vital to the Russian Revolution ... No Lenin didn't manifest this on his own!

Conclusion: The Challenge of Asymmetric Leadership

This case study shows how contemporary leadership is asymmetric, rather than symmetrical, rational, individual and hierarchical. Asymmetric leadership references the multiplicity of actors, leadership and followership relations, individual, group and mass interactions, and the emotional and symbolic that are part of leadership processes and activity. In contemporary society with the expansion of IT and virtual spaces, leadership and followership becomes ever-more intricate, enmeshed and nuanced, it has less and less logic or symmetry, it is not easily definable and does not easily sit within prescriptive frameworks. The contemporary world presents us with asymmetrical challenges, and this requires asymmetrical leadership responses. This was true in the turbulence of the Russian Revolution and it is true in the turbulent world of today. The excerpt from my colleague Philip Boxer's blog in Box 8 is helpful when thinking about asymmetrical leadership drawing on Lacanian thinking.

> **Box 8   Asymmetric Leadership: Entry from Philip Boxer's Blog, 19 October 2011**
>
> **The Asymmetric Leadership Forum**
>
> What's it like where you are leading at the moment?
>
> - Is the relationship between your organization and its customers in balance, or are you having to work out how to handle your customers' contexts in a more and more ad hoc way – riding your bicycle while redesigning it?
>
> - Are the outcomes your customers want highly dependent on others' services as well as your own – do you need to align purpose & activity with other complementary suppliers?
>
> - What about the challenge & imperative of delegating more leadership and authority to those dealing directly with your customers, moving power to the edge of your organization where your customers interact directly with you ...?

If any of this is recognizable to you, then you are at work as a leader in an environment of asymmetric demands, where situational judgements, exceptions, variety, differences – all of these are more like the facts-of-leadership-life than predictability, balance, controls, planning. We call this asymmetric leadership.

As an asymmetric leader you are likely to be working with some combination of:

- Customers' escalating demands within increasing uncertainty and complex contexts.

- The challenges of personalization & individualization by an increasing number of providers' networks.

- Aligning through-life support and condition management for the customer across organizational boundaries.

- Reducing duplication and eliminating waste, whilst increasing the emphasis on early intervention to secure long-term benefits.

- Trying to improve outcomes, especially in the case of complex needs.

- Facing increasing pressure to develop greater resilience and to contain upredictability.

But how do you think and act in a context like this? What are the ways in which you can conceptualise what is happening that can provide some traction, give you a handle on the situation and create opportunities for improving the economy of your leadership effort?

We have some concepts and analytic tools, which we think can help you:

- Map the ecosystem of organizations, customers and contexts within which you increasingly need to decide how to act.

- Consider how to strengthen horizontal accountability in ways which hold accountable the individuals who are dealing directly with customers.

- Develop the fractal resilience of the service systems you design and lead to cope with variation in the scale and scope of individuals' needs.

- Establish economies of governance in the way resources can be brought together and combined in individual interventions.

Define the indirect value for your customers beyond immediate value arising from their involvement with your services.

My consulting work in organizations constantly addresses the question of how to lead in an asymmetric environment, and the first thing we do is de-myth the symmetry of leadership. Then we begin to create local and networked approaches of leadership from within their context. This is practical work, applying theory to practice and learning from practice.

This case study helps reveal how leadership is enacted in the contemporary world, in asymmetric and complementary ways. Efforts to tame leadership, to essentialize it and measure its impact, are wholly inadequate responses to today's leadership and organizational challenges. The map is not the territory, and unfortunately the maps we often use to understand leadership are over-simplified and prejudiced towards certain symmetrical biases, in order to make us feel more in control, as if we are managing the unmanageable.

Asymmetrical leadership acknowledges that leadership is not a mechanistic and functional object. It is multifaceted and operates at multiple levels simultaneously, as the analysis of Trotsky's text demonstrates. Individuals and collective actors are interdependent, separate entities and yet paradoxically entwined in a process of organizing and influence. Understanding this asymmetric approach to leadership is a key contemporary leadership challenge.

Suggested Readings

- Heifetz, R. (1994) *Leadership Without Easy Answers*. Boston, MA: Belknap Press.

- Lilley, S. and Platt, G. (1997) 'Images of Martin Luther King', in K. Grint (ed.), *Leadership: Classical, Contemporary and Critical Approaches*. Oxford: Oxford University Press.

- Pye, A. (2005) 'Leadership and organising: sensemaking in action', *Leadership*, 1 (1): 31–49.

Reflection Points

- Reflect on the implications for organizations if leadership is asymmetric and multilayered.

- Reflect on the seven themes presented in this chapter and try to prioritize them to reflect the leadership you most commonly observe.

- Try to identify an example of mass leadership that has occurred in the past few years.

Sample Assignment Question

This chapter offers seven leadership themes: choose the three that stand out for you because you have experienced them. Explain the impact of each leadership theme on you, others, and the organizational or social setting. The impact should include the emotional responses as well as practical effects.

4 Against Leadership: Autonomist Leadership

> **Chapter Structure**
>
> - **Introduction**
> - **Is 'Leaderless' Possible?**
> - **Leadership, Power and Authority**
> - **'Bad Leadership': Despots, Dictators and 'Our Boss'**
> - **Autonomist Leadership: Anarchists Lead the Way**
> - **New Social Movements: Leadership for Postmodern Times**
> - **Conclusion; Networked Autonomist Leadership**

Introduction

Don't follow leaders, watch out for parking meters.

(Bob Dylan, 'Subterranean Homesick Blues')

This chapter gives space for the voices of dissent, those against leadership, and those who wish to reform and reimagine the idea of leadership. The dissenters have in common an aim for more egalitarian forms of organizing in order to create a fairer, better society. A long history of dissent against leadership exists, some dissenters are utopian-inspired, others pragmatists.

Many egalitarian-inspired individuals and social movements are distrustful of leadership, pointing to the many examples of abuse of power by despots and dictators with devastating consequences; millions of lives being lost in the last century alone through the leadership of Mao, Stalin and Hitler for example. Misuse of power by leaders goes beyond the evil worst and is commonplace in organizational life, whether through nepotism, bullying or more subtle forms of coercion. We all have experiences of leaders who don't make the grade.

Dissenters claim that leadership inherently creates a power imbalance between leaders and followers, and that leadership itself is the problem. They say that corrupted individuals and groups easily take advantage of, and exacerbate, the power imbalances that are produced by leadership. They claim that because power is located in an elite leadership, the majority are by contrast diminished, reduced in their capacity to be fully human, and reach their full potential. From a societal or organizational perspective, they claim effectiveness, creativity and engagement is lost, not because of poor leadership, but because of leadership itself.

This chapter reflects on the dynamics of leadership power and authority and questions how these lead to 'bad leadership', from the extreme despots and dictators to the 'bad boss'. The idea of 'autonomist leadership' is explored drawing on anarchist and egalitarian experience and theory, before turning to new social movements that offer new leadership for new times.

Is 'Leaderless' Possible?

The term 'leaderless' seems as contentious as the term 'leadership'. Leadership dissenters often try to operate within an ideal of being leaderless. Yet under scrutiny 'leaderless' appears more of a utopian desire, or a misnomer, than a reality. When formal leadership is abolished, it seems that informal leadership thrives within 'leaderless' movements, as organization and negotiations take place to sustain them (Katz, 1981; McAdam, 1982). Helen Brown (1989) found that little had been written or researched about the process of 'leaderless' movements with the exception of Gerlach and Hine (1970). Brown (1989: 231) researched the women's movement and Greenham Common peace camp that strived for 'leaderless groups', and she found that:

> Leadership is not absent but it is understood as a set of organizing skills, skilful information search, interpretation and choice. The application of these three is necessary for the successful accomplishment of organization.

She cites Kerr and Jermier (1978), who suggest that leadership in the traditional hierarchical sense becomes redundant in certain settings – when participants find the task intrinsically motivating and have all the skills and knowledge they need.

> Leadership [or organizers] in a hierarchical sense are not necessary for the achievement of social organisation. What is necessary is that participants devise a means of engaging in leadership acts and thus acting as skilled organizers which is legitimate in terms of shared values. (Brown, 1989: 227)

Brown goes on to discuss a distributed leadership:

> Leadership is perceived here as acceptable influence, which is legitimated by the agreed values of distributed leadership [where everybody has a

right and responsibility to contribute]. Authority resides in the collective as
a whole. (p. 235)

Brown's research findings are similar in concept to Starhawk's (1986)
description of 'leaderful' instead of leaderless groups, where the leadership
is distributed throughout the movement or group. Douglas observes that,
'there is no such thing as a leaderless group, only groups with different
degrees of leadership residing in the actions of one person or several'
(1983: 43). Leaderless groups often utilize leadership under another
name, and are in denial of leadership because of a misunderstanding that
assumes all leadership is about power and position, i.e. they perceive all
leadership to be classical rather than autonomist (see alternative
leadership approaches such as autonomist leadership – discussed later in
the chapter).

When leadership is denied, these different outcomes may occur:

- Leadership reappears under a different name.

- Experimental forms of organizing, leadership and followership take
  place, that can be more mutual, fluid, adaptive and creative.

- The denial of leadership creates a shadow, distorting power and group
  dynamics often in a negative way, and allowing informal oligarchies to form.

The desire for unity and equality can push difference and power beneath the
radar. Utopian ideals often hide a shadow side that denies aggressive
tendencies, which then arise often in very hurtful ways. The shadow side of
libertarianism is the unconscious desire for belonging and conformity. An
interesting spectacle on peace or anti-capitalist demonstrations are the
anarchists, claiming to be ultra-libertarians, against all authority, demanding
individual liberty, hating conformity, yet they appear as the most
homogeneous group of all. Dressed in their 'black-bloc' uniforms, they offer
us the parody between autonomy and conformity. In *The Tyranny of
Structurelessness*, Jo Freeman (1972–1973) articulated her observations and
experiences of leaderless groups in the feminist movement:

1 '[S]tructurelessness' becomes a way of masking power and within the
   women's movement it is usually most strongly advocated by those who
   are the most powerful.

2 Awareness of power is curtailed by those who know the rules, as long
   as the structure of the group is informal.

3   The most insidious elites are usually run by people not known to the larger public at all. Intelligent elitists are usually smart enough not to allow themselves to become well known.

4   Friendship and informal power networks dominate and exclude 'out-groups' within such movements and organizations. (1972–1973: 156–157)

Freeman's main concerns about leaderless groups are regarding the issues of power, transparency and accountability, which occur due to hidden elites wielding unchallenged and unaccountable power. Indecisiveness, a group narcissism focusing on internal dynamics rather than external tasks, and impotency could also be added here from my own personal experiences of groups which advocate leaderlessness or simply deny leaders in favour of egalitarian approaches. A typical example is the refusal of a work-team to have a leader, and instead to select a rotating-facilitator role. The person who is the facilitator can be handed a poisoned chalice, with responsibility and accountability yet no authority.

Freeman argues for rules and formalized structures in non-hierarchical movements, in order to prevent such leaderless tyranny. However, whilst clarity of structure and decision-making is helpful, the bureaucratization of leadership is a folly. Conflict is avoided to prevent the disruption of the ideas of unity, and consensus is attempted through time-consuming negotiations over each contested area and decision. These organizations often rationalize themselves into rigid and bureaucratic structures. Michels argues that leaderless groups can become dangerously authoritarian organizations:

> Organizations that start out with egalitarian or anarchistic political values tend to become as, or perhaps more, authoritarian and alienating than the organizations they were designed to reform or replace. (Michels, 1915, in Grint, 1997: 284)

Much of the debate contests the type of leadership rather than actual leadership itself. Authoritarian leadership and power are the underlying issues. Many new social movements aim to create organizational forms that challenge those that characterize and wield power in modern society. They have shown some success but also demonstrate some of the challenges and problems of idealizing the leaderless group. The contemporary anarchist Chaz Bufe argues that leadership is inevitable in groups:

> In the 60s and 70s many leftist, anarchist and feminist groups agonised over how to eliminate leadership, equating all leadership [including

temporary, task-based leadership] with authoritarian leadership. Their fruitless efforts confirm what the more astute anarchists have been saying for over a century – that it's a mistake to think that any kind of group or organization can exist without leadership; the question is, what kind of leadership is it going to be? (Bufe, 1988: 21)

The choice then is not leadership or leaderless but 'what sort of leadership', and the challenging task for egalitarian movements is how to create and support non-oppressive leadership. To achieve this the relationship between leadership, power and authority requires constant review and we turn to this next.

Leadership, Power and Authority

Authority

> My authority is total because it's the owners authority … They [the players] don't have to back my project, it's the owner who backs my project.

These are the words of André Villas-Boas, when manager of Chelsea Football Club, reported in the *Guardian* newspaper on 17 February 2012 (www.guardian.co.uk/theguardian/sport). When reading this I felt sure the football manager was doomed, as his misunderstanding about authority was a fundamental mistake. Perhaps he had authority from the owner, attained through position power, but without the respect of his players, he had very little real authority. A leader needs followers, and a mandate from above is not enough. Three weeks later the headlines read: 'André Villas-Boas sacked after eight months and 40 games'. Authority comes not only from above, but also from within ourselves, laterally from peers and from 'below', i.e. those we lead. Amongst the leaders I coach it is quite common for them to experience 'imposter syndrome' and some struggle to find the inner authority to act with confidence in their role. Other leaders suffer from the opposite challenge, an omnipotent form of feeling entitled and always authorized (even when out of their depth in a role or situation). Position power may authorize a leader to make decisions about resources, e.g. people and money, yet the backing from above does not give a leader total authority. In fact a leader never has total authority, it is always partial, always in the process of negotiation within oneself and with a team of peers or followers. The nearest a leader gets to total authority is in a totalitarian situation, and even then their authority is fragile. Leaders can be de-authorized by followers and sometimes by ghosts from their past, or events in the present. A confident leader can be undone by a situation that evokes a regressive experience from the past. One leader I coached excelled at public speaking, and dealt with her CEO very confidently, but in interview situations and in the boardroom, she experienced a negative regression to being at school, and her reaction was to show signs of stress and respond with poor answers and in a defensive tone. Recall an anxious teacher in an unruly classroom: they are authorized from above, they have position power and sanctions, yet unless they can gain respect from the class, they are de-authorized and are helpless before the rule of the mob. Haile Selassie, the former Emperor of Ethiopia, ruled his court like an ancient monarch: he had total power, and many believed he was authorized by the greatest power, God. He assumed total authority and power, commanding all the resources in Ethiopa, but in Kapuscinski's excellent book *The Emperor* (1984) (a must-read for leadership scholars and leaders) his authority is exposed as partial and fragile, always dependent on courtier factions, manipulations, coercions. Haile Selassie with his grand titles, the King of Kings, Elect of God, Lion of Judah, His Most Puissant Majesty and Distinguished Highness, always lived with the fear that his authority could dissipate at any time, and sure enough, the contradictions between his rule and social poverty finally revealed this fragility and he was 'de-authorized' and deposed.

Anton Obholzer discusses authority and its relation to power: 'Authority, without power, leads to a weakened, demoralized management and power without authority leads to an authoritarian regime' (1994: 42). Obholzer says that role and title indicate the power a leader has, therefore, the title of dictator indicates that power is the essential component; whereas manager or director indicates a mix between power and authority, and the title of coordinator indicates very little power, relying on consensus from the group (which Obholzer says is a very unlikely phenomenon).

Power

Aspiring democratic organizations are often troubled by the concept of power (and by the term 'leader') because it is defined in management literature as coercive, i.e. the ability to make another person do what they would not otherwise do, overcoming some resistance (Pfeiffer, 1978; Weber, 1947). The philosopher Ricoeur (1990) calls this 'power over' but points to three other modes of power:

- **Power-to-act**: personal agency, our capacity 'to do' which constitutes the basis of our ethical beings.

- **Power-over**: where one exerts their will over another, and Ricoeur claims this is the basis of violence.

- **Power-in-common**: power with others, to act as community, which shows the desire to live together.

- **Power-of-productivity**: the power of creativity to produce.

Ricoeur acknowledges that there are tensions between these modes of power and that it is almost impossible for a person to act without exerting some power over another. All of these modes of power are clearly aspects of leadership, followership and teamwork. Power is not something to be disdained or denied; when this happens it simply goes underground, usually with very negative effects. Foucault's insights into power are very helpful as he says that power is not situated only in elites, in leaders, but exists everywhere, and that power and resistance are complementary:

> Where there is power there is resistance, and yet, or rather consequently, this resistance is never in a position of exteriority in relation to power …

> These points of resistance are everywhere in the power network. Hence there is no locus of great refusal … or pure law of the revolutionary. Instead there is a plurality or resistances, which by definition … can only exist in the strategic field of power relations. (Foucault, 1980: 95–6)

Power and authority reside everywhere, whether or not there is a hierarchy or explicit leadership. So, for Foucault, power and resistance are one, they are interdependent, and power is not simply repressive, or at the top of a hierarchy it is everywhere and fluid. Authority and authoritarian become conflated leading to misunderstandings. Taking up personal authority as a leader is different from being authoritarian. The former is to take up one's legitimate agency, perhaps on behalf of others as their representative, whereas being authoritarian implies abusing one's power and position, being repressive and using some form of coercion.

A popular belief in the Human Relations tradition is that a leader should empower employees (Bennis and Nanus, 1985; Kanter, 1979). Yet the meaning of empowerment has not been systematically articulated; it is a nice idea, yet leaders are uncertain how to empower employees without diminishing their own power. Others claim that empowering others is patronizing, and that power cannot be given away, only taken, undermining the notion of empowerment. Harmony and the absence of conflict are often seen as desirable, the fantasy being that power is removed. However, the absence of conflict means that demands are not being made, and that compliance and obedience are the result of a totalizing power, however benign. Sometimes the absence of conflict reveals a fear of questioning authority; at other times culture control utilizes hidden power through the control of discourses and culture, whereby members of an organization adhere to unspoken rules and behaviours without the capacity to question them (see Messiah Leadership, Chapter 11).

Power can also be inspirational and a force for positive activity. We receive power from the support of friends or a group in material and non-material ways; a political leader is mandated power and authority, and an athlete or sports team works to maximize the power of each individual and the team to achieve success. Power and authority are neither good nor bad, but how they are attained and used is the question. On a daily basis, we all face an existential choice as to how we use our power; we all have the power to make differences to others' lives. Leaders usually have positional power and personal power and are authorized to make decisions and influence change, which paradoxically places them in a vulnerable position … what choices will they make? How will they use this power? This vulnerability often creates anxiety and can lead to a misuse of power. Coercion and bad leadership most often come from a place of insecurity and fear, rather than security and confidence.

Bad Leadership: Despots, Dictators and 'Our Boss'

When God is unhappy, he sends a blind shepherd.[1]

Most leadership texts write about leadership as a 'good object', a desirable thing; and bad leadership is often attributed to an individual's deficit, a personality disorder such as narcissism. Yet bad leadership is commonplace and it is structural and systemic. This means that context and cultures produce 'bad leadership' and create the spaces that bad leaders step into. Bad leadership means two things; firstly ineffective leadership, and secondly unethical leadership (Kellerman, 2004). Unethical bad leadership can be very effective leadership in many ways and provides secondary pay-offs for followers:

> Followers follow bad leaders not only because of their individual needs for safety, simplicity and certainty but also because of the needs of the group. … Bad leaders often provide important benefits … maintain order, provide cohesion and identity, and do the collective work. (Kellerman, 2004: 24–25)

---

[1] I am told this quote comes from the Talmud.

These pay-offs are often at the expense of a persecuted out-group, used by the leader to create unity and identity in their followers. The classic is when fascist leaders use race and immigration to inspire fear and hatred to unite their followers. This phenomenon is alive and well: in the first round of the 2012 French presidential election during the economic crisis in Europe, the rightwing anti-immigration candidate Marine Le Pen received nearly 20% of the French vote (*Guardian*, 2012).

Developing Kellerman's thinking, the following contribute to bad leadership:

- Context fosters bad leadership behaviour – a country in which corruption is rife will foster corruption.

- Leaders are led astray by the influence of others, and poor/corrupt advisors.

- Leaders are led astray by an inability to control their internal desire, e.g. power, narcissism, greed.

- Power corrupts – (1) through promoting grandiose feelings, (2) senior leaders can find themselves isolated and separated from reality, without enough checks and balances to help good decision-making.

- Follower demands – strong leaders and simple answers are demanded especially in a crisis.

We Get the Leaders We Deserve (and the Leaders We Desire)

Most texts on bad leadership focus on a uni-directional flow of power from leaders to followers and again need challenging. When reviewing dictators and despots, it is important not to universalize their leadership traits and personalities any more than we can for 'good leaders'. Each situation is local and specific, containing multiple causations and influences. There is a scale of 'bad leaders', from murderous dictators to the 'bully leader' at work. Followers don't blindly and passively follow bad leaders, they also produce and uphold them (not always consciously). Some reflect this by saying we get the leaders we deserve, and we also get the leaders we desire (albeit often unconsciously). Followers of despots acquiesce for many conflicting reasons; some from fear and coercion, some for self-interest, some for ideological belief. Kellerman (2004: 24–5) divided the Nazi followership into three groups, whilst acknowledging that this might be over-simplifying, to give a flavour of diverse responses to despotic leadership:

- By-standers – who went along with Hitler for reasons of self-interest, who felt cohesion as being part of a national group.

- Evil-doers – such as the SS, some of whom had sadistic personalities or believed that they were dealing with vermin.

- Acolytes – fervent believers in Hitler's ideology.

It is shocking how 'charismatic' and transformational leadership ideas continue to be propagated in light of the damage done through charismatic, despotic leaders. Continuing to promote transformational and charismatic leaders who create strong, 'cult-like' cultures, to which loyal followers align themselves, is clearly dangerous. Kapuscinski (1984: 149–50) quotes one of Haile Selassie's courtiers: 'Life inside the palace seemed strange, as if existing only of itself for itself.' This statement could probably apply to financiers working in Wall Street before the collapse, who were living in cultures created by financial leaders who were in denial of the external reality. Kellerman (2004) cites Machiavelli, who warns 'if we choose freedom we choose it at our peril', and she argues this means that leadership is always a tradeoff: 'less freedom for more security' (2004: 16). Anarchists would respond, 'the only security we have is self-reliance, mutuality, maximizing autonomy and resisting leadership that tends towards power imbalances', and we have witnessed the consequences!

Autonomist Leadership: Anarchists Lead the Way

I use the term 'autonomist leadership' to describe the leadership of egalitarian-inspired social movements, and more recently it can be found in organizations that are attempting to rethink it leadership, distributing it more freely and without the formality of role. Autonomist leadership is becoming increasingly important in all aspects of organizational and social life, yet is very under-researched and theorized. This new leadership approach draws upon a century of anarchist and libertarian thinking, and an even longer heritage, as shown by the Quaker case study in Box 10.

Autonomist leadership is informed by anarchist thinking. Anarchists wish to remove all authoritarian forms of social organization and replace them with non-hierarchical and non-authoritarian forms, which challenges the classical idea of leadership. The anarchist cry of 'No God, No Master' sums up their disdain for authoritarian leadership; however anarchist theorists provide interesting and polemic ideas that paradoxically inform contemporary society about leadership. Many anarchists claim to 'reject all leadership' yet what they actually reject is domination and subjugation to the authority of another, as the anarchist Mikhail Bakunin explained in the mid-nineteenth century:

> At the moment of action, in the midst of the struggle, there is a natural division of roles according to the aptitude of each, assessed and judged by the collective whole: some direct and command, others execute orders. But no function must be allowed to petrify or become fixed and it will not remain irrevocably attached to any one person. Hierarchical order and promotion do not exist, so the commander of yesterday can become a subordinate tomorrow. No one rises above others, or if he does rise, it is only to fall back a moment later, like the waves of the sea forever returning to the salutary level of equality. (Joll, 1979: 92)

For anarchists and others from autonomist, libertarian and other new social movements leadership exists but not in its classic form. It is a fluid entity, functioning not as positional power, and not with authority over others. Bakunin's description reflects what I call 'autonomist leadership', a form of leadership imbued with mutuality and autonomist principles.

Box 9   Classical vs Autonomist Leadership

The formula below differentiates classical and autonomist leadership:

Classical leadership = Person + Position + Authority

Autonomist leadership = Spontaneity + Autonomy + Mutuality

Classical leadership focuses on a person called a leader, who inhabits a position (role) that gives them power (and resources) to exert authority to lead others.

Autonomist leadership has three principles:

1 *Spontaneous leadership*: Leadership arises spontaneously, emerging when necessary, and falls away when not needed. Leadership is not fixed or static, it is not the property of one person, group or role, but is fluid, moving between people.

2 *Autonomous leadership:* The principle of autonomy applies to both leaders and followers. Anybody and everybody can take up leadership, there is no ranking or hierarchy, it is freely available to all. Neither leader or follower are coerced into their role, all act with autonomy.

3 *Mutuality:* Leadership is enacted with mutual consent and for the mutual benefit of the group. Followers will choose to follow a leader when it is in the best interests of all.

To cite Bakunin again:

> I receive and I give – such is human life. Each directs and is directed in his turn. Therefore there is no fixed and constant authority, but a continual exchange of mutual, temporary, and, above all, voluntary authority and subordination. (Bakunin, 1871)

A spontaneous leader carries transitional authority arising from their expertise or capability; it must be voluntarily sanctioned and for the benefit of the group. Leadership resides with one person or a group, only for as long as is necessary and useful. All participate as potential leaders and followers, all work for a common aim and for the mutual good of all. When autonomist leadership works well, it does not preclude the tensions of leadership, i.e. human dynamics such as envy and rivalry or power issues, but works with them as transparently and openly as possible. It helps to have a shared desire for mutuality, co-operation and an overriding common aim.

Autonomist leadership is not a utopian dream, nor it is easy, and it has a long history, with mixed success. Autonomist leadership happens all of the time: we self-manage, self-organize and self-regulate most social and work situations (even when explicit management and leadership exist). Autonomist leadership can be informal and formal, and it works best when it is explicitly named and thought through. One of the challenges for autonomist leadership is how it gets mixed up with leaderless ideas, and the shadow side of social dynamics that arises because of this.

In Box 10 I outline two examples of autonomist leadership.

Box 10   Autonomist Leadership: Case Studies

The Quakers

The Quakers emerged during the English civil war from aspirational groups such as the Seekers, Levellers and Ranters, in a climate of millenarian hope that the 'world would be turned upside down' and a new kingdom was about to arrive. The Quakers attempted to live as if the new kingdom had come, being a pacifist and radically egalitarian community. The Quakers discovered an experiential spirituality; they read the scriptures as words of liberation and experienced direct mystical spirituality that freed both men and women alike. In the 1650s Quaker women were able to preach the gospel the same as men, a scandalous thought at the time (even for some churches today!). They preached that no professional preacher was necessary, that God himself would teach his people, without a mediating priest, and they would rid themselves of legalistic and ritualistic forms

(Continued)

(Continued)

of religion. Furthermore, they believed in a universal deity, 'that of God in everyone', meaning that anyone could experience the 'seed of God' within them, whether Christian, Turk or American Indian; this too was radical theology overthrowing the Calvinistic belief that only a chosen few would be saved as 'the elect', and that the written word, the scriptures, were the true Christian path to God. The Quakers were accused of wanting to ban the priesthood, but they claimed to do the opposite and wanted abolition of the laity, creating a 'priesthood of all believers' (Quaker Faith and Practice, 1995: 11.01, see BYM, 1996).

Today the Quakers still operate with the same organizational form and basic principles as they did 350 years ago.

The Quakers provide a 350-year case study of a successful organization that is participative, and whilst they are not strictly leaderless (they have elders and clerks of meetings in temporary roles), they do not elect leaders through voting, and all decision-making is made through a mutual process of spiritual-consensus. At Quaker worship meetings people sit in silence, and anyone is free to minister or speak. The elders' role is to close to the meeting on time with a handshake. At Quaker business meetings all are free to speak, and the aim is to reach a spiritual consensus. At their annual meeting all members are invited and in Britain up to 1,000 can be present, discussing and praying that they will be 'led' to the right decision. Interestingly, whilst this process can feel slow and frustrating, it has led to radical actions. The Quakers are social reformers, leading change in slavery, prison reform, urban housing and the working conditions of the poor, and mental health provision, and most recently they were the first UK church to accept gay marriage.

Paradoxically their religious 'business methods', kinship networks, adherence to hard work, honesty and simple-living, plus their persecution that banned them from education and professions, led them to great success in business. Starting small they became great industrialists, forming companies such as Barclays bank, the chocolate-makers Cadbury and Rowntree's, and Clark's shoes (see Walvin, 1997).

The Quakers enact the principles of autonomist leadership, in that there are no fixed leadership roles in ministry, and anyone can speak/minister at Quaker meetings. Ministry leadership is temporary and spontaneous. They aim to uphold each other in roles (mutuality) and their purpose is to benefit and improve all society.

Other leadership roles such as elders (supportive roles) and clerks of business meetings (facilitating roles) are temporary, and those who have role are elected through a collective yet autonomist process of mutual consent (without voting). For further reading see Moore, 2000, and Dandelion, 2008.

Autonomist work groups

The second example derives from a comparative study of work organization made by the Tavistock Institute in the late 1950s, and reported in E. L. Trist's *Organisational Choice*, and P. Herbst's *Autonomous Group Functioning*.

They reported on the composite work group in coal mining, describing how the group takes over complete responsibility for the total cycle of operations involved in mining the coal-face. No member of the group has a fixed work role. Instead, the men deploy themselves, depending on the requirements of the on-going group task. Within the limits of technological and safety requirements they are free to evolve their own way of organizing and carrying out their task. They are not subject to any external authority in this respect, nor is there within the group itself any member who takes over a formal directive leadership function (cited in Ward, 1966).

Composite or autonomist work groups challenged the traditional form of controller leadership and organizing work through rewarding individuals for individual productivity (piece rates) and utilizing controller leaders to supervize and monitor work. This famous case study, cited in business schools, revealed that productivity increased when teams worked in cohesion rather than competing individually with each other, and the removal of supervision allowed adaptivity and creativity to achieve the task more efficiently. Motivation is also increased through encouraging autonomist teamwork.

Cole (1989) writes that these Tavistock methods were adopted particularly in Scandinavia in the 1970s, led by the charismatic and visionary Norwegian scholar Einar Thorsrud (Thorsrud and Emery, 1969).

In the early days of the movement, Thorsrud was known in Sweden as 'the foreman killer'. We can see this challenge in the 'psychosocial job design criteria' laid down by Thorsrud and his collaborators in the early 1960s (which assume that acceptable levels of income and job security have already been achieved). These criteria were expressed somewhat differently from publication to publication, but they typically included the following:

1 Freedom on the part of workers to make decisions about how to do their work.

2 A meaningful set of tasks, offering some variety and some free space to develop the job over time.

3 Opportunities for learning on the job and to continue learning on the basis of feedback of results and future needs.

4 Freedom to give and receive help on the job and to establish mutual respect between people at work.

5 Recognition and social respect outside the workplace for doing a useful job.

6 Some form of desirable future at work, not only in the form of promotion.

(Cole, 1989: 90–1)

(Continued)

> *(Continued)*
>
> Freedom on the part of workers to make decisions about how to do their work sets the tone for an approach to work design that is diametrically opposed to the control system of traditional bureaucracy. Volvo were one of the companies to utilize these methods that encouraged autonomist leadership (albeit not in a purist way, as company leadership existed as well).

The pursuit of autonomist leadership in workplaces was founded on the vision of a more democratic society, however the tensions between democratizing the workplace and extracting more labour from workers led to the demise of this movement in the 1980s. Yet new forms of autonomist leadership have arisen at the turn of the century. No longer focusing on autonomist teams and small group functioning, autonomist leadership now emerges within the Eco-leadership discourse (Chapter 12), where production and organizational forms change, and leadership occurs in networks rather than teams.

New Social Movements: Leadership for Postmodern Times

Rapid social, environmental and technical changes are taking place that are transforming the very co-ordinates of how we organize and what kind of leadership is needed in the 21st century. Post-industrialism, the knowledge economy, globalization, environmental change, the hi-tech revolution and network society, digital labour, cognitive labour and the nomadic and virtual worker, all reference a new zeitgeist that demands new leadership and new organizational forms.

The Eco-leadership discourse describes these changes in detail, but in this chapter I want to stay with dissent against classical leadership and reference the new social movements who are the 'new dissenters', and who offer and strive for new forms of autonomist leadership.

The New Dissenters

New social movements (NSMs), such as the environmental and anti-capitalist movement, are challenging the status quo, and at the same time have sought new ways of organizing and leading their own movements. Their belief is that we must 'become the change we desire', which has meant that they enact the egalitarian social ideas they profess. Alongside activist groups in the West, the Arab Spring revolutions also occurred through new forms of organizing. Traditional resistances had been eliminated or contained, such as leftist political groups, trade unions or Muslim brotherhood activities, yet unregulated autonomist leadership sprang up in spontaneous waves; triggered by events in one country, the uprisings spread with a speed that has led to the fall of regimes in Egypt, Tunisia and Libya, and struggles occurring elsewhere. The success of these new social movements comes paradoxically through organizing without formal leadership, but utilizing new technologies to create networks, hubs and collaborations, that enable a rapid response and maximize participation.

The leadership literature has by and large overlooked the influence of NSMs, many of which organize in forms that global corporations would be delighted to emulate. For example, many of the anti-capitalist and anti-global movements organize with a committed and loyal 'membership', are extremely flexible, fluid and responsive, are very entrepreneurial, and act through autonomous organizing principles. Large corporations, internet and creative industries, and small IT companies, have been attempting to mirror these structures and flatten hierarchies, disperse leadership, and create network and matrix structures with self-managed teams that can respond rapidly at local levels with committed and loyal employees.

To reimagine leadership it is useful to go beyond the mainstream leadership literature and briefly review new social movements, to open up our potential for learning from difference.

Networked Autonomist Leadership

New social movement theorists offer a very rich source of insights that are applicable to new attempts to create collectivist forms of organization elsewhere. New social movements are wide-ranging, from feminist to environmental to anti-capitalist movements, and they represent new forms of collective action (Castells, 1997; Della Porta, 1999; Giddens, 1991; Melucci, 1989), attempting to create non-hierarchical movements/ organizations. They differ from the traditional workers movements in organizational form as they do not organize within rigid structures, and unlike Marxist inspired movements that herald leadership, and formal organizational discipline as a key aim (i.e. organizing the masses with leaders and vanguard parties), NSMs regard this as elitist and counter-productive.

Traditional social movements aim to mobilize others to win control of material resources and political power. NSMs reflect postmodernity's concerns, and organize informally to gain influence over truth production, identity and culture. Their organizing principles reflect technological changes, they utilize technological networks and organize in networks; they work in virtual spaces, and organize virtually, often with seemingly no tangible spokesperson, figurehead or leader.

There are sharp differences between NSMs and organizations such as corporations, but also growing areas of cross-over: for example, in corporations their move away from hierarchy and towards dispersed leadership, self-managed teams, normative control, matrix structures, understanding complex systems that operate without clear structures, addressing global flows, and using social networking technology, suggests much can be learnt from the NSM research carried out by sociologists, anthropologists and ethnologists. NSMs arise as communities of resistance to what they perceive to be a threat (Castells, 1997; Etzioni, 1993; Melucci, 1989). The sociologist Alberto Melucci's work on NSMs says that moving beyond grand narrative and single order systems of explanation opens up possibilities to move from reductionist theories to those that attempt to account for complexity.

The Movement Is the Message

Marshall McLuhan famously claimed the 'medium is the message' and that 'all media work us over completely' (McLuhan and Fiore, 1967). He was indicating the growing power of communication and media in our lives, claiming that meaning was no longer communicated simply through the content of what was said, but more importantly through how (i.e the medium) it was communicated. Melucci (1989: 206) claims that new social movements operate in this way too, as a 'message' or a 'sign' to society:

> From their particular context, movements send signals, which illuminate hidden controversies about the appropriate form of fundamental social relations within complex societies. (Melucci, 1989: 206)

> Participation within movements is considered a goal in itself. Actors practice in the present the future social changes they seek. (Melucci, 1989: 5–6)

Melucci describes how 'the message' operates for new social movements:

> The very forms of the movements their patterns of interpersonal relationships and decision-making mechanisms operate as a 'sign' or 'message' for the rest of society. E.g. the women's movement for instance, not only raises important questions about equality and rights. They also, at the same time, deliberately signal to the rest of society the importance of recognizing differences within complex societies. (Melucci, 1989: 5–6)

Melucci (1989) proposes that new social movements have three forms of symbolic challenge:

- Prophecy: the act of announcing, based on personal experiences, that alternative frameworks of meaning are possible.

- Paradox: the reversal of dominant codes by their exaggeration.

- Representation: the movement plays back to society itself, revealing contradictions and irrationality.

NSMs can be understood if they are observed through two lenses:

1 **Explicit aims:** The stated political and social goals of the movement.

2 **The signifying message:** How the movement presents 'signs and messages' for society at large. The forms they take represent the message: how they organize their communities and their collective actions, specifically the conflicts they choose to contest, reveals the tensions and hidden power structures within society.

If we apply this to organizations, similarities apply. Companies state their explicit aims – 'to be the best computer company in the world' – yet their signifying message comes through their enticing products, slick company offices, brand advertising, and their manufacturing of stories about the company and their heroic leader's journey. This signifies something else: 'identify with our company, brand and leader; and you will be a smart, cool and happier person'. Apple have been masters at working this signifying message, and it has made them the world's richest company in 2012.

New social movements can help us unravel the knots we have tied ourselves in over leadership. Organizations can learn about working in the symbolic domain ethically and creatively. Their task is to create organizational forms that will carry a message to society, providing products and services that are not just ethical in a material sense, but also ensure their form and their medium evoke ethics, sustainability and community building etc. Many companies who do this in-authentically to mislead, overstate their environmental and social concern, but are at risk of an increasingly discerning and concerned public and consumer base, i.e. the consumer social movements and activists that can bring them to their knees very quickly. Those companies who work in the symbolic realm authentically and become networked organizations, leaning towards autonomist leadership, will be the leading companies of tomorrow.

New Eco-leaders can learn from new social movements in (a) how they organize in non-traditional, democratic and networked ways; in (b) how they operate in the symbolic realm; and in (c) how authentic beliefs in an ethical cause can engage and provide meaning in ways that simply striving for profit cannot.

Conclusion: Networked Autonomist Leadership

Dissenting voices challenge classical leadership, yet leadership, it seems, doesn't disappear but changes, from formal to informal, from individual to collective, from static to fluid, from classical to autonomist. Dissenting voices challenge us to question how leadership influence is attained, and examine power and authority relations. Yet removing formal or classical leadership doesn't remove power and authority. The most democratic leadership (or leaderless) approaches can hide power relations that entrap employees and followers through hidden social influences. The literature on adaptive, systemic, informal and democratic leadership often neglects to undertake a deep analysis of power and authority, leaving gaps that hinder progress in this direction.

When first writing this chapter the intention was to give voice to dissenters, highlighting the negative aspects of leadership. Yet the research revealed that, paradoxically, dissenting voices point the way to tomorrow's leadership. Leadership from the edge is an aspect of Eco-leadership described later in the book, and dissenters from the past anarchist traditions and contemporary new social movements offer us new forms of 'leadership from the edge'. These new visions and attempts at networked and autonomist leadership are emergent and part of the Eco-leadership discourse. There is also a tension between organizations and particular corporations, who draw upon networked and autonomist approaches only to maximize productivity and profit. To successfully allow autonomist leadership to flourish, is to work towards the three autonomist principles: spontaneity, autonomy and mutuality. Without doing this, duplicity of purpose will undo a company in the end.

Suggested Readings

- Bakunin, M. (1871) 'What is authority?', from *Dieu et l'état* (1882). Retrieved from www.panarchy.org/bakunin/authority.1871.html (4 February 2013).

- Gemmil, G. and Oakley, J. (1992) 'Leadership – an alienating social myth?', *Human Relations*, 42(1): 13–29.

- Kapuscinski, R. (1984) *The Emperor.* New York: First Vintage Books.

- Reedy, P. (2002) 'Keeping the black flag flying: anarchy, utopia and the politics of nostalgia', in M. Parker (ed.), *Utopia and Organization*. Malden, MA: Blackwell. pp. 169–88.

Reflection Points

- Leaderless groups are never leaderless; diverse forms of leadership always exist.

- Leadership is much more complex than position, power and personal charisma.

- Understanding the diversity of authority and power is key to understanding the diversity of leadership.

- Autonomist leadership reveals how leadership can be spontaneous and mutual, undoing the idea that it is fixed and hierarchical.

- Reflect on your organization and try to identify leadership that goes unnoticed.

Sample Assignment Question

Define classical and autonomist leadership, and give an example of each, reflecting on the strengths and weaknesses of both forms.

5 Leadership and Diversity

Figure 5.1   Demonstration in Trafalgar Square, London, 2011

Chapter Structure

- **Introduction**
- **Locating Ourselves, to Recognize the Other**
- **Space Invaders**
- **The Diversity Business Case: Beware!**
- **Gender and Leadership: The Essentialist Debate**
- **Conclusion: 'Rainbow-Wash'**

Introduction

One of the challenges in dealing with diversity in the workplace is that because it is complex and emotionally charged, it is often addressed in a simplistic and idealistic way. This chapter will attempt to highlight key issues connected with leadership, raising a few of the important questions, rather than seek comprehensive answers to the questions raised by diversity. Leaders are becoming more aware of both the 'business case' of addressing diversity, and the moral case; yet there is still much to do. The business case grows stronger in a global and increasingly competitive environment. It can be summarized thus: true meritocracy is a means to competitive edge, excluding people for irrelevant reasons because they are different prevents us from being the best we can be, and monocultures limit creativity, which is a by-product of diversity.

Addressing leadership and diversity raises two questions. How can leaders improve their organization's capacity to:

1 embrace diversity?

2 recognize the challenges facing marginalized and diverse groups to take up leadership roles?

The first question raises issues of education, understanding the challenges, the power relations and the unconscious dynamics that, in spite of goodwill, still make embracing diversity challenging. The second question emanates from the first, but carries with it specific issues about leadership. For example there has been a lot of progress in gender equality in many areas in the workplace, yet in boardrooms women still are very marginalized.

Locating Ourselves, to Recognize the Other

To address diversity is to acknowledge difference. To acknowledge difference we have to firstly recognize and locate ourselves. We all carry personal, social and historical culture/baggage within us, and however 'PC' (politically correct) we are, however progressive or liberal, we all belong to social groups, which exclude others, and we all make value judgements on a daily basis, often at unconscious levels. Some differences are easily recognized – gender and ethnicity – yet even here we can be tripped up, making assumptions about another, when less obvious differences also exist. To address difference we must first 'decriminalize bias'[1], not trying to eliminate difference but to recognize we are all different and we all carry biases within our cultures and ourselves. Biases do not just belong to 'evil racists', and bias itself is not the problem. When bias gets used to oppress, to marginalize, it becomes a problem. Becoming more conscious of our unconscious, personal assumptions and biases is important if we are to become more aware of others' experience. Our social and cultural bias is more difficult to see as it becomes 'normative'. A gay friend of mine in the USA told me how he watched the first gay marriage ceremony on television (which he had long supported), and he described how he was shocked by his own homophobic response: 'Two men in tuxedos kissing at the town hall ... it just didn't seem right'. Even when we are part of an activist group that is discriminated against, even when we are aware and supportive of the issues, social norms instilled in us since childhood still inhabit our lives, thoughts and our bodies. We carry around our histories, social class, ethnicity, physical ability/disability, gender, sexuality, and religious beliefs, and we notice difference in others.

Anybody in a leadership position needs to realize that they and their team will be working from a set of assumptions and biases based on personal and group experience and social location. This includes one's physical ability, ethnicity, nationality, religion, age, faith, sexuality and class that are inscribed with social meanings. These meanings are enacted by us, and by others who encounter us. Our assumptions from a dominant group gel into our culture and behaviours and become taken-for-granted 'norms'. Butler (2004: 41) points out that norms can be explicit but are usually implicit, 'this is just how things are', and those that deviate from this are made to feel wrong, excluded and imbued with a sense of failure.

---

[1] A term given to me by a colleague, Pooja Sachdev.

Difference, Leadership and Projection

It is not possible to be a leader or follower and work openly with difference unless we can first locate ourselves. Unless we are self-aware, knowing what we are carrying with us and have an awareness of what others may see in us, we will always be 'reactionary'. An emotionally charged reaction to the difference we see in others, and to their reactions to us, results in unconscious discrimination and exclusion taking place. When undertaking diversity training I always begin with an exercise where participants 'locate themselves', identifying their own place and locating myself as an example.

I write as a white, heterosexual, English male. I carry with me the history, social and cultural meanings, stereotypes, power and privileges and disadvantages, associated with this position. I attended a 'working-class' school that offered a very poor education. I dropped out of school and didn't get to university. I accessed higher education in my thirties. This experience gives me a heightened awareness and sensitivity towards issues of class, the elitism of education, and a less personal experience of issues such as disability. When working as Director of Coaching at Lancaster University Management School, taking on a role and the title 'Dr Simon Western', I had a heightened awareness of the powerful unconscious projections I received. These projections towards an 'academic' clashed with the internalized sense of an 'uneducated' self I had grown up with.

These projections arise because of what I represent to others, in my body, personality and university role. Depending on others' personal emotional and developmental histories and social location, will depend on how they respond to me. This is a two-way process, a dynamic that is both conscious and unconscious. I have observed that these projections are triggered through five key sources (see Box 11), which I believe are also applicable to leaders working in other contexts.

Box 11   Leadership and Projection

Sources that stimulate projective responses in leaders

1   **The Institution and Context**: In my case this is the University, which carries with it the history of academia and elite knowledge, which I represent in the 'here and now' when standing in front of a lecture theatre. Each leader will have a specific context that 'speaks through them'.

(Continued)

(Continued)

2 **'Embodied and Cultural Self'**: For example, my whiteness, my sexuality, being British, my accent denoting class and region, my maleness, age, 'able-body'; each individual carries in their embodied self a cultural self that stimulates reactions in others.

3 **Personality**: Personality traits, 'charisma', quietness, calmness, intellectual capability, elements that make us distinctive. Each personality will trigger some people's feelings in powerful ways, positive and negative, and in others they will have a bland reaction.

4 **Expertise**: I teach Coaching at Master's level, drawing on my psychoanalytic and systemic background. Coaching and therapy can carry the mystique of the 'shrink' or of a secular priesthood, and with it the fear/curiosity of being able to read the hidden unconscious, or people will expect me to be a caring, holding figure for them. The expertise signifies meanings: a physics or maths lecturer will stimulate different reactions, an engineer or nurse different reactions again.

5 **Role Power**: As Course Director I have the power and authority to assess students, and position power and influence in the lecture theatre: my voice may be given more weight than others. Leaders must recognize power relations if they are to overcome bias discussions or worse, 'silent organizations', i.e. organizations with employees who speak but in public say nothing of importance or do not voice their dissent.

Leaders and followers should reflect on these five areas when in role at work, to begin to understand what they carry with them, how they use it, what biases they have, and how others react to them.

People respond to me differently, depending on their own social and historical location. In my case, mature executives with little academic experience can be daunted by 'the University'. This can be very displacing, moving from an important role, to a role where you feel like you know very little, and you do not understand the language, the academic writing rules, and the higher educational systems such as the library. They can respond by becoming infantilized very quickly. In a teaching context this is sometimes projected onto me, sometimes as anger, when they feel impotent, or they can become very dependent and needy towards me, and I can feel like a 'nursing mother' or 'all-knowing Guru'. Other students I supervise, from China and Korea, often come to me with great deference. Their approach is clearly not about me personally, but about me in a role and their cultural normative response to the student/professor relationship. My subject expertise impacts on others, and this links to my personal teaching style. I work differently to many professors, drawing on my experience as a psychotherapist; I deal with emotions and the unconscious in the classroom. I am also aware of the classic 'patient/analyst' relationship as one of dependency and how easy/dangerous it is to enjoy projections of idealization. Having some awareness of my own social location gives me more room to mediate on how I deal with different individuals. I do not take their anxiety and projections personally and can distance myself from them, protecting myself from the feelings of omnipotence or from being paralysed by negative projections. Being able to reflect on the biases and projections with my students is an important learning experience, and we explore diversity in way that makes it part of the whole rather than an add-on at the end of the course. I ask students to observe their own responses and we agree on a learning contract: 'this classroom is a learning laboratory, all experience is data for learning … including your feelings … be aware of your responses to each other and to me.' For leaders this ability to understand projections and the idea of social location is very important when dealing with difference.

A fundamental principle that applies to leaders is that too much followership dependency undermines critical and innovative thinking, and creates a climate that eradicates dissent, or even the exploration of difference. It may feel good to a leader to have a dependent followership, but it is not a healthy or sustainable dynamic. Without critical thinking, awareness of role, social location, the issues of power, patriarchy and diversity will never be addressed.

Space Invaders

Nirmal Puwar's book *Space Invaders: Race, Gender and Bodies Out of Place* (2004) eloquently describes this process that marks establishment spaces, and excludes those bodies that are not part of this space. We particularly notice 'otherness' when difference transgresses normal spaces. My own experience alerts me to this as I have transgressed normative gender boundaries, working as a nurse at a time when it was a 95% female profession, and as a home-parent walking into mother and toddler groups in the early 1980s as the sole male figure. My experience of this was that I was not treated as 'me' the subject, but as an 'object' either to be feared – a threat of contamination to the homogeneous group (asked to leave some nursing lectures on gynaecology, not being allowed to work on female wards) – or in the mother and toddler group to be treated as an exotic sexualized object to be flirted with, or an object of pity to be 'mothered'.

Puwar cites Winston Churchill's reaction to Nancy Astor, the first woman MP to enter the House of Parliament:

> I find a woman's intrusion into the House of Commons as embarrassing as if she burst into my bathroom when I had nothing with which to defend myself, not even a sponge. (Winston Churchill cited in Vallance, *Women in the House*, 1979; in Puwar, 2004: 13)

Frantz Fanon in *Black Skin, White Masks* writes about arriving in France in 1950, from Martinique, a French colony, and describes his experience of transgressing boundaries and the effect of the 'gaze' of the other:

> The movements, the attitudes, the glances of the other fixed me there, in the sense that a chemical solution is fixed by a dye ... sealed into that crushing objecthood the look imprisoned me.'

He relates this experience to a 'Historic-racial schema ... a racial epidermal schema'. He was assigned ethnic characteristics, through which, he says:

> I was battered down by tom toms, cannibalism, intellectual deficiency, festishism, racial defects, slave-ships ... I was told to stay within bounds, to go back to where I belonged ... dissected under white eyes, the only real eyes, I am *fixed*. (Fanon, 1970: 109–16, in Puwar, 2004: 39)

Fanon's accounts are visceral and insightful from the perspective of how people react to 'otherness' and how this becomes internalized. One of the most important issues when dealing with leadership and diversity is to look at the spaces in the workplace. Who inhabits which spaces? Who is excluded and what happens if the space is transgressed? What happens when a woman walks into a boardroom full of men? What happens when a black person enters an all-white establishment? Does the 'other' have to be assimilated? Do they have to learn to be like the majority group, women executives proving their maleness, or black executives their whiteness? Is there a negotiation and co-existence tacitly agreed whereby the 'other' conforms to the norm whilst becoming the 'exotic other' and performing 'otherness' for the majority? (See Said, 1973.)

Diversity is truly complex, and even those of us committed to equal opportunities, to working with difference, even those in minority groups striving for equality, get tripped up in dynamics that reproduce normative behaviours. Being politically correct can also propagate hidden discrimination. Leaders should reflect deeply about what happens in their workplace, what language is used, how they and their teams react to difference, when a 'strange body' enters their work space.

Puwar finds that in Britain our colonial past stays with us like sediment:

> Black bodies are represented as coming from uncivilised spaces,
> wildernesses where people are savages and need taming ... whites are
> associated with spirit and mind, representing the flight from the body.
> (Puwar, 2004: 21)

Whilst ground has been made on these issues, unconscious gender, sexual,
disability and racial stereotyping is still very much with us.

Whiteness

Whiteness is a term that aims to make white people visible to themselves as
a racialized category (Andermahr et al., 2000). White people have viewed
themselves as racially neutral, which it has been claimed gives them power.
Invisibility is, as noted by Burgin, a general instrument of power:

> *White* however has the strange property of directing our attention to color
> while in the very same moment it exnominates itself *as* a 'color,' for we
> know very well that this means 'not white.' ... To speak of the color of skin
> is to speak of a body. (Burgin, 1996: 130–1, in Puwar, 2004: 58)

This is important for critical leadership especially when dealing with a
corporate European-American 'Axis of Maleness and Whiteness' (or as some
feminists put it 'pale, male and stale'). Power and patriarchy are still
intimately linked, and whiteness is still regarded as neutral and normative,
especially in corporations, although some progress has taken place in the
public sector in the UK. The task for those in leadership is to recognize this
state of affairs and address it with urgency. When locating ourselves, the
concept of whiteness can help bring 'normative' European-American
behaviours and assumptions into focus.

Diversity Education

Marginalized minorities face discrimination in subtle and indirect ways,
Treacher discusses the difficulty of addressing difference because it is 'subtle
and yet pervasive'. She refers to:

> a series of mantras being repeated ... it is not that I think these are
> inadequate or wrong but that they operate as shutters against thought,
> feeling and recognition of how we are all implicated in fantasies of self and
> other. (Treacher, 2000: 12)

The only possible way to address diversity is from a perspective that begins with ourselves, recognizing our individual and collective social location and historical-cultural position. Unless leaders can do this, then they address these difficult issues with huge blind-spots triggered by their defence mechanisms. Yet many diversity education settings provoke defences rather than build trust. Discussing diversity is problematic, as it inevitably threatens one's identity. When discussed in leadership circles dominated by white men, diversity also asks uncomfortable questions about privilege and power. My experience of workplace diversity and equality workshops is that they often raise anxieties and create defensive responses amongst the participants who are most in need of change if a culture change is to occur. These defences are displayed as either passive-aggressive responses or total compliance. Silent resistance occurs that emerges as vocal resistance in small groups over coffee after the event, or aggressive-defensive behaviours, such as 'we are all individuals here and nobody is treated differently' or 'are you calling me a racist?'. Building trust in order to have more transparent conversations is the only possible way to make progress. As every good psychoanalyst knows, pushing at resistance only creates more resistance. When discussing diversity issues it is vitally important not to lose the ability to think or to speak. Diversity policies have made language central to their attempts to change behaviour; however this has a double edge. It does help to improve negative images of racial and gender stereotypes but it also has other consequences. Andrew Cooper points out, 'one of the unintended consequences of Political Correctness is that it has bred a generation of stutterers' (Cooper, 1996: 2). People become afraid to speak, for fear of saying the wrong thing, and being accused of being racist or sexist. It is almost impossible to be 'politically correct' because there is no 'correct', and for those outside the diversity discourse the nuances and changing terms and acronyms used to describe diversity are very challenging. For example, what does LGBT mean and whom do I apply it to? Should I say gay or homosexual when addressing this issue? Should I use black, person of colour, brown, mixed-race, African-American, Asian, Indian-British? What is accepted in some countries, regions and contexts is wrong in others, and finding a common language becomes increasingly difficult. Those outside of the latest agreed terms of reference find themselves stuttering or silenced. Engaging people to change from all sides of the diversity spectrum means building trust, openness and understanding.

I am concerned about this alienation that occurs during 'equal opportunity and diversity purges' in the workplace, which can close down rather than open up dialogue. Learning the mantras is easy: 'celebrate difference', 'empower everyone'. Yet if real change is to occur, leadership is required to bring the discussions and debates back to practice, and to tolerate mistakes, slips and misunderstandings in order to surface what is really happening, the subtle discrimination, and to identify where change is needed and the process that will achieve this. Diversity is as much about inclusion as it is exclusion, and this needs to be enacted in diversity education; creating an elite from those who can command the diversity language and agenda creates new barriers, and is not underpinned by the principles of maximizing inclusion.

Using personal experience to locate 'personal and shared' ideas of normative behaviour and defences is the only starting point when dealing with diversity and difference. Addressing systems and power structures, normative attitudes, discourses and behaviours that exclude and diminish minority and marginalized groups is vital to this debate.

Successful future leaders will be those who are able to cope with diversity and difference, as the globalized world demands it.

The Diversity Business Case: Beware!

Diversity issues are marginalized in management circles and business schools. When they are dealt with it is too often as an 'add on' to placate the liberal 'politically correct' lobby. Kandola and Fullerton (1994) take another approach, which emphasizes the business case for managing diversity:

> ... that there are visible and invisible differences, sex, age, background, race, disability, personality, work-style ... harnessing these differences will create a productive environment in which everybody feels valued, where talents are being fully utilized and in which organizational goals are being met. (Kandola and Fullerton, 1994: 47)

R. Roosevelt Thomas Jr (1991: 16–17), a US diversity consultant, makes the business case, and argues in more concrete terms that managing diversity is

> not about a moral responsibility to do the right thing ... it is not a civil rights or humanitarian issue ... it is about maximising employee effectiveness and retaining competitive advantage when working in a global economy with an increasingly diverse workforce. (cited in Fulop and Linstead, 1999: 56)

This utilitarian 'business case' for managing diversity in order to improve efficiency is important as it adds to the argument: for example, in recent work in an international bank with a patriarchal culture they were slow to realize the ethical case, but quickly grasped that their competitors were gaining an advantage by employing women at senior levels, because without doing so 50% of the talent pool was being missed. Yet the utilitarian case is also naïve and dangerous when separated from ethical and human concerns. The business case (creativity, the retention and recruitment of talent, maximizing the potential of the workforce etc.) is important but it cannot be the only argument. Unless there is a deeper ethical belief in a diversity agenda it is unlikely to be successful, as privileged elites will repeat the mantras but not change the structures that exclude disadvantages and minority groups. What happens when research shows that the most effective workforce consists of homogeneous groups? Bond and Pyle (1998) researched workplace diversity in the USA: 'A predominant research finding shows that whilst diverse teams can be creative, they also tend to experience less cohesion and greater turnover than more homogeneous work groups' (Bond and Pyle, 1998: 591). Using Thomas's rationale, the business case would now argue for diversity in areas that require creativity, such as design teams, and homogeneous teams for production. My guess is that it would have a pretty devastating effect on employee moral if the company divided teams by race, sexuality and gender, citing efficient working teams as the reason. Martin Parker in *Ethics and Organizations* suggests that utilitarianism is in a sense the logic of organization (Parker, 1998), yet utilitarianism without ethics can have devastating consequences. This is where a critical leadership is called for: to challenge value-free policies that ignore ethics in favour of efficiency, without looking at the whole system ramifications and the human implications.

Gender and Leadership: The Essentialist Debate

Historically women have struggled for equality; to not be essentially defined by their biology or the traits that society considers inherently female or feminine, but to be considered as equals in all regards. Leadership roles exemplify this challenge as women are still under-represented at the highest positions of power in politics, business and religious institutions.

Feminism and the struggle for women's rights has a long history. An early example comes from the Quaker movement in the 1650s. Margaret Fell was an important Quaker leader and organizer, and married George Fox, the founder of Quakerism. Their belief was in equality, that no hierarchical priests could be appointed, that all could minister the word, and this meant women as well. Fell wrote a public pamphlet called 'Women's Speaking Justified':

Those that speak against the power of the Lord speaking in a woman, simply by reason of her sex, or because she is a woman, not regarding the spirit ... such speak against Christ. (Margaret Fell, cited in Trevett, 1995: 57)

Mary Wollstonecraft wrote her *Vindication of the Rights of Women* in 1792. It has been a long struggle for gender equality; if this awareness was available in the 1650s, our progress has been very slow!

Essentialism

Essentialism is the view that the body provides the raw materials from which cultures craft their own interpretations and elaborations of gendered identities. Social construction is the view that gendered identities are formed as a result of cultural and psychosocial processes through which men and women are socialized into gender-specific constructions of how males and females are to act, think and feel (Tolman and Diamond, 2002: 37–8).

Lynne Segal in *Straight Sex: Rethinking the Politics of Pleasure* (1997) finds that the female body is socially equated with passivity, receptivity, and penetrability, and the male body with activity, directness, determination, impenetrability and so forth. Segal says that whilst these representations may be sexist and seem stupid we cannot ignore them, as they are inscribed onto us through social discourse, and they become part of the lived experience (Sullivan, 2003: 128). Contemporary feminist theorists claim that 'essentialism' hinders the progress toward liberation (Butler, 1990; Rich, 1980). This argument is important in the leadership context as many perspectives presented on women in business take an essentialist stance. For example, Professor Lynda Gratton, as head of the Lehman Brothers Centre for Women in Business, the first research centre dedicated to this issue in Europe, when interviewed said:

The sort of things women are good at – innovation, getting work done at the same time as getting on with people – are increasingly valuable as we move into a world in which flexibility and knowledge-sharing are a key ... women are good at networking, they just tend to network with people they like, men tend to network with more powerful people ... if we make organisations more humane, guess what? They suit women. (*Guardian*, 3 November 2006)

The problem with these essentializing statements is that they box women into fixed roles and traits and by implication men also. Essentializing gender is problematic because it is binary and reductionist – 'Men are from Mars, Women are from Venus' – creating a polarization between genders. The idea that 50% of a population have the same essential traits is frankly absurd. Feminists have long argued that fixed women's identities based on their reproductive roles, as mothers, nurturers and carers, have trapped them in social positions of limited freedom and power. It is very problematic then to claim that in the contemporary world these essentializing characteristics give women a leadership advantage. This view that women's natural traits and strengths, listening, caring, relational, are going to give them an advantage in the post-heroic leadership world of the 21st century is supported by Sally Helgeson in her book *The Female Advantage* (1990) and Judy B. Rosener in her book *America's Competitive Secret: Women Managers* (1995).

Challenging this essentializing and binary viewpoint, Simone de Beauvoir's classic statement that 'one is not born, but rather becomes a woman' (1949/1972: 295) indicates that woman is as much socially constructed as biologically determined. Clearly biology plays a part in gender difference, but gender is also socially produced and performed, and as social attitudes change, perceptions of gender and roles change too. Judith Butler claims that there is no natural identity and no essence to gender. Gender is always in the process of becoming, never fixed. It is through repetitive individual and social performative acts that gender and identity become normalized (Butler, 1990). Arguing that women make better modern leaders because of their specific essentializing traits is therefore reductionist, keeping women in fixed stereotypes they have been struggling to liberate themselves from, and continuing to reproduce social norms that are no longer appropriate or fixed. As demonstrated from the following quote, these essentialist norms are also colour-blind and culturally situated, offering a hegemonic Westernized view. A woman's fixed identity immediately becomes problematic when location, ethnicity, culture and race are introduced:

> In the Indian context, woman has not been so neatly defined: she is made up of many attributes, ... as both goddess and dangerous power (*shakti*), as virtuous wife and dangerous evil, both pure and impure in her embodiment, to be revered and worshipped but also to be controlled through direct regulation of her sexuality. (Thapan, 1997: 4)

This deconstruction of gender, sexuality and race fuelled by post-structuralist theory has created new insights but has also fragmented a notion of the universal. Thereby when we speak of women, who are we speaking of if there is no essential gender? How can women fight for equality and liberation if the concept of woman itself is in flux?

Women are making ground in the corporate world, and the 'Gap between salaries of men and women is at a record low' (*Guardian*, 27 October 2006). Walby (1997: 64) notes that

> massive changes are taking place in women's employment and education which are transforming gender relations, for example, increasing their presence in professional and managerial positions in national and local government in the UK by 155%, science education and technology 72%, in literary arts and sports by 54%. (in Fulop and Linstead, 1999: 52)

Yet a huge gap still exists:

> The percentage of women on US corporate boards has been stuck at around 11–12% over the last decade. Boards must realize 'not just what women bring to the table when [on boards] but what is missing when not,' said Gail Becker. … Countries including Norway, Spain and France all have opted for quotas that require women to hold a certain percentage of corporate boards' seats (usually 40%) …

> 'No company will remain competitive for long if it ignores half of its available labor pool,' states the CED report. (Taylor, 2012)

When researching this chapter it became clear that whilst gender in leadership has a higher profile in academia and the media, the other diversity issues are still marginalized. Sexuality, class and race, for example, rarely figure in management and leadership literature, and leave a gaping hole in creating more humane and inclusive workplaces:

> Whilst the glass ceiling has been cracked quite significantly with gender, for race the concrete ceiling has just been chipped ever so slightly. (Puwar, 2004: 7)

Conclusion: 'Rainbow-Wash'

When coaching, educating and consulting with senior executives, it has become clear to me that issues regarding empowerment, inclusion and diversity are integral to all the other issues companies face. Yet whilst diversity is highly visible in the corporate and public sector agenda, like those discriminated against, diversity itself gets marginalized from strategic, cultural and policy changes that would really make a difference. When companies talk big but do very little about sustainability, activists and campaigners accuse them of 'greenwash'. I use the term 'rainbow-wash' to describe and challenge companies when diversity and difference are highly visible in the company rhetoric, but very little happens. I apply this to companies that claim to be 'colourful rainbows' filled with diversity, progressive and dynamic, yet in reality are monochrome, bland and monolithic in their attitudes and culture.

A colleague of mine, working in OD and passionate about diversity issues, writes of her experience of working in Canary Wharf:

> There has been a lot of effort and focus on diversity policies and metrics in organizations in recent years, but real change is very slow to come. I feel this is because we have been focused on diversity for the sake of diversity, and many simply pay lip service or add it on as an afterthought. We need to look at diversity, not as an end in itself, or as a separate task where the box needs to be ticked. It should be about how we do everything else – hiring, decision-making, leadership – it's an indicator of as well as a precursor to an effective, engaging and fully-functioning organization. (Sachdev, 2011)

The links are clear: the ethical case for diversity and inclusion must drive change or otherwise diversity becomes an afterthought and little changes. Yet those companies who take diversity seriously will also benefit in multiple and often unexpected ways, both directly and indirectly. The task for leaders and organizations is to make inclusion and working with difference a core part of the company culture. When this happens difference itself becomes a strength rather than a problem.

Difference is the underpinning dynamic in the diversity debate: can we tolerate, live with, accept, enjoy 'the other'? Or are we always retreating to homogeneous groups, grasping for familiarity and sameness, staying with those who offer no threat but also little creativity?

In relation to leadership, particular issues arise relating to diversity, such as which social groups can be tolerated as leaders, and how can structural changes be made to prevent elite groups dominating the highest leadership positions in companies?

When working in organizations it is important to address diversity as a part of the whole; for example, when supporting a company making the transition from a command and control hierarchy to a more dispersed leadership, I take the opportunity to ask these questions because in order to distribute leadership as they claim to desire, they have to address these issues:

- Who is sitting at the leadership table and who is absent?

- Who can speak and who can't?

- Whose voices are heard and whose aren't, and why?

- Whose values and interests are being represented?

- Which groups are being marginalized and how does this impact on organizational success?

I coach leaders to observe their meetings, to observe their organization, to notice what happens in meetings and within themselves, using questions like these to stimulate awareness of the structural power issues that exist. They often come back to the next coaching session with some powerful insights: 'At the board meeting there were 10 men and 1 woman'; 'We had a meeting and the CEO spoke and the meeting went silent, people listened. When the HR director [a female] spoke people interrupted, went to the restroom, got coffee'; 'We really try hard to be inclusive in this company, but we find at the European–Asian summit it is English and German voices which never shut up. The Asian leaders are much less quick to speak, and they don't often get the opportunity.'

These questions open up the normative and structural issues; they go beyond the content of the meeting and ask the deeper question about power, norms and representation in the organization. As will be addressed later in the Eco-leadership chapter, these questions also go beyond the organization, to the stakeholders, the local community and the ecology and network associated with the organization. Increasingly the task of leaders is to realize that it is not only within the company boundaries that these issues arise, but that they also have to account for supply chains and other stakeholders. The working conditions in which Chinese employees are making Apple products matter, both from an ethical perspective and a brand and business perspective. To deal with difference and diversity is to face oneself, to question who you are, to accept that otherness is not straightforward, that it can be tough and challenge our own personal and social identities. Yet to do so is enriching.

Leadership teams who address diversity issues begin a process that inevitably evokes creativity across the organization. Conformity is born from sameness, and it is from the tensions and beauty of diversity and difference that new thinking and new understandings are born.

Suggested Readings

- Butler, J. (2004) *Undoing Gender*. New York: Routledge.

- Fanon, F. (1970) *Black Skin, White Masks*. London: Paladin.

- Puwar, N. (2004) *Space Invaders: Race, Gender and Bodies Out of Place*. Oxford: Berg.

Reflection Points

Choose a work meeting or university lecture, and observe and reflect on diversity and leadership issues. Ask yourself:

- Who has a voice and who doesn't?

- Whose voices are heard, when they speak, and whose aren't, and why?

- Whose values and interests are being represented? What vested interests are being defended?

- Which groups are being marginalized and how does this impact on organizational success?

- Are some people or groups deferential followers to others ... if so why?

- Does healthy conflict exist, or is the meeting compliant?

Reflect on your own unconscious discriminating tendencies. Think about your social upbringing: which social groups were you socialized to discriminate against, however subtly? How does this impact on how you think about or react to different leaders, e.g. male or female leaders, old or young leaders, ethnically different leaders, able-bodied or disabled leaders?

Sample Assignment Question

Gender and ethnicity are differences that are easily identifiable when thinking about diversity. Reflect on an organization you know well and describe other differences that exist which create hidden discrimination or tensions but aren't spoken about? Make some suggestions as to how these unspoken differences might be addressed, with a particular reference to leadership and power.

6 Leadership and Organizational Culture

Introduction

Organizational culture is deemed to be the heartbeat of company success, and organizational culture is believed to be susceptible to leadership influence. Mainstream leadership thinking claims that successful leaders in the 21st century are 'cultural engineers' (Kunda, 1992), charismatic, strong leaders who can change the organizational culture. This marks a radical shift in the expectations of what senior executives should be doing in leadership and management roles. Traditionally, senior personnel were trained and expected to manage in a material way – to manage people and resources, to organize material things to raise material production. In the post-industrial climate, senior managers are renamed as leaders, with the expectation that instead of managing resources, they manage meaning. The concept of leadership is now taken beyond material governance and into new realms of symbolic activity. Now leaders lead culture. For example, Bass and Avolio (1993: 113) claim that transformational leaders build 'highly innovative and satisfying organizational cultures … Leaders who build such cultures and articulate them to followers typically exhibit a sense of vision and purpose (p. 113).

Whilst Bass et al. recognize that culture also shapes leaders, they perpetuate the comforting idea that a gifted individual leader can 'build' a culture. The phrase 'building a culture' materializes culture, making it an 'object' to be created, transformed, or changed. The Westernized cultural norms that privilege individualism and leaders with heroic agency are joined with the modernist ideas that humans can master both the natural world and human nature. As we can see these underpinning assumptions extend to a desire for heroic leaders to master culture as well.

The idea that leaders stand outside of culture and change is, however, flawed. The large number of failures in mergers and acquisitions due to the unforeseen difficulties and failures of leaders to change organizational culture (Tichy, 2001) show how challenging culture change is. Changing culture is hugely problematic when it is attempted in this direct way because (a) culture is not a 'thing' to be changed, and (b) leaders as change agents are imagined as being outside of culture, using their 'helicopter vision' to look down and see what needs changing. This is to misunderstand culture and leadership. The relationship between leadership and culture change is much more nuanced. Leaders today must be cultural influencers and cultural transmitters, yet to be successful they first have to understand their reflexive positions, i.e. that they are swimming in the sea of culture, that they embody and enact culture, they are not separate from culture.

The other important aspect of organizational culture is to debunk the idea that an organization has a culture that is separate from the wider culture. The way leadership and organizational culture are treated in many business schools and companies follows the metaphor that an organization is like a glass-house, and culture is like the plants inside. This creates a closed system, and the leader then controls the light, the heat, the plant feed, the water, etc. to nurture the culture they desire, killing unwanted pests and weeds as they go. Whilst it is true organizations do have nuanced cultures, they are not closed-systems but interdependent with wider social and corporate cultures. These wider aspects of social culture influence them far more than is acknowledged. Yes, leaders are engaged in the symbolic activities of working with culture. No, leaders do not have the power to change culture *per se*.

To become a leader is to be a 'cultural carrier'; the leaders who get to be top leaders are those who are most embedded in contemporary culture. To become a leader you will be formed through attending the right school, being exposed to networks and business schools, and working and fitting in well within the corporate culture.

The key points about leadership and culture made by this chapter are summarized in Box 12.

Box 12   Leadership and Culture

- Leaders do not speak from outside or above culture but from within it.
- The idea of leaders being 'engineers of culture' misleads, as culture is not an object to be manipulated but a nuanced collection of meanings.

- Leaders are selected as leaders because they fit with an organizational culture, rather than because they are radical, cultural change agents.

- Cultural avatars: leaders act as cultural avatars, acting on behalf of wider and dominant social-cultural forces.

- Culture speaks through us: leaders speak from within 'the unchosen principle of all choices' (Bourdieu, 1990: 61), i.e. the choices and agency that leaders enact are shaped and limited by the confines of what culture permits and demands.

- A talented leader is a skilled transmitter of culture: this is where individual agency comes into play.

What Is Organizational Culture? 'The Way Things Feel Around Here'

Edgar Schein (1988: 9), a prolific scholar on culture, describes culture as a 'pattern of basic assumptions that a given group has invented', whilst Mats Alvesson explains that culture is 'a tricky concept as it is easily used to cover everything and consequently nothing' (Alvesson, 2002: 3). Deal and Kennedy's (1982) straightforward description of culture as 'the way we do things around here' is popular due to its simplicity. However, Alvesson (2002) believes that when culture is over-simplified people should use terms like 'social norms' as culture itself is a more complex phenomena. 'The way we do things around here' suggests that culture can been seen in a material sense, yet culture is more symbolic and tacit than this functionalist description, it is more about feeling than doing, meaning rather than materialism, and I would argue that a more accurate simple description would be *'culture is the way things feel around here'*. Culture is not a material phenomenon, it is how material things, such as rituals and artefacts, are manifested collectively in our minds, how we interiorize and experience these things. Culture organizes disparate phenomena, offering us models from which we collectively, and unconsciously, interpret meaning. The phenomena that express 'culture' are commonly thought of as architecture, rituals, art, religion, music, folk 'tradition'. In organizations, culture is manifested in company buildings, internal architectures (open-plan offices, dining areas), seasonal rituals, workplace practices, dress and behavioural codes, 'company speak' (i.e. the in-language, so if you work for Google you are a called a Googler), and the company mantras, narratives and discourses express and shape the culture.

Culture is both a model of reality and a model for reality (Geertz, 1973), meaning that culture offers us a model to make sense of reality, and tells us how things should be and how we should act.

Organizational cultures change mostly when economic and social change requires new organizational forms, new ways to organize the process of production (or service provision). Leadership plays a part in developing these new forms and cultures that respond to the social and economic changes. Examples are Cadbury's Bourneville village in England, Fordist factories, and Volkswagen's Dresden plant (which makes the entire production process visible and transparent). These companies created new organizational spaces, and new manufacturing processes, from which new cultures emerged. These new cultures also shaped new forms of management control, from which new forms of employee resistance arose. When a new culture emerges it quickly spreads to other organizations working in similar fields. Leaders and others then transmit these cultures from one site to another.

Culture: A Non-neutral Force

Culture is often perceived as a neutral force, something that reflects a nation or organization, yet culture is very 'non-neutral'. Martin Parker (2002: 25) refers to Mathew Arnold's 1867 *Culture and Anarchy*; Arnold claimed that the right culture, established by a moral elite, could be embedded in the masses, and thus provide a defence against moral anarchy. This mirrors contemporary leadership goals in organizations to establish or sustain the culture that 'controls' the masses of employees, ensuring they are 'on task', and working hard for the company goals. This may or may not be malevolent control, it may be more focused on motivation, but the end-game is raising productivity.

Alvesson points out that culture has a dual capacity – to create meaning and to control:

> *simultaneously* to create order, meaning, cohesion and orientation, thus making collective action, indeed organizational life possible, *and* to restrict autonomy, creativity and questioning, thereby preventing novel, potentially more ethical thought through ways of organizing social life to be considered. (2002: 13)

By connecting the terms leadership and organizational culture a tension is set in place, as leadership infers acting upon, or shaping, organizational culture. Kets de Vries and Miller (1984) argue that a leader's neurosis can be mirrored in the organizational culture, for example creating narcissistic and paranoid cultures. Strong leaders do enact their inner-theatres on their organizations, however how much they actually influence the culture is debatable. Perhaps it is more accurate to say that leaders exacerbate existing (perhaps dormant) cultures such as an organization's grandiosity or paranoia. A dictator can perhaps create a paranoid culture, for example if they imprison and torture many people, but in corporate life, these cultures are probably more reflexive, with the leaders acting out the culture on behalf of followers, than simply dominating and dictating a certain culture. Handy (1996) offers four frames of organizational culture, 'power, person, role and task cultures', and claims that individuals fit with the culture closest to their personality. I believe the same applies for leaders, who select the culture they are comfortable in and replicate it.

Cultural Avatars: 'Leaders Shape Culture, and Culture Shapes Leaders'

> Through socialisation the individual becomes a part of the organization; but so, too, does the organization become part of the individual. (Gabriel, 1999: 196)

Leaders have a certain amount of agency and influence:; they can be powerful, yet they are better understood as skilled cultural 'avatars' than cultural engineers. Like avatars in a computer game, leaders act (often unconsciously) on behalf of other interests, they carry and transmit cultures on behalf of wider forces.

Culture is a wide coalition of effects and affects, that produces normative leadership and normative corporate cultures. In my work as a coach/consultant, I see clearly that leaders do not appear as neutral individuals from the skies, but undergo a formation process, in which culture shapes them. Most senior leaders are shaped by the industry, the sector, the region, the product, the department, the company, the MBA and the literature, i.e. the socialization process from the cultures in which they live and work. Rites of passage exist for leaders within companies and across companies (on training courses, conferences etc.) that ensure only the right leaders who 'fit' the culture are selected to senior positions. Many public sector CEOs will be sent on a 'leadership course' at that holy site of management, Harvard Business School. Those leaders who don't fit the company culture, or a wider corporate or public sector culture, are quickly spat out! Many organizations will select a talented leader from another company to change their cultures, yet they will face resistance from the very people who selected them; even those who consciously want change will often resist it at an unconscious level. Culture colonizes us, in ways we don't always appreciate.

Culture influences how leaders are selected and developed and creates boundaries and limitations regarding how they perform. The lessons are clear, we must remove the gloss of individual leaders riding white stallions into organizations and changing cultures. Cultures are too embedded and ethereal to be chased out of town so quickly. The best we can hope for from our leaders is that they will try to influence the culture, beginning by (a) recognizing their own reflexive positions as carriers of culture, and (b) recognizing that culture does not recognize organizational reception desks, that it does not stop and start at the company boundary but is everywhere, and an organizational culture is part of a greater social culture (organizations are ecosystems within an ecosystem).

Leaders such as the late Steve Jobs have carefully constructed images. Heroic narratives are repeated of the maverick leader raising a pirate flag, and the iconic pictures of relaxed CEO Steve in jeans and black polo produced a signifier that infered 'hyper cool', the non-conformist, renegade billionaire, who maintained social capital by raging against the corporate machine (whilst selling more machines than anyone else). In the formative years buying an Apple computer was not just to own a computer, but to join a cool, counter-cultural community. This is today's leadership, transmitting a culture to employees, and into the network of customers and shareholders as 'the brand'. However, by all accounts the organizational culture at Apple is not much different from other 'hi-tech' creative companies in Silicon Valley. Steve Jobs didn't invent this hi-tech corporate culture but he did carry it, contribute to it with others at Apple, and transmit it with panache. He and other image-makers created a narrative of 'think-different' Apple, challenging the totalizing big brother 'other', epitomized by IBM and Microsoft. This was brilliantly captured in their most famous advert, the 1984 Mac advert.[1] The culture Apple transmits to its employees, however, is not that cool or original, but reflects the essence of a hi-tech, Silicon Valley, corporate culture. Apple do this very well, hence their huge success, and yet the organizational culture in Apple seems to have the same totalizing influences as other global corporations. We don't hear of Apple employees dissenting against the exploitation of their Chinese fellow workers in Foxconn (the production arm of Apple, renowned for poor conditions, that are likened to a labour camp, and have driven employees to suicide and riots[2]). If Apple were a cool, liberal company, a lot more complaints would be heard, but my guess is that at Apple this dissent is forbidden. Steve Jobs' brilliance wasn't creating an Apple culture, it was to be completely focused on a vision of integrated and aesthetically beautiful products that were exceptionally simple and intuitive to use.

---

[1] see www.youtube.com/watch?v=OYecfV3ubP8.

[2] http://news.cnet.com/8301-13579_3-57515968-37/riots-suicides-and-other-issues-in-foxconns-iphone-factories/.

Postmodernity and Leadership Culture

Postmodernity throws us out of modernity's structured and boundaried lands, and sends us into exile. We find ourselves in strange lands of hyper-reality, in globalized workplaces that are de-territorialized (Baudrillard, 1983). Our lives are saturated with media and images, where the real and the image merge and become the same. Money before 1971 had an exchange value linked to gold, then Nixon de-coupled money from the 'gold standard' and it is now free floating. Vast sums of 'electronic money' are traded, won and lost in seconds, as electrical numbers flit across computer screens. This virtual gambling game, however, has real consequences for those families who lose houses and jobs during financial crashes. The real and virtual merge in networks that become enmeshed knots, feeding and constituting each other. In this hyper-real world a 'consumer culture' exists, where it is no longer the utility that is of value, but the sign:

> The term consumer culture points to the ways in which consumption ceases to be a simple appropriation of utilities, or use values, to become a consumption of signs and images in which the emphasis upon the capacity to endlessly reshape the cultural or symbolic aspect of the commodity makes it more appropriate to speak of *commodity signs*. (Featherstone, 1995: 75; emphasis in original)

When the sign becomes more valued that the product, and the perception of brand value drives the actual company valuation (Steenkamp et al., 2003), a new form of leadership is required. In these new cultures leaders can no longer focus on the material, but have to focus on the culture, perceptions and the symbolic.

Corporate leaders operate in this new realm as cultural experts, sending symbolic signs and messages that shape the perceptions of employees, customers and shareholders. Their task is to change and shape the organizational culture, brand perception and 'reality' itself. Enron leadership took the global corporate cultural norm, of transmitting conformist totalizing cultures to excess (see Messiah Leadership, Chapter 11). The leaders of companies like Enron and the banks didn't invent these compliant corporate cultures; they transmitted what had become normal, taking them to extreme levels that led to tragic failures. Post-modern leaders are skilled at using the signifying tools of media and communication, to help shape internal culture and external perception.

However, a paradox exists: individual leaders are rewarded with huge 'packages' because of their perceived capacity to manipulate and engineer organizational cultures that encourage hard work, conformity, high performance, and therefore success for shareholders. Yet these 'Messiah leaders' are not above culture, they are not 'masters of culture' but are themselves products of culture. Leadership is a facet of contemporary culture, and leaders are enmeshed within culture.

Messiah leaders are 'hyper-real' leaders, created by images and signs to become cultural icons, and therefore their capacity is not to engineer a culture, but to transmit a culture (of which they are part). Successful leaders utilize their agency as 'cultural transmitters' (Alvesson, 2002) to impact on local culture (i.e. organizations). They are skilled at transmitting the dominant cultures that the wider corporate world, supported by business school and consultancy firms deem the best for our times.

Leadership Cultures

The rise of leadership as a term in organizational life reflects how leadership itself is a signifier of organizational culture. Organizations with managers and supervisors sound like yesterday's companies and have been usurped by CEOs, senior leaders and team leaders. This new 'leadership culture' in organizations is part of the wider goal of producing a new employee for the 21st century. Alvesson and Willmott (2002: 3) describe positive meanings associated with leadership and how these impact on employee identity:

> Consider, for example, the now widely used terms 'leader' and 'team leader'. The commonsensically valued identities associated with such discourse, which appeal to the positive cultural valence assigned to discourses of supremacy and sport, have replaced less 'attractive' titles such as 'foreman', 'supervisor' or even 'manager'. We interpret such moves as symptomatic of efforts to secure organizational control through the use of cultural media – in this case, the positive and seductive meanings associated with leadership. (Alvesson and Willmott, 2002: 3)

Creating distributed leadership is argued from the position (which I agree with) that leadership needs to be everywhere in post-industrial workplaces, as central control is not adaptive enough for organizations. However, the flip side of this is where team managers are renamed as leaders, without being given more opportunities for creativity or responsibility. Leadership is then utilized as a form of culture control, harnessing employee identification with being a leader (a hero, a courageous person) in order to maximize their contribution, hoping they will extend their hours, and attempting to get the extra mile from their team in order to improve productivity. Unless leadership means leadership, you have the rhetoric of a leadership culture and the practice of a management, controlling culture; this schism and dissonance leads to cynicism and a lowering of morale.

Cultural Contagion

Taking a bigger-picture look at organizational culture, it cannot be separated from social culture or other company cultures in the same sector and region as they share the same local and global flows of influence. Organizational cultures are not closed systems, and whilst companies have specific subcultures, they also import cultures from wider social and cultural forces. Isomorphism (DiMaggio and Powell, 1983) is a powerful force whereby organizations mimic those around them who are most successful; this creates a cultural contagion. The culture of banking, for example, changed from 'low risk, high stability', i.e. banks were the safe and secure places for depositing money, and would lend to those deemed financially secure to repay the debt, and from the 1980s onwards the banks, one by one, mimicked others in the financial industry where the culture was 'higher risk for higher profit'. Banks became virtual financial trading companies, risking and ultimately losing huge sums. The culture of banking had changed, not because of a maverick leader taking a decision to change the culture, but by isomorphic pressures to conform to the most successful norm, to keep up with the other banks/financial traders that were making vast profits quickly.

Despite the talk of diverse company cultures, in reality there is much homogeneity within corporate and public sector life. Working as a consultant and visiting diverse corporate offices internationally, I experience the monotonous uniformity of 'corporate culture', which, like airports, shopping malls and business hotels, creates a 'depressing sameness'. Global corporations carry a particular minimalist, modernist aesthetic, sharing a culture of conformity. When open-plan offices become the fad, all have open-plan offices. When inside companies, subtle cultural nuances begin to emerge, that arise from the type of work, company history, the product and sector, the organizational space and architectures, national and regional differences, and the leadership, amongst other influences. Globalization and the emergence of corporate power are, however, eradicating cultural difference very quickly, in a process that Ritzer (1993) calls 'the McDonaldization of society'. These totalizing organizational cultures are especially dangerous because those employees inside them are often unaware of their entrapment, reducing the potential for resistance or change. Chapter 7 addresses these 'fundamentalist tendencies' in more depth.

Conclusion: Start from a New Place

This chapter has reviewed leadership and culture, arguing that individual leaders do not lead culture change as the transformational leadership literature claims, but are more likely to be 'cultural avatars', acting on behalf of cultures that animate them as leaders. They become skilled transmitters of the cultures in which they 'swim'. Leadership is one of many factors that influence organizational culture. You cannot protect the intellectual property of your organizational culture because it is not yours, and it is not definable. Cultures are too complex, and too diffuse for leaders to create or master them, and over-simplifying the relationship between leaders and cultures may be reassuring, but inevitably leads to problems.

There are worrying signs that 'cultures of conformity' within corporations and public sector organizations are at dangerous levels, and current leadership adds to this problem as it supports strong unified cultures. Hidden beneath the rhetoric of dynamism, entrepreneurship and creativity is a malaise that lies deep within contemporary organizational culture. In corporations, schools, hospitals, and banks, I have experienced employee compliance and conformity at unprecedented levels. These embedded cultures have fundamentalist tendencies which are a deep concern, and in Chapter 7 we shall seek to better understand this 'corporate fundamentalism'.

What Can Leaders Do?

There is an old Irish joke:

> A lost traveller asks a farmer how to get to Galway.
>
> After thinking for a long time the farmer replies:
>
> 'Well, I wouldn't start from here.'

I am suggesting that we take this joke seriously, and begin from a new place, as starting from where we are implies starting with two false assumptions: (a) that leaders can change cultures, and (b) that cultures are things within organizations that can be changed. So if leaders cannot change cultures *per se*, what can they do?

Starting from a new place is to discard the conventional leadership view that 'we are above culture, let's map it out, then plan how to change it'. Each leader must discover their own new starting places, but below are some provocative suggestions:

- Forget grand culture change plans.

- Remember that leaders and organizations exist in culture; they are part of it, not above it or outside of it.

- Cultures are diverse and plural, not monolithic and singular.

- Culture change comes indirectly, asymmetrically, and is emergent; it cannot be planned.

- Leaders should lead a cultural resistance against hegemonic social and corporate cultures.

Taking the above suggestions, a key leadership task is to lead a cultural resistance against hegemonic social and corporate cultures, rather than be captured by them and simply reproduce them. Such cultural resistance by employees in organizations is rarely explicit in corporate life (as it will be quashed, or militants fired) but it is always present to different degrees. Forms of underground resistance mirror how powerless groups resist domination in other social situations. Scott describes forms of peasant resistance:

> The ordinary weapons of relatively powerless groups: foot dragging, dissimulation, false compliance, pilfering, feigned ignorance, slander, arson, sabotage and so forth. They require little or no coordination and planning; they often represent a form of individual self-help; and they typically avoid any direct symbolic confrontation with authority or elite norms. (Scott, 1985: 32)

In the workplace some resist the culture with an 'ironic knowing', others resist the culture simply because they are discontented with the company and work. Casey (2000) claims this 'non-work' is part of a growing disillusionment with corporate culture. Organizations can fail through death by a thousand cuts, i.e. a low-morale workforce finds many minor ways to resist, that together destabilize and undermine a totalizing or oppressive company culture.

Leaders can learn from this process of cultural resistance. A damaging dominant culture cannot be changed or defeated head-on, but it is possible to build coalitions to mitigate against these cultures such as those that demand employee conformity. Taking an asymmetrical and multi-positional approach can lead to growing resistance that destabilizes dominant cultures and can contribute to creating developing competing cultures. I am claiming that cultural resistance by leaders and followers is the first step, because resisting the colonizing effects of oppressive cultures is the first act that leads to potential new cultures emerging.

Leaders can use the dominant corporate/social culture to undermine itself. Irony and humour are great weapons against dominant cultural forces, as testified by those in Eastern Europe during the dominant Soviet system, and used by anti-capitalist provocateurs such as Adbusters. Using the psychoanalytic method in organizations as a consultant, I am always struck by the power of naming the unconscious in the room, saying the unsayable that everyone is thinking. Leaders too can take up this role; if everyone is tired of moronic vision statements, but are still performing 'good employee' in meetings playing along with something nobody authentically believes in, it's better to name this. Leaders must be more courageous and imaginative in this sense. Had critical dissent been a part of organizational cultures in the banking and financial sectors, the worst economic crisis since the 1930s would have been avoided.

David Harvey, author of 'Rebel Cities', thinks that a healthy civic life is built on dynamic battles and negotiations. He writes:

> A conflictual city is always a much more engaging thing … the big problem is to have a conflictual city where people are not killing each other. (Harvey, 2012)

The same applies to organizations: distributing leadership will be essential in order to create more engaging and adaptive organizational cultures. Yet this also means enabling and accepting more 'conflict'. Perhaps a leader's task is to create 'conflictual organizations' where people don't metaphorically kill each other. To achieve this means to act before things get too stuck and too difficult to change because dissent has been repressed for too long. Leaders can provide containment to encourage 'healthy levels of conflict', enabling true diversity, free thinking and autonomist leadership to develop.

Leaders cannot create new cultures, but they can resist dominant trends that create 'silent organizations' where dissent (and by default, creativity) has been outlawed by cultures of conformity (Tourish and Robson, 2006).

Leaders cannot change cultures by themselves, nor can they manipulate culture at will. They can, however, support their companies to find creative and symbolic waves to ride an hegemonic culture, resist the worst aspects, and open spaces that will allow new and healthier cultures to emerge.

Suggested Readings

- Alvesson, M. (2002) *Understanding Organizational Culture*. London/ Thousand Oaks, CA: Sage.

- Kunda, G. (1992) *Engineering Culture: Control Commitment in a High Tech Corporation*. Philadelphia, PA: Temple University Press.

- Schein, E. (1988) *Organizational Culture and Leadership*. San Francisco, CA: Jossey–Bass.

Reflection Points

- This chapter argues that leaders are shaped by culture as much as they shape it. Reflect on the idea that leaders are not above culture, pulling the strings, rather they are *in* culture. Culture creates order and meaning, and it also constrains and limits individual and collective autonomy.

- Identify two organizational settings: (1) where you see a healthy culture, (2) where you see the culture has become too strong, creating totalizing environments where people don't speak or think independently. Try to identify the differences in how these organizations feel, and how they work.

Sample Assignment Question

Identify a leader or team of leaders (either well-known public leaders such as national politicians, or from within an organization) and describe how they enact and perform a particular culture that shapes their leadership.

7   Corporate Fundamentalism

Chapter Structure

- **Introduction**
- **Reviewing Religious Fundamentalism**
- **Where Christian and Corporate Fundamentalism Meet**
- **Corporate Fundamentalism: Totalizing Cultures**
- **Conclusion: Fundamentalist Cultures Are Unsustainable**

Introduction

> Apple is one of those companies where people work on an almost religious level of commitment.[1] (Former Apple Employee)

This chapter offers new resources to understand how much of contemporary corporate culture has morphed to become a benign form of totalizing culture with 'fundamentalist' tendencies. As the Apple employee writes above, these organizational cultures mimic religious cultures in their intensity of belief and commitment.

This chapter explores these cultures finding they are informed by, and mimic, new religious fundamentalist movements, in particular Christian Fundamentalists in the USA. Fundamentalist movements often have charismatic leaders, skilled at communicating symbolic messages, with a dynamic, loyal followership committed to the vision and values of the leader and movement. This chapter reviews how corporations attempt to mimic aspects of these fundamentalist movements in order to maximize employee engagement, commitment and productivity.

The Corporate Holy Grail: Dynamic and Conformist Cultures

Corporate leaders were struggling to adjust to post-Fordist production and globalization, falling behind the Asian Tiger economies in the 1980s.

---

[1] http://appleinsider.com/articles/10/07/07/former_employees_shed_light_on_apples_internal_corporate_culture.html

They wondered about how to lead, control and motivate employees in this new globalized economy. The question they faced was how to create a cohesive company brand, with loyal, hard working and committed employees, who could work independently and autonomously in this post-industrial knowledge-led economy. This was a very different task from leading an industrial factory or bureaucratic office. Put simply, the Holy Grail these companies sought was to create workplaces that unleashed employees' dynamism, but that were also conformist, so that employees worked in a committed and engaged way and didn't question the company norms.

The success of Christian Fundamentalist churches in the USA offered a radical social movement that seemingly had achieved this holy grail of 'dynamic *and* conformist' cultures. Charismatic preachers inspired followers, creating a community of believers motivating and sustaining each other, in a world around them which was increasingly alienating and atomizing. These churches are full of energy, bubbling and alive, yet they are also monocultures, totalizing, free of dissent, and homogeneous. I have visited these evangelical Christian mega-churches, in London, California, North Carolina, and South Africa, and the monoculture is uncannily reproduced all over the world. The liturgy, the service, the message, the preachers, the body language and verbal responses are replicated everywhere. Even the facial expressions are the same, that evangelical 'I am filled with grace' look, is performed beautifully in all of the churches I have observed. The level of commitment, loyalty, energy and performativity these churches achieve set within an 'aligned culture' represents the dream employee base for global corporations. The control of these churches comes from culture, as the transactional or coercive levers of pay, conditions, and promotions of the workplace do not exist.

This chapter reveals how corporate fundamentalism emerged and how religious fundamentalism can help us understand the more complex and subtle dynamics within organizational culture. Religious fundamentalism is often very over-simplified and a misunderstood phenomena, and by addressing it with curiosity and openness, we can learn much about secular society and organizational leadership and culture.

The chapter works through four phases:

1 Reviewing religious fundamentalism: To reveal how these social movements are far from premodern antiquities, and are more akin to postmodern social movements, which use the past as a reference point to critique the failings of modernity.

2 Where Christian and corporate fundamentalism meet: Exploring the unconscious connections and cultural exchange between corporate culture and Christian Fundamentalist cultures.

3 Corporate fundamentalism – totalizing corporate cultures: Revealing how 'corporate fundamentalist' culture mimics the leadership and dynamics of religious fundamentalism, and creates totalizing cultures that entrap employees, most of whom do not see their entrapment, leaving them little scope to resist.

4 Fundamentalist cultures are unsustainable: Religious fundamentalism helps us to predict the decline (that is already happening) of corporate fundamentalist cultures and messianic leaders because of an inbuilt incoherence. These 'dynamic yet conformist' cultures are inherently unstable and unsustainable.

Reviewing Religious Fundamentalism

Fundamentalism is a disparate phenomenon – a confused category. (Hardt and Negri, 2001: 146)

Figure 7.1   A neon sign outside a fundamentalist church in California, USA, 2006

Insights into Religious Fundamentalism

Using the resource of religious fundamentalism and looking beyond the populist rhetoric about fundamentalism as a premodern, primitive movement, we discover new understandings that help explain postmodern forms of leadership and organization culture.

In spite of the claims that fundamentalists are conservative and backward-looking, they are also radically postmodern movements, that successfully challenge tradition and orthodoxy, restructuring their religious movements and creating dynamic new organizational forms. Religious fundamentalists have created highly active and effective dispersed leadership, and also managed to influence world affairs. This review is not praising the ultra-conservative aims of fundamentalists, but is asking the reader to put aside prejudice that gets in the way of understanding. To look beyond their reactionary aims and examine their organizational forms, leadership and culture from a sociological perspective that reveals new insights into contemporary society and workplaces, as the two are very much connected.

From a secular-liberal position, the arch-enemy of fundamentalism, one often gets a negative knee-jerk response. Barr reflects common perceptions, saying of Christian Fundamentalism that it carries the suggestion of 'narrowness, bigotry obscurantism and sectarianism, though this may be unpleasant it may also be true and just' (Barr, 1981: 2). However as Karen Armstrong (2000) explains, fundamentalism returned religion to the main political stage when it was in serious decline: its impact on the world's great religions, and national and international politics, as well as the personal lives of millions of people, is testament to its power and influence. Fundamentalism has shown itself to be a global phenomenon that is not restricted to 'less developed' nations, the USA being a clear example.

There are multiple understandings of what defines religious funda-mentalism. Castells writes 'that religious fundamentalism has existed throughout the whole of human history, but it appears to be surprisingly strong at the end of this millennium' (Castells, 1997: 13), whereas, Armstrong stresses that 'fundamentalism is an essentially twentieth century movement' (Armstrong, 2000: xi). Both, however, agree that religious fundamentalism is a reaction against modernism and secularism and that its contemporary rise has been remarkable and very successful. Barr maintains that Christian Fundamentalism is a particular kind of religious tradition that *controls the interpretation* of the Bible, rather than treating the holy book as the inerrant truth (Barr, 1981: 11). Frosh (1997: 422) agrees, saying that all sacred texts require an interpretation and it is the ownership of the texts and the authority to interpret them that is important, not the literalist adherence.

Armstrong and others point out that religious fundamentalists usually begin with a spiritual war within their own religious group but that fundamentalism itself is diverse: 'Each fundamentalism is a law unto itself and has its own dynamic' (Armstrong, 2000: intro). If we think of this in terms of corporate culture, there are clear internal battles for the control of the texts, e.g. which texts are taught at business schools, which gurus are chosen to represent business culture, and how these are interpreted and who interprets them, are core to holding cultural power. Box 13 outlines the fundamentalist mindset.

Box 13   The Fundamentalist Mindset

Common themes from different religious fundamentalist movements

Authority and truth

The movement's leaders have the divine authority to interpret sacred texts and formulate the truth from these texts. Within fundamentalism is the acceptance of absolute authority, interpreted by their leaders. There is hostility to modern theological and heuristic methods that reveal new and different interpretations of the holy text.

Militancy

Evangelical militancy often begins within the movement's own faith community, e.g. Christian fundamentalists condemn liberal Christians over issues such as biblical inerrancy, homosexuality or women priests before taking their concerns to other faiths. This militancy is then turned outward to the modern, secular world, or competing religious groups.

Leadership

Fundamentalist leadership is messianic, transformational, innovative and charismatic, rather than the institutional hierarchy of more traditional religious leadership. It usually has a male bias.

Anti-modern

Fundamentalists look to an idyllic past and claim to be against modernity. They revere mythos and distrust logos (rationality and reason). However, whilst anti-modern, they can also be seen as postmodern social movements, dynamic and reinventing their faith communities to meet contemporary needs. Unlike other social movements who are 'emancipatory radicals', fundamentalists are conservative and reactionary radicals.

The Remnant: the chosen community

Fundamentalists usually believe they are a remnant community: a remnant community is one left over after a catastrophe. This catastrophe is usually interpreted as God's divine retribution for a community that lived sinfully and unfaithfully. The Remnant is saved by grace and carries God's faith and hope for the future: a chosen people to enact 'God's' will for a purpose in the world.

Social change: creating the kingdom

Fundamentalists aim to change society, social codes, structures and constructs in line with their beliefs, creating a new social order within their community (the kingdom of God on earth) and colonizing other social spaces to achieve this.

Purity: fear of difference

Gender and sexual issues often feature highly, and childbirth and the role of women in society are prominent. Women are often both idealized by fundamentalists as mothers and 'bearers of culture' and also denigrated as 'other', i.e. as dangerous 'impure' sexual objects (Frosh, 1997: 422). Diversity is feared by fundamentalists as they find difference difficult to cope with, preferring monocultures and universal explanations and beliefs. The idea of pureness is central to their belief systems.

Martyrs and persecution

Fundamentalists attract persecution and idealize personal martyrdom and sacrifice, which binds them together as a group, and fits with a mindset of paranoia about the world as well as convincing them that they are on track with their mission.

Millenarianism and perfection

Fundamentalists usually have two core beliefs: (a) an 'edenic ideology', a belief in perfection from sin, and the imminent arrival of the 'kingdom' of God (articulated in different ways depending on the religion); (b) a vision and belief that we are in the 'end-times', followed by a golden period of perfection, for the chosen community of believers. This is enacted in diverse ways in different fundamentalist movements.

Fundamentalism: Premodern or Postmodern?

According to Castells (1997: 25), fundamentalism is a reactive movement, idealizing a past, and looking to a utopian future in order to overcome an unbearable present. However, the populist idea that religious fundamentalism is a premodern regressive force is one of the commonest themes refuted by scholars such as Karen Armstrong:

> The term also gives the impression that fundamentalists are inherently conservative and wedded to the past, whereas their ideas are essentially modern and highly innovative. (Armstrong, 2000: x)

John Gray claims that Islamic fundamentalism is mistakenly thought of as a return to medieval society. He claims that 'radical Islam' draws heavily on early modern millenarian movements, such as anarchists who rejected established authority (Gray, 2003: 20). Gray also sees links to radical liberation movements, saying that modern writers such as Frantz Fanon and the existentialist Jean-Paul Sartre have inspired Islamic fundamentalists. Islamic fundamentalism's radical movements such as al-Qaeda have gone beyond the usual boundaries of fighting within one's own religious tradition and nation state and are examples of how, far from being medieval, they have embraced contemporary globalization. They have taken their fight beyond national borders to challenge the global hegemony of Westernization and have created innovative networked organizing forms, utilizing modern communication technologies and media images, to create an 'asymmetric warfare where the weak seek out to exploit the vulnerabilities of the strong' (Gray, 2003: 82).

Frosh discusses religious fundamentalism as a specific anti-modern movement: 'A response to the crisis of rationality which draws on the same emotional forces as do feminism and postmodernism but to different ends' (Frosh, 1997: 417). Frosh describes modernity inflicting a fragmentation of social life, which produces uncertainty, 'the sense of tragedy, degradation and annihilation being just around the corner' (p. 417). He then makes the unlikely link to postmodernism:

> Fundamentalism is like postmodernism in that it is a response to the crisis of rationality to the despair of modernity. Fundamentalism responds in a time honoured way; it refuses them absolutely. (p. 417)

Hardt and Negri (2001: 146–7) agree, saying fundamentalism 'is not a re-creation of a pre-modern world but rather a powerful refusal of the contemporary historical passage in course'. They claim that 'Post modern discourses appeal to the winners of the process of globalization, and fundamentalist to the losers' (p. 148).

Armstrong uses Khomeini in Iran to further the point that fundamentalism is much more than it appears on the surface and has a revolutionary and innovative side as well as a reactionary one:

The Ayatollah Khomeini was essentially a man of the 20th century. Instead of harking back to the Dark Ages, he was really introducing a revolutionary form of Shi´ism that was, in fact, as innovative as if the pope had abolished the Mass. But most of us didn't understand enough about Shi´ism to appreciate that. (Armstrong, 2002)

Religious fundamentalism today usually takes on the paradoxical position of being innovative in its anti-modern stance and radical in its conservatism. Corporate fundamentalism replicates this stance, adhering to neo-conservative values, yet radical in its neo-liberal ambitions.

Communities: A Fundamentalist Challenge to Individualism

Modernity's success limits traditional sites for community and the increasingly atomized social fabric means that the very idea of community has become counter-cultural, surpassed by the dominance of individualism. A 'fundamentalist' church community, sharing a collective identity and strongly held values and beliefs, stands as a symbolic witness to the power of the group. The Christian Fundamentalist discourse celebrates individualism, which is deeply embedded in both Protestantism and American culture, yet their individualism is a core attribute of collective identity (Castells, 1997; Lasch, 1979). The Christian Fundamentalists have created a very strong collective identity, with individual salvation, to be 'born again' as one of its bedrocks. One of their primary tasks is to evangelize individuals. Addison Leitch writes:

> There is no salvation by way of the social gospel, but only in the individual's call to Christ. But there is no such thing as an asocial Christian. (Leitch, 1956)

However, whilst the language fits with the culturally dominant view of individual freedom being sacrosanct, the practice is very much one of building a community represented by 'the true church'. The Christian Fundamentalist community cleverly utilizes individualist rhetoric as part of the cement that binds the collective together. As a community they are 'the chosen people', fulfilling God's will on earth.

Etzioni (1993, 2002) has long called for communitarianism and praises religious communities:

> Compare social conduct in strong communities like Mormon Utah, the Hasidic neighborhoods of New York City and Israeli kibbutzim to behavior in our prisons, where the state oversees individuals in the most direct way.

> When communal bonds are tight and belief (religious or secular) is fervent, we find that abortion, drug and alcohol abuse and violence are rare and that voluntarism and social responsibility flourish; the state plays a small role in sustaining the social order. (Etzioni, 1993: 56)

Critics of this type of communalism reference oppression to individuals over abortion and gay rights, for example. Christian Fundamentalists' communitarian side is powerfully present and active. Putnam's (2000) book *Bowling Alone* powerfully depicts the atomization in the USA and he shows a decline in civic engagement in America. Membership of clubs, voting in elections, going to meetings and also socializing with friends have all decreased. Putnam says these activities grew in the first part of the 20th century but have been on the decline since the 1960s. However, one reversal of this trend is the evangelical Christians, who, he points out, were traditionally a Protestant Quietist movement:

> Religious conservatives have created the largest, best-organised grassroots social movement of the last quarter century. It is, in short, among evangelical Christians, rather than among the ideological heirs of the sixties, that we find the strongest evidence of an upwelling of civic engagement. (Putnam, 2000: 162)

Roger Scruton points out the contemporary dilemma that takes place around individual freedom and the community:

> The question that I raised in "Communitarian Dreams" is precisely the one that Etzioni has not answered: namely, to borrow his own terms, how do we fashion a viable "we" in modern conditions, while retaining the sovereignty to which the "I" has become accustomed. (in Etzioni, 1997: 72)

This question is fundamental to the corporate leader who wishes to create strongly aligned cultures and also encourage individual creativity. Christian Fundamentalists have attempted to address this, by harnessing the 'I' (personal salvation) as the essence of their discourse – yet the 'I' becomes the bedrock for a very powerful 'we', the chosen community, the true church.

The corporate transformational leader pursues ever-increasing commitment and loyalty that attempts to replicate the solidarity, clannish culture and strong emotional bonds between employees that are exhibited in fundamentalist communities. Belonging is key to the success of these corporate cultures. One of the stated aims of transformational leadership is to give followers something to believe in beyond themselves:

These leaders will generate awareness and acceptance of the purposes and missions of the organization and stir the employees to look beyond their own self-interests for the good of the overall entity. (Bass, 1990a)

The Christian Fundamentalist movement managed to produce a style of transformational leadership that offered a vision and a clear set of beliefs from which emerged a dynamic and collective actor. Individuals, however, retain an identity of personal special-ness, a personal relationship with Jesus (and their pastor). This individual and collective sense of belonging and meaning is converted into commitment and action. This is precisely what the transformational leaders are attempting to replicate in corporate organizations; individuals and teams with high levels of dynamic autonomy, free to bring their creativity to the company, balanced by unquestioning loyalty and commitment to the brand.

Where Christian and Corporate Fundamentalism Meet

The transformational leader, charged with creating new collectivist corporate cultures, became prominent in the USA during the late 1970s (Burns, 1978). This was immediately precipitated by the Christian Fundamentalist revival (epitomized by the Moral Majority), that became a force so powerful and successful, that it impacted on the whole of American society, directly seen through the elections of President Ronald Regan.

Box 14 gives a brief overview of the Christian Fundamentalist revival.

Box 14   The Christian Fundamentalist Revival

After half a century where Christian fundamentalists had withdrawn and become inward-focused and quietist, mainly in the southern and mid-American states, they found a new strength and confidence to become visible, externally focused and politically active. Led by Jerry Falwell, the Moral Majority, formed in 1979, symbolized this growth. Karen Armstrong (2000: 308) notes that three professional right-wing political organizers inspired this movement. They wanted to build a conservative alliance to oppose the moral and social liberalism which had grown since the 1960s. They noted the strength of the evangelical and fundamentalist Protestants and saw Jerry Falwell as perfect for their needs, with his huge, ready-made constituency. The Moral Majority went beyond Protestant fundamentalists and included

(Continued)

(Continued)

other denominations and other religions, including Catholics, Jews and Mormons, who shared the Protestant 'conservative fundamentalism'. Armstrong notes that, 'militant Christians began to colonize mainstream institutions for the next decade'.

The Christian Fundamentalists' rise was phenomenal; by the late 1970s the most successful charismatic leaders had celebrity status, with mass TV followings, and were courted and taken seriously by the political establishment. They were also creating new mega-churches, which stood outside traditional church governance, crossing denominations. This led to new cultures forming within these religious communities and the Christian Fundamentalist movement as a whole.

This religious fundamentalist revival 'was declaring war on the liberal establishment and fighting a battle for the future of America' (Armstrong, 2000: 110).

The Christian Fundamentalists believed in biblical inerrancy and were politically radical conservatives. The Moral Majority impacted on millions and grew through expert communicators, using the media in new ways (televangelism) and offering a transformational, visionary, charismatic leadership based on moral 'family and traditional' values.

It has been estimated that 4 out of every 10 households in the USA tuned into Falwell's TV station during the 1970s and the top ten Christian television empires took over a billion dollars each year, turning out a very professional product (Armstrong, 2000: 275). The Fundamentalists interpreted their financial success and growth as evidence that God was on their side. Pat Robertson, a leading Christian Fundamentalist preacher, claimed that in the Kingdom of God 'there was no economic recession, no shortage' (Robertson, 1982: 108–9).

The Christian Fundamentalist movement has been hugely influential within American economic, social and political institutions, as a very powerful lobbying force and through grassroots activism. Fundamentalists funded right-wing think-tanks, such as the Heritage Foundation, the American Enterprise Institute and the Hoover Institute. The Moral Majority was disappointed in Jimmy Carter, for whom, as President, they held high hopes but who did not take a radical evangelical stance in office. They then backed Regan and later George W. Bush, supporting them to victory. In 1986 the movement felt powerful enough to support Pat Robertson to make a serious attempt to stand as President. The influence this movement has on American policy through the White House and the wider business community is widely discussed. Today the power of the Christian right has perhaps waned, but it remains a powerful lobbying force. In a Gallup poll in 2000, 44% of people in the USA describe themselves as born-again or evangelical Christians. Putnam writes that in an unexpected turn-around, the liberal and progressive social movements born in the 1960s are now far less influential than the conservative Christians, who are now some of the most politically active in the USA (Putnam, 2000: 161).

The similarities between 'messianic' leadership approaches and the 'organizational' cultures they created, within both religious and corporate 'movements', lead to the conclusion that through informal and indirect social processes, they were reflexively influential in co-creating each other.

During my research on the rise of transformational leadership and the strong collectivist cultures such leaders form, I found the explanations as to how US-based companies turned to mimic Japanese collectivist culture inadequate and partial. There was an unexplained gap between the individualistic culture of American society, and the more collectivist cultures of Asia. My research question was how did American individualistic culture embrace these new collectivist Asian workplace cultures, that turned companies into communities, as the literature claimed? A critical perspective must 'look awry' and seek explanations beyond the limited view of looking at organizational cultures as if they are closed systems. One key factor that influenced the dramatic change in corporate culture yet has been missed in the literature comes from the Christian Fundamentalist movement that took place outside of the business world. If we conceptualize organizations as 'ecosystems within ecosystems' rather than closed-systems, it explains how organizations interact interdependently with social phenomena. Organizations, conceptualized as ecosystems, operate locally and globally and are influenced by macro-ecosystems (global communication flows, natural disasters, carbon prices, social, economic and political trends) and micro-ecosystems (the local and regional economy, education systems, natural and social changes etc.). In turn, organizations reflexively influence the ecosystems in which they exist in an interdependent dynamic. This implies that organizations cannot be understood from research that only takes place within organizations; a broader social perspective has to be taken. When I researched US social trends external to the business world, it became clear that a parallel social movement was developing just before the emergence of the rise of transformational leaders within corporations. This social movement was Christian fundamentalism, broadly known as the Moral Majority, and its impact was immense. This movement provided an indigenous model, an example of a very successful collectivist culture, where messianic leaders created visions that inspired followers, and where followers joined conformist communities.

Corporate cultures mimicked Christian Fundamentalist leadership styles and cultures (unconsciously and through cultural transmission), replicating their visionary evangelical language and the collectivist, conformist and dynamic cultures they created. The Messiah discourse (Chapter 11) describes in detail the religious and prophetic rhetoric used by transformational leaders, and the cult-like cultures in which they operated. The Christian Fundamentalist movement provided a template for the corporate cultures, and Box 15 shows the similarities between the two movements.

Box 15   Similarities between Christian Fundamentalism and Corporate Culture

Transformational leadership

Based on mythos, symbolic leadership and culture control, these leaders claim to create conformist 'strong' and yet dynamic monocultures. This leadership in both realms is predominantly male, charismatic, visionary and messianic.

Conviction of righteousness, certainty of the truth

Corporate culture believes 'there is no other way' but the neo-liberal, free-market, and Fundamentalist Christians believe that 'there is no other way' but their interpretation of Christianity.

Intolerance of difference, refuting pluralism

The only pluralism accepted by corporate America is the pluralism within the limits of a Westernized, capitalist, free-market democracy. Other forms of governance and economic functioning are blasphemous, and conflict is encouraged to defeat opposing ideologies that challenge the hegemony of their belief systems. Christian Fundamentalists are convinced they are the chosen people and refute a liberal approach that accepts other belief systems.

Growth

Both Fundamentalist Christians and corporations aim for growth and global expansion through gaining a 'greater market share' on their own terms.

'Religious' evangelizing zeal

Leaders in both camps have evangelic zeal in abundance, and both aim to convert/conquer new markets and new believers (employees, customers, converts).

Organizational form

Both exist with charismatic leadership and flattened hierarchies. They organize around family-sized teams and dispersed leadership, unified by a shared belief and values. They are held together by the leadership/company vision and culture control.

> **Organizational glue, as a community of believers**
>
> Employees and church members identify with their company/church and leader, and their peers form a community of believers, working towards common aims and goals.

The Formation of a New Leadership Discourse

Christian Fundamentalism initially provided a site of resistance to liberal Christianity and secularism and its adherents separated themselves from the sinful world, becoming inward-looking, hierarchical and rigid organizations. When new leaders emerged, they went on the offensive to fight to change the world, which meant engaging with the secular world, and learning about finance, marketing, and especially media and communications. The leaders began to open their boundaries, allowing a flow of knowledge, leadership skills and culture exchange, both within the political-social environment and with corporate organizations (where many of them worked).

Likewise corporate organizations, when confronted with the new challenges of the global economy and having to face their lack of success, opened their boundaries to learn from others, importing ideas from Japan and from anthropology (Ouchi, 1981). They also opened their boundaries to the home-grown Christian Fundamentalist movement. The transformational leadership style and strong collectivist cultures of the Fundamentalists were everywhere in the US ecosystem, on TV, news, active in local communities and in prayer groups and bible meetings inside corporate America. To understand the social processes of how two cultures transfer and learn from each other, without a conscious or deliberate strategy, we must turn to the theory of isomorphism.

Isomorphism

It is claimed that successful organizations have forms that are isomorphic with their environments (DiMaggio and Powell, 1983). This means that the environment 'selects in' successful organizational forms with characteristics that match their environment, discarding others that aren't successful (Nelson and Gopalan, 2003: 1118). Alvesson (1996) points to the connections between national culture and organizational culture, yet Nelson and Gopalan were surprised that this connection was so under-researched:

> Given the logical connection between national and organizational culture via individual socialization and institutional forms, one would expect

organizational theorists to have already explored this in some detail. (2003: 1116)

Because of this lack of research, the connections between the powerful social movements of Christian Fundamentalism shaping American organizational culture are missed. The isomorphic process between successful religious and secular organizations cannot be ignored within the American context. Isomorphism is more likely to occur between secular and religious organizations in countries where religion flourishes, and the USA is the

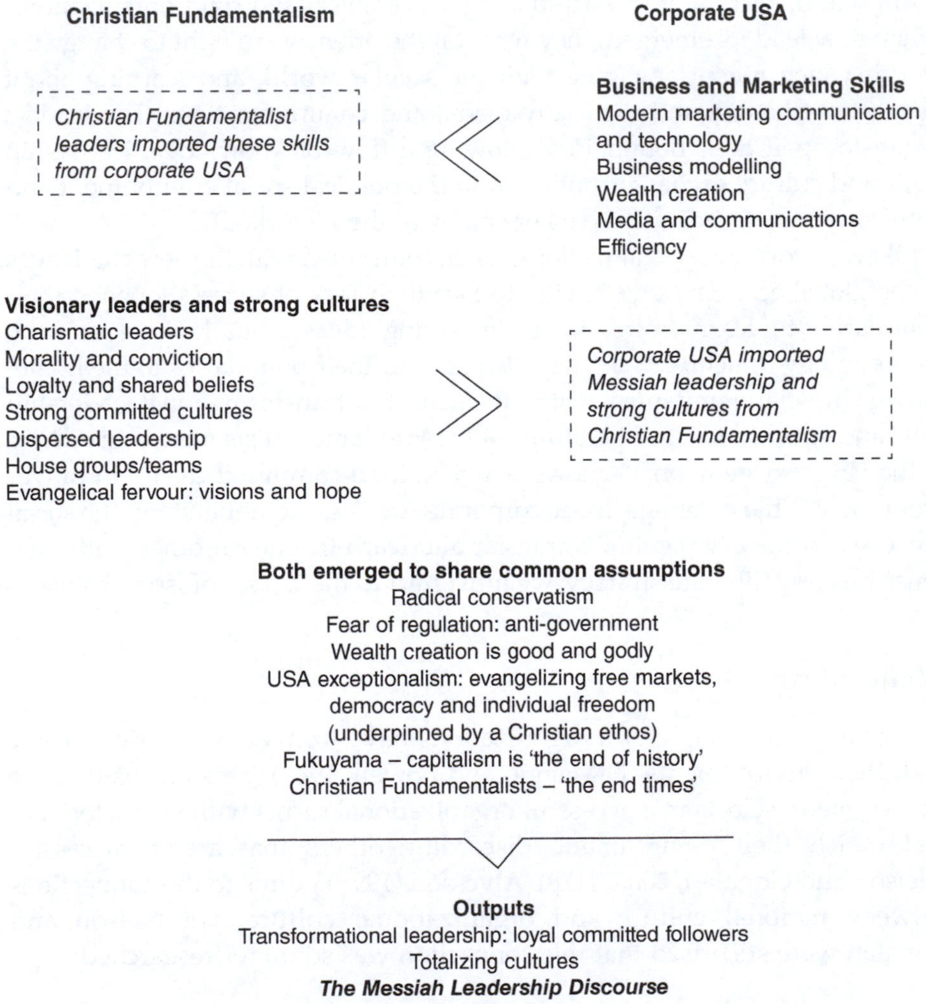

Christian Fundamentalism   **Corporate USA**

Business and Marketing Skills
Modern marketing communication
and technology
Business modelling
Wealth creation
Media and communications
Efficiency

*Christian Fundamentalist
leaders imported these skills
from corporate USA*

Visionary leaders and strong cultures
Charismatic leaders
Morality and conviction
Loyalty and shared beliefs
Strong committed cultures
Dispersed leadership
House groups/teams
Evangelical fervour: visions and hope

*Corporate USA imported
Messiah leadership and
strong cultures from
Christian Fundamentalism*

Both emerged to share common assumptions
Radical conservatism
Fear of regulation: anti-government
Wealth creation is good and godly
USA exceptionalism: evangelizing free markets,
democracy and individual freedom
(underpinned by a Christian ethos)
Fukuyama – capitalism is 'the end of history'
Christian Fundamentalists – 'the end times'

Outputs
Transformational leadership: loyal committed followers
Totalizing cultures
The Messiah Leadership Discourse

Figure 7.2 The cultural exchange between Christian Fundamentalism and Corporate USA

most religious country in the Western world. Christian Fundamentalism was on every American TV screen and radio show; it was entering the political stage. In every American workplace, born-again Christians attending the new mega-churches and house-groups, and being influenced by the religious transformational-style leaders and internalizing the culture, must have had an influence on corporate America and the arrival of the transformational leader.

Figure 7.2 shows the process of isomorphism and the two-way culture exchange that took place.

The exchange of culture, expertise and leadership style meant a realignment in values across much of the USA. Leaders who ran successful companies, like preachers who ran successful churches, became role models. Evangelists displayed wealth and proudly boasted of their million dollar churches and TV empires. The old Protestant work ethic did not fit this morality, the 'eye of the needle' has widened and entry to heaven for those who follow the path is less anxiety-provoking and persecutory than through the old Calvinist route. In the USA, a new Protestant work ethic transcends the churches and enters the wider culture accommodating these changes.

Box 16   The New Protestant Work Ethic

Working hard beyond one's calling

The old Protestant ethic meant that a person worked hard at their 'calling' but never questioned it. In the new ethic, individuals work constantly to achieve beyond their calling, because to reach salvation is to fulfil one's dreams.

Personal salvation comes through 'working on oneself'

The old ethic meant toiling and working externally, the new ethic connects internal and external work. Personal salvation and personal growth merge. Working on oneself becomes a purifying act, a way of becoming whole (at one with God) again.

The Prosperity Gospel: Blessed are the wealthy

The old ethic called for hard work but an austere lifestyle. The new ethic claims that material acquisition and wealth are a sign of God's favour. 'God's promise of abundant life becomes a promise of a life of abundance' (Gwyn, 1989). The big house and wealthy church show God is rewarding the righteous.

(Continued)

(Continued)

Conservative values

The piety of the old Protestant ethic now shows itself through a political/social conservativism, e.g. supporting perceived traditional and American family values.

The poor shall *not* inherit the earth

The undeserving poor must work harder to reach salvation, only they can save themselves; to help them would be violating God's will.

Too much governance is dangerous

National government, and especially international regulation from agencies such as the IMF, United Nations and World Bank, is viewed as infringing on individual rights, preventing free trade and as part of a liberal/leftist secularist conspiracy to rule the world, and should be resisted. Having faith in God and the free market is the way forward.

This new Protestant work ethic has grown and mutated from the Calvinist one, and has become a mainstream part of American culture and beyond. The radical and selective vision of this ethos uniquely supports both the corporate neo-liberal and the Christian Fundamentalists' agenda. Casey acknowledges what she calls the neo-Protestant work ethic, in this advanced industrial milieu:

> The corporation revives and restores the Protestant cultural forms that have been obscured and faltered under the culture of narcissism of advanced industrial society and its therapeutic salvation. (Casey, 1995: 181)

Casey then argues that this neo-Protestant work ethic recovers the elements of order and a dedication to work (duty), rational submission to a higher authority and self-restraint from the old ethic.

Corporate Fundamentalism: Totalizing Cultures

The challenge for leadership at the turn of the millennium was how to influence a diverse, expert and knowledge-based workforce that was globally dispersed within multinational companies. The answer seemed to be a paradox; to create dynamic *and* conformist cultures. Religious fundamenta- lism offered one source of answers to this dilemma, however early success did not mean sustainable success. Their vision of 'harmony, and cultural alignment' effectively eliminates difference. Walking into a corporate business, whether in India, America, a big town or small town, there is an uncanny and haunting lack of difference in the physical environment. Casey's research into corporate culture describes the effect of this colonization on employees' souls:

> The new corporatization of the self is more than a process of assault, discipline and defeat against which employees defend themselves. It is a process of colonization in which, in its completion, assault and defeat are no longer recognized. Overt displays of employee resistance and opposition are virtually eliminated. Corporatized selves become sufficiently repressed to effectively weaken and dissolve the capacity for serious criticism or dissent. (Casey, 1995: 150)

These 'corporatized selves' unite behind a leadership that subtly demands and gains an active followership and allegiance to the company's vision, goals and values. Smith and Wilkinson's (1996) research takes us to a progressive non-hierarchical company, 'Sherwood's', and provides a concise example of the totalitarian nature these cultures can produce; similar research supports these findings (Axtel Ray, 1986; Casey, 1995; Kunda, 1992). Smith and Wilkinson say that 'Sherwood's' is a company that shines as a beacon within the new collectivist organizational paradigm. Employees pursue 'furious interaction' in open plan offices with a religious fervour, job functions rotate between managers in an anti-bureaucratic milieu, and consensus and cooperation have been institutionalized. Smith and Wilkinson describe this as a totalitarian culture with nightmarish qualities due to the tight control that co-exists within a high degree of autonomy. They make an analogy with a penal institution, saying it is like an open prison. The lack of privacy precludes dissent, control is not located specifically but generically, 'everyone is at the heart of things but everybody also has several others within their gaze and everybody is clearly observed by others' (1996: 106–107). There is an obsessive degree of quality control within the company and conflict is apparently obliterated. They are paid above the industry norms in order to keep them in 'golden handcuffs' and 'they are their own policemen' (1996: 106–107). They say that when people join 'Sherwood's' they think it 'a bit funny at first, but then soon see it as normal' (1996: 106–107).

What exists is an internalized culture of control, a surveillance culture, policed by the self and the social group, in which to be different is not an option and, more worryingly perhaps, is not even a thought. This type of organization, with its many cultural variations, is one of the ascending visions within contemporary management literature for company cultures and management approaches. These cultures resonate with those of religious fundamentalist movements who win souls through charismatic leadership and as a result create self-regulating monocultures, which demand commitment and allegiance to the movement. Others claim that these new organizational cultures are far from totalitarian but are flexible, dynamic, non-authoritarian and improve productivity. The latter two claims are not absolute opposites.

The rise of the transformational leader in the management world followed closely on from the success of the Christian Fundamentalist leaders, and a Japanese 'conformist and collectivist' work culture. Both cultures now seem in transition; in Japan the traditional conformist roles are no longer deemed sustainable and the economy is struggling, and a turning point may have been reached in the Fundamentalist churches in the USA. Christian leaders are becoming disillusioned with politics, and whilst fundamentalism is still a powerful force, continued gaps in moral preaching and personal behaviours threaten to undermine the movement further. For example, Rev. Ted Haggard, leader of the biggest church in the USA, the huge Evangelical Alliance, who it is claimed had a weekly phone call with President Bush, resigned in 2006 due to his long-term relationship with a gay prostitute. In Haggard's own words:

> The fact is I am guilty of sexual immorality. And I take responsibility for the entire problem. I am a deceiver and a liar. There's a part of my life that is so repulsive and dark that I have been warring against it for all of my adult life. (Fox News, 2006)

Also there are real concerns over the future. A leading article in the *New York Times* in 2006 stated:

> Despite their packed mega-churches, their political clout and their increasing visibility on the national stage, evangelical Christian leaders are warning one another that their teenagers are abandoning their faith in droves. (Goodstein, 2006)

Casey (1995) identifies that there has been a 'southern style revivalism' with the sexual energy of charisma and conversion displayed by the corporations' leaders. This creates the 'magic of a turned-on workforce' (Peters and Waterman, 1982), which comes from meaningful team relationships and loyalty to the company. However, Casey critiques these totalizing cultures. They do not immediately reflect a 'big brother' culture and can be dynamic, high energy and often initially successful, with a 'charged up' 'feel great'-type culture, as described by Peters and Waterman (1982), where employees unleash their energy and talent for the company. But, as Peters and Waterman discovered, their excellent companies were not the most sustainable.

Casey describes how her ethnographic research showed that these employees developed a 'new-colluded self', which she describes as 'dependant, over agreeable, compulsive in dedication, diligent and passionate about the product and company' (1995: 191). This new-colluded self has an alter ego that is consistently in a state of capitulation, which leads to a 'wearied surrender' because it 'implicitly recognizes but denies the process of discipline, enforced self restraint and evangelical optimism' (p. 191).

These cultures aren't 'big brother', authoritarian regimes; more 'little brother' (Žižek, 1999), where peer- and self-surveillance ensures order within family-team groups, and where any real conflict is eliminated and difference is hidden or denied. This culture idealizes harmony, but within it there is a hint of paranoia and grandiosity that comes from idealizing oneself, one's team and one's organization. Alongside the harmony there exists a new kind of dependency culture, different from the patriarchal and hierarchical leadership cultures of the past. In the new cultures one appears to be much more autonomous, but nevertheless a psychological dependency exists on the community. It is this subtle dependency that prevents individuals from accessing real autonomy or being able to question the culture itself. Those who resist the culture are ejected or marginalized. Most frightening is the lack of recognition of one's entrapment within this culture. Reflexivity, the ability to see oneself clearly as an individual or sub-group within these strong cultures, is very difficult, as their *raison d'être* is to increase conformity, commitment and compliance.

The Desire to Belong: Community, Families, Teams and Clans

The community, team and the family were metaphors that were promoted (Ouchi, 1981; Peters and Waterman, 1982) as one of the basic structural forms of social organization to achieve these company goals. Kunda's (1992) research into a high-tech company he renamed 'Tech' found employees using the family as an oft-cited metaphor about their teams and their relationship with their company. Casey (1995) found that the family metaphor was not optional but essential for these progressive companies, and is now part of the architectural design of organizations. Casey went onto describe how strong team mindsets broadened participation in management leading to employee empowerment. The Japanese culture, such as quality circles, was another example, with another closer-to-home model being the successful *church house-group movement*. The Fundamentalists, acting against a failing and staid institutional church, distributed leadership through dynamic house-groups. Members found themselves at the centre of worship, rather than watching a performance like an audience when in the mega-churches. Some of these house-groups formed cell churches and worshipped without any formal leadership or ministers. The dynamic house-church movement precedes what Casey calls the new architectural design of organizations (which uses this same formula), with small family-sized groups, a flattened hierarchy, and commitment to and sharing in the vision and values of the larger 'parent' organization.

The family metaphor seems purposively chosen by business transform-ational leaders to create associations with the idealized family, which would help create the solidarity: 'The family metaphor actively evokes pre-industrial romantic images of human bonding and shared struggles against adversity ... employees assume family-like roles with each other and are managed by family rules and processes. The family is also hierarchical, paternalistic and deferential to higher external authorities' (Casey, 1995: 113).

Ouchi (1981) called these processes 'clan control', as they produce a deep loyalty and dedication to the team. Kanter claims that work in these new company cultures maybe the closest they will get to an experience of 'community' or total commitment for many workers, 'a dramatic, exciting and almost communal process brought to the corporation' (Kanter, 1983: 203). The use of family as a metaphor and organizing into house-groups and family-teams had similar and powerful cultural impacts in their respective environments.

Neo-liberal Fundamentalism

In a broader sense the term 'corporate fundamentalism' describes not only the internal workings of organizations but also the meta-picture, as the new breed of global corporations became the main collective actors of the neo-liberal agenda, which itself has a totalizing tendency within global politics. Corporate commercial advertising through the TV, the internet and billboards is accused of colonizing and 'polluting' public spaces. Out-of-town shopping malls make car ownership essential, leaving behind empty shops in local streets and a diminished sense of community:

> I picture the reality in which we live in military occupation. We are occupied the way the French and Norwegians were occupied by the Nazis

during World War II, but this time by an army of marketeers. We have to reclaim our country from those who occupy it on behalf of their global masters. (Ursula Franklin, Professor Emeritus, University of Toronto, 1998, cited in Klein, 2000: 311)

Klein (2000) argues in *No Logo* that the commercial pressures put upon artists, advertisers and filmmakers leads to an increasing level of censorship by retailers and the end result is a colonization of everyday life. The expanding power of the corporates, set within a neo-liberal framework, is a powerful socio-political as well as economic force. The intellectual 'left', anti-capitalist movement and diverse political and religious movements critique this trend, which they call free-market or neo-liberal fundamentalism. Naomi Klein used the term 'McGovernment' to describe the free-marketeers rampant march:

This happy meal of cutting taxes, privatising services, liberalising regulations, busting unions, what is this diet in aid of? To remove anything standing in the way of the market. Let the free market roll and every other problem will apparently be solved by trickle down. This isn't about trade. It's about using trade to enforce the McGovernment recipe. (Klein, 2001: 87)

The opponents of neo-liberalism argue that an Orwellian double-think (Orwell, 1949) takes place, whereby freedom, democracy and individualism are espoused, whilst at the same time thought, dissent and action are repressed, through the colonizing of public and private space. The anti-capitalist movement claims that the economic-political system produces a fundamentalism as the corporate wealthy own the media, fund election campaigns and politicians, and undermine dissent. Madeline Bunting calls it a Westernized fundamentalism:

A westernised fundamentalism believes that historical progress is most advanced in the west and the neo-liberal agenda attempts to bring underdeveloped nations up to a higher (more civilised and economically developed) level. The west is tolerant towards other cultures only to the extent that they reflect its own values – so it is frequently fiercely intolerant of religious belief and has no qualms about expressing its contempt and prejudice. (Bunting, 2001)

Corporations and multinational companies led by transformational leaders are identified as the main collective actors within this neo-liberal agenda. It is argued that they create a dominating power elite, which is global, beyond nation-state control and largely unaccountable. Some view them as a hugely successful economic force set within democratic structures and a means of providing wealth and economic growth throughout the world. Others see them as 'fanatical preachers of neo-liberalism' (Ali, 2002: 312), a hegemony, with totalitarian tendencies. It is not only anti-capitalists and other 'leftist' critics' who use this language; the influential and Nobel Prize-winning economist Joseph Stiglitz writes:

> The scandals over conflicts of interest in accounting and banking were predictable fruits of 'market fundamentalism'. The image is Adam Smith the reality is Enron ... We live in a world driven by economics. Liberal democracies use it as a theology to justify taxation policies, the ownership of the media, immigration policy and an unelected official's ability to overrule the manifesto of an elected president. (Stiglitz, 2003)

The neo-liberal project is in the ascendancy and operates from an ideological position which its exponents believe to be righteous. It leads them to protect their existing 'free market' economies and to export their economic and political system in order to protect and export democracy and freedom itself. Habermas (1987) calls this process the 'colonisation of the lifeworld', and others agree, using a different language, as their book titles demonstrate: Hertz (2001) *The Silent Takeover*; Hardt and Negri (2001) *Empire*; and Monbiot (2000) *Captive State: The Corporate Takeover of Britain*. The claim has been made that, at a meta-political level, the neo-liberal agenda also has fundamentalist overtones.

Conclusion: Fundamentalist Cultures Are Unsustainable

Corporate fundamentalism has been explored in this chapter using the lens of religious fundamentalist cultures, drawing on religious sources to open and reveal new insights into totalizing corporate and organizational cultures. The Messiah discourse (Chapter 11) will further explore the links between transformational leaders and the cultures described in this chapter.

These totalizing cultures need messianic leaders to symbolically hold them together, and some leaders are very astute at playing this significant role. However, as soon as serious economic or other troubles occur, and culture change is needed to address the challenges, these messianic figures are often powerless to change their company cultures. The myth of Messiah leadership is then unveiled. These hopeful, communal, evangelical, 'dynamic-conformist' cultures, both in religious circles and corporations, are initially dynamic and often begin with huge energy and commitment. Yet they inevitably slide towards totalizing fundamentalist cultures, that internally destroy themselves and are unsustainable, because inevitably their conformity kills dynamism. Set out below are some of the common ways companies who adopt these cultures either fade and demise slowly, implode, or find ways to change.

1. Passive-Resistance

Employees become tired of the evangelical rhetoric, cynical of the visions and values which are increasingly seen as a veneer, and sceptical about the authenticity of the passionate leadership. Fundamentalist cultures are then resisted by employees, who take a path of passive-resistance. Outward revolt is unusual (people need to keep their jobs), so they perform 'good employee' but passively resist the culture, the work demands and the leadership. Sending cynical emails, undermining the establishment with humour, taking sick leave, displacing their energies towards their own interests rather than the company. These companies either fade and decline or a new leadership and culture emerges to displace the fundamentalist one.

2. Conformity Outlasts Dynamism

Energy drains when the culture expels and marginalizes difference, the organization increasingly becomes an homogeneous monoculture, and the dynamic energy begins to fade. These companies then begin to mirror stale bureaucracies, and dissonance between the visions and realities demoralizes workforces. Conformist cultures continue, usually without a transformational leader, who no longer is required to 'transmit culture that is endemic and embedded'. While the economy grows, things are maintained, but these conformist cultures cannot adapt to change due to their cultures. A great many of the excellent companies named by Peters and Waterman (1982) which claimed they had the right recipe for success fell into this category, 'including such stalwarts as Sears, Xerox, IBM, and Kodak [which] had faced serious hardships in the 20-odd years since' (Sheth, 2007).

Scenarios 1 and 2 are often complementary.

3. Implosion

Finally, Enron and the financial crash of 2008 signify what happens when fundamentalist, totalizing cultures carry on unchecked: an implosion takes place. Misjudgments are rife, ethics disappear, and nobody is left to question malpractice. Constructive dissent has been abolished by the passionate loyal culture that blindly marches onward. Within these cultures, there is also a lot of psychological and emotional suffering by individuals who get damaged and hurt on the way to the implosion.

4. From a Fight–Flight Culture to Maturity

Creativity and dynamism are born through hope and libido; companies are energized by hope to fulfil a mission, which unites members, and often a fight–flight culture emerges. Fundamentalist cultures depend on an external enemy to unite their people. However, this is unsustainable in the long term, and successful companies are those that transcend this fight-flight culture and take on a more mature and collaborative position.

When this hope begins to fade leaders often tactically pick fights in order to re-energize members/employees and create a new solidarity and dynamism, using fight–flight rhetoric in order to galvanize this draining energy. Steve Jobs and Ryanair CEO Michael O'Leary were master craftsmen in picking fights to galvanize employees:

> Jobs liked to see himself as an enlightened rebel pitted against evil empires, a Jedi warrior or Buddhist samurai fighting the forces of darkness. (Isaacson, 2011: 136)

However, fundamentalist tendencies not only distort organizational cultures, they also distort leaders' judgements. Leaders pick the wrong fights, take too many risks as they believe in their own omnipotence and rhetoric. Jerry Falwell and Pat Robertson, two leading evangelical and Fundamentalist Christians in the USA, immediately after 9/11 claimed that America deserved this attack, due to its secular and liberal lifestyle: i.e. it was God's intervention against a sinful nation (Žižek, 2002). This example identifies how the fundamentalist mindset works, identifying an enemy and then relating every event to this; it moves towards paranoid tendencies. Initially this can create a mobilized followership, but it is never sustainable and inevitably self-destructs.

These companies either fail or change. Apple began its life as many entrepreneurial companies do by taking a fight–flight attitude, inspired in this case by a visionary and aggressive leader. Steve Jobs' surprisingly (thereby disappointing his loyal and passionate followers) shifted his fight–flight rhetoric towards Microsoft (one of their chosen demons) during his second spell in charge of Apple, but this new mature position enabled Apple not only to increase its business share, it also symbolically shifted Apple from being the outsider fighting against the world, to a more mature, market leader aiming to dominate the market, and if this meant collaborating with an old enemy, that was a cultural shift worth making.

This chapter has revealed a continuing desire that cannot be fulfilled in corporate life, to create dynamic-conformist cultures. This is further elaborated in the chapter on the Messiah discourse, and following this the chapter on the move towards Eco-leadership describes new forms of leadership that offer alternatives to Messiah leaders and totalizing cultures.

Suggested Readings

- Armstrong, K. (2000) *The Battle for God*. London: HarperCollins.

- Casey, C. (1995) *Work, Self, and Society: After Industrialism*. London and New York: Routledge.

- Tourish, D. and Pinnington, A. (2002) 'Transformational leadership, corporate cultism and the spirituality paradigm: an unholy trinity in the workplace?', *Human Relations*, 55(2): 147–72.

Reflection Points

- Christian fundamentalism produced leadership and cultures that closely matched the desire of corporate leaders to create both 'dynamic and conformist' cultures. Reflect on why these cultures are attractive but not sustainable.

- Reflect on how social phenomena may be influencing corporate life today.

- Can you think of examples from your own workplace of totalizing influences that limit dissent and constructive criticism?

Sample Assignment Question

Corporate fundamentalism emerges from strong aligned cultures that become extreme. Describe what is attractive about these cultures for corporate leaders and employees, and the dangers that exist. Try to give examples from organizations you are familiar with.

Part Two

Reconstructing Leadership

8   The Four Discourses of Leadership

Introduction

Beginning with the question 'What is discourse?', this chapter explores how discourses shape how we act and think in 'normative' or taken-for-granted ways. Lessa (2006: 288) summarizes Foucault's use of discourse as 'systems of thoughts composed of ideas, attitudes, courses of action, beliefs and practices that systematically construct the subjects and the worlds of which they speak".

Leadership has its own discourses, which shape how we think about leaders and the power we give to them. However, there is not a singular leadership discourse, but four dominant discourses that have formed over the past century: the Controller, the Therapist, the Messiah and the Eco-leadership discourse are set out in Figure 8.1 and are described in depth in the following chapters. These discourses will impact differently on how leaders and employees behave depending on which is dominant in an organization.

This critical discourse analysis takes a broad historical overview of leadership theory and practice over the past century. These discourses emerge through wider societal phenomena, beyond the world of organizational and leadership theory, which is the focus of most business school scholars. Economic, social, political, technological and historical factors influence leadership discourses, as business and organizations are not a separate entity from these social factors.

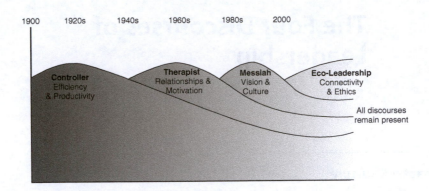

Figure 8.1   The four discourses of leadership

The aim of the following discourse chapters is to identify the dominant discourses that have determined and reflect the commonly held perceptions, assumptions and power relations of leadership. These four discourses offer a heuristic tool and shared language to reflect on how leadership is being taught, discussed or practised.

I have used the term *characters of leadership* to describe how an individual leader embodies a discourse of leadership, making the link between individual leaders and discourses, and drawing on Alasdair MacIntyre's (1985) work on characters. The approach to critical discourse analysis is then discussed utilizing a psychosocial perspective, before naming the four discourses to be reviewed in the following chapters.

What Is Discourse?

Discourse has different meanings: it refers to language, and can be simply a linguistic representation of how we speak, or it can infer an institutionalized way of thinking, a taken-for-granted (or normative) way of being, that is determined by language, communication and texts. This book uses discourse in the second way, and is influenced by Michel Foucault, who transformed discourse from a purely linguistic formulation. Johnson explains:

> Michel Foucault (1972) ... rigorously identified and typologized the structures of discourses, emphasizing how discourses affect everything in our society while remaining nearly unobservable ... For Foucault, discourse

is necessarily tied to systems of power insofar as the elite is able to maintain power by controlling what can be said. ...

Foucault identifies three types of exclusion that can be used to control discourse: rules that prohibit what can be said, rules that distinguish reason from madness, and rules that determine truth and falsity. (Johnson, 2005)

Discourse is related to power, as a way to control and normalize ways of thinking and being; as Butler says, discourse defines the 'limits of acceptable speech' (2004: 64). A discourse determines what can be said and also what cannot be said; it impacts on our views, our self-perceptions, and it is not possible to escape discourse:

We embody the discourses that exist in our culture, our very being is constituted by them, they are part of us, and thus we cannot simply throw them off. (Sullivan, 2003: 41)

Stakeholders in society and organizations therefore have vested interests in maintaining certain discourses while marginalizing others. It is difficult to grasp how a discourse confines us, as they often represent what seems normal, and are therefore out of consciousness. Yet through being unseen, discourses maintain social relations with little reference to critique.

The critical theory task is to reveal discourses so we can begin to analyse their impact. Discourses, which on the surface appear helpful and empowering, can be structurally disempowering. For example, counselling is a 'taken-for-granted' helpful practice; someone in distress is offered a counsellor, who is seen as unquestionably good. However, the therapeutic discourse which produces counselling can have the impact of making people more vulnerable and more self-obsessed, and it is argued that counselling can reinforce individualism and professionalize helping and caring relationships, that previously would have been an essential part of community life, and that therefore community itself is undermined (Furedi, 2003). Counselling *per se* is not good or bad, but the therapeutic discourse that underpins its logic has many social consequences beyond just being a force for good, including the ideas of therapeutic governance where the discourse produces acceptable and non-acceptable ways of being, of behaving in society (Rose, 1990, 1996).

Acknowledging and naming an underlying discourse can itself be liberating: for example, understanding the discourses around sexuality and how 'hetero-normative' discourse which marginalizes and undermines single and gay people can be liberating for those individuals who previously internalized the feeling of being failures, and misfits for not fitting into this pervasive discourse. Once a discourse is revealed it can be resisted, shaped, or simply lose some of its power over us. Halperin (2002: 21) claims that it is the hidden power of discourses that can be damaging, and not power itself, because discourses create truths, which become the accepted norms. Discourses act in plural ways and they co-exist (as we shall see in the leadership discourses); they exist in multiplicities, they merge and flow, as described by Foucault:

> To be more precise, we must not imagine a world of discourse divided between accepted discourse and excluded discourse, or between the dominant and the dominated one; but as a multiplicity of discursive elements that can come into play in various strategies. (1978: 100)

Discourses are not conscious and planned by some elite power; yet powerful elites do shape and reproduce those discourses that support their power. For example, the discourses of patriarchy have been reproduced by church, business and state, in favouring the existing male elites in power. And whilst discourses are instruments of power, they are also sites of resistance, offering spaces to contest power and providing:

> a point of resistance and a starting point for an opposing strategy. Discourse transmits and produces power, it reinforces it, but it also undermines and exposes it, renders it fragile and makes it possible to thwart it. (Foucault, 1978: 101)

These points are important when reading the following chapters. The leadership discourses set out are not rigidly fixed, either historically or in any given setting, and nor do they occur in isolation from one another. These discourses will merge and exist in tension with each other. There is not a right and wrong discourse either, but each does have strengths and weaknesses in any given context, and each asserts a form of 'organizational control' on employees through the leadership stance taken.

The Characters of Leadership: The Link between Individual Leaders and Discourses

The term 'character' used here draws on Alisdair MacIntyre's (1985) book *After Virtue*. A problematic gap exists in the literature between the notion of individual leaders and leadership discourses, dynamics and processes. A split often occurs between individual leaders and leadership, as discussed in earlier chapters. MacIntyre's notion of characters offers a structure to help explain how an individual leader embodies and performs a particular discourse. To be a social *character* is different from taking up a role, or a particular leadership style; it is to internalize an archetype that embodies a specific discourse. To name somebody a 'leader' signifies a specific meaning within the organization; the discourse defines and limits this meaning. This empowers but at the same time entraps the 'leader' in a symbolic position in relation to others. MacIntyre links the *character* to the dramatic tradition, citing Japanese Noh Plays and English medieval Morality Plays as examples, because they have a stock set of characters that are immediately recognizable to the audience. These *characters* partially define the plots and action, and through knowing the symbolic *characters*, the audience has a means of interpreting the behaviours of the actors who play them. A similar understanding informs the actors themselves, and other actors' responses to the *character* they inhabit. MacIyntyre suggests that certain social characters hold the same purpose within particular cultures:

> They furnish recognizable characters and the ability to recognize them is socially crucial because a knowledge of the character provides an interpretation of those actions of the individuals who have assumed those characters. (MacIntyre, 1985: 27)

MacIntyre views a social character as a signifying force within society; for example, the English gentleman in the nineteenth century represented to society elitism, power and honour.

Applied to organizational life, if we imagine the workplace as a theatre, a leadership discourse will impose and establish the ground rules – what can and cannot be said and what can and cannot be done – and define who are key actors (leaders) and who makes up the audience (followers), and this will set the scene for the narrative to unfold. A leadership discourse establishes norms, and expectations, and will influence how work processes unfold. The dominant discourse will then be embodied by one of the four *leadership characters* (the Controller, Therapist, Messiah or Eco-leader) who will signify a certain expectation as to how social relationships will take place. The Controller leader character will signify a transactional and coercive response for example, whereas the Messiah leader will evoke dependency and loyalty in their followers. However, MacIntyre does not provide a full account of the social process taking place, and turning to psychoanalytic theory, Jacques Lacan's work further illuminates this process. Lacan theorized that the primacy of the signifier entails 'the domination of the subject by the signifier' (Dor, 1997: 49). Lacan's use of the term 'signifier' complements MacIntyre's description of *character* and helps explain how *characters* engage and impact on society. The character embodies the discourse, enacting an unconscious signifying role that gives the character its power, dominating a field of social interaction. This signifying role dominates the subjects involved, both the leader and the followers; their relations are determined by the signifying qualities found in the particular discourse of leadership.

Each individual brings their specific attributes to the *leader character*: embodying and performing the discourse, they represent it in their personal way. However a codified way of relating takes place. A Controller leader will engage very differently to a Therapist leader, and employees will expect them to engage in this specific way. This process is relational and not uni-directional, and the employees' expectations are not passive but shape the leader's actions and thinking. Consciously the leader character is thought of by employees, stakeholders, as simply the CEO, as an 'uncontested figure'. Unconsciously the leader character signifies the specific discourse, and the tensions between discourses, reflecting and shaping workplace dynamics.

What has surprised me in five years of teaching, consulting and coaching drawing on these leadership discourses and characters is how quickly people recognize and identify with them. I have worked in Russia, the USA, Eastern Europe and Western Europe (and with Asian employees and Chinese students[1]) and no matter what sector or region, it seems these discourses are clearly identifiable, and the *leadership characters* that embody them signify a set of relations and expectations in the workplace.

The Critical Discourse Analysis Approach

The discourses outlined in this text are mainly a report on my doctoral research on leadership texts, and most importantly on my field-work, from my organizational and strategic consultations, my teaching engagements in executive education, my in depth coaching sessions with individual leaders and teams, and my personal diverse leadership and organizational work experience. This combination of theoretical research and practitioner-observation through multiple lenses, and a wide and diverse exposure to organizations from different sectors and countries, has provided rich research data.

The discourses have been articulated through theoretical, social and textual analysis, although I follow Nicholas Rose, who explains in the introduction

---

[1] The Asian and Chinese students I work with often have more trouble recognizing the Therapist and Eco-leadership discourses in their cultures; the Controller and Messiah they find clearly recognizable.

to his book *Governing the Soul* that a formal methodology is not applied, but a number of dimensions are used, which I set out below:

> I am not particularly keen on attempts to derive a formal methodology for this kind of 'history of the present' and it would be misleading to claim that this study is the application of any such methodology. Nonetheless, speaking roughly, it is possible to identify a number of dimensions along which this analysis is conducted. (Rose, 1990: xi)

This critical discourse analysis utilizes theory that draws on Fairclough (2001), Foucault (1977/1991) and Latour (2005) and Law (1993), who offer ethnographic actor-network perspectives. Norman Fairclough (1995), a leading figure in the development of critical discourse analysis, identified three dimensions of discourse analysis that I have found useful:

- Analysis of discourse carriers (e.g. speech/texts).

- Analysis of discourse production (e.g. how texts are produced and consumed).

- Macro-level analysis (e.g. societal and wider contexts).

I also bring psychosocial approaches to my research. For example, drawing on my psychoanalytic and therapy training I use counter-transference as a means of investigating the subjectivity, affects and unconscious dynamics with those whom I consult and coach. Organizational psychoanalytic observation techniques (based on infant observation) were developed at the Tavistock Clinic where I studied and taught, and I adapted these using actor-network ethnographic approaches to extend observations beyond human dynamics, and to account for the human and non-human interactions in the networks observed.

I draw upon my diverse personal work experience, particularly from working as a family therapist and from working in public sector institutions, such as mental and general hospitals, thus allowing me to bring personal experience and subjectivity to the research, that enables unconscious and emotional nuances in organizations to be picked up. For example, working in mental hospitals has alerted me to the nuances of totalizing institutional cultures, and the behaviours and resistances that occur. When consulting in a global HQ of an international bank, the experience of totalizing cultures and institutionalized behaviour I experienced in the asylum was reawakened in me. I spent time observing the open-plan office spaces, the peer surveillance, the lack of personal privacy, whispered interactions, the dress codes – the uniformity of dark suits for men and women. I read and observed the texts of speechs, memos, reports, emails. In the canteen were slogans on every table promoting diversity, or as the leader who introduced this 'culture change' intervention called it 'diversity propaganda'. All this has become research data, and as a participant-observer I am able to share and engage in dialogue with my clients, helping them make sense of their work. This dialogue then enables me to reflexively test observations and hypothesis with leaders and followers in the workplace, and later with academic colleagues.

Engaged Observation

I was inspired by Bruno Latour's (2005) advice to 'follow the actors', meaning that the task is not to arrive with preconceived ideas of what you will research or observe, but to follow the leads, follow the actors; and the actors are both humans and non-humans in these settings. I arrive at appointments early and spend time observing the architectures and comings and goings in the reception areas. I take the opportunity whenever I can to 'walk the floor' to get close to the work itself. In a fertility clinic consultation I spent time observing the work of creating life in the laboratory, and contrasted the scientific-laboratory cultures, from the medical, administration and nursing cultures, outside the laboratory walls. In a horse-racing drugs testing laboratory I observed the detailed methods and processes, the collection and recording of data, the human and machine interactions.

When attending senior management meetings I note who's at the table and who's not, who speaks, who's heard, what emotions and rhetoric are used, what team dynamics take place. I emotionally feel the experience, watch the bodies as well as the words, and observe my own reactions as part of the research. Both the content of the conversations and the power relations are observed. As an executive coach I have access to the in-depth emotional and subjective data leaders carry within them. In my recent book *Coaching and Mentoring: A Critical Text* (2012) I reflect on how coaching has become a postmodern confessional, a new space at work where leaders feel compelled to confess their desires and their contemporary 'sins'. These sins break the code of leaders in workplaces, such as lacking self-confidence, feeling like imposters, out of control, lacking passion, being unhappy, recognizing the dissonance between the rhetoric they use as leaders and how they feel about what's really happening. To speak openly about these things at work is a sin, and not 'being passionate and engaged' may be punishable by missing the next promotion or pay rise. The coaching confessional also reveals very personal issues and desires; clients reflect on their identities and the meanings of their work and lives, revealing great hopes and often sadness when the coach is trusted as a 'Soul Guide' (Western, 2012: 132).

The critical discourse analysis here is derived from this rich observational and subjective data, arrived at through engagement, as well as observation.

The critical approach means to apply the four critical frames, discussed in Chapter 1, to this process:

1 **Emancipation** – examining whether underlying the dynamic surfaces of these organizational cultures, they serve to produce autonomous and free thinking individuals and groups, or whether they promote tacitly oppressive or conformist cultures.

2 **Depth analysis** – drawing on psychoanalytic and hermeneutic frames, unconscious and under-the-surface themes are explored.

3 **Network analysis** – examines the social structures, the wider systemic implications beyond micro-leadership practices and skills.

4 **Looking awry** – brings our awareness to new possibilities, that will provide new resources to examine existing texts and practice.

These frames are applied to:

- *Written texts:* academic texts, websites, institutional texts, company branding, professional bodies, advertising, conference papers, journals.

- *Spoken texts:* in management meetings, informal dialogues, conferences, coaching dialogues, executive education.

- *Leadership micro-practices*: analysis of the form, techniques and methods of what happens in the micro-practice of leadership (using observation and consulting to and coaching leaders).

- *The macro-social*: analysing and observing how the institutions that promote leadership, business schools, consultancies, and companies and organizations, utilize leadership to promote the different expectations and agendas they seek to achieve.

I test my observations with colleagues, clients and academics, to discern meaning and cross-check my findings. I do not use discourse analytic software in my work. Core to this particular critical approach is to bring subjectivity to the research, and to begin from practice and experience. As Miller (2011) writes:

> The first time Lacan tried to speak of psychoanalysis, he didn't start from Freud at all, but from his practice.

Lacan proposed a phenomenological description of analytic experience; thus from the beginning it was a matter of identifying the data of experience. Beginning from experience is a different starting point from beginning from theory or knowledge, and it is experience I begin from and return to, whilst acknowledging our experience is shaped and filled with knowledge, theory and discourse.

The findings of this analysis reveal four dominant discourses within leadership. I do not claim these are the only discourses within leadership, nor that they are absolute or stable, but they are present, and offer insights into how leadership has underlying forms that dominate how it is taught, thought about and practised.

The Four Discourses of Leadership

This book identifies four main discourses within organizational leadership in the past century:

1 **The Controller leadership discourse:** 'Controlling resources to maximize efficiency'. Controller leadership is underpinned by scientific rationalism, and the drive for efficiency and productivity. It became dominant as industrialization took place and after a demise returned in a new form of leadership control through audit and target cultures.

2 **The Therapist leadership discourse:** 'Happy workers are more productive workers'. Therapist leadership focuses on relationships and motivation. It emerged in the post-war period reflecting the endeavour to humanize and democratize the workplace and society. It became dominant after the 1960s boom in individualism and therapy culture entered the workplace through the human relations movement.

3 **The Messiah leadership discourse:** 'Vision and strong cultures'. The Messiah leadership focuses on transformational leaders who provide vision and lead by creating strong corporate cultures. The Messiah discourse began to dominate from the early 1980s.

4 **The Eco-leadership discourse:** 'Connectivity and ethics'. Eco-leadership is characterized by new understandings of organizations as ecosystems within ecosystems. The focus is on networks, connectivity and interdependence, where new forms of distributed leadership occur within organizations, and new connections with stakeholders and wider society take place. Ethics is at the heart of Eco-leadership.

The following four chapters will describe the historical and social influences on workplace leadership over the past century from which these discourses emerged, and describe the effects of these discourses on leadership and organizations. Chapter 13 will then offer an overview of the discourses, summarizing their essence as well as their strengths and weaknesses, and showing how they interact, as these discourses are not separate entities but work alongside each other and often merge.

Suggested Readings

- Fairclough, N. (1995) *Critical Discourse Analysis: The Critical Study of Language*. London/New York: Longman.

- Foucault, M. (1980) *Power/Knowledge: Selected Interviews and Other Writings, 1972–77* (ed. Colin Gordon). London: Harvester.

- Rose, N. (1990) *Governing the Soul*. London: Routledge.

Reflection Points

Discourses are not easily observable, but once identified we are more able to contest them or change our relationship with them.

- Reflect on the leadership discourse most dominant in your workplace, or place of study.

- Discourses create our social assumptions, i.e. they frame our perceptions and thinking, defining what we take for granted as normal.

Sample Assignment Question

Judith Butler says discourse defines the 'limits of acceptable speech' (2004: 64). Discuss and give examples from your own experience of how the gender discourse shapes how people think and act as men and women.

9 The Controller Leadership Discourse

Controlling Resources to Maximize Efficiency

Figure 9.1　Controller leadership

Key Words

Science

Rationality

Control

Efficiency

Productivity

Functionalism

Task

Chapter Structure

- Introduction
- Modern Times: The Context
- The 'Efficiency Craze': Taylor's Scientific Management
- Migrating Control from Factories to Offices
- Leading by Numbers: The 21st Century Revival of the Controller Discourse
- Case Studies of Controller Leadership
- Conclusion

Introduction

Figure 9.2 shows a hierarchical pyramid, typical of the organizational form of Controller leadership.

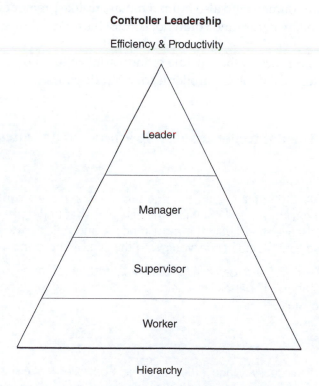

Controller Leadership

Efficiency & Productivity

Leader

Manager

Supervisor

Worker

Hierarchy

Figure 9.2 Controller leadership organizational form

The Controller leadership discourse emerged from (and helped develop) the 'modern' workplace environment. This first leadership discourse of the

20th century contrasted with prior ideas about leadership, rooted in the 'great man' heroic tradition, where leadership was associated with elitism, privilege and class. The Controller discourse emerged alongside the application of scientific rationalism to the workplace, that led to industrialization, urbanization and new social roles and identities.

The Controller leadership discourse is not only about the coercive control of employees (although this plays a part), it is also underpinned by two faiths. Firstly, the faith in the scientific method that advocates controlling an environment to minimize variants. Secondly, the faith in rationalism i.e. modernity is informed by rationalism, which in essence has a controlling ethos, working on the principle that human progress and happiness depend on the capability to rationally be in control of our passions and desires, instead of being at the mercy of our passions and the wildness of nature. Machiavelli began this modernist thinking, rejecting Aristotelian idealism about politics in favour of a utilitarian approach. Machiavelli believed an aim of politics was to control one's own chance or fortune, and that relying upon providence actually would lead to evil (Strauss, 1987). Modern man was rational and could master the natural environment and also human nature, unlike premodern man, who was determined by nature and could not control his own wildness and animal instincts. These beliefs arising from the Enlightenment became solidified at the turn of the century in the crucible of industrialization. Box 17 sets out the ethos and outcomes of the Controller leadership discourse

Box 17   The Controller Leadership Ethos and Its Outcomes

Ethos

1 Science: Applying the scientific method to the workplace – controlling the environment to test and minimize the variables that undermine efficiency. Also to discover and apply the most modern and efficient ways of using technology and human endeavour, with the aim of improving productivity.

2 Rationalism: Utilizing reason to understand, and therefore be in control of, the natural and social environment, overcoming unwanted passions and natural obstacles to progress.

Outcomes

1 Improved productivity and efficiency: The Controller leadership discourse remains necessary in any workplace (alongside other discourses that we discuss later). To control resources and waste, to measure success and

> outcomes, to seek efficient ways of working are vital. The huge gains from industrialization and modern scientific methods, including improved health-care and cheap consumable goods, have raised living standards immensely.
>
> 2 Instrumentalism: The leadership application of scientific-rationalism in the workplace inevitably leads to instrumentalism, i.e. the aims of increasing efficiency and productivity justify and override the means of achieving this, which include coercion, exploitation and a dehumanizing of the work-place. Instrumentalism often leads to inefficiency, due to functionalist and siloed thinking, rather than taking a more systemic perspective. This approach often privileges efficiency over human behaviour, without accounting for the impact of low moral.

At the turn of the 20th century, leaders of industry applied these ideas to the workplace. Workers were considered to have a base human nature that required controlling by leaders of the 'scientific-management' movement. Employee control became a key organizational concept, and remains so today, and the Controller leadership discourse emerged to achieve this. These leader-ship objectives did not always set out to be coercive or exploitative to workers (although many did), but some had higher aims as a social progressive force. The Controller discourse is underpinned and justified in both a moral and utilitarian sense. Even today the magical words used by politicians and busi-ness leaders 'we need to modernise' are a moral and utilitarian argument that is undisputable in most circles. The moral explanation is thus: when work is rationalized it improves performance and productivity, and also improves the moral good of workers by applying discipline and rules, and this benefits everybody, both contributing economically and improving society and the common good. Controller leadership did lead to huge social and economical benefits, however; worker conditions in the early industrial factories were very poor. The act of controlling others deemed lesser than those leaders con-trolling them cannot escape ethical questions, even when the aims were pro-gressive. From the beginning, there have been many critics of the application of science and rationality to work and society, and its instrumentalism and de-humanizing effects, including Rousseau, Kant and the Romantic move-ment, which critiqued the coldness of rationalism and modernity and cham-pioned nature, beauty, poetry and the soul, which they saw as becoming overwhelmed by the machine of modernity.

This chapter offers an overview of the historical, social and economic con-text at the turn of the 20th century, describing how Controller leadership emerged through scientific-rationalism being applied to industry, to transform workplaces to make them run like efficient machines. Controller leadership then migrated from factory conditions to a bureaucratic office culture, but became an 'outdated' leadership approach in the post-1960s, overtaken by the dominant Therapist discourse. However, it underwent a revival at the turn of the 21st century, when leaders found new ways of utilizing the formula of scientific-rationality to control employees and improve efficiency, through imposing target and audit cultures, where everything that mattered was measured, and was therefore controllable.

Modern Times: The Context

The Controller leadership discourse emerged as the Western world embraced modernity with gusto. The idea of meritocratic leadership grew, especially in the USA, slowly replacing feudal, epic and class models of leadership. To become a leading economy and progressive nation meant ensuring that talent was harnessed beyond the elite rich classes. Tennyson's famous poem 'The Charge of the Light Brigade' (1854) highlighted the folly of elite class-based leadership, which led 600 soldiers to ride to a futile death:

> Theirs not to reason why,
>
> Theirs but to do and die:
>
> Into the valley of Death
>
> Rode the six hundred

At the turn of the century democratic ideals emerged in the West, whilst in the Soviet Union egalitarian hopes flourished within their socialist revolution. While these societies organized along different political and economic principles, they both shared the philosophy of modernity, privileging science and rationality as the drivers of progress (Gray, 2003). In the Soviet Union this took a utopian (and later dystopian) form, and a utopian belief in science, rationality and progress prevailed also in the West. Being modern was seen as a true implementation of the Enlightenment, where the pursuit of reason could improve human affairs and transform society:

> Scientific knowledge would engender a universal morality in which the aim of society was as much production as possible. Through the use of technology, humanity would extend its power of the earth's resources and overcome the worst forms of natural scarcity. Poverty and war could be

abolished. Through the power given to it by science humanity would be able to create a new world. (Gray, 2003: 2–3)

The Enlightenment promised much, using science and rationalism as its tools, linked to the values of toleration, democracy, personal freedom and human equality. Unfortunately the ideals of democracy and personal freedom were marginalized in the workplace in favour of coercion and efficiency. Economic wealth increased and living standards improved through industrialization after brutal and exploitative beginnings.

In the late 19th century rural and peasant Europe was being transformed as urbanization and industrialization forged ahead; modernity and the machine were the transforming forces. The '"romance" of technology abounded, rail travel connected the "new cathedrals" of the 19th century, Euston, St Pancreas, Penn Station' (Hughes, 2005: 11), and today's ambivalence about the machine was rarely present:

no statistics on pollution, no prospect of melt-downs or core explosions on the horizon … The machine meant the conquest of progress and only very exceptional sights, like a rocket launch can give us anything resembling the emotion with which our ancestors in the late 1880s contemplated heavy machinery'.

This was personified perhaps by the Eiffel Tower, built for the Paris World Fair in 1889. The use of industrial materials to celebrate the nation state symbolized a new modern era. This iconic building enabled millions of people to see Paris from a new perspective, giving the masses a new futuristic vision. In 1855 Eiffel said his tower would symbolize 'not only the art of the modern engineer, but also the century of Industry and Science in which we are living, and for which the way was prepared by the great scientific movement of the eighteenth century and by the Revolution of 1789, to which this monument will be built as an expression of France's gratitude' (Loyrette, 1985: 116).

The Eiffel Tower reflected the zeitgeist and 'summed up what the ruling classes of Europe conceived as the promise of technology to be: Faust's contract, the promise of unlimited power over the world and its wealth' (Hughes, 2005: 11). To lead this march of progress, the ruling class required new meritocratic leaders of industry, yet these leaders substituted class and their elite control of feudal workers, for a new form of control of industrial workers. Their task was to engage workers to behave like the machines they worked alongside, with obedience, following standardized procedures; the whole process and environment required scientific control. The Leader as Controller discourse had arrived.

In the workplace, Chaplin's classic film *Modern Times* (1936) captures viv-
idly the essence of the new productive process: workers tied to monotonous
tasks on assembly lines, with a cold and distant leader controlling the process from offices beyond, and supervisors and foreman coercing the workers
on the production lines. The workplace became a site of economic and
human struggle; those nations able to develop the economy most effectively
could also lead in scientific research, further boosting the economy and also
weapons development, which was hugely important in the first part of the
20th century and arguably still is. New forms of work produced a new
worker and a new work regime. Rationality and efficiency produced the factory, the assembly line, the mass-production of goods and the industrial
labourer. These ideas were developed in the USA but were also embraced by
Lenin. The Bolsheviks believed human emancipation required industrialization (Gray, 2003: 8):

> American efficiency is that indomitable force which neither knows nor
> recognizes obstacles; which continues on a task once started until it is
> finished, even if it is a minor task, and without which serious constructive
> work is impossible ... The combination of the Russian revolutionary sweep
> with American efficiency is the essence of Leninism. (Hughes, 2004: 251)

Socialist Realist art portrayed the new workers as 'heroes of labour', building a new socialist utopia, whereas in the West, the factory workers were less
iconic and worked in transactional relationship – their labour and time in
exchange for a wage. From the outset disputes occurred over harsh conditions and low wages. The leadership belief was that through rationalizing
work, and control of the resources, processes and employees, new modern
institutions would emerge and a new modern society would be created.
Even benevolent and socially transforming leaders such as the Quaker
chocolate magnates operated from within the Controller leadership discourse. These philanthropists knew what was good for people and did not
see any inherent conflict in driving this forward in a top-down, controlling
manner. The Quakers (the Cadbury and Rowntree families) made exceptional progress in workplace conditions: for example, the Bourneville 'factory in the garden' in 1878, was a huge leap in progressive social conditions
for workers. Their industrial policies mimicked the Quaker communities'
emphasis on social control of their own domestic and church affairs, focusing on simplicity, hard work, austerity and purity. The Quaker industrial
policies attempted to align morality with profit. Walvin notes:

> The Quaker magnates tried to maintain a distinct moral tone at work. ...
> The Rowntree family insisted on decorous behaviour to and from the
> factory ... recruited workers from 'respectable homes' ... and refused to

employ married women in the belief that they should care for hearth and home; single mothers were never employed. (Walvin,1997: 183–91)

Controller leadership can be benevolent, or harsh, and the Quakers and other philanthropists pioneered new moral forms of industrial management and radically improved new workplace conditions. Interestingly, it was another Quaker (less heralded in Quaker hagiography) who had the greatest impact on industry, and whose work more than any other contributed to the emergence of the Controller leadership discourse.

The 'Efficiency Craze': Taylor's Scientific Management

The Worker Becomes a Cog-in-the-Machine of Production

New technologies, machines and modes of production demanded new forms of leadership and management as the industrialization process changed society. As science and modernity raced forward, Taylor's book *The Principles of Scientific Management* (1911) articulated this for industry. Taylor's leadership provided clear arguments for applying the scientific method to rationalize the workplace and make it more efficient and productive. In 1908 the Harvard Business School 'declared Taylor's approach the standard for modern management and adopted it as the core around which all courses were to be organised' (Barley and Kunda, 1992: 370). Scientific-management became the first American business fad, which historians call 'the efficiency craze'. Taylor's work was hugely influential and was also immediately challenged as being dehumanizing. Taylor's principles began with systematic observations that were translated into laws, rules and mathematical formulae:

> The main elements of the Scientific Management are: time studies (e.g. screw on each bolt in 15.2 seconds), standardization of tools and implements, the use of "slide-rules and similar time-saving devices", instruction cards for workmen (detailing exactly what they should do), task allocation. Taylor called these elements "merely the elements or details of the mechanisms of management"
>
> Another central tenet of scientific management was task allocation and labour division, where larger tasks were broken down into smaller tasks, enabling them to be done repetitively and more efficiently.

Another principle was for managers 'to study the character, nature and performance of individual workers so that they could scientifically select those most suitable for performing a particular task' (Fulop and Linstead, 1999: 210).

Taylor (1911) believed it was rational (in their own self interest) for workers to use their knowledge to avoid work rather than increase production. He called this work-avoidance 'soldiering'. He believed 'soldiering' could be eliminated through standardizing tasks and increasing the division of labour, therefore removing opportunities to deviate from productive work. Close supervision of workers was required, and scientifically trained managers, the new experts, would oversee this process. Workers were now under the control of supervisors, who themselves were under the scrutiny of 'expert' managers.

In effect, Taylor believed that workers should leave their sense of identity at the factory gate, and so be prepared to fit whatever 'mould' had been prepared for them by management (Kenny et al., 2012: 5).

Taylorism had a profound impact both on work and the wider society; 'managerialism' and management-science became a dominant feature of the 20th century. The new managers were scientific experts, morally neutral and apolitical characters, except for their one undisputable moral aim, to deliver efficiency and effectiveness in universal conditions (MacIntyre, 1985: 30). Taylor's cold assessment of humanity caused labour disputes and the Human Relations movement castigated his work as 'inhuman, reducing workers to the level of efficiently functioning machines' (Pugh and Hickson, 1971: 93). Whilst Taylor has been demonized, his work must be seen in the greater context of mechanization and how this shaped labour relations; and these methods have been (and still are) widely used in car plants, fast food chains, airlines, retail, hospitals, and athletic and sports training.

Fordism

Henry Ford epitomized the success of Taylor's approach by introducing the mass production of cars created in new industrial landscapes and applying new management technologies, such as de-skilling work and the massification of work conditions. Henry Ford symbolically offered the large wage of $5 a day to attract and retain workers on the monotonous production lines. As industrialization increased and became more efficient, this led to higher income and lower-priced goods: for example, the price of Ford cars fell from $780 in 1910 to $360 in 1914. This led to a cycle of production and consumption, producing a new consuming class which has been the basis of expanding economies ever since.

The management style was, in Etzioni's (1961) terms, 'utilitarian control', where power is based on a system of rewards or punishments. The threat of unemployment and hunger was very real in the first part of the 20th century and workers were controlled both in the workplace and through a fear of harsh social conditions if they lost their jobs. The Controller leadership discourse operates from within this social and the organizational field. The threat of losing wages and housing or healthcare benefits if the work regime is resisted supports the internal workplace controls.

Within the Controller leadership discourse, socially recognizable characters emerged: the controlling supervisor was caricatured as the 'tough foreman'; in the factory head office sat the cold and efficient 'bureaucratic manager'; and the company owner became the 'fat cat' boss. Workers were at the bottom of the hierarchy; losing their identities and skills as craftsmen and tradesmen, they became faceless and mindless workers in overalls, and with this came disillusionment, alienation and 'disenchantment'. Workers, unhappy with being treated like robots, turned to trade unions and labour disputes to improve their working conditions. My first job, at the age of 17, was in a paper bag-making factory in the late 1970s, and I recall a song that highlighted the delineation between workers and first-line management. It was sung by the shopfloor workers after a few pints on a Friday night, to the tune of 'The Red Flag':

> The working class can lick my arse,
>
> I've got a foreman's job at last.

The force of modernity demanded progress, and industrialization became a signifier of humans' power over nature. Controller leadership is not restricted to one sector, although manufacturing industry was the starting point and it continues unabated in the manufacturing sector, particularly in the expanding Asian manufacturing sector with conditions that mimic Tayloristic harsh approaches. Peng (2011: 726) describes 'sweatshops scattered around southern China where scholars have explored the despotic nature of labour control'.

The Controller leadership discourse was both a producer and an outcome of the industrialization process. It reflected and created the dominant workplace ethos that meant tight control of the production process and the workers on the production lines. Rationality, standardization and efficiency were key to industrial leadership in the early part of the 20th century.

Migrating Control from Factories to Offices

Changing Times: Post-War Social Change, Rethinking Controller Leadership

During the Second World War this model of rationalization, efficiency and mass production produced the weapons that changed the face of war. Taylorism and Fordist methods were much admired by Hitler (Gray, 2003) and the concentration camps utilized the factory model and scientific rationalism as their organizing means. The Nazis despised the democratic and liberal aspects of the Enlightenment but, like the Soviet Communists, they shared the Enlightenment's most hubristic hopes, believing that the power of technology could be used to transform the human condition, including the power to commit genocide on a hitherto unprecedented scale (2003: 13). Science, technology and the ideology of modernity had been exposed as a force that could produce efficiency and high production, but this did not necessarily deliver the hoped-for industrial, modern utopia. Worse still, science and rationalism became linked to the dystopia that was perpetrated by the Nazi regime. Zygmunt Bauman argued in *Modernity and the Holocaust* (1989) that the Holocaust, rather than being a specific German problem, was a result of modernity and bureaucracy, which had created unintended conditions that led to a demise in moral responsibility:

> The Holocaust is fully in keeping with everything we know about our civilization, its guiding spirit, its priorities, its immanent vision of the world. (Bauman, 1989: 8)

Science had produced the atomic bomb, and with Hiroshima, Nagasaki and the image of mushroom clouds and human devastation fresh in people's minds it became clear that science was not a straightforward force of progress and salvation – it was also a force for destruction on unimaginable scales. Karen Armstrong (2000) points out that the Holocaust took place next to one of the world's oldest universities and was planned by some of the most educated people in Europe, using rationality as their guiding light. The faith that science and rationality would produce a more modern, reasonable, progressive and civilized world was no longer sacrosanct.

Factory mass production lines had dehumanizing implications and the machine metaphor of efficiency and rationality was in desperate need of change. The Controller leadership discourse was no longer tenable in this form. A better paid and better educated workforce demanded new social relations, ' a world fit for heroes'. Alerted and worried by the socialist revolutions in the early part of the century, industry and political leaders feared a worker backlash against harsh conditions and that organized unions could rise up. Post-war hopes of a better future in the West meant improving workers' morale and preventing industrial conflict as well as continuing to drive for efficiency and increased productivity. Two leadership responses emerged in post-war Europe and the USA. Firstly, a new leadership discourse emerged – the 'Therapist', to be discussed in the following chapter. Secondly, in spite of the anti-Taylorist sentiments, Controller leadership remained strong but adapted itself, becoming less harsh: a new polite form of coercion and control fit for an office culture.

'The Bureaucrat': Controller Leadership in an Office Culture

In the 1950s and 1960s the rise of the office and the white-collar worker saw the Controller discourse migrate from the factory to the office. Modernity's dream of progress still underpinned the Controller discourse in offices, but the heady dreams of creating utopian, modernist futures disappeared, leading to a more utilitarian-focused society – one that was not without hope, for the 1950s were good times for the Baby Boomers, but without a utopian hope. The Controller leadership discourse privileges the language of science and rationality, yet controlling factory processes and people was only the beginning. Max Weber's (1930, 1947) influential writings advocated that bureaucracy is like a modern machine, while other organizational forms are like non-mechanical methods of production. Weber argued that bureaucratic organization is the most technically efficient form of organization possible, as it is based on 'rationality', but he was also wary of the dehumanizing aspects of this rational and efficient organizational form, which he said threatened the freedom of the human spirit and the values of liberal democracy; hence his view that bureaucracy and the modernizing process could easily turn into an 'iron cage'.

As workplaces developed and more white-collar jobs appeared, the Controller leadership discourse easily migrated into the new offices. The leadership aims were to produce office cultures and processes that could deal with mass information and produce their outputs efficiently, through the standardization and tight control of people, process and procedures. Bureaucracy today has a bad name, signifying slow and inefficient processes, yet in the 1950s it was (and still is under different names) considered to be the modern-efficient way to do business and run organizations. Controller leaders embodied the character of the discourse. They were the archetypal bureaucrats depicted by Whyte in 1956 as 'Organizational Man', who enjoyed a good life both in the office and in their suburban domestic lifestyles; 'for them society has been good, very, very, good' (Whyte, 1956: 395). Whyte also noted the lack of autonomy and the conformist culture that ensnared them at home and at work:

> Most see themselves as objects, more acted upon than acting – and their future therefore is determined as much by the system as by themselves. (Whyte, 1956: 395)

The office became a functionalist place of work, a reliable place where if you kept to the rules, and were polite and obedient to the leadership, you were rewarded with a job for life and a pension. The new burgeoning middle class would work 9 to 5 and then enjoy suburban leisure pursuits such as consumerism, home-making, cars, dinner parties, bowling, the cinema and holidays.

The Controller leader, whilst softer, still retained the cold scientific approach. Leaders of industry kept tight control of their domains. Managing directors sat in big offices on the top floors of their empires, like benevolent dictators establishing their top-down command and control cultures, promoting the loyal, and expecting compliance and even obedience from employees. Saul describes the dominant figure of rationality as the modern technocrat whose 'talents have become the modern definition of intelligence' (Saul, 1992: 106–7). On the other hand, bureaucracy cannot be dismissed as a dysfunctional system. In spite of reservations and many problems, public services have benefited immensely from applying rational and bureaucratic approaches to deliver change. Paul Du Gay, in his book *In Praise of Bureaucracy*, challenges accounts that dismiss bureaucracy as anti-human, or argue that it is no longer relevant in new hyper-capitalist turbo-charged cultures. Du Gay maintains that 'the bureaucratic ethos' remains relevant to the achievement of social order and good government in liberal democratic societies (Du Gay, 2000).

The 1960s brought social change, with an individualistic focus, and 'people power' social movements began to rail against hierarchies of power and the depersonalization created by 'faceless bureaucracies'. Demands for work to provide opportunities for personal development grew, and the need to motivate workers rather than control them led to the Therapist discourse flourishing in this new climate. The Controller discourse slid into a demise, but without disappearing, and it remained strong in particular sectors such as manufacturing and banking. It also remained important in different functional parts of organizations, such as finance departments where control of financial resources was vital. Control leadership generally was seen as a crude form of running an organization, one that was not suited to more human or post-industrial times. At the turn of the new century, however, it re-emerged unexpectedly.

Leading by Numbers: The 21st Century Revival of the Controller Leadership Discourse

Nothing can be known unless it can be quantified. (Gray, 2003: 38)

In the past few years, I have taught, trained, coached and consulted, using the four discourses of leadership, across sectors and with international clients, and I share my research observations that the Controller discourse faded after the 1960s when therapeutic culture and individualism led to the rise of the Therapist leadership discourse. This often evokes a strong and emotional reaction from individuals, who agree that the Therapist discourse became strong and is present, but point to the experience in their everyday working lives, which they see as a new onslaught of the Controller leadership discourse. They recognize immediately the rationalization, standardization and efficiency language of the Controller leader in their 21st century workplaces. The revival of Controller discourse began in the very late 20th century, and it stands in sharp contrast to two other rising discourses – Messiah leadership and Eco-leadership. This rise of the Controller aligns with my own experience and observations, particularly in large institutions, in both the public and private sectors, and the new form it takes is 'Leadership by numbers'.

The revival of the leadership Controller discourse emerged surreptitiously, under the cover of audits, measurement, targets and numbers. Rationality had previously indicated the need for leadership and management control to be imposed on workers. Now rationality itself was directly being used as a technology of control. Nikolas Rose explains the power of numbers in society:

> Numbers have an unmistakable power in modern culture … they achieve a privileged status in political decisions, yet they simultaneously promise a de-politicization of politics ... by purporting to act as automatic technical mechanisms for making judgments, prioritizing problems and allocating scarce resources. (Rose, 1991: 673–4)

When numbers are cited in workplaces they are often accompanied by scientific titles such as 'evidence-based' practice or accountancy terminology. They are presented as sacrosanct, factual accounts, an independent truth, free from the social-political contexts in which they are produced. Yet numbers are not free from ideology, politics, inaccuracy, abuse or morality. Michael Power's book *Audit Society* (1997) reports on the explosion of audits as a systematic form of social organization and control. Power points to the pervasive rise in auditing across all sectors, from charities to schools, from global corporations to national governments. Leading and numbers always sounds convincing yet the numbers are used as a form of organizational control, in an instrumental way, often to achieve 'political' ends.

A Critique of the Scientific Meta-theory Used by HR and Managers

Scientific rationality makes everything quantifiable, turning services and actions into numbers. In the social field this is problematic, the wrong meta-scientific theory is being used to measure something that is often immeasurable, and is always unpredictable:

> In the social world, prediction is virtually impossible although in some parts of the natural and man-made (e.g. engineering) world prediction is possible. So whilst prediction might be nice, it is not possible. Those that hint at prediction in the social world are almost always operating with an implicit idea of (some) natural science in the 'back of their minds'. (Fleetwood and Hesketh, 2006)

HR departments are wedded to the scientific meta-theory, and attempt to measure causal relations between people and performance outcomes. Fleetwood and Hesketh (2006) demonstrate the inadequacy of this position, claiming that it has led to bad science and weak outcomes. Finding a causal link is problematic because (a) there is never a simple causal link to be researched, there are always many others; and (b) any 'proof' of a causal link still doesn't offer an explanation of this association (2006: 681). Bhaskar (2010) supports this view, arguing that causal links in closed system experiments do not give 'laws' or sustainable knowledge in open (human) systems.

Reductionist scientific approaches do more damage than simply getting a lot of things wrong; they shape the way leaders, managers and employees think and act. Collinson notes, 'Through measurement and assessment, surveillance systems render individuals "calculable"' (2003: 535).

Collinson makes two points about Control by numbers: firstly that individuals become calculable and measurable by 'the management system'; secondly they collude in their own subordination, i.e. no longer do you need managers and supervisors to control workers, the weight of numbers shapes workers to control themselves. Reductionist science becomes reductionist thinking and practice. 'Micro-thinking' and number crunching dominate, micro targets and goals are focused on, whereas systemic, holistic and strategic 'macro-thinking' is undermined.

Economics and the Politicization of Numbers

The 'scientific' methodology does not distinguish natural science from social science and the model for both is mathematics (Gray, 2003). Economics takes this model and it becomes politicized to result in the free-market economics of the neo-liberals, whereby a political faith is developed believing that a free-market increases efficiency, productivity, growth and democracy. This free-market economy is a based on a positivist ideology, i.e. leading by numbers. Joseph Stiglitz, World Bank Chief Economist and Vice

President (1997–2000), describes how this method is used by the IMF apparently to assess a country's needs, yet the mission of economists sent into countries to do the numbers becomes a farce, as the neo-liberal solutions are pre-ordained: austerity measures, public sector reductions, a liberalization of markets and de-regulation of labour. Stiglitz writes:

> When the IMF decides to help a country, it dispatches a 'mission' of economists. These economists lack extensive experience in the country; they are more likely to have knowledge of its five star hotels than of the villages that dot its countryside.
>
> They work hard poring over numbers deep into the night. But their task is impossible. In a period of days or, at most weeks, they are charged with developing a coherent programme sensitive to the needs of the country. Needless to say a little number crunching rarely provides adequate insights into the development strategy for an entire nation. Even worse, the number crunching isn't always that good. The mathematical models the IMF uses are frequently flawed or out of date … country teams have been known to compose draft reports before visiting … [Stiglitz adds they even have been known to substitute one country for another in the report]. (Stiglitz, 2000: 5)

The dominance of the neo-liberal economic agenda stays with us. In spite of the failure of their best economists and business leaders to predict and prevent the financial collapse in 2008, they proclaim more of the same, more extreme Controller leadership to solve the crisis. Italy and Greece both suspended democracy to be controlled and governed by 'neutral' technocrats imposing austerity measures dictated by the IMF, European Commission and European Central Bank, to ensure these countries efficiently controlled their budgets. As the *New York Times* (2011a) put it, 'roiling financial markets have upended traditional democratic processes'. David Skelton (2011) writes in the *New Statesman*:

> Government of the technocrats, by the technocrats, and for the technocrats is hugely undesirable and, by its very nature, bad for democratic legitimacy ... Rule by technocrats has replaced rule by the people – with unelected, economically orthodox international bodies like the European Commission and the IMF working with unelected technocrats now heading up national governments to implement tough austerity measures that have never received public backing.

The abandonment of democracy in favour of technocrats demonstrates the faith in the Controller discourse in spite of the failures that led to the financial crisis. The game of numbers extracted from reality, the application of 'instrumental rationality', the chasing of the ends (short-term profit) without reflection on the means, to impact on business and society in general. What became apparent was the irrationality of this 'rational' number chasing approach. The banks lost their identity and focused on their core business, i.e. as safe places to invest money, and became sites of commerce, and, worse, casinos, gambling with and losing our pensions and savings. Numbers showed huge success, and numbers also managed to hide huge risks and debts. A failsafe system based on logic, mathematics, computerized risk-assessment, with complicit 'independent' credit agencies, proclaimed the banks safe until days before they fell. In simple terms, the increasing mountains of debt were unsustainable and in retrospect sure to fail. When leading by numbers becomes divorced from the social, from people's lives, there seems to be a snowball effect, and those involved lose sight of what's important or real.

Case Studies of Controller Leadership

Three short cases studies below describe how the Controller leadership discourse plays out in organizations today. The first case studies offer critiques of how controller leadership undermines creativity and autonomy, and more importantly how it distorts the real focus of the work. In the hospital, numbers become more important than individual patient care. The other two case studies show how Controller leadership produces commercial success whilst always raising concerns about what happens to humans in these companies.

Box 18   Case Study (1): Leading by Numbers in the NHS

Public sector modernization

In the public sector, the Controller discourse re-emerged with a vengeance in the 1990s as the 'modernization' of services meant a transfer of power and control from clinicians to managers and other experts. At the heart of this process are numbers, and the focus shifts from patient care to hitting targets. Focusing on targets is to focus on the ends rather than the means, i.e. how to achieve results then becomes distorted. Shortcuts are taken, numbers are prioritized over clinical decisions and cuts are made to make efficiencies, yet the holistic impact of the cuts is not accounted for.

Leading by numbers was initially planned to enhance leading with professional expertise, bringing best practice from the private sector to the health service, with the authentic aim to make it more efficient, productive, accountable and transparent for users.

However, this approach soon became a classic example of 'instrumental rationalism' and disenchantment set in. A similar modernization experience took place in Canada, with similar results. It seems that however good the intentions, when leaders control by numbers, the workplace becomes less human; and this can also have a detrimental effect on results. In the NHS it became essential for managers to produce the right numbers; everything that mattered was measured, including the government itself, which imposed its own targets on healthcare: waiting lists and waiting times were to be reduced, and operations increased, all by the next election. The government's hold on power was at stake and it impressed this on the new CEOs of hospitals.

The government appointed expert consultants to advise NHS leaders. Their ideological advice comes from neo-liberalism and is uniformly the same whatever industry or sector; it is an unrelenting message: the rationalization of services and encouraging a free market to increase competition and choice. In this case it was an internal market that created false splits and an unnecessary layer of bureaucracy. The classic top-down Control leadership discourse quickly pervaded the health service, using numbers, targets and measurement as the key control mechanisms. The aim was to put pressure on those delivering care, to deliver faster and more efficiently. These aims were morally indisputable; to improve services meant to impose a more accountable, efficient and rational system. Clinical staff agreed with the aims, but the application was more complex, as healthcare is not a car factory and lean technology may inform healthcare, but must not dominate it.

A battle raged between this new onslaught of managerialism and clinical leadership, led by medical consultants whose power was being challenged. These medical consultants were deemed not fully accountable as they exercised power through an non-standardized application of expertise, utilizing clinical experience that did not always accord with rationalizing and standardizing healthcare. Many health employees had some empathy with this position; some consultants were too powerful, unaccountable and idiosyncratic, and there was waste in the system. Yet nurses and healthcare professionals also knew that control by numbers and reducing healthcare to audit control, treating a hospital like a supermarket, were not the answer.

This modernization process was supported by a huge government investment, which included importing new 'experts' into the system – consultants, accountants from the big consultancies who had experience in the private sector, who claimed to know how to run businesses efficiently. The target culture produced new layers of bureaucracy and soon clinicians found themselves as 'bean counters'. Worse still, a gap appeared between the local and global, with professionals making decisions close to their patients and Controlling leaders setting targets and measuring numbers from afar. Training programmes expanded to educate managers and clinicians in number crunching methods, e.g. leading change, lean technology, healthcare MBAs, and

(Continued)

(Continued)

performance management courses were everywhere. Clinical leadership meant setting targets and evaluating outcomes; to manage was to measure. Accountability used to mean taking responsibility for healthcare, but Control leadership accountability meant to do the accounts and get the numbers right, and a new order of control was established.

From covenant to contract

The patient–doctor/nurse relationship is based on a social covenant, a shared trust that is underpinned by ethics and compassion. The customer–provider relationship is based on a transactional contract, underpinned by market forces. In the latter, patients first become customers, then become objects, units valued in monetary and numerical terms. An ex-colleague of mine spoke of her experience as a clinical leader:

> My job used to be caring for people, now I feel like I am running a production line, all we are concerned about is getting the waiting times down, if we don't, our funding is reduced. The leadership here talks about creating a culture of trust, empowering us to do our jobs, but in reality they are the most controlling leaders we have had in my 24 years of service. (Ward Charge Nurse, NHS hospital, September 2005)

Breaking the social covenant undermined staff moral, took decision-making away from the experts and de-humanized healthcare with devastating consequences in some places. Patients were moved from emergency rooms prematurely and left in corridors as staff were under pressure to meet treatment targets. The pressure was immense and mistakes were made. The Stafford Hospital scandal revealed how bad things got, with a public inquiry that reported in a February 2013 hearing how between 2005 and 2008 between 400 and 1,200 more patients died than would have been expected when 'nurses and doctors were put under pressure by managers to ensure official targets were achieved, even when that meant patients were put at risk' (*Daily Telegraph*, 2013).

Conclusion

The vision was sincere, governments wanted to improve services, and it would be wrong to claim that no progress was made. Many services were improved through Controller leader techniques, and rationalization does have its place; efficiency drives and accountability that are quantifiable are important. The danger is when the Controller leadership discourse dominates completely. This brief case study highlights that problems arose when numbers unhinged patient care. Patients require thoughtful, expert, high quality, compassionate *and* efficient healthcare services.

Another side of the Controller leadership discourse shows how it plays a big part in highly successful companies in many sectors, such as engineering, pharmaceuticals, manufacturing, food industry and retail. The following short case studies describe two well-known companies, McDonald's and Ryanair.

Box 19   Case Study (2): McDonald's – the World's Biggest Food Chain

The resurgence of the Controller discourse

Note: All quotations and statistics are taken from the McDonald's official website www.aboutmcdonalds.com

McDonald's is perhaps the best example of the Controller leadership discourse in action. It is an organization driven by a faith in functionalism, leading through rationality and efficiency, and applying tight controls to people and processes. Its success is phenomenal:

> McDonald's is the leading global foodservice retailer with more than 34,000 local restaurants serving nearly 69 million people in 119 countries each day.

The company has 1.8 million employees. Its leadership focus is on the mass production and distribution of 'good' quality, cheap food. The philosophy of its founder, Ray Kroc was:

> to build a restaurant system that would be famous for food of consistently high quality and uniform methods of preparation. He wanted to serve burgers, buns, fries and beverages that tasted just the same in Alaska as they did in Alabama.

Borrowing heavily from scientific management and utilizing Fordist assembly production techniques, the food is produced in a standardized and tight for-mulaic way, leaving very little room for human error (or human creativity). Efficiencies are made everywhere: the kitchen design ensures staff complete their tasks within two steps of the machines they work with, saving time and costs. They even have a 'Hamburger University' established in 1961, where franchisees and operators are trained in the scientific methods of running a successful McDonald's.

To deliver this success on a mass scale Kroc's philosophy was to establish control systems across the three key parts of the business he called 'the three legged stool', i.e. suppliers, franchisees and the McDonald's corporation. Kroc

(Continued)

(Continued)

believed the stool was only as strong as its three legs. Utilizing and rewarding entrepreneurial spirit through the franchise, yet creating strict formulaic practices through central control, was the perfect recipe for success, with the final part ensuring that the supply line was as efficient as the restaurants, ' creating the most integrated, efficient and innovative supply system in the food service industry'.

McDonald's leaders, whilst embedded in Control leadership, have proved to be adaptive to social change: their invention of the Drive Thru epitomizes their business, serving reliable food from a limited menu, so fast and efficiently you don't even waste time stepping out of your car. Paying attention to current social changes, their restaurants offer reliability and continuity whilst absorbing changes such as the cappuccino culture, and offering health options in their menu. And in France, for example, they serve only French beef to accommodate local demand. McDonald's are paying attention to customer demands and protecting their brand by signifying their intent in five key areas:

Nutrition & Well-Being

Sustainable Supply Chain

Environmental Responsibility

Employee Experience

Community.

McDonald's has it critics and for many it represents all that is wrong with popular culture, i.e. the dominance of global corporations, and commodified modern living. The Mclibel case highlighted these issues: complaining that amongst other things McDonald's offers an unhealthy diet that also misleads people, exploits workers, is cruel to animals and seriously damages the environment (see www.mcspotlight.org/campaigns/current/wwwmd-uk.pdf). Another argument is that cheap prices through mass-production techniques undercut local businesses and restaurants, undermining local shops and diversity. Others provide counter arguments supporting MacDonald's, pointing to the fact that they employ many low-educated employees in poor areas and offer a career ladder to the top of the business, and provide a popular and cheap 'quality' service to millions of happy customers.

McDonald's symbolizes the triumph of the Controller discourse: hugely successful, providing consistently cheap and reliable quality burgers across the globe. Yet conformity comes at the expense of diversity, efficiency at the expense of local quality and aesthetic beauty, and low cost food has high cost environmental impacts.

At McDonald's there is the comfort of knowing precisely what you are going to get, no matter where you are in the world; and this obviously appeals to millions.

Box 20   Case Study (3): Ryanair – Europe's Most Successful Low Cost Airline

> Our strategy is like Wal-Mart, we pile it high and sell it cheap. (Michael O'Leary, 1994)

Michael O'Leary presented himself a robust Controller leader – and a very successful one. As Ruddock (2007) says, O'Leary was 'a combative, cost-effective and lemon-squeezing business leader.' He worked on the premise that if he provided an efficient enough service with the lowest prices, then customers would fly Ryanair, and thus far he has been proved right. Ryanair began its operation in 1985 with a 15-seat turboprop aircraft. Their success is illustrated by this summary from their website:

Ryanair is the world's favourite airline operating over 1,500 flights per day from 53 bases on 1,500 low fare routes across 28 countries, connecting over 168 destinations. Ryanair operates a fleet of over 290 new Boeing 737–800 aircraft with firm orders for a further 13 new aircraft … Ryanair has a team of more than 8,500 people and expects to carry over 80 million passengers in the current fiscal year. (www.ryanair.com/en/about; accessed 11 March 2013)

Ryanair mixes Control leadership with an acute business strategy, that aims not only to make the airline efficient, but the airports and passengers too. Changing passenger and airport behaviour has been part of the success story. For example, limiting baggage weight and charging for extra baggage brought extra revenue and changes in behaviour, as people travelled lighter, improving loading and unloading and helped speed up turn-around times. Flying to secondary airports means avoiding the huge gate and landing charges demanded by the major airports, and Ryanair picks up subsidies for bringing new business to regional airports. Passengers book their own tickets, print off boarding passes, and self-manage much of what used to be done by airline staff. Working with airports to speed up passenger transition times has also been important part of Ryanair's strategy. Efficiency savings come from offering a limited service and flying only one type of airplane, reducing maintenance costs. Small gains are made everywhere: no reclining seats means less maintenance, no magazine pockets means less rubbish and less cleaning time, and therefore a quicker turn around. Keeping planes in the air is their target: the more time they are carrying passengers, the less waste and the cheaper the fares. Ryanair, however, like most Controller leadership approaches, has trouble with the people side of the business, both in terms of a reputation for poor customer service and poor staff

(Continued)

(Continued)

morale. An article in *The Economist* (2007) entitled 'Snarling all the way to the bank' explains:

> That is the paradox of Mr O'Leary's Ryanair. It is hugely successful. It has brought flying within the reach of people of the most limited means. It has helped to change the economic prospects of neglected parts of Europe by bringing passengers and their money to underused provincial airports. But at the same time Ryanair has become a byword for appalling customer service, misleading advertising claims and jeering rudeness towards anyone or anything that gets in its way ...

> Since Mr O'Leary is worth £420m, according to this year's *Sunday Times* Rich List, he can certainly afford to go. Only when he does will we know whether a kinder, gentler Ryanair can be as profitable as his snarling creation. Sadly, the answer is probably no.

Ryanair is a fly-away success and thus far has not made any great attempt to accommodate customer and staff complaints, but this surely is not sustainable and O'Leary recognized this, saying that in the future 'Ryanair would need to trumpet attributes other than cheap fares – such as its young aircraft fleet and "terrific" in-flight service' (*Observer*, 2010).

Summary of Case Studies

Ryanair and McDonald's show how the Controller leadership discourse can produce business success. However, both companies will need to adapt and accommodate some of their critics to remain successful. Whilst the Controller leadership discourse can drive a successful business by focusing on efficiency, competitiveness and reducing costs, this discourse alone can rarely sustain success. People matter, and both McDonald's and Ryanair have begun to address issues of customer care, in different ways. There are ethical questions to answer, and cultural ones when addressing the Controller discourse. Do we want a McDonaldization of society (Ritzer, 1993) where shopping malls across the globe look the same, and offer the same global brands? Do we want cheap and familiar, rather than diverse and interesting? Low cost, mass-produced rather than locally grown/made? For millions who enjoy popular culture it seems the answer is yes; for cultural critics who fear that the losses are too great and the long-term results undermine the 'good society', it is a resounding no.

Conclusion

The Controller leadership discourse has gone through three phases:

1 *The efficiency craze:* Emerging at the beginning of the 20th century Controller leadership dominated industrial workplaces, and was best articulated through Taylorism and Fordism.

2 *Bureaucratic leadership:* Control leadership migrated to 1950s offices; with leaders and bosses implementing control through bureaucratic culture.

3 *Leading by numbers:* After a period of demise it re-emerged at the turn of the 21st century, through 'leading by numbers', establishing target and audit regimes, using data and audits as a new form of organizational control.

Much of today's workplace is still underpinned by the ethos and promise of rationality and therefore the Controller leadership thrives, yet without the hubristic hopes of the early modernizers.

Box 21 briefly summarizes the archetypal character of the Controller leader.

Box 21   The Character of the Controller Leader

Controller leadership operates with two core aims: efficiency and productivity. Controller leadership also operates through transactional and functional approaches. These leaders are not charismatic, innovative, dynamic, passionate or creative – all those words we often associate with leaders. For the Controller leader the task is much less romantic, more utilitarian and focused. Controller leadership puts in place processes that drive forward efficiency within a system of clear roles and tasks, overseen by structures of governance and control. These leaders are today's 'organization men or women'. They expect workers to behave like them, to follow rules and procedures, to respect position power as people must know their place in the hierarchy. These leaders believe that control resides with the position more than the person. Promotion goes to those who follow the rules, those who conform. Some Control leaders humanize this process as much as they can, others distance themselves from the human side, focusing only on performance outcomes and results (numbers); this depends on personality and context.

The social gains of Controller leadership cannot be underestimated. Mass production has created untold opportunities to obtain cheap and available material goods, including cheap food, and service industries such as hospitality have also benefited. Underpinned by science and rationality, with the aim of improving productivity and efficiency, this leadership discourse brings a clear focus that has proven very successful in organizations. Controller leadership can not only improve productivity, it can also raise standards, and improve safety and quality. Yet the dangers are self-evident: people are not numbers or machines, and the dangers of instrumentalism and dehumanizing organizations are ever-present. Also the focus on detail, measurement and control undermines more holistic and systemic approaches to leading organizations.

The Controller leadership discourse is an important part of how leadership is undertaken. However, if it dominates an organization without being balanced by other discourses the outcomes are likely to be dehumanizing and will lack the strategic agility required by leaders in today's fast-changing world.

Suggested Readings

- Du Gay, P. (2000) *In Praise of Bureaucracy: Weber Organisation Ethics*. London: Sage.

- Fulop, L. and Linstead, S. (1999) *Management: A Critical Text*. London: Macmillan. pp. 210–24.

- Parker, M. (2002) *Against Management: Organization in the Age of Managerialism*. Cambridge: Polity Press.

- Power, M. (1997) *The Audit Society: Rituals of Verification*. Oxford: Oxford University Press.

- Taylor, F. ([1911]1997) *The Principles of Scientific Management*. New York: Dover Publications.

Reflection Points

Controller leadership applies scientific rationalism to the project of leading organizations. Human and non-human resources are controlled to maximize efficiency and raise productivity. Ethical questions arise from over-zealous

Controller leaders, where humans are treated as cogs-in-the-wheel of the machine, and efficiency and productivity override human concerns.

• Reflect on a familiar organization and think about how dominant or not Controller leadership is. Can you envisage an organization without some form of Controller leadership?

Sample Assignment Question

Summarize the Controller leadership discourse identifying its strengths and weaknesses, drawing on examples you have experienced or observed to support your case.

10 The Therapist Leadership Discourse

Happy Workers Are More Productive Workers

Figure 10.1 Therapist leadership

Key words

Relationships

Motivation

Teamwork

Personal growth

Therapeutic culture

Emotions

Subjectivity

Chapter Structure

- Introduction
- The Context: 'The times they are a changing'
- The Human Relations and Human Potential Movements
- The Triumph of the Therapeutic
- Wounded Self and Celebrated Self
- Therapeutic Culture Enters the Workplace
- Executive Coaches: Therapeutic Experts for the Workplace
- 21st Century Therapist Leadership
- Conclusion

Introduction

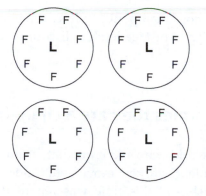

Therapist Leadership
Relationships & Motivation

Team Leadership

Figure 10.2   Therapist leadership organizational form: organizations are shaped around team leaders and their followers

The second leadership discourse, the 'Therapist leader', emerged from the influences of post-Freudian psychology, post-war democratizing movements and the growth of individualism in the West. Dominant social cultures infuse workplace cultures, and in this chapter we clearly see how a therapy culture colonizes the workplace. The Therapist leadership discourse

mirrors the 'subjective turn', described as 'the defining cultural development of modern western culture' (Heelas and Woodhead, 2005: 2–5). Prior to
this, life was 'lived-as', i.e. we belonged to an established order, and life was
scripted by external forces; after the 'subjective turn', life was 'lived subjec-
tively', a life shaped by our emotional experience where we learn to adapt
ourselves to a changing world (2005: 2–5). A 'life-as' shaped by external
forces fits with the Controller leader: employees' lives shaped by the factory
and office rules, routines and rituals, with workers following instructions
from an external hierarchy. This new 'subjective life' was more complex, it
required expert help, and a new array of 'soul directors' emerged (Western,
2012). Professional helpers such as psychologists, social workers, therapists
and counsellors pioneered and responded to the new phenomenon of therapeutic culture pervading society (Rose, 1990).

The workplace required a new leadership discourse to meet new social
expectations. The Therapist leadership discourse emerged as a people-
focused, emotionally literate leadership within this changing social context.
The underpinning ethos is that to run an organization successfully, it's the
people you have to focus on, and it's the psychological and emotional that
are important, not just managing people as functional objects or 'human
resources'.

This chapter explores how therapeutic culture emerged and entered the
workplace, and how the Therapist leadership discourse became dominant in
the post-1960s.

The Context: 'The times they are a changing'

The period between the world wars and immediately after the Second World
War was extremely turbulent; workers movements and socialism were gaining momentum. Leadership at this time was regarded as important but
problematic. Classical leadership and trait theories dominated, and these
produced 'great men' and hero leaders such as Winston Churchill and
Gandhi – but they also produced Hitler and Stalin.

Those returning from service in the Second World War demanded a 'land
fit for heroes' and returned with a new confidence and raised expectations,
no longer willing to put up with pre-war class and social divisions and dire
working conditions: 'The new rhetoric focused on entitlements and improved
working conditions ... the upshot of which was the birth of personnel
administration' (Barley and Kunda, 1992: 372). Fearful of another rise in
fascism or the rise of communism, social scientists and political figures
worked on building a new post-war society with democratic social structures

and institutions. This included changes in the workplace. The aim was to avoid a class war, and prevent a social revolution, which were fuelled by poverty and anger at poor working and living conditions and mistreatment at the hands of controlling leaders and exploitative capitalists. Another aim was to empower previously passive followers, in the hope of undermining their tendency to behave like compliant actors blindly following Controlling leaders (as seen in fascism). Democratizing the workplace meant democratizing leadership, and Box 22 briefly reviews this process.

Box 22   Democratizing Leadership

The distrust of leadership became widespread after the Second World War, when Hitler epitomized its dangerous potential. The socialist Left also became disenchanted following their aspirations being dashed by the communist dictatorships of Mao and Stalin. The impact of the Vietnam War also eroded many students' and young people's attitudes towards the 'democratic leadership' in the USA and beyond. The post-war reaction to leadership was highlighted in the 1960s with the anti-authoritarian hippie movement and the liberation-focused social movements that emerged, such as the youth, peace, feminist, and lesbian and gay movements. The Bob Dylan lyric in the heading to this section neatly captures the sentiment of the time, which berated leaders, and with them any form of authority. Many activists who were influenced by these movements remain distrustful of leadership and associate it with authoritarianism, manipulation and coercion. Others became the next generation of political, social and business leaders, many bringing reformist ideals of democratizing and improving society, and trying to offer a more democratic and collaborative leadership approach.

Moves to find more democratic and egalitarian forms of organizing emerged from this distrust. Democratic and participative leadership styles became widely accepted, overcoming overtly hierarchical and coercive Controller leadership. Democratizing the workplace through democratic leaders echoed the social zeitgeist. Gastil writes of Kurt Lewin's work:

> He argues that democratic leadership relied upon group decision-making, active member involvement, honest praise and criticism and a degree of comradeship. By contrast, leaders using the other styles were either domineering or uninvolved. (1997: 157)

A more democratic style also appealed to workers who preferred to be motivated than coerced. Gastil states that one of the democratic leader's functions is to sustain the democratic process and prevent undemocratic

(Continued)

(Continued)

structures from forming. Democratic leadership aims to share decision-making and give employees responsibility and a degree of autonomy to bring about double benefits: satisfaction for the employee and increased output. Participative management (Likert, 1961) and Servant leadership (Greenleaf, 1977) are forms of leadership that claim allegiance towards 'Democratic leadership'. Kurt Lewin and colleagues produced work on democratic leadership (Lewin and Lippett, 1938), separating it from autocratic and *laissez-faire* leadership, and proposed the argument that democratic leadership was not only morally correct, it was also better leadership. In democratic bodies, the authority given to a leadership position has to be circumscribed, so a line is drawn as to which decisions can be taken by the leader and what needs further approval from the group. Formal and informal structures and rules come with this territory.

Co-operation and competition

Tjosvold and Field sharply contrast cooperative and competitive people and goals:

> People with highly cooperative goals discuss their opposing ideas and positions directly, examine each other's perspectives and work for mutual benefit. With open minds, they understand the opposing positions, integrate their ideas and achieve a mutually acceptable, high-quality decision. People with competitive goals are reluctant to discuss their views directly and may belittle and attack another's position. (Tjosvold and Field, 1984: 28; Tjosvold and McNeely, 1988)

When democratic approaches are sought, there can often be what Kurt Lewin called a 'pseudo-democracy', which paralyses decision-making and prevents leaders from taking up their authority. Elliot Jaques' Glacier Investigations found that the need for clarity of role and status for individuals and their colleagues was paramount. Organizations that identified themselves with democratic ideals or consensus decision-making often undermine a leader's ability to take up authority and lead. The results can be sabotage, confusion and frustration (Jaques, 1955).

Many organizations whose ideals are democratic and egalitarian, or whose members aspire to this, are often hybrids, hierarchical in structure but consensual in aspiration, or consensual at some levels but accountable to a hierarchy of leaders. In organizations/teams that pursue democratic ideals for ideological reasons they can become engrossed in their own internal processes. I have experienced this in the public sector where envy and rivalry are often rife, and when this happens, the organization is underpinned by emotional insecurity.

There are four leading types of organizations with aspirations for more democratic leadership and participative engagement:

1 **Co-operatives and not-for-profit organizations**: charities and self-help organizations, which aspire to more democratic structures, sharing profits, sometimes with rotating leadership roles, attempting to limit hierarchy and disperse power wherever possible with various degrees of success.

2 **Religious, spiritual, utopian-inspired communities** with egalitarian leanings from both traditional and 'new age' backgrounds.

3 **Large companies such as the John Lewis Partnership** who structure their ownership in ways that offer employees participation in ownership/decision-making and shared-reward schemes.

4 **Public sector teams with vocational staff** who identify with the ideals of service provision and attempt to lead their work teams in participative and collaborative ways.

Democratic ideals mean less focus on position power, instruction and explicit controlling, and more on participation and relationships. Achieving democratic leadership, therefore, inevitably means supporting the rise of the Therapist leadership discourse – a discourse that focuses on people, people, people.

The Therapist leadership discourse's greatest influences can be traced back to the human relations and human potential movements which emerged as a reaction to the devastating trauma of two world wars and reflected the growing individualistic nature of society. They also acted as counter-movements to the alienating aspects of modernity.

The Human Relations and Human Potential Movements

The human relations movement aimed to soften the harshness of scientific-rationalism that paid no attention, and the Controller discourse that didn't pay enough, to human needs in the workplace. The human potential movement occurred as prosperity and individualism opened up new opportunities to reflect on the self, and it 'preached' the gospel of 'human potential', i.e. that we could achieve great things for ourselves, with the ultimate goal of finding inner happiness. The Therapist leadership discourse can be traced back to these two movements.

The Human Relations Movement

Elton Mayo is widely held to be the founder of the Human Relations movement. He was appointed to the faculty at Harvard and brought multi-disciplinary perspectives to the problems of industry. Gareth Morgan points to motivation and the relationship between individuals and groups as the important issues arising from Elton Mayo's Hawthorne experiments in the 1920s and 1930s. These experiments raised questions about informal as well as formal organization, and placed the importance of human relationships in the limelight, which dealt a blow to classic management theory (Morgan, 1986: 41). Mayo argued that group processes amplified an individual's psychopathology and that a first-line supervisor was the most influential change agent in the workplace. The Human Relations movement was clear about its task, and was well funded and supported. In post-war Britain, the Tavistock Institute was formed to work on these democratizing organizational issues, bringing together social scientists, psychoanalysts, biologists and anthropologists in a multidisciplinary effort to make social changes, focusing on the workplace.

The Human Relations movement shifted the focus from the pre-war ideas of paternalist duty and industrial betterment led by philanthropists, to an ideal based on a win–win situation. Production would improve as 'happier workers are more productive workers'; to get happier workers meant improving democratic structures, to include them in decision-making processes. Motivation linked to productivity was the key, set within greater democratic structures, more worker autonomy and greater satisfaction at the workplace. The Human Relations movement was led by Mayo and influenced by Kurt Lewin. Early success came through the Tavistock Institute's researchers Trist and Bamford (1951), who pioneered new 'open socio-technical' systems after researching the coal mining industry. They applied the biologist Von Bertalanffy's open systems theories to organizational theory, linking the interdependent relationship between technological changes and the human–social system. They found that bringing new technology to work without taking into account the social and psychological effects was problematic; however accounting for the social and technical would provide much greater success.

A paradigm shift took place in leadership thinking. The leadership role was no longer to coerce and control the workforce but to motivate the workforce. Good industrial leadership meant privileging employee social and psychological welfare over controlling their behaviour. New technology in the coal industry had brought in new work practices, initially inspired by scientific management, which were causing many difficulties. Trist and Bamford designed and restructured working relationships, creating autonomous self-regulating teams, which they called 'composite work-groups'. Workers gained satisfaction from completing whole tasks together in teams, and were paid team bonuses on what they achieved together. This was the antithesis of the Controller leadership approach that deconstructs tasks and divides labour, in the name of rational efficiency, but does not account for the human aspect and the benefits of teamwork. Trist and Bamford's (1951) work proved very successful and offered a model that was widely copied, particularly in Scandinavia.

A cultural ideology swept across the USA and Western Europe; democratic societies that protected and enhanced individual freedom would underpin the betterment of the human race. In the workplace, these democratizing forces were matched with an economic striving for socio-technical systems, which took Human Relations into account.

1960s Human Potential Movement

The 1960s gave birth to a new counter-culture, further challenging any notion of Controller and authoritarian leadership. Emerging from the beat generation, the human potential movement formed at Esalen, California, bringing together a diverse group of psychologists and alternative thinkers:

> ... including Fritz Perls, Timothy Leary, Abraham Maslow, and Carl Rogers who constituted a kind of brain trust for the Esalen Institute in Big Sur, California. Esalen was a great cross-roads, beginning in 1962 when it opened, for these already established scientists of human consciousness who were joined by people like Carlos Castenada, Alan Watts, Ken Kesey, Jack Kerouac, Maharishi Mahesh Yogi and Aldous Huxley, all who took an interest in re-awakening the life of feeling ... Esalen is remembered for generating what came to be called the human potential movement. (Cobb, 2005: 256)

A counter-culture flourished and the personal growth movement (Maslow, 1968; Rogers, 1961) epitomized the new focus on the self and on 'feeling', completely counter to the previous dominant ideas that rationality and science were the progressive forces. This counter-culture in its less extreme forms soon became mainstream. Salvation would no longer come through organized religion, but through personal therapy techniques, eastern philosophy and spirituality that would reveal the 'true-self'. Authority and the Controller leadership discourse was being openly challenged both in the workplace and politically. The 'patriotic' Vietnam War was undermined by students and activists, as new media technology bringing instant film reports meant that for the first time the horror of war was shown to the masses at home, and many rebelled, eventually creating a movement so strong that the war was ended.[1] A counter-cultural movement arose and peaked in social unrest of 1968, that created a wave of social change, including change in the workplace:

> Boltanski and Chiapello (2006) write of the emergence of a third 'new spirit' of capitalism that emerged as a response to social and artistic critiques of capitalism in France following the social unrest of spring 1968. Capitalism absorbed these critiques by appropriating their demands for personal authenticity and emancipation, making them central to the tenets of its 'new spirit' that promised managers work that would excite and provide security and a moral framework for their work in project-based organizations that are flatter, leaner and more flexible. (Cullen, 2009: 1243)

In the late 1960s the 'self' became an icon, which required nurturing. Collective activity became a struggle for identity and equal opportunity. New social movements such as feminism, the environmental movement and the peace movement grew and their influence shifted from the politics of the social to the politics of identity (Castells, 1997; Diana and Eyerman, 1992; McCarthy and Zald, 1987; Melucci, 1989). The slogan 'the personal is political', highlighted this cultural shift.

As the workplace became an increasingly important site of community and identity formation, so personal growth became aligned to workplace ideology, supported by the Human Relations movement. Abraham Maslow was a key influence as management theorists took on board his work on self-actualization:

> Early research into the psychology of work undertaken in the 1950s stressed communication processes and individual adjustment needs and worker motivation. Following Maslow's hierarchy of needs schema (1954, 1956) researchers tried to find ways in which workers' higher needs, for self-esteem and self-actualization, could be met at work. (Casey, 1995: 79)

Maslow's work was formative and popular, leading to research in participative and democratic leadership to improve worker motivation. Healthy relations between individuals and groups, and taking a developmental model of human potential, harnessing social and psychological theories, became mainstream organizational preoccupations. The Human Relations movement reflected

---

[1] This lesson has been learnt by political leaders. In the Iraq and Afghanistan conflicts strict media control was put in place to prevent the public from seeing American casualties or brutal scenes of war inflicted by the USA/Allies.

the personal growth explosion, privileging the emotions and personal identity. This was fed by the socially pervasive 'therapeutic culture'.

The Triumph of the Therapeutic

Therapeutic culture pervaded the West, transcending the therapist's couch and colonizing all aspects of life (Giddens, 1982; Lasch, 1979). The workplace became the modern site for community, a place to develop relationships, self-esteem and identity. Under the Controller leadership discourse people exchanged labour and time for money. In the post-1960s workplace people wanted a better quality of life, and this meant financial rewards, better working conditions and also the opportunity to develop themselves at work. Employees would no longer be cogs-in-the-wheel of the machine; they were emotional beings, not rational objects. Change was needed to address the cold rhetoric of scientific management and the dehumanizing aspects of modernity. Social and economic conditions changed, a prosperous period of growth was coupled with social transformation. This meant a new discourse of leadership was required, a discourse that resonated with the changing times. The Therapist leadership discourse was born.

The American psychologist Philip Rieff announced in 1966 'The Triumph of the Therapeutic', claiming that therapy wasn't any longer a psychological practice but a culture that had migrated from the therapist's couch, to a culture that now dominated society. Critiques of therapy culture claim this has led to an 'ever-widening definition of psychological distress' which requires some form of therapeutic intervention (Furedi, 2003: 111). Furedi calls this an age of traumas, syndromes, disorders and addictions, which give rise to a culture of fear and vulnerability, and the pathologization of emotions. In turn this has led to a huge increase in counsellors, therapists and self-help books, to offer expert help with these burgeoning problems. Therapeutic culture has gone beyond the realm of treating the suffering, and those supporting this culture claim that 'Therapy is too good to be left to the ill' (Dineen, 1999). Therapy has gone beyond treating the ill in four ways:

1 The definition of 'illness' became much broader with new 'illnesses' being recognized such as post-traumatic stress disorder, attention deficit disorder, multiple personality disorder. These are syndromes rather than illnesses and with them huge rises in diagnostic rates (and interventions) took place.

2 Other areas of 'ordinary' life, one's self-esteem, relationships, bringing up
   children, all became potential areas of concern, and therefore areas
   accessible to therapeutic intervention.

3 Recognized 'illnesses' such as depression found a much wider constituency.

4 What in the past was understood to be grief, misery or melancholy
   became treatable illnesses, such as depression and anxiety, all encouraged
   by the pharmaceutical industry. The results were a mass market for
   treatments such as Prozac and Valium, and also therapeutic interventions.
   In Britain depression accounted for 1% of the population born before the
   First World War, 5% in the Second World War, and jumped to 10–15% in
   the 1960s. In the USA, 20% of the population suffer from prolonged states
   of depression at some stage in their lives (Furedi, 2003).

5 Therapy culture entered healthy social arenas and became 'a way of
   thinking rather than a way of curing psychic disorder' (Bellah et al., 1996
   in Furedi, 2003).

Fitzpatrick writes:

> A therapeutic culture has become pervasive. It is apparent in the
> emotionally charged speeches of the Prime Minister, in the conduct of
> royal funerals, in the numerous confessional TV shows, in the shelves full
> of self-help manuals in every bookshop. It seems that everybody now
> speaks the language of 'self-esteem' and 'support'; displays of emotional
> incontinence and claims of victimhood are guaranteed social approval.
> (2000: 64)

The 1960s, which led to the explosive growth of the Human Potential movement, helped create a culture that Lasch (1979) describes as individualistic
and narcissistic. The focus on identity and self-realization has been successful in liberating individuals and their particular collective movements from
the baggage of traditional, religious and social constraints. However, as
Moskowitz (2001) points out, the progressive forces which focused on identity and aimed at personal liberation and acceptance of diversity led to
something quite different: 'The identity politics of the 1960s laid the ground
for America's obsession with feelings in the 1970s'. Frank Furedi (2003)
argues that the optimistic 1960s became less radical and less optimistic, creating today's therapeutic culture of vulnerability. Heelas (1996: 146) writes
that the torrent of advice from the self-help industry 'generates a climate of
discontent', while Beradi (2009) claims that the 'happiness imperative' (that we
should all seek to be happy) also creates a sense of failure, as the bombardment

of advertising, TV and films and social demands that we should strive to be happy leaves us feeling even more wounded, as it is impossible to live up to the illusive demand and media images of happiness and success.

When researching my book *Coaching and Mentoring: A Critical Text* (Western, 2012), I explained that coaching had become successful because it successfully bridged two facets that therapeutic culture has produced: the wounded self and the celebrated self.

Wounded Self and Celebrated Self [2]

In the workplace the Therapist leader was expected to work with emotions, and this meant to work with both the wounded self and the celebrated self.

Wounded Self

> The 'wounded self' refers to a self that is damaged, fragmented or emotionally hurt and is the domain of psychotherapists and psychologists. Psychotherapists look for the 'wounded self' – this is their expertise, their business – in order to offer therapeutic intervention (the talking cure) and reparation. (Western, 2012: 4)

Modern identity is to have a part of oneself that is a 'wounded self'. From childhood to adulthood we are working on our 'damaged' selves, overcoming our emotional injuries, our loneliness, our obsessions, addictions, depressions and anxieties. We use friends, family, partners and an array of therapeutic experts to confide in, to talk about our issues. Critics claim that the therapeutic culture administers to, and also produces, this wounded self.

Other scholars challenge this polarized view, claiming that a complex, modern society does produce real psychological problems:

> The vast differentiation of modern life, the multiplication of roles and social masks each person is called to assume and the burdens of making choices quickly create enormous psychological tensions. (Melucci, 1989: 141)

Melucci claims the continual diffusion and penetration of therapy into daily life is a symptom of these tensions and provides necessary support to deal

---

[2] See the Introduction to Western (2012) for a full account of the wounded and celebrated self.

with them (1989: 134). Anthony Giddens (1991) goes further, believing that therapy actually helps make the modern individual:

> This is where therapeutic cultures can be helpful, according to Giddens, since they provide both solace and resources for self-formation. Solace is needed in his view, because the modern self is much more insecure. ... Therapeutic cultures, in his view, do not destroy the self, and its relationships, but make them. (Swan, 2006: 4)

Nikolas Rose also observes how therapy can help individuals' well-being:

> ... the psychotherapies of normality, which promulgate new ways of planning life and approaching predicaments, and disseminate new procedures for understanding oneself and acting upon oneself to overcome dissatisfactions, realize one's potential, to gain happiness and achieve autonomy. (Rose, 1999: 89–90)

The 'wounded self' is a feature of modern society, whether a therapy culture helps individuals or whether it reinforces the creation of the 'wounded self', and with it a 'victim-society' is debated.

Celebrated Self

A contemporary turn in the 21st century has been the growth of the celebrated self. This has been fuelled by individualism and positive psychology (Seligman) and New Age spirituality. The celebrated self offers a hopeful optimization of the self, the potential to grow and improve our happiness and well-being. Arising from the human potential movement, at the turn of the 21st century the celebrated self has become a central idea of self-hood, which is very strong in the USA. The central idea of the celebrated self is that within ourselves lies a true and authentic self, which if it is celebrated, listened to and nurtured will allow us to achieve deep happiness and great success. Cobb explains:

> Trust your feelings, have faith in yourself, follow your bliss, do your own thing, listen to your inner child, do what feels right, be true to yourself. These messages are offered as formulas for salvation. ... Therapeutic values that are worthy of organizing one's life around, such as self-esteem, self-fulfilment, self-realization and self-expression have come to be accepted as axiomatic, occupying the normative heights once controlled by such counter values as self-discipline, self-control and self-denial. (Cobb, 2005: 252)

The gurus of the self-help movement, once counter-cultural actors, have paradoxically found themselves as key influencers in the world of business and leadership:

> Heelas pays much attention to the 'prosperity wing' of the New Age whose trainers, writers and consultants have assumed the role of clergy in enabling people, especially business people, to experience spirituality. (Carrette and King, 2005: 1246)

Adam Bright writes of Echart Tolle, a New Age guru:

> He breathes in. He breathes out. He waits. Something comes, and he leans over the desk to write the words that will form the core of his teaching: 'you are not your mind' … Tolle borrows from nearly every tradition (spiritual and religious) but does not belong to any of them. (This institutional nimbleness helps him win followings in unexpected communities; I'm told he's especially popular with the MBA crowd). (2009: 11–16)

Stephen Covey became a best-selling author with *The 7 Habits of Highly Effective People* (1989), and then cleverly bridged the gap between self-help, new spirituality and managerialism. Micklethwait and Wooldridge (1996) reported that Covey's management training business employed 700 people, had declared revenues of around $100 million and clients comprising 50% of the Fortune 500 companies in 1996. In an appendix to *The 8th Habit* (2004), Covey reports that the numbers employed had risen to 2000 and the client base included 90% of the Fortune 500.

Cullen (2009: 1246) offers a textual analysis of Covey's work, showing how *7 Habits* clearly exhibits the components of 'self-spirituality', mapping his work against Heelas's (1996) key definitions of New Age teachings:

> 1) *Your lives do not work:* Covey accentuates disappointment space as described above. After stressing eight 'human challenges' in the foreword, Covey begins the first full chapter with a set of quotes from individuals suffering from various personal and professional disappointments.
>
> 2) *You are gods and goddesses in exile:* The social and conventional world limits our capabilities. The inner authentic self is the only source of true happiness and sanctity. Covey warns against the 'social mirror' of the world, urging readers to act according to principles and values and not social expectations.
>
> 3) *Let go/drop it:* People have learned to behave in certain ways on the basis of their upbringing. Covey advocates a path by which individuals can utilize the space between stimulus and response to *choose* their actions.

> (Cullen, 2009: 1246)

As this reveals, the Therapist leadership discourse is alive and well in the twenty-first century, absorbing both the subjective and the spiritual turn. Therapist leaders offer solace to the wounded self, and motivation to the celebrated self. To be a leader of people today, is to have the insights and qualities of a coach or therapist.

Therapeutic Culture Enters the Workplace

With the loss of traditional sites of community, the extended family, life-long neighbours and the demise of the Church, the workplace has become an ever-important communal site where social engagements and psychological tensions are played out. The new Therapist leader had to be capable to motivate employees, and to support entrepreneurial hi-performing, motivated employees (the celebrated self). They also had to offer solace to the distressed, the over-worked, to deal with difficult group dynamics, and to manage emotional discontent in the workplace (the wounded self). The Therapist leader required therapeutic expertise. They received this through management and leadership training programmes filled with the therapeutic discourse, drawing on Maslow's hierarchy, psychometrics, self-awareness and group dynamic training. This training was supported by an array of experts who entered the workplace.

Initially a positive movement, aiming to motivate and help employees self-actualize, it began to reflect the tensions and culture of wider society. Concerns grew as the use of psychology and emotional management, drawing on therapeutic language and techniques, was being used to manipulate workers in order to increase productivity. Barley and Kunda (1992: 375) write:

> Managers all the way down to first line supervisors were said to require communication skills, sensitivity in interpersonal relationships, methods for instilling if not inspiring motivation and knowledge of how to mould the dynamics of a group.

The use of emotional labour and emotional management (Hochschild, 1983) is seen as a worrying development where employees are pressed to utilize their emotions in a performance to help sell goods, for example. The Human Relations movement opened the way for leaders to become active agents in the management (and manipulation) of the emotions. The therapeutic technologies of liberation were now seen as technologies for control and domination. Zaleznik (1997: 56) cites a CEO who likened the leadership role to running a clinic:

> Nevertheless, the Human Relations school was right in that organizations are indeed social systems and are arenas for inducing cooperative behaviour. As such, they are quintessentially human and fraught with all the frailties and imperfections associated with the human condition. So much so, in fact,

that one especially wise chief executive officer once commented, 'Anyone in charge of an organization with more than two people is running a clinic.'

Nikolas Rose (1990) points out: 'The management of subjectivity has become a central task for the modern organization'. The contemporary leadership role has shifted from leading a functional machine, to leading a therapeutic clinic, and managing the emotional lives of their employees.

To be a successful leader is to expertly manage emotions, not only the emotions of others, but also the leader's own. Heelas (2002) describes how managers/leaders have to develop an ethic of self-work in order to adapt themselves to changing others, and changing environments. The emotional work of leadership entails engaging, understanding, intervening and managing emotions in the different contexts set out in Box 23.

Box 23   The Emotional Work of Leadership

Leaders work with their emotions and those of others, in the following ways:

- **Self-work***: managing personal emotions and developing reflective insight to cope with challenging work situations.

- **Relational-work**: managing the emotions that arise through demanding relationships with peers, followers and their seniors.

- **Team-work***: managing the emotions that are evoked in team dynamics – e.g. envy, rivalry and competition.

- **Authority-work***: there are specific psychodynamics and emotions involved in the authority and power relationships that leadership has to address.

- **Diversity-work***: managing the emotions of difference is an increasingly important task. Globalization increasingly puts leaders in positions of working with diversity, e.g. gender, ethnicity, age, physical-ability, class, and also the unseen everyday differences. Diversity issues engage emotions, and leaders have to manage and work with them.

- **Cultural-work***: cultural forces place emotional demands on the role of being a leader. Tensions arise pending on the particular culture leaders work within. Sometimes they have to resist these cultures if they are negatively impacting on work, at other times embrace them. Leaders have to manage the emotional tensions that arise within and between competing organizational cultures.

Emotional Intelligence

The therapeutic culture within the leadership discourse has blossomed. Emotional intelligence (EI), popularized by Goleman (1995), has become an everyday expression and today's 'good' leader is expected to have a high emotional intelligence. Mayer and Salovey, who first used the concept and term Emotional Intelligence, describe EI as:

> A type of social intelligence that involves the ability to monitor one's own and others' emotions, to discriminate among them and to use the information to guide one's thinking and actions. (1993: 433)

EI has been changed in many directions but these five headings are common to its essence:

1 *Self-awareness*: Observing yourself and recognizing a feeling as it happens.

2 *Managing emotions*: Handling feelings so that they are appropriate; realizing what is behind a feeling; finding ways to handle fears and anxieties, anger and sadness.

3 *Motivating oneself*: Channelling emotions in the service of a goal; emotional self-control; delaying gratification and stifling impulses.

4 *Empathy*: Sensitivity to others' feelings and concerns and taking their perspective; appreciating the differences in how people feel about things.

5 *Handling relationships*: Managing emotions in others; social competence and social skills.

Essentially EI has been developed by Daniel Goleman and others to fit the business mindset and highlights the use of the management of emotions as the primary tool of the leader. Many assessment and training techniques are available to support this type of leadership work. Mayer and Salovey have criticized Goleman for his expansion and distortion of the term and theory they founded:

> What makes you smarter is understanding your own feelings better, argues John Mayer. Goleman has broadened the definition of emotional intelligence to such an extent that it no longer has any scientific meaning or utility and is no longer a clear predictor of outcome. (cited in Schwartz, 2000: 296)

The contemporary popularity of EI reflects trends in American human psychology as it offers a positivistic, empirically measurable and developmental model (even if, as Mayer points out, the science is unscientific). The subject can measure their personal levels of EI and attend training to improve their intelligence. This is seductive and naturally creates a marketplace in assessment and training tools and offers HR leaders the measurable outcomes they need to justify their budget expenditure. EI cleverly links the competing leadership discourses, combing both the scientific-rational and the emotional rhetoric (Barley and Kunda, 1992), which make those on both sides of the debate happy. There is, however, a growing scepticism about measuring EI and its unsubstantiated claims (Mayer et al., 2000).

The McDonaldization of Emotions

Emotional management is the attempt to manage employees' emotions to improve productivity. In his paper 'Emotional balancing' Huy advocates that 'to maintain operational continuity in a radical change context, recipients' emotions also have to be carefully managed' (2002: 33). Huy, in a three-year research study, praises middle managers' ability to manage competing emotional demands as they experienced a severe downsizing of the workforce. He praises them for working 80–100 hours a week, over a three-year period, 'to implement change whilst simultaneously attending to their work-groups' operational continuity and their subordinates' emotional stability' (Huy, 2001: 49). Huy calls this 'emotional balancing' but this ignores questions about the emotional balance between work and home life, and the state of these managers' mental and physical health after this long slog. The middle managers, he claims, balanced the emotional pressures coming from senior management, and from below, their reportees. At one point a memo was sent from senior management to middle management, articulating that 'expressions of cynicism will not be tolerated. We are in positions of leadership and must display enthusiasm at all times to everyone' (p. 49). Huy goes on to describe a manager leading an 'emotion-attending' training session which followed a morning's communication briefing regarding turbulent changes where job losses were raised. Huy writes that, despite his scepticism of 'touchy feely' approaches, these subsided when he interviewed workers following this session. In the 'emotional attending' session employees were asked to draw their collective experiences of the work situation: 'Anxious people in lifeboats, caravans lost in deserts and big thunderstorms began to appear and were displayed around the room and individuals started to realize how similar they were and they started to laugh and joke about them' (p. 52). The consultant running the session then showed them a model of transition and explained how it was 'normal and common to have these feelings' (p. 52). Huy goes on to draw on psychological literature to support the notion that expressing one's feelings is healthy. In Huy's study, he says the outcome of these sessions produced more work from the employees and less absenteeism. However, the evidence linking these types of 'emotions sharing' sessions with increased productivity is very weak. The empirical evidence for the success of therapy or that expressing one's feelings improves mental health is contested (Eysenck and Hans, 1953; Masson, 1990). The superficiality of an afternoon's 'emotional session' is unlikely to have any deep personal impact and, worse, can create cynicism. It is a weakness throughout the management literature that the successful claims regarding emotional intelligence and emotional management are accepted with little critical attention. Writing as an experienced psychotherapist, it is difficult for me to hear management trainers and coaches who make outlandish claims about their 'life-changing', transformational programmes. Human change is hard, personal change is a struggle, emotional patterns go deep. As all practising therapists know, change occurs but it is often slow, arduous and not guaranteed.

Emotional labour is 'to create a publicly observable facial and bodily display' (Hochschild, 1983: 7) or 'to mask all emotions and intention behind bland smiling and agreeable public faces' (Jackall, 1988: 128). The aim is an attempt to create the correct company persona. R. Janie Constance writes about best leadership practice and cites the Chief Executive of Yum Brands (Taco Bell, KFC, Pizza Hut, etc.) as an example: 'Each person is trained to be a customer maniac. Yums' goal is to train all 750,000 [a global workforce] to have a customer maniac mindset' (Constance, 2003: 47). There is nothing in her article to suggest the coercion involved in this process of getting low-paid employees to learn how to perform the emotional labour required to be a 'customer maniac'. The Yum employees are rewarded through patronizing tokens of recognition that are described as best practice in this article, e.g. prizes and email congratulations. This is reminiscent of the discredited behavioural therapy used in psychiatric institutions (Goffman, 1961), e.g. cigarettes were given for 'good' behaviour and were withdrawn for 'bad' behaviour. The employees are expected to mirror the Tayloristic, uniform and controlled production approach, with a *McDonaldization of emotions*, to create a monocultural workforce of 'customer maniacs', eliminating global difference: give the customer a uniform burger with a uniform smile, and a uniform 'Have a nice day'.

Executive Coaches: Therapeutic Experts for the Workplace[3]

The growth of coaching in recent years shows how the Therapist discourse retains its power in the workplace, and it has a particular role in

---

[3] For an in-depth account of coaching see Western (2012).

shaping today's Therapist leaders. Coaching is clearly a manifestation of the 'talking cure':

> Two people sat in a room talking. One charges the other for their time and skills. The 'expert' listens to the 'client' and is expected to help her/him, hence the financial exchange. This scenario describes a number of activities, for example, executive coaching, life coaching, counselling, psychotherapy or individual consultancy. While these activities have a different emphasis, what they have in common is a direct lineage to what became known through the work of Sigmund Freud as the 'talking cure', i.e. psychoanalysis. (Western, 2006: 31–4)

Coaching has become big industry and is particularly focused on leadership.

> What is clear is that the market has spoken. Many of the world's most admired corporations, from GE to Goldman Sachs, invest in coaching. Annual spending on coaching in the United States is estimated at roughly $1 billion. (Sherman and Freas, 2004: 83)

Why Is Coaching Such A Success Story?

The Therapist leader has a very difficult task and a new form of help was needed: a specialized expert who could help the leader manage their own emotional lives at work, and the emotional lives of the individuals and teams they led. Western (2012) explains the explosive rise of coaching in the late 20th century because it bridges the therapeutic divide, addressing both the wounded self and celebrated self: coaching for motivational and performance enhancement and helping individuals to live more fulfilled lives (the celebrated self) whilst also offering a supportive and listening ear to the lonely CEO, to the overwhelmed employee, to the tearful HR Director who has just gone through a divorce (the wounded self). Coaching has also became the postmodern confessional (Western, 2012), providing a much-needed space in the workplace for employees to be heard by a caring witness, a professional ear. It offers a space to disclose one's innermost desires and problems; a sacred-confidential space. In late modernity it seems we badly need a confessional space, and the workplace lacked this until the arrival of coaching:

> Confession is deep rooted in the Western cultural psyche, and has taken on new populist forms in the past two decades. Coachees find themselves often unwittingly confessing their desire and/or anxieties to a coach. (Western, 2012: 147)

Box 24   Executive Coaching: Therapy Culture in the Workplace

1. Coaching: Bridging the wounded and celebrated self

Coaching is a talking cure for our times; it utilizes therapeutic techniques to bridge the wounded self of therapeutic culture, allowing clients to work on their issues, to undertake reparation and reflective work (the wounded self).

Coaching also works on the celebrated self. Drawing on positive psychology, New Age and Eastern spirituality, and a bricolage of techniques and approaches, e.g. NLP, CBT, solution-focused coaching, all of these aim to help the individual discover, celebrate and harness their authentic inner selves, to attain the success and happiness to which they are entitled.

2. Postmodern Confessional

Coaching provides a new site for individuals to confess and to redeem themselves. It offers a contemporary replacement for the 20th century dominant confessional characters of (a) the pathologizing therapist – 'you are wounded and if you tell me all, I can alleviate your pain' – or (b) the powerful priest – 'tell me your sins and as God's representative I can offer you redemption'. The coach does not have the same social power as the priest or therapist, so they offer a less authoritarian and more egalitarian and collaborative confessional. The postmodern confessional is a much more forgiving space, and a space of mutual exploration, a space where the client creates themselves through the process of confessing, beginning with sharing what's wrong, telling of their disharmony and of their secret desires. Redemption that comes from within the client, simply through sharing and confessing unhappiness and unspoken hopes and desires, is a liberating process, one that can lead to sense-making and also to action to put something right, or do something to fulfil oneself.

Leaders are often lonely; their domestic lives may be as busy as their work lives, and who has the time or the emotional space to listen in today's manic world? In my coaching experience, the coaching space at some point always becomes a confessional space. Clients feel the compulsion to confess, and this is a very healthy use of coaching, albeit an unspoken one.

Coaching has other lineages and influences as well as the confessional, and in my book *Coaching and Mentoring: A Critical Text* (2012) I offer a genealogy of coaching, tracing links back to the premodern helping relationships and to friendship itself. Coaching is not so much a new practice, but is better understood as a hybrid of practices, merged to produce an adaptive postmodern form of professional helping.

The Coaching Sphinx

> Coaching has emerged from a multitude of personal dyadic helping relationships, beginning with friendship. Like a mythical sphinx, a coach has the head of a friend, the body of a psychotherapist, the feet of a manager, the tail of a consultant and the face of priest. (Western, 2012: 159)

A leader's role is filled with ambiguity, with diverse and hybrid demands, and requires a flexible expert to help them in their challenging roles. This hybrid practice fits well for 21st century Therapist leaders, who need coaches who can listen, reflect, be sounding boards, motivate them, offer them insights, help them think about strategy. Coaches offer a variety of approaches but the best coaches do one thing well; they help leaders make sense of and process their experiences. By doing this they allow the leader to think about their experience, and to return to the workplace more integrated and with a greater capacity to relate to others thoughtfully and in a contained way, rather than just react to them.

Figure 10.3   The Sphinx of Tahargo (Egyptian, 680 BC, British Museum, London)

Coaching Leaders

Coaching (therapeutic) skills are also becoming essential for today's managers and leaders. Company cultures are now being told that they should embrace 'coaching cultures', that they should become leader–coaches. This website reflects this position:

> Coaching is becoming a new model for leadership. A leader–coach actively works with their staff to help them be more productive and satisfied. Coaching improves the quality of managerial ability, which subsequently improves employee and customer satisfaction. Coaching really is a win/win. (www.odysseycoaching. com, accessed 12 September 2006)

The 'leader–coach' is perhaps the final confirmation, if needed, that the Therapist leadership discourse remains alive and well in the 21st century.

21st Century Therapist Leadership

The Therapist leadership discourse had been the dominant leadership discourse from the 1960s until it was overtaken in the 1980s by the Messiah discourse, discussed in the following chapter. However, it remains a strong leadership discourse, evidenced by the rise in coaching and a continued focus on subjectivity and identity at work. Eva Moskowitz (2001) claimed that therapy was a new religion and cited that in the 1990s Americans spent $69 billion a year managing their feelings and attending to their emotional health, and as this chapter makes clear, a therapy culture remains endemic in the workplace.

A populist example expressing the therapist discourse is Dr Noel Nelson's e-book with Harvard, *Make More Money by Making Your Employees Happy*. Nelson is a clinical psychologist importing therapeutic techniques to create happy employees to make money, making the case that 'happier workers are more productive':

> … companies that effectively appreciate employee value enjoy a return on equity & assets more than *triple* that experienced by firms that don't. When looking at *Fortune*'s '100 Best Companies to Work For', stock prices rose an average of 14% per year from 1998–2005, compared to 6% for the overall market. (Nelson, 2012; cited by Cooper, 2012)

She offers examples of leaders drawing on the Therapist discourse:

> Paul O'Neil took the reigns of Alcoa in 1987, the world's leading producer of aluminum; O'Neil announced that his sole priority was to increase

worker safety. A shock to his board room. O'Neil understood, however, that safety was a major concern for his workers. Over the next 13 years employee productivity soared as accident rates decreased from roughly one per week per plant to some plants going years without an accident. When O'Neil stepped away just over a decade later, Alcoa's annual income had grown 500%! (Cooper, 2012)

This simple equation 'happy employees are more productive employees' may seem like a win–win for all, yet connecting happiness and profit can also be manipulative and problematic. Nelson offers another example, where Starbucks chose to train staff to manage difficult customer situations rather than punish them for getting stressed with customers. She writes, 'If you put the compassion first the profits will follow'. It was not compassion that drove Starbucks to train staff better, it was utilitarianism, and common sense, i.e. better customer service means better business. Employees who feel they are being emotionally manipulated soon become cynical, and there is always a tension between the Therapist leadership discourse promoting employee welfare and happiness and the business demand to increase profit and productivity. There can be a win–win, but only if both issues are addressed explicitly and with transparency, otherwise attempts to engage employees emotionally can quickly backfire.

In a postmodern, post-industrial world, subjectivity and identity are at the heart of the human condition and in the workplace. We live in vulnerable and turbulent times that require emotionally sophisticated leaders to manage this vulnerability (Dartington, 2010). Employees work with cognition and affect, they have to bring themselves to work rather than get paid for their labour, and in return they demand better support and opportunities for personal growth and identity formation to take place. The Therapist leadership discourse is especially important in this context, and also especially important at a middle manager and team leader level, as these leaders are best placed to offer individuals and teams interpersonal, supportive and relational leadership.

Box 25 Case Study: The Two Sides of Therapist Leadership

A case study of a multidisciplinary mental health team

Working in a multidisciplinary CAMHS team (child and adolescent mental health team) for ten years, provided me with a case study that revealed the two sides of the Therapist leadership discourse. The team consisted of consultant psychiatrists, social workers, speech therapists, psychologists and psychiatric

(Continued)

(Continued)

nurses. The ethos was strongly collaborative and democratic, underpinned with a politically correct ideology, feminism (8–10 members were women) and leftist leanings. Leadership was not a welcome word, it was associated with power over others, and the management function was weak and somewhat derided by clinicians who felt they did the 'real work' and managers didn't understand things well. The work was immensely difficult, as the client group were self-harming, suicidal, had eating disorders and suffered abuse. We were working at the extreme end of mental health and with the marginalized and the extreme urban poor (a northern post-industrial UK inner city in the 1980s).

Each profession had its own hierarchical structure, diverse training backgrounds, and there were huge pay differentials, and yet we worked together doing the same work, delivering assessments, family therapy and psycho-therapeutic interventions. Interestingly, working with emotionally troubled young people, the work is 95% emotional, psychological and social, eradicating the need for the medical model except in the remaining 5% of cases. This put our consultant psychiatrists in a double-bind: they believed in the therapeutic, non-medical approaches such as family therapy (and trained in these methods) but were paid much more than others in the team because of their medical training. To justify their positions they had to abandon their true belief in the therapeutic approach. Also the tension was about power; they invest and train to be 'leaders' in medical settings, and then find themselves as peers to 'lesser' professions such as nursing and psychology. In some multidisciplinary teams, medics assume or are explicitly given the lead; in others they are not. The Therapeutic leadership discourse advocates democratizing approaches, whereas workplaces inherently have hierarchies based on pay and power. When working in a cooperative or a social movement these issues are transparently addressed; when working in the public or private sector the tensions are present but unspoken, and often surface in challenging ways. There was no formally agreed management structure within our team, just a departmental management structure covering four regional teams.

Therapist leadership delivering success

Collectively we worked as therapists and our shared underpinning ethos for organizing the work was the Therapeutic discourse. Initially when these four teams were established they worked with rotating facilitators, who operated democratically, facilitating decision-making to organize our clinical tasks and in doing so, denying the need for leadership. This worked up to a point, but decision-making was slow, progress was arduous, waiting lists grew and general discontent set in. Our team then broke away and internally elected a pair of team leaders, myself (family therapist and nurse) in partnership with a consultant psychiatrist. This partnership worked exceptionally well; as a pair we worked together to push forward important initiatives, supported each other, established better clinical supervision, offered a high-quality client service and lowered the waiting lists. We were highly motivated and engaged, and pioneered interdisciplinary collaborative work with social work and education professionals. The team were relieved that leadership was clear yet collaborative. This Therapist leadership approach, in a democratic and collaborative atmosphere, worked very well. We were very successful as a team, we collaborated and supported each other, we learnt from each other, we shared the burden of the work. For two years we worked mostly as a 'successful and motivated team', an excellent example of Therapist leadership in action.

Chronic Niceness – Acute Nastiness: The Shadow Side of Caring Cultures

However, as a clinical nurse I was leading the team but without a clear mandate. In effect, I was taking a lot of responsibility, I was authorized by the team, but without any clear authority from above, which meant working without the time allocated for managerial tasks, and without remuneration for this role. The consultant psychiatrist I worked with was part-time, leaving me alone working with a large clinical case load of high-risk patients, supervising others, leading team meetings, and organizing regional events. When responsibility is given without authority, roles are not mandated and clear, the work is emotionally stressful, and diverse professional groups have their own agendas, then trouble awaits. Envy and rivalry bubbled beneath the surface, psychologists began to compete with and undermine psychiatrists, other professionals resented being led by a nurse. Nurses and speech therapists felt underpaid and undervalued as they did the same tasks as higher-paid psychologists and psychiatrists.

When a new psychiatrist arrived, bringing with her the traditional medical model (Controller leadership) in contrast to the Therapist leadership approach, the problems really began. She resented being led by a nurse and saw her role as team leader. The focus shifted from the task of helping the children and families to avoiding this difficult emotional work and focused on in-fighting. Two psychiatrists began competing, and the power agenda shifted for the whole team. Previously good working relationships fragmented and the psychiatrists united – too destructive to fight each other they defended their position and turned on me and others who challenged them, but in a non-direct way. The results were that stress levels went through the roof, and three excellent team members were 'forced' to leave in very unhappy circumstances.

What is interesting about the caring professions is how they can be extremely cruel places; the shadow side of 'chronic niceness' in the caring professions is 'acute nastiness'. This shadow side is found in religious organizations, charities and workplaces where caring and collaboration are at the centre of the work.

(Continued)

(Continued)

My experience is that when working in a factory, on construction sites, or the business world for example; competition is much more explicit, and gets overtly expressed. It can be hard but it is more open, whereas the 'therapeutic' ethos of collaboration and caring suppresses competition, envy and rivalry and they emerge in very destructive ways, that often severely damage individuals who become scapegoats for a distorted dynamic.

Those perpetuating such destructive behaviours can never admit to themselves that they are behaving in such negative ways, as their identities are so tied up in being 'caring' and doing good. Therapist leadership demands collaborative and democratic work, which means to reveal one's strengths and weaknesses. Yet as Woodhouse and Pengelly (1991: 29) point out:

> If collaborative work is to take place in a group, each member is confronted with threats to his sense of 'self'. This sense of self is their most precious possession. It is bound to be defended stoutly.

Reflections

The therapist leadership discourse requires a clarity of role and authorization to work well. Therapist leadership in practice creates many challenges as it works with the emotions in the group. This requires excellent leadership and active followership, to contain the emotional dynamics that arise between team members. A lack of clear leadership creates a lack of containment, and when working with suicidal teenagers, staff need containing leadership more than other workplaces. For two years we succeeded, and this could have continued if the leadership roles were properly mandated, as the ambiguity led to the roles being undermined. Without a leadership that offers psychological containment for staff, the stresses of the work get into the team dynamic, which become toxic. It is with great sadness that I have experienced time and time again how caring workplaces turn from 'chronic niceness to acute nastiness', seriously damaging individual staff members who have been committed to caring for others, and find themselves bullied and discarded without any care at all.

This case study reveals the strengths of the Therapist leadership discourse, providing engagement, support and collaboration in the face of very difficult work. It also reveals the weaknesses, where the Therapist leadership discourse idealizes democratic processes while at the same time denying envy, competition and rivalry. These bubble away beneath the surface, creating unspoken tensions, and often emerging with explosive force like a pent-up volcanic explosion, doing a lot of damage.

Conclusion

The Therapist leadership discourse brought a more humane approach to the workplace, chiming with the times, but it was also a discourse that focused intently on improving productivity, and it supported huge economic growth in the West. Therapist leaders aimed to raise morale, and motivate, democratize and encourage more autonomy, cooperation and teamwork, with the intention to create happier and more engaged individuals and teams. Embracing the pervasive therapeutic culture in wider society, Therapist leadership transformed the workplace culture, particularly between the 1960s and 1980s, from a place of control, domination and rationalization, to one of democratization, engagement and collaboration. The underpinning unconscious metaphor for the organization is the 'therapeutic clinic' where leaders act to ensure the environment is therapeutic in order that workers maximize their productivity.

> ## Box 26   The Character of the Therapist Leader
>
> The Therapist leader character is a leader who listens, cares and encourages, and is usually a leader who is liked and admired, because they understand, praise and support, and stand by their people. This leader takes care of the team, creating a subtle therapeutic dependency, becoming the unconscious 'good father/mother'; when absent, they are missed. They lead through caring not charisma, and find time to be with team members, but are less focused on strategy and less good at organizational politics. They are 'development devotees', believing in personal growth as a way of being, always trying to develop themselves and their team, and are fond of the latest literature on leadership development, organizational and positive psychology and coaching approaches. They advocate psychological feedback and team process sessions using Myers–Briggs, 360 degree feedback, and other psychometric tests. These leaders work on the sole premise that people are the most important asset.

The Demise of the Therapist Leadership Discourse

The Therapist discourse ran into problems in the late 1970s. Despite America's cultural and economic dominance, which placed them as leaders in the field of management thinking and practice, the country's economic performance was falling behind and faced a severe challenge. A new leadership discourse was needed to stimulate organizations as they faced an increasingly competitive and turbo-charged, global economy. The attention of Therapist leadership was too focused on individual motivation and teamwork. What was missing were leaders who could develop company visions, be strategically agile and focused on the bigger picture. The Therapist leadership discourse also struggles to address the big and complex ethical challenges such as sustainability and corporate responsibility. Lasch believes that 'therapeutic morality encourages the permanent suspension of the moral sense' (1979: 389) which supports the view that the Therapist leadership discourse is that of the technocrat, aiming to create efficiency through skilfully manipulating and influencing emotions and relationships. Human Relations theorists helped the passage of individualism and the pervasive therapeutic culture into the workplace, which brought with it liberal permissiveness and the rise of individualism, which undermined socially consensual morality. This left a moral vacuum, or at least a confused and unclear view of what constituted morality.

Global corporations and large public sector organizations such as vast hospital complexes required more than good people skills. Companies were becoming more global, and work patterns were changing from institutionalized teams and departments that suited the Therapist leader to more fluid and knowledge-based work that required nomadic workers, flexibility and temporary project teams, which meant the leader's relation with their team was less stable; people were less available for therapist leadership approaches. The therapist leadership discourse remains powerful and vital, especially in 'people-services' such as education and retail, for example, and is more relevant and suited to middle management and team leadership roles, and stable organizations. The Therapist leadership discourse is embedded in our social structures; we now expect our leaders to be humane and relationally skilled in handling their employees. However, Therapist leadership alone would not be sufficient to deal with the new challenges ahead.

The surge of new technology and the focus on knowledge meant that new organizational forms emerged and a new leadership was required to influence these fast-changing environments. The American economy was falling behind rising Asian Tiger economies and the Therapist leadership discourse was no longer sufficient to deliver on its own. A leader who could utilize culture as the mode of control and influence and who could offer inspirational leadership to dispersed employees was required. The following two chapters describe the leadership discourses that emerged to compensate for the gaps left by the Therapist and Controller discourses, as the workplace changed once again.

Suggested Readings

- Binney, G., Wilke, G. and Williams, C. (2004) *Living Leadership: A Practical Guide for Ordinary Heroes.* London: Pearson Books.

- Furedi, F. (2003) *Therapy Culture.* London: Routledge.

- Goleman, D. (1995) *Emotional Intelligence: Why It Can Matter More than IQ.* New York: Bantam Books.

- Greenleaf, R. (1977) *Servant Leadership.* Mahwah, NJ: Paulist Press.

- Kets de Vries, M. (2006) *The Leader on the Couch.* San Francisco, CA: Jossey–Bass.

- Maslow, A. (1968) *Toward a Psychology of Being.* New York: Van Nostrand.

- Rieff, P. (1966) *The Triumph of the Therapeutic: Uses of Faith after Freud.* London: Chatto & Windus.

Reflection Points

- Therapist leaders have excellent soft people skills. Do you believe a good leader can operate without some influence from the Therapist discourse?

- The Therapist discourse focuses on individual motivation and psychology, relationships and team dynamics. Team leadership skills are often very challenging. Think of team meetings you have been in, and reflect on the leadership approach: how much Therapist leadership was present?

- What are the weaknesses of the Therapist leadership discourse? Where are the gaps?

Sample Assignment Question

Summarize the Therapist leadership discourse, offering examples of Therapist leaders you have encountered and describing how they led their teams and what was the impact of their leadership approach. Identify both strengths and weaknesses in their leadership approaches.

11 The Messiah Leadership Discourse

Visionary Leaders and Strong Cultures

Figure 11.1 Messiah leadership

Keywords

Transformational leaders

Charisma

Vision and belief

Strong cultures

Loyalty

Conformist cultures

Dynamic engagement

Chapter Structure

- **Introduction**
- **The Context**
- **A Critique of the Transformational Leader**
- **Engineering Culture**
- **Cult-like Cultures**
- **Conclusion**

Introduction

Messiah leaders are charismatic figures and organize the workplace with flattened structures, utilizing culture control to influence employees.

The Messiah leadership discourse resurrected leadership itself. The rhetoric of management became challenged in the early 1980s when the rise in transformational leadership epitomized the new interest in leadership as a cure for workplace ills.

In response to a sharp economic decline in the USA and Europe, and with rising Asian Tiger economies outperforming the West, and also to accommodate the increasing impact of globalization and post-industrial organizations, the old way of leading organizations was no longer sufficient.

The Therapist and Controller discourses simply were not delivering success in this new climate. Messiah leadership very quickly became the dominant leadership discourse. The leaders that emerged were proclaimed as being charismatic, visionary, and able to transform followers and organizational cultures to produce outstanding company success (Peters and Waterman, 1982).

Messiah Leadership

Vision & Culture

L

FFFFFFFFFFFFFFF

Leader & Flat Structure

Figure 11.2   Messiah leadership organizational form

The Messiah discourse signified a shift away from bureaucratic and managerial control (Controller discourse) or therapeutic governance, through motivating and supporting individuals and teams emotionally and psychologically (Therapist discourse). Workers needed to work more independently, to self-manage their work, and this could only be possible through new forms of culture 'control'. Strong cultures were required in which employees could feel they were part of a progressive vision, part of a community, and because they shared the values and vision of the leader they would work long hours and bring their whole selves to work. Motivation and control came from within individuals and from peers who shared norms set by the culture of the company. To establish these strong and seductive cultures, charismatic leaders were required who could set out visions and values persuasively, gaining loyalty and commitment from employees.

Where there is no vision, the people perish:

but he that keepeth the law, happy is he.

Proverbs 29: 18

This proverb speaks to the two sides of Messiah leadership. Speakers on leadership often use the first line of this biblical quote, which reflects the ancient desire for a visionary leader. What they omit is the second line, that sets out the role of followers in relation to the visionary leader. The first part speaks to the universal desire for Messiah leaders to offer visions to save the people. The second part speaks to the role of followers. To 'keep the law' is to follow in obedience, and to feel happy. In contemporary organizations a transformational leader provides the vision, and the follower acquiesces to the conformist cultures that these leaders create, whilst also being 'happy', i.e. the follower is motivated and engaged. Messiahs need disciples, and in spite of the rhetoric of transformational leaders to empower followers, critical approaches reveal that these leaders are the change agents who act on their 'conformist disciples'.

A key difference to the heroic leaders of the past is that these new Messiah leaders did not set out to create a *non-thinking*, obedient and dependent followership. Their task was more complex, because for an organization to be successful followers had to bring their intellect and dynamism to the company. A knowledge economy demanded knowledge workers, not people who were controlled, dependent and behaved without thinking. At the same time a company didn't want too much dissent, too much difference, it wanted homogeneous, agreeable and hardworking employees who could provide conformity across different business sites. Messiah leaders it is claimed created strong organizational cultures that bound workers together on a common mission, motivating followers to work towards a common cause, using all of their abilities. These transformational leaders have been heralded by some as the answer to contemporary organizational dilemmas because they offer new ways to overcome the inertia of bureaucratic forms of traditional organization (Kanter, 1983; Naisbitt, 1982; Ouchi, 1981; Peters and Waterman, 1982). By others they are critiqued as promoting totalizing monocultures, through a process of culture control (Axtel Ray, 1986; Casey, 1995; Kunda, 1992).

This new leadership promised a lot; what it really delivered will now be explored. There is a large gap between reality and rhetoric; what it is claimed these leaders can do and what actually happens in practice are highly contested. The emotive and grandiose rhetoric that underpins this discourse leads to its name, the Messiah leader.

This chapter will critically review the Messiah leadership discourse, tracing its rise and its impact, and challenging its proponents' more extravagant claims. The transformational leader was the leading exponent of this discourse, and is critiqued below, after describing the context in which Messiah leadership arose.

The Context

The late 20th century brought the new challenges of increasing globalization, exponential technological and communication advances and changing social and work conditions that demanded a new leadership discourse. Western economies were in demise and experiencing some shock at being overtaken by Asian Tiger economies. A leader with a greater vision was required, and a new 'heroic leadership' figure arose like a phoenix from the ashes. In the late 1970s the Messiah discourse came to prominence, and a hero leader had been 'resurrected', epitomized by the *transformational leader*.

Leadership theorists point to three areas that influenced the emergence of the new transformational or 'Messiah' leadership and these are set out below, and I also mention a fourth influence.

1. Asian Influence

During the 1970s and 1980s, the Japanese had the world's fastest economic growth, and their phenomenal success, particularly in areas previously dominated by the US economy, e.g. car production, challenged American theorists and practitioners to review what they were doing and to find out what was making the Japanese economy so successful. Ouchi's (1981)

Theory Z is the best-known work that attempted to learn and translate the Japanese model of management and integrate this with the American way of leading and managing companies. Ouchi found that Japanese success was attributed to their collaborative working methods, based on companies working with collectivist cultures. The American/Western axis of individualism was put under scrutiny: Therapist leaders motivating individuals were not producing enough. The Japanese model emphasized strong cultures focusing on family teams, flexibility, quality and service. Loyalty and commitment underpinned these company cultures, which opened up a new way of thinking about organizations. Previously culture was thought of as something a company had, but in the late 1970s (at the same time as the rise of the transformational leader) theorists were viewing 'organizations as cultures'.

A debate over how much of the Japanese success was cultural and how much structural followed. Whitley (1992) claims social, political and economic institutions were more important. Wilkinson (1996) believes that both cultural and institutional theorists overplayed their hands, and that groups of actors embedded in certain cultural, political, economic and institutional contexts have the greater impact. Interest was also shown in Scandinavia, where Volvo's car plants had a long tradition of collaborative working, establishing work-group autonomy and an holistic approach (Berggren et al., 1994). The Japanese economy has struggled more recently and the reversion of Volvo's plants back to less radical and more traditional practices has meant that practitioners' interest in these practices has waned. Like many other management fads, the quality circles, the move towards the 'Japanese social groupism' and Swedish style job-designs had faded. What survived and has grown from the Japanese and Scandinavian experiences is the premise that strong corporate cultures are vital to success. Transformational leadership was deemed as the way to achieve these much sought-after strong cultures.

2. Anthropology Influence

The second influence came through anthropology. Theorists argued that organizations should be viewed socially, as cultures and as constructed systems of meaning, rather than as material structures filled with individuals. This changed the 'social field' of where leadership should aim to influence and act. The emphasis changed from leaders working to control workers through transactional levers (Controller leadership), or on the psychology and dynamics of influencing individuals and teams (Therapist approaches), towards how to influence culture-as-a-whole. Culture would then impact, shape and control how individuals, teams and organizations could be influenced as social systems. To create and shape these cultures, the business world turned to the Messiah leadership discourse.

3. Practitioner Influence

The third influence came through consultants and applied researchers studying leaders in practice. Their arguments were more pragmatic (these consultant–practitioners were also influenced by the Japanese success). The changes in work practices, such as the rise of the knowledge economy, new technology and new globalized forms of organization, had consequences for leaders. The new organizational forms that emerged to address these changes meant that leaders were unable to control or motivate and influence individuals and teams as before. Three main changes made previous leadership practices inadequate: (a) teams became increasingly specialist and their expert and technical knowledge made individuals more autonomous and empowered; (b) flattened hierarchies removed a middle and lower order of therapist team-leaders and supervisory managers who were becoming obsolete; (c) leaders often worked with teams spanning global sites, making face-to-face contact more difficult.

The question arose as to how to lead and influence these newly de-centralized, nomadic, technically specialist and self-managing teams. Peters and Waterman (1982) identified that this de-centralization was not a one-way process as they had imagined. They found that both a centrali-zation and de-centralization occurred in the 'excellent companies' they studied. At the heart of the centralizing tendency was a powerful leader-ship figure forming a culture of excellence. (Peters and Waterman claim they came to find this centralizing leadership figure unexpectedly and reluctantly.) They found that the leader established cultural norms and an ethos that helped enable a de-centralized workforce to self-regulate its activity. Deal and Kennedy's *Corporate Cultures* (1982) and Peters and Waterman's *In Search of Excellence* (1982) became bestsellers, promoting their ideas drawn from practitioners' research.

4. American Social Influence: The Rise of Christian Fundamentalism and Its Influence on Corporate Life

This fourth influence is not found in the mainstream leadership literature, which focuses on what's happening inside of organizations to find its answers, and therefore misses these external social factors.

Chapter 7 describes how the corporate hopes of finding charismatic leaders to create strong cultures mimicked the success of the Christian

Fundamentalist church cultures that grew exponentially during the 1970s and 1980s: a two-way transmission of culture that took place between American Christian Fundamentalism and corporate culture, with each feeding off the other, each learning from the other, with Messiah leadership, strong cultures and loyal devoted followers a central feature of both. Messiah leadership was also affirmed by political leaders of the time. During the 1980s when Messiah and transformational leadership were rising, two political 'Messiahs' were espousing polemic views. US President Ronald Regan, referred to as the crusader by Kengor (2007), oversaw an economic recession turnaround, and the fall of communism. The Christian Right supported Regan, as he preached simple messages with conviction, drawing on his acting background. The American dream, individual freedom, small government, free markets and democracy were his central themes. Here was a living model for Messiah leadership, a screen hero president, taking on the economy and communism, and winning. In the UK in the 1980s Margaret Thatcher triumphed over the trade union movement, fought and won a war in the Falklands, supported Regan in international affairs, and transformed Britain more than any recent prime minster. Regan and Thatcher were polemic leaders, loved or despised depending on your political views. They were celebrated as Messiah leaders for free-marketeers in the business and financial world, and also for many in eastern Europe, who had finally escaped Soviet control and imposed communism. Transformational leadership began through a desire for salvation from economic recession, and flourished during a period of economic growth and political success.

A Critique of the Transformational Leader

The transformational leader was at the centre of the Messiah discourse, yet whilst very successful in terms of rhetoric, influence and popular training courses and book sales, the concept of transformational leadership is clearly problematic. I will now identify key themes arising from the transformational leadership literature, and critique the grandiose claims made for it.

> **Box 27   The Grandiose Claims of Transformational Leadership**
>
> Journals, articles and books continue to peddle omnipotent and exceptional claims about transformational leadership. Here are two examples, found in

two of the best-known management journals, the *Harvard Business Review* and the *Academy Management Journal*:

> Transformational leaders exhibit charismatic behaviours, arouse inspirational motivation, provide intellectual stimulation and treat followers with individual consideration. These behaviours transform their followers helping them to reach their full potential and generate the highest levels in performance. (Dvir et al., 2002: 736)

Changing people is a tough business and always meets resistance; to be able to transform large numbers of people is a grand claim. Bennis and Thomas, in a *Harvard Business Review* article entitled the 'Crucibles of leadership' (2002), write about leaders as though they are magical, with Peter Pan characteristics, and support their theory by using the language of scientific rationalism to add legitimacy to their claims. They discuss four essential skills they believe great leaders possess:

1 the ability to engage others in shared meaning

2 a distinctive and compelling voice

3 a sense of integrity (including a strong set of values)

4 'adaptive capacity', an almost magical ability to transcend adversity, with all its attendant stresses, and to emerge stronger than before.

They continue:

> But by far the most critical skill of the four is what we call adaptive capacity. (Bennis and Thomas, 2002)

The idea that heroes transcend adversity to become stronger is recycled theory. From a philosophical perspective, the existentialist view of Nietzsche clearly sums up the idea of their 'crucible' as 'that which does not destroy me makes me stronger' (Nietzsche, [1899]1996: 297). Nietzsche wrote this in the context of the 'superman' (*Ubermensch*) who, having rid himself of God, overcomes the limitations of man:

> There are no higher men, we are all equal, man is but man, before God – we are all equal. Before God! But now this God has died. And let us not be equal before the mob. You Higher Men, depart from the market place! (p. 297)

Bennis and Thomas's contemporary transformational leader is similar to Nietzsche's superman: one that must rise above the mob and leave the public place for a higher calling. But Bennis and Thomas's article outlines a leader

(Continued)

(Continued)

who is more than a tough cookie, who also has values and integrity, and is a great communicator. However, even this is not enough. What makes this leader really different is the magical quality of staying youthful and gaining immortality; like Peter Pan, these leaders just refuse to age:

> To understand why this quality [youthfulness] is so powerful in a leader, it might help to take a quick look at the scientific principle behind it – neoteny as an evolutionary engine.
>
> It is the winning, puppyish quality of certain ancient wolves that allowed them to evolve into dogs. (Bennis and Thomas, 2002: 43)

They offer examples of these leaders with Peter Pan characteristics:

> Robert Galvin, former Motorola chairman now in his late 70s, spends his weekends windsurfing. Arthur Levitt, Jr, former SEC chairman who turned 71 this year, is an avid Outward Bound trekker. And architect Frank Gehry is now a 72-year-old ice hockey player. But it's not only an affinity for physical activity that characterizes neoteny – it's an appetite for learning and self-development, a curiosity and passion for life. (p. 43)

What you have is a new mythical leader, a new 'superman' who has overcome ageing, and is able to transform the worst situations into the best. Interestingly the title of Bennis and Thomas' article, 'Crucibles of leadership', exposes the reality: the leaders go through an epic struggle and are transformed into these youthful and dynamic leaders: 'We came to call the experiences that shape leaders "crucibles," after the vessels medieval alchemists used in their attempts to turn base metals into gold' (p. 43). However, as is well known, the alchemist's crucible never did produce gold from other metals. Youthfulness does not last forever, despite cosmetic surgery, medication, fitness regimes, or specific leadership qualities, and the super-hero leader described is no more real than the alchemist's gold. This example demonstrates how the Messiah leader discourse has taken hold. This description of an individual heroic leader sells leadership books and courses, and it appeals to base instincts, to the ego and narcissism of those in leadership roles (the dreams of being heroic) and the dependency instincts of followers, who would like to be saved/led by Messiah leadership characters, and to shareholders, who would like their money to be in the hands of a great leader.

The transformational leader was initially contrasted with *transactional* leadership (Bass, 1985). Transactional leadership is based on an exchange relationship between the leader and follower, i.e. the leader offers incentives and in return the job is done efficiently. The transformational leader was said to possess new behaviours and qualities that won 'hearts and minds' and to work on different assumptions that are more suited to the high-tech, knowledge-based organizations. Burns' ideas were expanded by Bass and others, and since the 1980s the interest in transformational leadership, and leadership itself, has been explosive (Bass, 1985; Conger and Kanungo, 1987; House, 1977; Shamir et al., 1993; Tourish and Pinnington, 2002).

The Components Parts of a Transformational Leader

We are offered a breakdown of the component parts, the 'behaviours and actions', that represent transformational leadership, commonly known as the four 'I's:

1 **Idealized influence or charisma:** Measured by the followers' reactions to the leader, leaders are thoroughly respected, trusted, have much referent power and high standards, and set challenging goals for their followers, i.e. 'the leader has my trust to overcome any obstacle'.

2 **Inspirational motivation:** The leader uses symbols and images and simplified emotional appeals to increase awareness and understanding of mutually desired goals and to focus followers' efforts. He/she elevates followers' expectations.

3 **Intellectual stimulation:** Followers are encouraged to break with the past and to question the old way of doing things. They are supported in questioning their own values, beliefs and expectations as well as those of the leader and the organization.

4 **Individualized consideration:** Followers are treated differently but equitably on a one-to-one basis. Needs are recognized, perspectives raised and their means of more effectively addressing goals and challenges are dealt with.

The four 'I's are the best-known criteria with which transformational leaders are researched through the Multi-factor Leadership Questionnaire (Bass and Avolio, 1994). However, as with most competency and trait approaches, they take a reductive stance and look towards the attributes of individual leaders, omitting important aspects of transformational leadership found elsewhere in the literature:

• Promoting a common culture.

• Aligning moral values.

• Creating a compelling vision.

These and other wider goals are difficult to encapsulate when reductionism to behaviours and actions takes hold of a research and development agenda (Yukl, 1998).

A One-Size-Fits-All 'Hero' Leader

An overview of the transformational leader literature suggests a larger-than-life, one-size-fits-all, hero leader who seems to excel in all four identified behaviours. This charismatic, visionary would, however, overwhelm many individuals, who may respond to a more sensitive personality, working quietly behind the scenes to make things happen. Essentially, a leader cannot be 'all things to all people' or all things to all contexts and situations. Transformational leadership is critiqued for ignoring the contingency theorists who argue that different situations determine appropriate leadership approaches (Fulop and Linstead, 1999).

Schein (1988) and Alvesson (2002) place leadership in a cultural context, which is largely ignored in much of the popular transformational leadership literature that focuses on the traits of the leader. Schein says that different organizations require different leaders and draws on Etzioni's (1961) basic types of organization – coercive, utilitarian and normative. Organizations whose task does not require high levels of involvement would not respond to a charismatic leadership. He gives the examples of a company manufacturing textiles or a government bureaucracy and says a charismatic leader could not transform these into 'normative' organizations (controlled by culture) because they are fundamentally utilitarian organizations requiring a different leadership style. To sum up his position, Schein writes, 'Leadership is partly a cultural phenomenon and must be analysed within a given cultural, political and socio-economic context' (1988: 110).

Learning Charisma: Is Mass Ability Possible?

Charisma is regarded as another key attribute of transformational leadership. Bass (1999) chose to substitute the term *idealized influence* (meaning being influential about ideals) for charisma in an attempt to diffuse some of the criticisms that surround charismatic leadership and to link charisma to ideals and morality.

Bass felt that charisma could be used to manipulate and even indoctrinate followers who were lacking a moral stance. Charismatic leaders have been defined as exceptional leaders who, by force of their personal abilities, are capable of having profound and extraordinary effects on their followers (Steyrer, 1998). Weber links the idea of mission to the charismatic leader: 'the bearer of charisma enjoys loyalty and authority by virtue of a mission believed to be embodied in him' (cited in Bryman, 1993: 292). A transformational leader is a special type of person, being visionary and charismatic. One of the claims for transformational leadership, which separates it from the hero leader of old, is that it should be a dispersed leadership, i.e transformational leaders should be throughout an organization and not just at the top. To achieve this, it is proposed that transformational leaders can be trained, but Bass (1999) acknowledges that, to date, scant research attention has been devoted to the issue of training. This sets up a paradox for the theorists, which has not been resolved, that transformational leaders should be both common (distributed everywhere) and at the same time exceptional. Distributed leadership is a viable goal, but distributing transformational leaders operating with the traits of the four 'I's, makes no sense. Exceptional charismatic leadership cannot be mass-produced, and if it could be the results would be disastrous and chaotic!

Follower Compliance

Psychoanalytic theory claims that charismatic leaders create an unconscious fantasy of a saviour figure, a Messiah who will provide refuge and safety in a world full of turbulence, upheaval and uncertainty. It was no surprise that this leadership approach arose following the economic downturn in the late 1970s. This critique stems from the notion that individuals become regressively infantilized when a charismatic leader creates a psychological dependency in their followers (Hirschhorn, 1988; Kets de Vries, 1991; Masson, 1990). Bion (1961) clearly articulated this unconscious phenomenon by describing how groups operate with a Basic-assumption Dependency (BaD):

> In BaD the group acts 'as if' the leader will protect and sustain the members and will make them feel good. The group members avoid the responsibility of developmental activity and individual responsibility due to a pathological dependency. This group seeks an omnipotent and omniscient leader. (Western, 2005: 286)

Coopey (1995) points to research showing that leaders crave power, and says that their need for positive affirmation from their followers therefore distorts the claims made in transformational leadership research. A leader with power, who needs affirmation, creates follower dependency, which constrains creative or critical thinking. This may produce a highly cohesive group; however, individuals who wish to express alternative solutions to an emerging group consensus will be silenced or banished. The dangers presented by charismatic leaders are the creation of an 'idealized transference' where followers will do all they can to please the leader (Coopey, 1995: 207).

Empowerment

In contrast to early charismatic theories, transformational leadership emphasizes follower empowerment over automatic followership. The transformational leader's aim is to 'elevate followers' expectations' to go beyond what they expect of themselves. To empower is 'to give power or authority' (*Collins Dictionary*, 1992) but as Eric Miller explains:

> The notion of giving power is inherently patronising – it implies dependency – and hence is itself dis-empowering. Power cannot be given, only taken. (Miller, 1993: xvi)

Empowerment can be manipulative and disempowering, especially if the motives are to increase productivity or to enhance a leader's career. When working in Kosovo and Sudan training UN and Red Crescent senior leaders, I was forced to reconsider empowerment through the policies of 'capacity building'. Empowerment cannot be separated from the context. Trying to build capacity in contexts that are structurally disempowering because of contradictory international policies means that Western aid becomes complicit in structural disempowerment (Chandler, 2010). Likewise when leaders claim to empower followers, this is self-evidently disempowering, as the follower is clearly affirmed as the less powerful recipient of something being given by a more powerful leader.

Transformational leadership literature promotes a leader who 'sees beyond what the followers can see for themselves'. The transformational leader takes the follower beyond his or her own visions and goals to a higher level of emotional, moralistic (and perhaps spiritual) maturity. The leader clearly knows best. This is reminiscent of Victorian paternalism that attempted to impose a new morality on the working class. Yukl critiques transformational leadership because its aims are leader-focused, and don't encourage thinking, self-learning or critical thinking in followers:

> Inspirational motivation includes encouraging subordinates to embrace, disseminate and implement the vision, but not encouraging subordinates to challenge the vision or develop a better one. Intellectual stimulation includes communicating novel ideas to a subordinate, but not providing opportunities for subordinates to learn from experience and helping them interpret experience in a meaningful way. (Yukl, 1999: 38–9)

The empowerment ideology which is central to transformational leadership conveys a unidirectional process and does not offer the intellectual space for a real exchange of ideas or for the leader to learn from followers.

Morality: The Raising Up of Leadership

To be transformational one must be morally uplifting. (Burns, 1978)

For transformational leaders to be authentic, they must incorporate moral values as a central core. (Bass and Steidlmeier, 1999: 210)

Burns (1978) cited morality as a quality transformational leaders must possess and Bass claims morality is a main differential between transactional and transformational leadership. Focusing on leader morality is important and welcome, but if leadership morality is used to improve profits and productivity, questions arise as to whether this can be moral. Bass discusses morality as an uncomplicated 'mother and apple pie' sense of goodness, and writes as if parents are teaching moral codes to children:

Leaders are authentically transformational when they increase awareness of what is right, good, important and beautiful, when they help to elevate followers' needs for achievement and self-actualization, when they foster in followers higher moral maturity and when they move followers to go beyond their self interests for the good of their group, organization or society. (Bass, 1998: 171)

The linking of morality to charismatic personalities is dangerous territory. Transformational leaders with charisma represent a full range of personality types. Cuilla discussed 'The Hitler problem' (Cuilla, 1995) asking if Hitler can be viewed as a transformational leader and if not, who would set the standards as to what constitutes morality. Enteman claims that if leaders are too moral they cannot use their expertise because it reduces their ability to make the organization more effective, and therefore they lose their source of authority (Enteman, 1993: 163).

Despite claims of moral authority through developing individuals, transformational leaders are constrained by the goals of 'efficiency and effectiveness', to maximize profit or output at minimum cost, rendering the leader compromised and associated with, as MacIntyre puts it, the 'manipulation of human beings into compliant patterns of behaviour' (1985: 74). Leaders face dilemmas: 'It is not always in the best interests of employees to maximize benefits for other stakeholders [such as owners or customers]' (Stephens et al., 1995). If the leader is acting morally, do they act morally in favour of the employees or the owners? As Tourish and Pinnington (2002: 149) ask: 'Downsizing, delayering, multi-skilling, re-engineering and job enhancement are venerated by some and reviled by others, what is good or moral?'

Milton Friedman takes a polemic view, claiming that within a corporation it is moral to maximize profit and immoral to consider anything else. The corporate executive is an agent, serving the interests of his principal and the stockholders (Friedman, 1970), and thus:

> there is one and only one social responsibility of business – to use its resources and engage in activities designed to increase its profits ... (1962: 132)

He goes on to say that trends such as social responsibility, 'undermine the very foundations of our free society' (p. 132).

Drucker takes the opposite view:

> The rhetoric of 'profit maximization' and 'profit motive' are not only anti-social. They are immoral. (Drucker, 1973: 810)

One of the givens in organizations is that leaders and employees are easily substitutable, which limits their moral stance:

> Individual office holders are in principle replaceable by other individuals without affecting the continuity or identity of the organisation ... any individual is dispensable and replaceable by another. (Ladd, 1970: 488–9)

A transformational leader taking a moral stance faces a postmodern challenge. Leaders may act with moral certitude in a society with a moral social consensus, yet liberal and postmodern attitudes promote diverse views 'which undermine the assumption of a consensus on what constitutes moral integrity in society' (Furedi, 2003: 96). The transformational leadership theorists attempt to speak of morality without addressing the complexities and tensions that need addressing.

If leadership is to influence employees with morality, then it is vital to account for the power relationships and competing motives (their own gains, the company profits/bonuses). That leaders can impart their morality, and know what's best for a hugely diverse workforce, seems an outrageously dangerous claim. Transformational leadership and corporate leadership have not yet matured to address the deeper systemic and structural ethics, and this has led to an environmental crisis and financial crisis, and is leading to a widening social crisis. The Eco-leadership discourse is now on the rise, addressing these ethical and systemic challenges (see Chapter 12).

Engineering Culture

Those who champion transformational leaders claim they produce success-ful dynamic cultures that encourage worker autonomy and creativity. Criti-cal theorists find that transformational leaders use the rhetoric of liberating talent, whist actually creating cultures that enforce conformity and limit dissent and creativity. Kunda (1992) claims transformational leaders attempt to 'engineer culture', where an implicit form of culture control is taking place. Casey (1995) finds these cultures produce 'designer employees', who lose their capacity to see their subjugation. Carol Axtel Ray (1986) describes contemporary corporate culture as the ultimate form of manipulation, argu-ing that the culture espoused by transformational leaders is one that seeks devotion from employees with the aim of getting them to love the firm and its goals. Culture control is the ultimate form of control, because it comes from within the individual and peer group themselves, making constant surveillance unnecessary, and requiring no external policing. Howard Zinn, in *Declarations of Independence* (1991), explains:

> If those in charge of our society – politicians, corporate executives and owners of press and television – can dominate our ideas, they will be secure in their power. They will not need soldiers patrolling the streets. We will control ourselves. (Zinn, cited in Snow, 2002)

In return for devotion and loyalty to the company, employees receive the benefits of sharing collective values, and feeling a part of the community. Edwards finds a totalitarian scenario:

> Under normative control the workers owe not only a hard day's work to the corporation but also their demeanor and affections. Control tends to be a more totalitarian system – totalitarian in the sense of involving the total behaviour of the worker. Hard work and deference are no longer enough; now the 'soulful' corporation demands the workers' soul, or at least the workers' identity. (Edwards, 1979: 148)

Kunda's ethnographic study describes life in a hi-tech engineering com-pany, exposing the subtlety of the new culture control:

> Tech culture is not a prison and its managers are not jailers or tyrants in the simple sense of the word, but it does, nevertheless, represent a subtle form of domination, a 'culture trap' combining normative power with a delicate balance of seductiveness and coercion. (Kunda, 1992: 224)

It is claimed that the transformational leader creates these cultures. How-ever, in Chapter 6 I claimed that these cultures create the leader; they do not stand above the culture but are entrapped in it, in the same way as their employees. These cultures are not run by explicit dictatorial regimes, but subtly eliminate difference and critical thinking, from the top to the bottom, and impose control through culture and self and peer surveillance. Foucault makes an important contribution to this debate on surveillance and control:

> He who is subjected to a field of visibility, and who knows it, assumes responsibility for the constraints of power … [becoming] the principle of his own subjection. ([1977] 1991: 202–3)

Foucault uses the idea of Bentham's Panoptican to describe how surveillance and control have become the dominant social force of control. For Foucault,

> The principle of the Panopticon can be applied not only to prisons but to any system of disciplinary power (a factory, a hospital, a school). And, in fact, although Bentham himself was never able to build it, its principle has come to pervade every aspect of modern society. It is the instrument through which modern discipline has replaced pre-modern sovereignty (kings, judges) as the fundamental power relation. (*Stanford Encyclopedia of Philosophy*, 2008)

Foucault's theorizing in *Discipline and Punishment* ([1977] 1991) makes uncomfortable reading in the contemporary work culture, which is imbued with surveillance and technology. The modern open plan office enables this culture control. The leaders too are situated in these offices, both observing and being observed: there is no escape! The office is open and gives individuals no private space; anybody can walk by at any time, observation by a boss or peer is constant and unpredictable. Peers work so closely that they can hear every telephone call. Diaries are communal, open to all, thereby your hourly activity is known, and employees know that any breach of company policy would mean their computer hard drive and e-mails could be historically searched. Individuals are controlled through 'the gaze' of others, and control themselves through the knowledge that they are forever being observed. Individuals internalize and conform to the norms established, self-control their behaviours and, more importantly from Foucault's perspective, their thoughts.

Organizational culture is too often disconnected and de-contextualized from wider social and cultural implications. The external socio-economic reality has a huge impact on employees, i.e. the fear of damaging future career progression and of unemployment needs to be taken into account when discussing cultures of compliance. To challenge, or even not to fit into, the company culture and the threat of job loss can have a devastating impact (losing healthcare plans, children's education, and one's home, social status and security). Nancy Snow, a teacher and author in the USA, describes her dilemmas on questioning cultural norms, when teaching students:

> I'd like to tell them that the body politic is more public square than Wal-Mart and that democracy is more an uproar than an unquestioning nod. But they pay good money for their educations and I wonder: what kind of career track decision would it be to think – or worse to speak – outside the all-American comfort zone? Two seconds later I hear a voice in my head. 'Look at all you have. Then look at the alternative. A or B freedom or terror'. (Snow, 2002)

Snow is an example of employees who resist these cultures but in a non-confrontational way in order to keep their livelihoods. Casey (1995) describes how passive resistance forms within organizations, and Melucci (1989) shows how resistant communities form and attempt to reclaim identity outside of organizational life. Some critics question the validity of these strong cultures established by transformational leaders, believing 'normative control' to be largely rhetoric and a disguise for more traditional practices (House and Aditya, 1997; Yukl, 2002) that control workers through transactions, for example. I see these corporate cultures constantly in my work, and I also see resistance to them.

Cult-like Cultures

The Messiah discourse is filled with religious imagery, as Box 28 shows.

Box 28   Hail the Messiah!

What made the most difference in having an enduringly great company was the greatness of the leader. (Collins and Porras, 2000)

The claims made about the Transformational leader are quite literally astonishing, drawing on religious imagery and cult-like conformity, with seemingly no concerns or reflections that cults with messiah leaders are highly dangerous. Below are a few examples from scholars describing the zeitgeist that produced the Messiah leadership discourse.

Grint writes:

During the 1980s, charismatic leadership returned with a vengeance, complete with all the accoutrements of biblical charismatics including visions, missions and zealot-like disciples. (1997: 13–14)

(Continued)

(Continued)

Barley and Kunda's research reveals;

> Management was advised to exorcise unwanted thoughts and feelings from the workforce to replace them with beliefs and emotions that benefited the organization. To make the point proponents employed an imagery of cults, clans and religious conversions [see Deal and Kennedy, 1982; Ouchi and Price, 1978]. Authors exhorted managers to become 'highpriests' of their organization's values to appoint mythic heroes and fabricate sagas. (1992: 383)

They outline three tenets of this new cultural leadership:

1 The company as community; the company being the main site for many employees to experience community – bringing pride and a feeling of belonging.

2 Strong cultures could be consciously designed and manipulated.

3 Conformity and emotional commitment would foster financial gain.

(1992: 383)

Ulrich (1984: 126) uses religious imagery to encourage Messiah leaders to 'take the role of missionary ... converting key personnel, to institutionalize new rituals, symbols languages and heroes'.

Peters and Waterman (1982), who were highly influential in the formation of this discourse, claimed that employee autonomy was increased within the confines of value conformity, because organizations with strong cultures could trust employees to act in the company's best interest.

This Orwellian double-think that 'conformity creates autonomy' is very troubling, and is repeated by Collins and Porras (2000) in their book *Built to Last* (first published 1994), who claim that:

> In short ... cult-like tightness around an ideology actually enables a company to turn people loose to experiment, change, adapt and – above all – act. (2000: 123)

Peters and Waterman (1982: 15–16) affirm this idea of cult-like cultures, with 'fanatic centralists around core value', but say, 'yet as one analyst argues "the brainwashed members of an extreme political sect are no more conformist in their central beliefs"'.

What they fail to address was how these conformist cultures would expel difference and eliminate dissent, creating homogeneous employees who are trapped in 'group-think' (Janis, 1972), and unable to critique their own entrapment. To utilize the ideas that cult-like cultures with great leaders bring success seems dangerously naïve, yet these authors' work were best sellers, and are still often cited in leadership circles.

Tourish and Pinnington (2002) describe the similarities between transformational leadership traits and leadership traits within spiritual cults (see Box 29).

Box 29   Transformational Leadership and Cults

Transformational leader trait 1: Charismatic leadership

Similar cult traits

Leader viewed in semi-divine light by followers.

Leader sole source of ideas.

Power increasingly concentrated in leader's hands.

Leader has privileges far in excess of other group members.

Transformational leader trait 2: A compelling vision

Similar cult traits

Vision 'totalistic' in its implications.

Agreement with vision for group membership.

Vision communicated uni-directionally from top to bottom.

Dissent from vision penalized.

Transformational leader trait 3: Intellectual stimulation

Similar cult traits

The vision presented as an intellectual key, unlocking secrets that others cannot comprehend.

The vision monopolizes the time, thoughts and physical energies of members.

Transformational leader trait 4: Individual consideration

Similar cult traits

Members rewarded for compliance and penalized for dissent.

Leaders maintain that the vision is tailor-made to meet the deepest needs of members.

Members encouraged to believe that the leader has a personal vested interest in their welfare.

(Continued)

(Continued)

Transformational leader trait 5: Promotion of a common culture

Similar cult traits

Members begin to copy some of each other's speech mannerisms, dress codes and non-verbal gestures.

Dissent from the common culture punished by the withdrawal of valued social rewards.

Common culture seen as essential precondition for the group's ultimate success. (Adapted from Tourish and Pinnington, 2002: 162)

The transformational leader aims to engineer and influence culture and win the loyalty and commitment of members to the organization, an area in which cult leaders have demonstrated a perverse excellence. However, despite the proximity of the leadership styles, cults do not easily translate to larger, secular, organizational forms. A better analogy perhaps is that corporations have fundamentalist tendencies similar to the more mainstream Christian Fundamentalist movement that became powerful in the USA (see Chapter 7, Corporate Fundamentalism).

Conclusion

> As despair and helplessness deepen, the search and wish for a Messiah [leader] or magical rescue [leadership] also begins to accelerate. (Gemmil and Oakley, 1992: 115)

The Messiah leadership discourse emerged in the early 1980s like a religious revival, bringing leadership itself back to the fore after a long period where leadership had been surpassed by managerialism. Leadership, discredited by great man theories, by dictators and despots, marginalized by a post-war democratizing movement and a bureaucratic workplace, was suddenly back at the top of the business agenda. On every company's wish-list was to find a Transformational leader, a CEO with charismatic qualities to renew, restructure, reform and transform the company. Emerging from the recessionary 1970s and 1980s new hope was needed, and new ways to run businesses in a fast-changing world. The Messiah discourse answered the call of the times; a saviour was required to turn around failing economies, then the recovery and the fall of communism inspired free-market triumphalism. Good had succeeded over evil, free-market capitalism over state control, and this translated into the grandiosity seen in the transformational leader rhetoric. Two key dynamics underpinned the success of Messiah leadership.

1. Desire

Messianic leadership is underpinned by an unconscious desire: the desire for a saviour to rescue us from crisis, for hope in the face of despair, to have faith in a mother/father figure who will care for us, for a hero we can identify with, to be inspired, and to be like the hero we imagine and believe in. As Rost puts it, 'the leader has been likened to a saviour-like essence in a world that constantly needs saving' (cited in Barker, 1997: 348).

Bion, as a psychoanalyst, identifies an age-old problem for messianic leaders, namely that 'the messianic hope must never be fulfilled, only by remaining a hope does hope exist' (1961: 151). This insight explains why messianic leaders fail, and then new ones appear. Hope is the real desire, not the leader, who is a replaceable. The Messiah character reflects back to society its own vulnerabilities, anxieties and desires.

2. New Leaders, for New Times

Messianic leadership answered unconscious desires, but it also did more: it provided a rationale for leading organizations facing the new conditions of globalization and the post-industrial knowledge economy. The rationale was that transformational leaders would create new cultures that freed employees from the need to be managed. These new cultures would both inspire employees and act as a control mechanism. If employees believed in the leader's vision, if they felt they belonged to the company as if it was a community, they would work harder for the collective good of the company without having to be monitored by a manager. The recipe for transformational leadership success was both simple and ingenious: create a culture that inspired dynamism, and at the same time was conformist, ensuring individuals acted in the company's best interests, and behaved within the limits and norms of the company's expectations. Chapter 7 highlights the folly of this position, showing how dynamism turns to conformity, creating totalizing cultures, and this process is described in the case study in Box 30.

Box 30   Case Study: The Messiah Leadership Discourse

Dynamic and totalizing cultures

This case study comes from a piece of consultancy work in a multinational fashion retailer. I worked with the global HR team and coached senior leaders. This case study comes from my observations and the insights I gained during this work.

The CEO began his career as a designer and whilst CEO he expanded the company to make it a globally recognizable business. It became clear that he strongly identified with the Messiah leadership discourse. His vision was that both great design and great leadership came through creativity and passion, and he 'preached' that company success was almost solely dependent on creativity and great design. He generated enthusiasm and loyalty from a dynamic, young and committed workforce and the company built up a strong brand followership. This period of success reflected studies written about transformational leaders and their capacity to inspire and create loyal and dynamic cultures.

Things started to go wrong, but went unnoticed, during a period of growth and success for the company. The CEO had been bolstered by his success and he used his increased leadership influence to hire people with the same style as his own. He led the company with creativity and passion and he employed people with creativity and passion. They identified with him as a fellow 'creative'. Paradoxically, whilst the designers were creative, this approach led to a monoculture forming. There was a uniformity about the company that mimicked their glamorous company advertising. The employees were very young, and visiting the company restaurant for a sushi lunch felt more like entering a young persons' club than a work-place. Cool designers are fine but the company was moving towards a totalizing monoculture that excluded anything else. From the outsider it looked like a buzzing creative company, but to those inside there was a culture of conformity and peer pressure to toe the leadership line. There was very little independent or critical thinking, no room for dissent. Everybody performed being 'cool designers', and other leadership cultures and employee identities and roles necessary to lead a multinational com-pany were obliterated. In this company the CEO was renowned for saying 'you either got it or you didn't'. Those who didn't get it, or questioned 'it', didn't last long.

After a period of huge growth the company found that it lacked the matu-rity and experience to balance the creative business with the process of lead-ing and managing a global business. To run a multinational the leadership culture needed to be more mature and more diverse. They lost their way, seeing a huge drop in share value, job losses, and eventually the departure of the CEO. The leader as messiah went from being untouchable to being 'sacrificed'.

My comment to the HR team during their successful period was that my counter-transference (see note below) told me that the company was like an out-of-control youth club and needed a 'Father', a paternal container, to bring structure and containment to balance the passion of youth.

The rebuilding job was to change the totalizing organizational culture led by a Messiah leader to a more balanced approach, which allowed diversity into the company, some Therapist leaders in middle management, Control leaders in production and finance, and at senior levels they needed an Eco-leadership approach to realize that running a global business meant to understand global flows and adapt to change and trends. They appointed a mature, experienced corporate leader as the new CEO to steady the ship, who took a less passionate and more stable and pragmatic leadership role.

Note 1: Psychoanalytically-informed consultants work with their counter-transference, i.e. what they experience and feel in themselves during the consultancy is read as an internal-emotional response to the projections and transference from those they work with. My internal experience here was of feeling 'out of control'. I felt excited and a little disturbed. There was lots of high energy, but a bit manic, unreal, and unsafe. My instinct was to ask where were the parents? Where were the structures and containment needed to create a safe space to think, to face the reality principle that would create sustainable business success?

In Defence of Visionary Leaders

This chapter has developed a critique of the Messiah discourse in contrast to the lack of critique in mainstream and populist literature. However, it is important also to acknowledge the agency of individual leaders who can and do impact on organizational success. Individual leadership agency is often over-stated, yet individual leadership agency does matter; symbolic acts, excellent communication, personal drive and resilience, creative thinking and strategic vision do matter. Individual leaders do make a difference; they can inspire others, they can symbolize the mood of the times, and develop successful strategies with others, but they don't create cultures from thin air, and they don't ever lead alone. The mistake is to over-hype the power of the leader, creating unreal expectations that undermine the task of facing the complexities involved in leading corporate cultures.

Box 31   The Character of the Messiah Leader

Messiah leaders are usually extroverts. They walk into rooms and get noticed; they are good at getting attention, filling a room with their presence, whether welcome or not. They often inspire devotion and loyalty from some, and are often disliked by others. They preach passionately about passion, usually their passion, reflecting their strong ego and a narcissistic streak. They demand loyalty and commitment from others and can be brutal in getting rid of those who show dissent, which they interpret as disloyalty (a weakness that often leads to their demise and company problems).

They often imagine themselves as preachers, doing good in the world and making a difference for others. They are happiest in front of an audience, winning hearts as well as minds.

When they fall they fall hard, reflecting their inbuilt conviction that they are born to lead, convinced that they were doing good and right: even when they clearly make errors they find these hard to accept. This confidence can be a strength and their greatest weakness.

There are other charismatic leaders who show less hubris, but the character of the messiah leader in business is usually that of the extrovert described above, fed by success and follower adoration.

The Demise of the Messiah Discourse

Despite the hype, confidence in this leadership discourse soon began to fade (Bolden, 2011: 32). Peters and Waterman (1982) believed they had found the recipe for success, although subsequently many of the 'excellent companies' they identified fell by the wayside. Maccoby (2000) claims that charismatic leaders often desert organizations after making changes that create toxic organizations; he cites Enron as an example of charismatic leaders making a toxic organization.

Another reason for its demise are the serious questions about the efficacy of transformational leaders, and indeed whether they actually exist at all. As Yukl asks:

> How many managers do you know that are really transformational, much less charismatic? In contrast to the survey research, descriptive research using observation and interviews to study Transformational leadership in managers found that they were not charismatic in the usual sense of the word. (2002: 38)

House and Aditya sum up this viewpoint:

> There is little evidence that charismatic, transformational, or visionary leadership does indeed transform individuals, groups, large divisions of organisations, or total organisations, despite claims that they do so ... There is no evidence demonstrating stable and long-term effects of leaders on follower self-esteem, motives, desires, preferences, or values. (1997: 443)

Finally, the demise of the Messiah discourse is connected to the shocking financial and economic crisis of 2008. Messiah leadership and the hubris and omnipotence of the corporate world have been shattered. No longer is free-market capitalism triumphant, as China becomes the new rising economic power. Hyper-change is taking place, in a very uncertain world. A new leadership discourse was required that could make sense of globalization, that could take a systemic view and bring a new ethical leadership to face the world's challenges. This leadership needed to understand the interdependencies that connect us to the environment, and to each other: if one falls, we all fall. The next chapter discusses Eco-leadership, a new discourse to meet these challenges.

Suggested Readings

- Axtel Ray, C. (1986) 'Corporate culture: the last frontier of control', *Journal of Management Studies*, 23(3): 286–95.

- Bass, B. (1990) 'From transactional to transformational leadership: learning to share the vision', *Organizational Dynamics*, 18(3): 19–31.

- Bass, B. and Steidlmeier, P. (1999) 'Ethics, character and authentic transformational leadership behavior', *Leadership Quarterly*, 10: 181–217.

- Conger, J.A. and Kanungo, R. (1987) 'Toward a behavioural theory of charismatic leadership in organisational settings', *Academy of Management Review*, 12: 637–47.

- Deal, T. and Kennedy, A. (1982) *Corporate Cultures*. Reading, MA: Addison–Wesley.

- Tichy, N. and Devanna, M. (1986) *The Transformational Leader*. New York: John Wiley.

- Tourish, D. (2008) 'Challenging the transformational agenda: leadership theory in transition?', *Management Communication Quarterly*, 21(4): 522–8.

Reflection Points

The Messiah leadership discourse reflects the rise of transformational leadership and other forms of charismatic and visionary leadership that focused on culture control. These leaders claimed to offer leadership that simultaneously inspired and controlled workers, without having to closely supervise them. This was perfect for globalized workforces, and for knowledge work that was harder to 'police'.

- Reflect on the leaders you have met. Are any of them transformational? Do they influence organizational cultures? Or do you think these leaders are mythical?

Paradoxes exist within the transformational leadership discourse. For example, they claim to empower followers, but the uni-directional power coming from leader to follower undermines this claim; leaders claim to create (conformist) 'aligned' cultures in order to liberate individual autonomy and creativity.

- Reflect on organizations you know and try to identify paradoxes, where the leadership rhetoric differs from practice.

- Do the company/leadership vision and values align with practice?

Sample Assignment Question

Summarize the Messiah discourse in your own words and think about whether you have experienced any leaders who are truly transformational. If you have, describe the strengths and weakness of this leader, referencing some of the critiques in this chapter. If you haven't, try to explain why and critique the notion of Messiah leadership.

12   The Eco-Leadership Discourse

Connectivity and Ethics

Figure 12.1   Eco-leadership

Key words

Ecosystems

Distributed and ethical leadership

Networks

Connectivity

Interdependence

Globalization

Technology

Sustainability

> **Chapter Structure**
>
> - Introduction: 'New Leadership for New Times'
> - A New Paradigm: The Context Informing Eco-Leadership
> - The Four Qualities of Eco-Leadership
> - Eco-Leadership in Practice
> - Conclusion

Introduction: 'New Leadership for New Times'

Eco Leadership
Connectivity & Ethics

Distributed & Network Leadership

Figure 12.2   Eco-leadership organizational form

The Eco-leadership organizational form is a network of distributed leaders. The Eco-leadership discourse emerged at the turn of millennium responding to a new paradigm that is also emerging as modernity exhausts itself. The natural environment faces real danger from irreversible climate change, urban pollution and diminishing natural resources. Serious social, political and economic consequences are unravelling from the 2008 financial crisis, yet another symptom of modernity and capitalism's vulnerability to a new order.

I named this discourse 'Eco-leadership' to reflect the growing use of environmental and network metaphors in the leadership literature. Eco-leadership is becoming the most important leadership discourse for our times, although it is not yet the dominant discourse. The prefix 'Eco' signifies how progressive leaders conceptualize organizations as ecosystems and networks, rather than closed systems. Organizations are rethought as 'eco-systems within ecosystems' meaning that:

- Organizations are webs of connections, networks that operate like ecosystems. The machine metaphor was for the factory; today's metaphor is to imagine our organization as an ecosystem. We can then realize how parts make up an interdependent whole, how change in one part of an organization impacts throughout, and how organizations cannot be led top-down, for an ecosystem requires nurturing not controlling.

• The organizational ecosystem is interconnected and interdependent within larger ecosystems, e.g. financial and economic ecosystems, social-political ecosystems, local and global natural ecosystems.

'Ecology is not the exclusive domain of the environmentalist' (Hasdell, 2008: 99), and the ecosystems I refer to are not only natural ecosystems, they are also hybrids, made up of nature, technology and the human/social. Eco-leadership therefore is not exclusive to environmental leadership, but applies to all leadership. It implies that leadership is governed by systems intelligence (Senge, 2006) and that leadership is dispersed throughout organizations rather than residing in a single individual. This enables organizations to better adapt to changing environmental conditions (Redekop, 2010: 305).

Our interdependence in a fast-changing world requires radical leadership rethinking. Globalization and the network society has wide-ranging impacts, reconfiguring how we organize, communicate and relate. Political impacts have also been wide-ranging, including the Arab Spring uprisings, and protest movements such as Occupy. Economically the de-regulation of markets and the virtualization of capital led to the 2008 financial crash, which in turn led to an ongoing social and political crisis (Castells, 2012; McDonald and Robinson, 2009; Sennet, 2006).

Sadly, organizational leadership has failed to keep pace with these changes, and the Eco-leadership discourse is widely discussed, but now needs to be adopted and developed quickly. Eco-leadership is gaining ground quickly, from fragile beginnings. Anita Roddick of the Body Shop, an early pioneer of the Eco-leadership discourse in business, said 'Businesses have the power to do good ... we dedicate our business to the pursuit of social and environmental change'. Her ideas were that business could be a part of the 'Green revolution' (Roddick, 2006). Richard Branson announced his environmental commitment at the Clinton Global Climate Initiative in 2006, pledging $3 billion of his transport business's profits over the coming decade to combat global warming and promote alternative energy. The profits were to be invested to find renewable, sustainable energy sources 'in an effort to wean the world off oil and coal' (*NBC News*, 2006).

Paul Polman, CEO of Unilever, perhaps the best-known commercial voice of Eco-leadership, says there is a 'fundamental readjustment going on as a result of the financial crisis, from a rules-based society back to a principles-based society' (Polman, 2012). He challenges leaders who say they have to put short-termism and shareholders first:

> What we firmly believe is that if we focus our company on improving the lives of the world's citizens and come up with genuine sustainable solutions, we are more in synch with consumers and society and ultimately this will result in good shareholder returns.

The Eco-leadership discourse is embraced also by politicians such Bill Clinton and his Global Initiative connecting environmental and social challenges, Mikhail Gorbachov and The Green Cross, and Al Gore who won a Nobel Peace Prize in 2007 for his campaign to tackle global warming and is a leading proponent of 'sustainable capitalism'. China's leaders have realized that protecting the environment is a living necessity for many of their citizens, and vital for their future. Thomas Friedman writes:

> Yes, China's leaders have decided to go green — out of necessity because too many of their people can't breathe, can't swim, can't fish, can't farm and can't drink thanks to pollution from its coal- and oil-based manufacturing growth engine. And, therefore, unless China powers its development with cleaner energy systems, and more knowledge-intensive businesses without smokestacks, China will die of its own development. (Friedman, 2009)

China is now leading the world in green technology with a 'remarkable 77 percent growth in production of green technologies a year according to [a] report ... commissioned by the World Wildlife Fund for Nature' (*New York Times*, 2011b).

However, there is too big a gap between those advocating environmental solutions, and the networked and distributed leadership necessary to transform organizations and society. This chapter aims to position Eco-leadership in this gap, as it is not possible to make the radical changes necessary without a radical revision of how organizations and businesses are led and run.

The Eco-leadership discourse emerges from the work of diverse scholars, politicians and practitioners (Capra, 1996; Castells, 2000; Lovelock, 1982; Polman, 2012; Senge, 2006; Wheatley, 2006). Redekop, writing for the *Berkshire Encyclopedia of Sustainability*, refers to the growing 'Eco-leadership' paradigm (where he also cites my own earlier work):

> Thus in contrast to the industrial paradigm of leadership, a new 'eco-leadership paradigm' is beginning to emerge among students and practitioners of leadership. The writer Simon Western goes so far as to suggest that 'the next [leadership] discourse will be that of the eco-leader [2008: 184]'. (Redekop, 2010: 305)

In management education leadership and sustainability courses are commonplace, and the literature on systems thinking, network approaches, complexity and sustainability in relation to leadership and organizations is growing prolifically. The 'One Planet MBA', a collaboration between Exeter University and the World Wildlife Fund, is a leading exponent of the Eco-leadership discourse, and a project they hope to extend to many other universities and countries. This chapter will now explore the context that informs this discourse, and then develop a comprehensive review of the Eco-leadership discourse.

A New Paradigm: The Context Informing Eco-Leadership

Things fall apart; the centre cannot hold.

W.B. Yeats in his poem 'The Second Coming' (1919) defined the tensions of modernism early in the 20th century and his work has proven prophetic. At the beginning of the 21st century, late modernity finds itself in crisis and the old order is clearly passing. Our challenge today is to grasp new reality, that in a globalized, networked world the centre can *never* hold, simply because there is no centre. The myth of central control has been exposed: the Soviet bloc, the Arab Spring, the financial sector – in each, central control has been undermined by informal networks that cannot be controlled. We face a social, political and economic paradigm change. The environment is under pressure: climate change and the realization that our natural resources are finite increase the imperative for sustainable solutions and transnational agreements. Water and food shortages are expected as population growth soars. The 2008 financial crash exposed deeper problems. No one is sure how to run the financial markets, everybody chases economic growth yet exponential growth across the globe leads to a host of secondary problems, and we ignore sustainability at our peril. The European project is under pressure and China is undertaking the biggest social, political and economic experiment the world has ever known, trying to deliver a capitalist economy in a state-controlled system. Whilst raising the living standards of millions, social inequity increases and the social and environmental implications of such rapid change are unknown. The rise of the 'BRICS' countries – Brazil, Russia, India, China and South Africa – redistributes power from the West and brings many out of poverty, but as these countries become increasingly wealthy, they consume more and use more fossil fuels, and the pressures on the environment and climate increase too. Social inequities between rich and poor continue to increase disproportionately: 'in the USA the portion of national income going to the richest 1% tripled from 8% in the 1970s to 24% in 2007' (Rachman, 2012). Over 50% of the world's population is urban for the first time. Slum housing filled with the urban poor creates peripheral communities without civil rights, legal status or basic infrastructures such as public transport, electricity, water and sewerage: 'the problem is not just that they are poor but that they are excluded, which is a more radical barrier than poverty' (McGuirk, 2012: 78). Globalization has many facets, as discussed in Box 32. It brings new opportunities and also huge challenges that feed the emergence of the Eco-leadership discourse.

Box 32   Globalization

Globalization can be interpreted in different ways: some argue for its benefits, others that it creates social divisions and global elites. Either way, globalization is with us, and requires leaders in all sectors of society to think and act in new ways. As Kiely (2005) says: 'The impact of global flows means that no "local society" or culture can exist in a self-contained way.'

Global flows

Castells (2000) claims that globalization changes power relations, and he argues that a shrinking world has led to social divisions where those who are insufficiently globalized are confined to living in the 'space of places': they live in urban ghettos, favelas and local communities. The poor may live next to wealthy neighborhoods and share the same cities, yet they might as well be living on different planets. The global elite are immediately connected to each other by ICTs (information and communication technologies) and live in global 'spaces of flows', disconnected from the 'spaces of places' by living in gated communities, and shielded from the place they actually exist in.

> [They] experience much of their life – both in work and leisure – in the 'spaces of flows' in which they link up with other, distant places, in order to make money and take expensive holidays. They still live in particular localities but are abstractly – and literally – fenced off from those confined only to the 'space of places'. (Kiely, 2005: 10)

Twentieth century globalization was linked to Westernization: Western countries exporting their economic, cultural and political ideologies and practices. Today globalization might be considered neo-liberal, exporting a pervasive world order of economics and ideology led by the triad of the World Trade Organization, the International Monetary Fund and the World Bank. But perhaps a twist is now occurring, led by China and India, producing a counter-Easternization global flow, with unknown outcomes. A further global flow emanates from anti-capitalist movements that arise in the margins, resisting the dominance of the market and increasingly having an impact. Localism also influences the global, as Gwynne et al. (2003: 37) write: 'The "local makes the global", e.g. when Japanese production methods spread across the globe.'

Globalization Creating or Alleviating Poverty?

A (2002) World Bank report defends globalization as a progressive force:

> A widespread view of globalization is that it makes 'rich people richer and poor people poorer'. This simply does not seem to be true: poverty is falling rapidly in those poor countries that are integrating into the global economy. (2002: 152)

Their argument is that we need more not less globalization. Critics of globalization focus on the 'facelessness and undemocratic nature of global capitalism' (Gwynne et al., 2003: 226), arguing that globalization causes a split between the 'haves and have nots', where countries and regions get caught at the periphery of globalization through no fault of their own and development and wealth by-pass and further impoverish them, as they become less and less able to compete or even contribute to the global economy.

What Does Globalization Mean?

It can mean global capitalism, and unelected supra-national institutions such as the WTO and IMF having immense power, dictating to nation states how to become neo-liberal economies. Transnational corporations have bigger budgets than nation states, so corporations and neo-liberal institutions share agendas and promote one-size-fits all solutions: privatization of public services, de-regulation, welfare cuts, increases in the cost of living, rationalization and debt reduction. In the hyper-globalization thesis (Ohmae, 1995) the existence of the nation state is undermined, resulting in:

1 The triumph of individual autonomy and market principles over state power.

2 The triumph of oppressive global capitalism, creating structural patterns of inequalities between and within countries.

Perhaps the financial crisis of 2008 has dampened this triumphalism of global capital.

(Continued)

(Continued)

Castells (2012) points to the network society being a force that cannot be reversed, but does change things. Economic collapse was due to the digitalization of finance plus the deregulation of financial markets, resulting in global trading that spun out of control. Part of this trend was the self-interest of traders, divorced from sustainable commitments to their banks or society. Castells also points to another trend arising in the aftermath of this crisis, whereby self-interest is being usurped by a growing idea of 'common-interest' using social media to bond around 'shared interests'.

Globalization is a plural concept; it has all of the effects mentioned here. What is certain is that it cannot be restrained; but how it shapes the present and future is dependent on activists and leaders to work towards a globalization that supports sustainable communities and environments, and develops social equity.

Three converging intellectual and social changes have created the new zeitgeist that underpins Eco-leadership. We look at these next.

The New Zeitgeist: The Context for the Eco-Leadership Discourse

Quantum Physics and New Science

New science challenged our dualistic and binary view of the world. Fritjof Capra writes: 'The new concepts in physics have brought about profound change in our worldview; from the mechanistic worldview of Descartes and Newton to [a more] holistic and ecological view' (1996: 5). Wheatley made a major contribution to the Eco-leadership discourse in her book *Leadership and New Science*, where she claimed we have 'Newtonian organizations in a quantum age' (2006: 27).

Globalization and Technological Advances

Globalization shrinks the world, connects many, and also creates new divisions. Communication technologies transform our personal, social and economic worlds, and the network society creates new cultures, new democratic potentials, new business and economic realities, and new challenges. Other technologies, artificial intelligence, human genome, bio-genetics, nano-technology and environmental/green technologies, all contribute to a new zeitgeist.

The Environmental Social Movement

This movement has raised awareness of finite natural resources, the imminent dangers of climate change, and the increasing loss of bio-diversity. Awoken by a minority of activists (the Seattle 1990 meeting of the WTO was a significant moment), the world suddenly realized the looming environmental challenges that it was facing.

The environmental movement (and other activist movements) also pioneered new forms of organizing. Utilizing social networking and social media, they developed new 'leaderless' non-organizations such as Anonymous (Castells, 2012), and Occupy, mixing face-time meetings in public squares and virtual organizing. This radical distributing of leadership and new forms of organizing has contributed to the Eco-leadership discourse, by questioning the norms, challenging convention, and developing real alternatives.

The new millennium and the financial crisis have refocused us sharply. Manuel Castells tells us:

> In this crisis, some people are trying to go back and other people are trying to discover what the future could be. What doesn't work any more is the present, for anyone. That's why it's Aftermath Time. (Aftermath Project, 2012)

In their book entitled *Aftermath*, Castells et al. claim that the post-crisis challenges are economic and cultural. The political-economic system has lost its cultural power which relied on people's trust that the economic and financial system was safe and reliable. Castells claims that 'disenfranchised masses no longer believe in their leaders; a civil society in disarray, as old social organizations become empty shells' (Castells et al., 2012: 308). New social actors of change are beginning to emerge, creating new cultures that refute *Homo economicus*, and are attempting to 'translate the meaning of life into economic meaning' rather than be dominated by market forces (2012: 308).

Form and Function – The Architectures of Eco-Leadership

Eco-leadership challenges the central modernist slogan *'form follows function'*. This ethos focuses on functionality, linearity and utilitarianism (the Controller discourse). We design organizations (forms) that are 'fit for purpose' to carry out their utilitarian function. This seems an obvious truism, except that the opposite statement is equally true: *'function also follows form'*. Modernity traps us in 'forms' that limit us, urban worlds of production lines, shopping malls, traffic jams, square boxes to live in, square screens, and public spaces that are colonized by mass advertising (Klein, 2000). This form of media advertising distorts our human desires towards consumerist goods which can never satisfy us, and these 'unfulfilled desires' provide the basic logic of late capitalism.

External landscapes shape our internal landscapes, influencing how we think, feel and perceive the world. In natural environments and in creative urban environments, our imagination is stimulated and unleashed.

We imagine ourselves as 'the creators', but we are also 'created', i.e. socially constructed by forms that shape and often limit our individual and collective potential. This is especially true of many workplaces. I recently worked as a consultant within a major bank in London, and my experience of getting to the meeting awoke me once again to the totalizing nature of contemporary workplaces (see Box 33).

Box 33   Emotional Architecture: A Linear Journey to the Glass Tower

I travelled on the crowded Underground, packed with thousands, passed through the ticket control, stepped onto a moving walkway before travelling up an escalator. I walked through a glass-covered shopping arcade, bombarded by consumer goods and advertising. I arrived at the bank security and was 'screened', before taking the lift to the 30th floor. Finally I arrived in a huge open-plan office with 300 uniform desks, and glass walls on three sides.

I was transported to my destination by moving stairways, in linear lines: I was being efficiently 'processed' as if on a production line, with thousands of other commuters and finance workers. When I arrived I experienced 'sameness', monotonous rows of linear desks compartmentalized by small screens. Employees in dark suits, men and women alike. There were explicit rules, no objects above a certain height on desks to maintain uniformity, along with implicit rules, maintained by peer and self-surveillance, for how long you stayed at the desk, how loud you could speak, and so on. There was nowhere to hide in this open-plan panopticon, every telephone conversation could be heard, and your computer screen was always public viewing. A senior leader I coached was told by his boss that there was too much laughter coming from his team and he needed to address this. The message for the leader to control his team so they display only uniform and monotone 'office' emotions, is indicative of a totalizing and conformist culture.

I had two associations to this. Firstly to a large Victorian factory, except the weaving machines had become computers, and a sterile cleanliness and white noise replaced the commotion and dirt of the old. Secondly to the mental asylum I worked in many years before, where patients and staff were totally institutionalized, and they too had no private sphere of living.

I found the experience dislocating and totalizing. I recalled other corporations I had worked in, and like the business hotels I stayed in, they are conformist, modern glass buildings, minimalist, utilitarian, white walls, open plan offices, with occasional grandiose spaces signifying power.

What do these organizational forms do to us? What do they do to our capacity to think creatively and relate to each other humanely?

Employees are so embedded in these normative corporate cultures, they fail to see their own capitulation and entrapment (Casey, 1995).

An organization's internal and external architectures commonly mirror its hierarchy and culture. The banks located within the skyscrapers of London's Canary Wharf have hierarchical structures and cultures, mirroring the building. On the very top floor, with a separate lift to access it, reside the CEO and the senior team, and power relationships internally are vertical like the building. The financial centre of any major city replicates 'phallic capitalism', represented to us in architectural form.

Likewise, the size of a church mimics the power of the leader. The Pope has his own city, and the grandiose Vatican represents the Pope's omnipotent power (directly elected by God and infallible). The Old Order Amish people have a much flatter hierarchy; their bishops remain local, are elected by their peers, and are independent of an extensive church power structure. In contrast they have no church buildings; instead they hold rotating Sunday services in different family homes, reflecting their belief system of humility and a plain and simple lifestyle. Quakers also have a flat structure without any clergy or hierarchy. For 350 years they have survived with an organizational architecture of spiritual consensus, 'a priesthood of all believers', whereby any person can attend their meetings and 'minister' in their meeting houses. When big decisions are taken at an annual gathering, all members are invited and all have a voice. Their meeting house architecture mimics this egalitarian approach: small simple buildings without steeples; a circle of chairs or wooden benches inside a plain room without ornamentation or religious symbols.

Eco-leadership in contemporary organizations must learn from new social movements, and diverse organizations and faith groups like the Quakers and the Amish who have managed to create diverse organizational forms, real and virtual, that enable them to operate in non-linear, non-hierarchical or specifically sustainable lifestyles. Satterwhite claims that to be a self-generating (autopoietic) system, 'the organization has to respond to external stimuli, which it can only do in ways that are consistent with its structure' (2010: 232). A core task of

Eco-leadership is to constantly work on form and structure to make them consistent with organizational purpose. Form and function are interdependent and connected. Leaders need to think differently about form and function, to think in terms of networks of connectivity and interdependence and shape their organizations so they are capable of organizing in new ways.

The Four Qualities of Eco-Leadership

There is much diversity within the Eco-leadership discourse but the essence can be found in the four qualities of Eco-leadership set out in Box 34.

Box 34   The Four Qualities of Eco-Leadership

1. Connectivity and interdependence

Eco-leadership is founded on connectivity, recognizing how the network society has transformed social relations, and it also recognizes our interdependence with each other and the environment. Eco-leadership focuses on internal organizational ecosystems (technical, social and natural) and the external ecosystems of which organizations are a part.

2. Systemic ethics

Eco-leadership is concerned with acting ethically in the human realm *and* protecting the natural environment. Systemic ethics goes beyond company values and individual leader morality, which conveniently turns a blind eye to the wider ethical implications of their businesses, e.g. by ignoring social inequality, the downstream impacts of pollution and supply chain workers, world poverty and environmental sustainability.

3. Leadership spirit

Eco-leadership acknowledges the importance of the human spirit. It extends its values beyond material gain, paying attention to community and friendship, mythos and logos, the unconscious and non-rational, creativity and imagination. It draws upon the beauty and dynamic vitally within human relationships, and between humanity and the natural world.

4. Organizational belonging

To belong is to be a part of the whole, it is to participate in the joys and challenges faced by communities. Businesses and corporations, like schools, banks and hospitals, belong to the social fabric of community, and cannot operate as separate bodies. Eco-leaders commit organizations to belong to 'places and spaces', developing strong kinship ties. Place refers to local habitat and community, and space to the virtual and real networks that organizations also inhabit. Organizational belonging means ending a false separation, realizing that company interests and societal interests are inter-dependent. Organizational belonging is to rethink organizational purpose and meaning.

These four qualities will now be explored.

Connectivity and Interdependence

Bill Clinton, interviewed about his Global Initiative Conference 2012, spoke of interdependence:

> Our world is more interdependent than ever. Borders have become more like nets than walls, and while this means wealth, ideas, information and talent can move freely around the globe, so can the negative forces shaping our shared fates. The financial crisis that started in the US and swept the globe was further proof that – for better and for worse – we cant escape one another. (Clinton, 2012: 26)

Ecosystems and ecology, systems thinking, fractals and complexity, self-organizing systems, ethics and sustainability, networks and connectivity are becoming commonplace ideas used in relation to leadership and organizations. What they have in common is a growing realization of the connectivity and interdependence referred to by Bill Clinton.

Hybrid Ecosystems

Eco-leadership addresses complex challenges using the ecosystem as a metaphor but with an expansive meaning of the term ecosystem (Love-lock, 1982). The social world, natural world and the non-human world of machines and technology are increasingly enmeshed in inseparable net-works, forming 21st century ecosystems that have interdependencies just like rain-forests and coral reefs. Hybrid ecosystems, made up of humans, technology and nature, form both organizational ecosystems and social ecosystems. Our individual and social interconnectivity to technology and machines is inseparable, leading Haraway to call us cyborgs:

> By the late twentieth century, our time, a mythic time, we are all chimeras, theorized and fabricated hybrids of machine and organism; in short, we are cyborgs. (Haraway, 1991: 151)

Humans and non-humans participate together to make things work. John Law explains:

> ... the social world is this remarkable emergent phenomenon: in its processes it shapes its own flow... so ordering has to do with both humans and non-humans. They go together. So it doesn't make much sense to treat them separately as if they were different in kind. (Law, 1992: 15)

Eco-leadership is to continually work within these multiplicities; leadership is understood within a network of other actors and agents (both human and non-human).

The hubris of modernity has made us anthropomorphic; we situate humans at the centre of everything, an outcome of our narcissistic society (Lasch, 1979). Science and rationality became the human tools to overcome nature. Premoderns understood the interdependencies with nature better than us moderns, and they created myths, narratives and gods to explain these. It is now the turn of postmoderns to reclaim this holistic understanding, to find new and relevant narratives that are fit for our times.

Power and Connectedness

Whilst Eco-leadership emerges from social activism it is not a woolly, feel-good approach to leadership. It is a serious and radical approach that challenges the very coordinates of current organizational theory and practice, including a critique of power relations. Power and authority do not disappear in some utopian dream when environmental awareness and social responsibility are addressed; they become more transparent. A valid critique of systems theory and environmental thinking in organizations is the lack of critical theory in relation to power. Coopey (1995) claims that Peter Senge's work idealizes community and over-plays the importance of dialogue without adequately addressing power. Guha (1989) critiques American deep ecology for its lack of power and social critiques, claiming that Third World perspectives have 'a greater emphasis on equity and social justice ... on the grounds that in the absence of social regeneration, environmental regeneration has very little chance of succeeding'. When systemic approaches are applied to organizations, power as well as communication patterns have to be addressed. Who has access to knowledge and resources? Which groups control resources and communication? Which discourses are privileged and which are marginalized? Post-structural theories help reveal hidden power dynamics, showing that power is more distributed and fluid than we think, and we mistake power at the centre as strength, and power at the margins as weakness, when neither is the case.

Systemic Ethics

Systemic ethics means to expand the boundaries of rights and responsibilities beyond the immediate and obvious (McIntyre-Mills, 2008). Companies and leaders often hide behind a shallow veneer of values. Coca-Cola states its values in a way that reads more like marketing sound bites, and seems to aim at branding Coca-Cola as a cool or good company rather than addressing seriously the question of systemic ethics:

Live Our Values

Our values serve as a compass for our actions and describe how we behave in the world.

- **Leadership:** The courage to shape a better future

- **Collaboration:** Leverage collective genius

- **Integrity:** Be real

- **Accountability:** If it is to be, it's up to me

- **Passion:** Committed in heart and mind

- **Diversity:** As inclusive as our brands

- **Quality:** What we do, we do well

(www.thecoca-colacompany.com/ourcompany/mission_vision_values. html; retrieved December 2012)

Values like these may be useful as an aspirational compass for employees, but should not be confused with describing the reality on the ground. Using the language of the 'preacher', i.e. 'to be committed in heart and mind', 'to shape a better future' when trying to leverage profit, can quickly bring cynicism rather than aspiration.

If the purpose of ethics is to inform moral conduct, then two clear questions arise. The first is well rehearsed: how can ethics inform the moral conduct of individual leaders? When business ethics are taught and discussed the focus is often at this 'close level'. By 'close' I am referring to ethics of proximity, of our actions which affect others near to us, those we are in contact with or those we are responsible for. For individual leaders, Aristotle suggests that ethics and moral actions can be cultivated: 'Virtues, by contrast we acquire, just as we acquire crafts … we then become just by doing just actions, temperate by doing temperate actions, brave by doing brave actions' (Aristotle, *Nicomachean Ethics*, Book 2, Chapter 1, cited in Morgan, 2011).

The second question is less well rehearsed in leadership circles, but is becoming more prominent. This takes ethics beyond 'close' relationships and accounts for the 'distant' relationships, those we are engaged with indirectly; for example outsourced workers in Asia, or our damaging impact on the environment that affects all humanity. Both close and distant ethics are required and this demands systemic ethical perspectives, taking ethics to mean that we all share a responsibility for the planet, and for the indirect consequences of our individual and collective actions.

Eco-leadership demands an ethical approach, which stands firmly against the ethic of Milton Friedman that dominated the last century. As we saw in Chapter 11, Friedman (1962, 1970) claimed that businesses serve society only if they focus on increasing profit. This ethic has led us to climate crisis, war, divisions between rich and poor, and individual alienation. A new ethic is needed in business and public sector organizations, one that subverts the logic of the market. Much of the leadership literature seeking an ethical stance unfortunately oversimplifies the challenge, and by doing so contributes to the problem. Servant leadership (Greenleaf, 1977), transformational leadership (Bass and Riggio, 2006) and post-heroic leadership (Binney et al., 2004) all promote individualistic approaches to leadership: they define the leader as an individual, and argue for a moral individual leadership. Bass, for example, argues:

> Leaders are authentically transformational when they increase awareness of what is right, good, important and beautiful, when they help to elevate followers' needs for achievement and self-actualization, when they foster in followers higher moral maturity and when they move followers to go beyond their self interests for the good of their group, organization or society. (1990: 171)

While this is important, it unfortunately does nothing to question the deeper structural ethical questions, and I would argue that this type of statement becomes part of the structural problem, because it creates a power imbalance: it situates goodness in a hierarchical, heroic leader, creating dependency and a disciple followership that inevitably create a silent and conformist organization.

Slavoj Žižek (2008) differentiates systemic and subjective violence. He claims that subjective violence (interpersonal violence) can indicate and also be caused by the much greater evil, systemic violence. News reports are 'fascinated by the lure' of subjective violence, the murder of a young person or the abduction of a child. Systemic violence, on the other hand, is invisible: it is the unseen and disowned violence that inhabits bureaucracies, institutions and governing structures. It is the violence of poverty that kills infants in thousands, the violence of oppression where immigrant workers get low pay and poor healthcare and suffer accordingly. It is the violence that surrounds us but becomes 'normal' and ignored. Much systemic violence is caused by corporations, and therefore a systemic ethical response is urgently needed. There is a problem when leaders espouse personal values but ignore the big picture: 'The hypocrisy of those who while combating subjective violence, commit systemic violence that generates the very phenomena they abhor' (Žižek, 2008: 174).

Systemic ethics means to take into account the impact of your organization on others and on the natural world, to account for the externalities, the toxic waste, the use of carbon fuel, the social justice to workers in the developing world who work for your supply chain. Eco-leadership situates ethics as part of an overall systemic approach, asking questions about the primary purpose of an organization, what it values, how it serves society and its impact on the natural world, before jumping to immediate assumptions about profit, output and growth.

Rethinking Value, Growth and Purpose.

The Eco-leadership approach is to take the ethical questions to the fundamentals of business, which means to rethink value, growth and purpose.

Rethinking Value

> The old way of measuring value is becoming irrelevant. (Al Gore, *Guardian*, 6 November 2006, p. 24)

Many companies look at their values, but not at the meaning of value itself. Success is measured in terms of financial value, without accounting for 'externalities': the costs of plundering our natural environment, the true costs of carbon energy and disposing of waste, the human costs of climate change, the real human and social costs of unemployment that occur to drive 'efficiencies' and re-engineer companies to make them more competitive. Beyond financial value, how can we value healthy communities and environments, creative workspaces, personal well-being? Organizations are not simply money-making machines, they are social enterprises (whether they acknowledge it or not), and what is valued as success must go beyond money. Valuing externalities is good economics, as it accounts for 'real costs'. Society has to pick up the costs of environmental damage, climate change, of social problems caused by unemployment or mental health problems through stress at work. The challenge is (a) to find ways to agree and measure externalities and diverse values, and (b) get agreement on re-valuing work, when so many organizations exploit a system that is currently biased towards their profiteering. Fortunately a growing body of serious work is emerging in green economics (for example, Schumacher College and the New Economics Foundation in the UK). I will give the last word on value to the agrarian writer Wendell Berry (1972: 164):

> There is only one value; the life and health of the world.

Rethinking Growth

Whilst I believe that Eco-leadership begins with ethics, which underpins and drives success and creativity, I always get asked by sceptics and those who want to convince their seniors about the 'business case' for Eco-leadership. There are two answers: the first sets out a 'business case' that demonstrates how sustainability and ethical approaches support organizational success and sustainable business growth (Unilever and Interface, Inc. demonstrate how this can work, see the case studies later).

The second answer is a more radical approach. Rather than argue that sustainable approaches can provide sustainable business growth (which I agree they can), this approach challenges the very notion of continued growth as a desirable goal. Questioning growth is taboo, says Tim Jackson, writing for the UK Sustainability Commission:

> Questioning growth is deemed to be the act of lunatics, idealists and revolutionaries. But question it we must ... The idea of a non-growing economy may be an anathema to an economist. But the idea of a continually growing economy is an anathema to an ecologist. (Jackson, 2009)

Growth is a founding principle of current economic ordering. The only solution to economic and social stability politicians and economists know is growth. The neo-liberal agenda led by the IMF, WTO, the World Bank, corporations, and national governments depends on growth. Growth ensures winners and

losers, simply because we cannot all win the economic game of outperforming the other, and growth demands ever increasing production, but this no
longer equates to employment. Castells notes that productivity growth is
now disassociated from rises in income and jobs: between 1988 and 2008
productivity grew by 30% in the USA whilst real wages rose by 2% over that
period (Castells, 2012: 157). Growth also demands consumption, and this
was fuelled in the past decade by credit on a mass scale, rather than earnings
and savings.

As I write in 2013 the losers in the dash for growth are numerous; for
example, Greece, Spanish youth who suffer 50% unemployment, those in
Italy, Portugal, Ireland, the masses who are unemployed and under-
employed throughout the USA and Europe, many suffering depression and
other mental illness challenges.

The alternatives to every country and company chasing economic growth
are argued by the New Economics Foundation in its 2010 report *Growth Isn't
Possible*. The report cites the work of Wilkinson and Pickett, who show that
economic growth is no longer doing us good in terms of quality of life. They
argue that it is not higher GDP that improves health and social outcomes but
more equality in income. It is income inequality that causes a greater range
of health and social outcomes (such as trust, the status of women, mental
health, drug use, educational attainment, murder rates, life expectancy and
obesity) (Wilkinson and Picket, 2009, cited by Robins, 2010).

Growth is a key issue, and ideally an holistic approach is required that
supports growth in developing countries to alleviate social exclusion and
poverty, and requires the rich nations to adopt zero growth policies, rethinking consumption, production and the use of resources to develop new
economies fit for the 21st century, that privilege social well-being and environmental sustainability first.

Rethinking Purpose

Rethinking value and growth leads to the inevitability of rethinking organizational purpose. Discovering organizational purpose is an ongoing process,
and entails taking a systemic ethical approach. When this process is begun,
it is surprising how unexpected organizational gains are made in diverse
areas, such as raising morale, discovering unexpected opportunities, and
developing new business models and partnerships, community and client
goodwill, the retention and recruitment of talented staff. Organizational
purpose will always include the company being successful in financial
terms, but it can also include much more.

Leadership Spirit

Leadership spirit means to draw from the spring from which the human spirit and ethics flow. The term leadership spirit in this context references the human spirit which (I hope) is universal, yet reflects the diversity of sources that inspire it, whether humanism, different religions and spiritual beliefs, or deep ecology for example. When tracing the emergence of the Eco-leadership discourse, workplace spirituality cannot be ignored as it has become a widening literature. Spirituality at work and leadership spirituality reflect a social desire to move away from rationalism and materialism, a reaction to traditional religious institutions and to address the alienation of modernity. In terms of leadership, employees are increasingly expecting their leaders to embrace a more holistic approach, to embrace subjectivity and spirituality, and to show a leadership approach that values the human spirit and well-being, as well as profit.

The mention of spirituality engages some and immediately disengages others. I am fully aware that the connections between spirituality, leadership and work are problematic, and that spirituality can be misused and distorted in this field, particularly when instrumentalized, i.e. used as a tool to increase performance and 'the bottom line'. Leadership spirit is vital yet intangible; it inspires and awakens the human capacity to strive for beauty and the 'good society', and to see beyond the clutter of activity, to reach out to others in friendship, to be good neighbours, to love, build community, and to be courageous and resilient when called to 'speak truth to power'. Leadership spirit isn't just the spark of an individual acting on others, it is a spirit that flows amongst us. Anti-slavery activists, environmental activists, the Arab Spring uprising are all inspired by and enact leadership spirit. The post-Marxist writer Žižek offers a materialist's view of the holy spirit, when addressing the Occupy supporters outside Wall Street:

> What's the Holy Spirit? It's an egalitarian community of believers who are linked by love for each other. And who only have their own freedom and responsibility to do it. In this sense the Holy Spirit is here now. And down there on Wall Street there are pagans who are worshipping blasphemous idols. (Žižek, 2012)

Of course leadership spirit can be misused and is dangerous when egotistical leaders believe forces beyond themselves inspire them. This can lead to further grandiosity creating defence mechanisms and blind-spots that can lead them and their companies into big problems.

Whilst intangible and subjective and therefore open to critique from rationalists and Marxists, leadership spirit, like wisdom, is something worth exploring. Drawing on my personal experience of coaching leaders, it is those who act with an inner and collective sense of leadership 'spirit' that are most engaging, purposeful and liked, from whichever source they are inspired.

Leadership spirit, like leadership itself, is collective as well as personal. Leadership teams and distributed leaders have to find their communal spirit to work well together, to embrace what is important. Much of my work as a consultant is to get groups and individuals to pause, to hesitate, to create a space not just for cognitive thinking or reflecting on a challenge, but also to re-engage as humans on a journey, to reconnect with each other, to share stories, and rediscover mythos and their leadership spirit.

Organizational Belonging

Gary Snyder, poet and environmentalist, writes:

> When an ecosystem is fully functioning, all the members are present at the assembly. To speak of wilderness is to speak of wholeness. Human beings came out of that wholeness and to consider the possibility of reactivating membership in the Assembly of All Beings is in no way regressive. (1990: 121)

Snyder, like many other environmentalists and deep ecologists, believes that humans have become dissociated from nature, and from place. When we lose our connection to place, to the natural environment, we lose our way, and finally we lose ourselves. We have not only become dislocated from the natural ecosystem, but also from others and from community through modernity's process of individuation and alienation (Putnam, 2000). This dislocation is not just individual phenomena, it is also organizational. Companies were located much closer to communities, drawing on local labour, often providing 'jobs for life', and because they were embedded in communities, successful business men and women often took public office. Strong connections existed and 'good' companies worked to improve their local communities, because they were part of the community. This is not to romanticize this relationship, as worker exploitation and local pollution also occurred in many workplaces. In a post-agrarian society, modernity was premised on separation. The private sphere was separated from the public domain, the church separated from the state, the body from the mind. The economy became separated from society, home became separated from work, and the concept of employment was born (Caraca, 2012: 45–7).

Globalization, multinational corporations, chain stores and global finance created new levels of separation, and new accountabilities and loyalties to distant shareholders, thereby cutting further any sustainable engagement with communities. The link between organization and place has been broken. Organizational belonging is now only for a minority of locally based organizations. Corporate business and financial organizations consider themselves a different category, separated from communities existing in a business 'bubble world'. There is a grandiosity in this bubble, summed up by the financial traders who call themselves 'Masters of the Universe'. This separation of business from the social frees them from responsibilities (e.g. tax avoidance, polluting, exploiting people who work in far-off lands) but it also denies them the benefits of 'mutuality and meaning' that 'belonging' offers. However, the split between the business world and the 'other world' of society is, of course, a myth.

Many of the corporations I work in exist in these disconnected business bubbles, detached from society. Canary Wharf, London's financial hub, is an eerie and sublime place, where beauty, power and conformity meet. A towering collection of glass towers, built on an 'island' in the East End docklands, and surrounded by some of London's poorest communities. It's a wonderful sight and a huge success story (pre the 2008 crash). Yet it has carries a dystopian sensibility. As you pass through the security barriers you enter a separate world, detached from the society around it, with its own rules and behaviours and dress codes. It is a hybrid space, a public space anyone can visit, yet with private security firms who watch over you and ban basic rights such as photography. Transparent glass buildings mock the transparency they are supposed to evoke. Banking employees shop in underground malls, travel on underground railways, exercise in gyms in their workplaces, eat in staff canteens, and are catered for in every possible way, for their comfort and at the same time ensuring they don't have to mix with the other world, the poor people on the outside of the island. This organizational detachment led to unchecked delusions. Individually and collectively traders and bankers crossed the line that led to the chaos and madness but there were no social checks to stop them. The delusion that organizations such as financial institutions and corporations operate in a business bubble, and are separate from society, was painfully exposed by the financial crisis that has led to a social and political crisis, with many suffering. There is no escape from organizational belonging.

Corporate Social Responsibility

Corporate social responsibility (CSR) and environmental concerns are now on the corporate agenda (Maak and Pless, 2006; Parker, 1998), and mark a move towards organizational belonging that is welcomed, but with a healthy scepticism. Mervyn Davies, chief executive of Standard Chartered bank and a director of Tesco, discusses the breadth of CSR:

> There isn't a management meeting in Standard Chartered where we don't talk about corporate responsibility and sustainability ... you won't survive in business if you are not environmentally responsible ... Every company in the FTSE 100 now produces a corporate responsibility report ... 80 of them have identified climate change as a business risk ... (cited in Armstrong, 2006)

CSR is distrusted by many activists. The environmentalist Jonathan Porritt is concerned that it's 'business as usual with CSR retrospectively welded on' (Armstrong, 2006). CSR and sustainability concepts in corporations are too often 'greenwash', a façade to keep the brand strong. Even when authentically applied, CSR often lacks the critical approach necessary to address the systemic ethical issues that require change. CSR still puts business outside of society; it emphasizes the costs of compliance and regulation, highlighting social imposed regulations, where companies are negotiating with society, rather than belonging to society. CSV (Creating Shared Value) gets closer to the notion of organizational belonging, as it looks to build social value into corporate strategy, realizing that corporate success and social success are interdependent.

CSR and CSV are steps on the way towards organizational belonging, with many scholars and practitioners aware of the pitfalls of 'greenwash' that uses CSR to hide rather than create real change (Bansal and Roth, 2000; Fry et al., 1982).

Three Principles of Organizational Belonging

- **Mutuality** is the foundation of organizational belonging. Mutuality infers this is a covenantal relationship rather than a transactional one, whereby there is a mutual promise of caring for the other, and for the planet.

- **Solidarity** implies that we stand alongside each other and in lateral fraternal relations, and not with one party above or below.

- **Engagement** means 'not to walk on the other side' but to engage, recognizing the obligation to our local and global neighbour. Our contemporary neighbour can be our networked global neighbour, the machine operator in China, the unemployed youth down the road, or the environment we share with others.

Organizational belonging means that organizations locate and commit themselves, to place and space. *Place* means engaging and working with local communities, being transparent about the challenges of getting rid of waste, of pollution, and helping build community. *Space* refers to networked belonging, to engaging in the extended networks the organization shares with international others, to best social and business practice, and developing sustainable business models.

Organizational belonging is to rejoin the assembly, and collectively we must find adaptive structures and processes to reconnect our organizations and businesses. This is a philosophical task, an ethical task and a practical task. Taking Eco-leadership from a theoretical context and putting it into practice is to develop the concept of organizational belonging.

Eco-Leadership in Practice

The Business Case and Examples of Good Practice

Some will say Eco-leadership is idealistic, that it's too futuristic, not practical for now. Yet the increasing recognition of social, environmental and economic interdependencies, and the implications of recent world events, point towards Eco-leadership responses that are self-evidently an urgent necessity rather than an idealist dream. There are two streams of thinking within the Eco-leadership discourse, usually divided between politicians and organizational leaders, who are **reformers**, and activists who are **radicals**. Radicals are anti-capitalists and other social activists who claim that it is necessary to radically change the political and economic structures that support existing elites. They say that reform merely prolongs a dying system. Reformers advocate *responsible* or *caring capitalism*, terms supported by progressive politicians, business and organizational leaders. They believe that capitalism can be reformed to align the purpose of organizations to accommodate the profit motive, and account for social and environmental responsibility. Box 35 sets out the reformers' business case for Eco-leadership approaches.

> ### Box 35   The Business Case for Eco-Leadership
> - **Protecting the brand** against social activism and negative consumer voices.
> - **Efficiency savings** by reducing energy bills and waste.

- **Talent attracted and retained.** Ethical practice and socially responsible companies are more attractive to bright minds.

- **Employee engagement and brand loyalty.** Employees and customers respond to companies that align 'good business' with 'doing good'. Cool companies are dynamic and ethical companies.

- **Organizational belonging and community engagement.** Creating 'social capital' is as important as financial capital; goodwill and engagement with local communities and global networks pay dividends in terms of good relations, reducing conflict and tensions, and also in unexpected ways, knowledge and ideas are shared, and the organizational network is distributed beyond company walls.

- **Anticipating regulation.** As natural resources decline and climate change increases, international and national regulation will increase. Eco-leaders lead rather than follow these moves; they anticipate change.

- **Adaptive organizations and emergent capability.** Distributing leadership and engaging employees in tackling the big issues create unexpected opportunities. Emergent strategies are formed from having open-communication across the networks. Opportunities arise from the cross-pollination of ideas, from patterns that emerge across the whole.

- **Diversity and inclusion.** Encouraging diversity and inclusion encourages both creativity and ensures the potential and talent of women and excluded minorities are engaged rather than disenfranchised, as happens in many monocultural male-dominated boardrooms.

- **New business models.** Business models are at the heart of success. Innovative new business models are emerging that replace traditional make-and-sell models. Google, Facebook and Apple are all new companies that have a huge market/share value, and operate with diverse and new business models. The challenge for them and for all companies is to connect these with more ethical practices.

- **Sustainable supply chains.** Engaging suppliers collaboratively and creatively to find sustainable solutions not only helps the environment it also creates good supplier relations and longer-term ethically-based contracts.

Reformers challenge the radicals, claiming they have yet to put forward a coherent and convincing case that offers alternatives to capitalism. However, in light of postmodern theories that discredit the notion of grand narratives, waiting for a 'new system' to be revealed is in itself old-paradigm, modernist thinking. Communism tried this route and was found to be self-destructive. Radicals claim the answer is in emergent small changes that challenge the status quo and will ultimately undermine it. Networked cultures shift from being self-interest driven to common-interest. Cardosa and Jacobetty (2012: 200) call these 'cultures of network belonging' with openness a core principle, citing YouTube, Twitter, Flikr and WikiLeaks as examples that change media power relations, and engage the multitude. Alternative economic practices are burgeoning, according to the research from Castells et al. (2012: 214), sometimes led by activists, and also by everyday folk in a response to a changing world and austerity cuts.

Below are brief case examples of Eco-leadership in practice, to show the diversity of practices. They are organized into three parts:

1 *Business sustainability and Eco-leadership* highlights leading corporations that are radically changing their business strategies and attempting to become more environmentally sustainable.

2 *Commercial Eco-leadership* offers Apple as an example of a company that applies Eco-leadership to commercial ventures, but hasn't yet matured to embrace ethical sustainability.

3 *Social Eco-leadership* briefly describes a not-for-profit hospice I work with that is attempting to radically transform hospice care using Eco-leadership principles.

1. Business Sustainability and Eco-Leadership

Unilever

The Unilever Sustainable Living Plan is a radical attempt for a company of such a size and impact to create a long-term plan that addresses environmental sustainability and protects social interests.

Paul Polman, CEO of Unilever, demonstrates Eco-leadership, claiming:

> People always think that to do the right thing costs you more. That is not true at all. It can actually ignite innovation and lower your costs. The alternative of not having sustainable sourcing, of having to deal with the effects of climate change, is a much higher cost on business ... It is time to change, that is why I am here. I want to live in a better world.

> ... The business case for growing Unilever sustainably is compelling. Consumers are asking for it, retailers demand it, it fuels product innovation, it grows the company's markets around the world and, in many cases, it saves money. (Polman, 2012)

In a March 2012 global sustainability report Unilever retained its top ranking and continued to perform well in traditional terms.[1]

Interface, Inc.

> Ray Anderson [was] often called the 'greenest CEO in America' for his crusade to turn his billion-dollar carpet company [Interface] into an environmentally sustainable enterprise. … 'I always make the business case for sustainability,' he told the *New York Times*. 'It's so compelling. Our costs are down, not up. Our products are the best they have ever been. … And the goodwill in the marketplace – it's just been astonishing.' (*Washington Post*, 2011)

I met Ray Anderson, who died in 2011, a few years ago at Schumacher College in the UK. I found he was genuinely surprised by the success of his 'mission', as he had encountered serious resistance at the outset. He expected to be making business sacrifices initially yet found himself making savings and improving business models, employee morale, brand reputation and profits too! His enthusiasm was contagious and he will be missed.

Other companies pioneering Eco-leadership approaches include Walmart, who set some fairly radical goals: Walmart's website states:

> Environmental sustainability has become an essential ingredient to doing business responsibly and successfully. As the world's largest retailer, our actions have the potential to save our customers money and help ensure a better world for generations to come. We've set three aspirational sustainability goals
>
> – To be supplied 100% by renewable energy
>
> – To create zero waste
>
> – To sell products that sustain people and the environment
>
> (http://corporate.walmart.com/global-responsibility/environment-sustainability; accessed November 2012)

Companies like Walmart have a lot of reparation to do! Their business has produced cheap goods, but with out-of-town supermarkets they have

[1] See www.globescan.com/commentary-and-analysis/press-releases/press-releases-2012/h84-press-releases-2012/181-experts-again-name-unilever-as-top-corporate-sustainability-leader.html

created big social problems by leaving whole communities without local shops who cannot compete with this giant retailer, and the company's carbon footprint is huge. There are critical voices against Walmart who claim their radical agenda is simply 'greenwash', pointing to the serious exploitation of immigrant agricultural labourers, 50% of whom earn below $5,000 a year, live in shacks and suffer poisoning by pesticides. This view reaffirms the need for the application of systemic ethics; it is no good doing good in one sphere, whilst exploiting in the other. The social and environmental agendas are inextricably linked. A 2007 analysis of Walmart's sustainability plans, by a critical coalition of labour, environmental and human rights organizations, criticized the plan as nothing more than a corporate ruse. Even if every possible target goal were reached, the plan would not make any 'real impact on global warming, employee health and welfare'. According to Walmart's own reports, total global operations in 2006 released 220 million tons of greenhouse gases, an amount that is more than 40 times greater than the emissions the company's sustainability plan pledges to reduce (Corella, 2012).

What is clear is that sustainability is at the top of the corporate agenda; the debate rages as to whether this is greenwash or serious attempts to change. I believe that both co-exist, and the task is not to polarize the debate into good activists, bad corporates, but to continually look at the structural and systemic ethics, and push for improvements.

2. Commercial Eco-leadership

Apple – not ethically there yet

Apple computers began their commercial activity by producing amazing computers but also working on business models that were out of sync with their inventions. The company adapted itself and its business models. Their move into music created a huge new business for Apple, and changed the way the music industry operated, changing how music was sold, bought and listened to. Digital distribution moved the music industry into the 21st century. Pressured by open-source activists sharing files, Apple found a solution where most people were happy to pay rather than pirate music, just so long as they could buy it at home, and download and listen to it in seconds as they could with pirated songs. Selling computers is now a sideline for a much more systemic business model. Another new key income stream has come from selling 'Apps' (applications). Here Apple changed from being imaginative but very secretive, to 'outsourcing' creativity and innovation from everyone. No longer do Apple alone create the content; consumers and competitors do too. Constantly updating Apps means more people want an

I-phone/I-Pad to access this flow of inventiveness. This is Eco-leadership in a commercial sense, democratizing creative leadership to anyone capable of invention, not just to creative employees. Eco-leadership is generative, it creates new capability, new creativity and adaptive new ways to do business. The challenge for Apple and companies like them is to discover the 'leadership spirit' and 'systemic ethics' and apply these to the Eco-leadership inventiveness that brings success. Without this change I predict that Apple will not be a sustainable success; consumers will increasingly demand better from them. To be a cool brand means to be a non-exploitative brand and Apple have serious issues in this domain. They face serious questions about the manufacturing conditions for workers in their Asian plants, and their environmental credentials are low on their agenda. They must also work hard to ensure their culture is dynamic and creative, but avoid becoming coercive and conformist. It's high time this innovative company, with a huge young consumer 'fan' base, took more seriously its capacity to influence social and environmental change. Apple can adapt, but can they belong?

3. Social Eco-Leadership

Hospice Care

This example of Eco-leadership is led by the CEO of a hospice[2] for which I consult. This hospice offers a fascinating example of an organization in transition. It has a radical aim to promote a 'social and inclusive approach' to caring for the dying. This applies Eco-leadership thinking to the social and economic challenges of providing the 'best possible death' to as many people as they can, and with specific aims of inclusivity, i.e. to reach out to excluded and marginalized groups who don't currently access this care. The ideals are excellent but the implementation of Eco-leadership principles is far from easy.

Distributing Care Means Distributing Leadership

In my work with the hospice CEO we are discovering together that to attain the vision of a 'social and inclusive approach', and to distribute care from the hospice to the community, a parallel transformation has to take place in the hospice. Power and leadership need to be distributed internally, freeing employees and volunteers to work and think differently. This means changing how people work together, creating networked and integrated relationships

---

[2] Barbara Gale, St Nicholas Hospice Care.

between diverse groups, which for some means challenging deeply held 'unconscious' assumptions about their professional identities and the nature of the work.

The hospice has six distinct sub-cultures:

1 Professional nurses/doctors: Hierarchical dependency culture

2 Fundraising department: Target-driven culture

3 Retail business (charity shops in the high street): Retail-commercial culture

4 Large volunteer workforce: Caring, 'doing good' culture

5 Managerial, admin', board and services: Bureaucratic/efficiency culture

6 CEO – Eco-leader: Social entrepreneurship culture

People work in different jobs for social and autobiographical reasons, rarely is it an accident of chance. We are drawn to roles and sectors due to a convergence of personal factors, and this is particularly so in caring professions and hospices. Our reasons are sometimes conscious and often unconscious, but most workers come to the hospice as they identify with dying, loss and 'doing good'. The overall culture in the hospice itself is pervasively one of a 'caring institution', a place of calm, dependency and quiet. It is a place where being kind, caring and considerate is the norm towards patients and relatives. There is always a shadow side in caring institutions, where anger, frustration and the sadness of the work seep out in displaced ways – not towards the patients but towards each other. The visitors, relatives and patients receive superb care, in an atmosphere of calm containment in the hospice and in the community. At this hospice they excel at what they do. Yet the CEO has a vision, believing that hospice care can be improved, and that their services can reach many more people, including disenfranchised people, if they change the way care is delivered. Below is a consultation note I wrote to help clarify their aims and reflect back to them their journey and challenges.

Consulting Note to Hospice Leadership Team
Social Hospice Care: Reconnecting Life and Death

The vision is to turn the hospice 'inside out' to deliver a social model of hospice care that engages family, friends, neighbours, local charities, professionals and volunteers. The aim is to transform the current idea of a hospice from being a building, a good place to die whilst nursed by angels, to the idea that a hospice should 'mobilize hospitality' to the dying and their relatives in the community. The care of the dying will be returned to those best placed to do the caring – family, friends, neighbours, community – supported by volunteers and vocational experts when needed.

The advantages of this model are manifold, but three key areas stand out.

The Moral Case: Expanding access

- *Getting more from existing funding.* Four per cent of those dying currently access hospice care. By enabling the community to do the caring, this percentage can be increased thereby maximizing the benefits from the same resources.

- *Engaging diversity.* Hospice care throughout the UK is taken up mostly by the white, middle classes. By engaging the community the hospice hopes to reach diverse and marginalized groups that currently don't access hospice care, such as the homeless, travellers and racially excluded groups.

2. The Quality Case: 'Light touch' interventions

By engaging the community a more personal, tailored care is given, and delivered in the person's home whenever possible. Professional expertise is used where necessary, but care of the dying is so much more than a medical intervention, or talking to a bereavement counsellor. A 'better death' means taking an holistic approach, drawing on all the resources available: family, friends, neighbours, familiar surroundings and expert help where necessary.

3. The Social Case: Reconnecting life and death

By returning the experience of dying to the community a process of reconnecting life and death takes place. Modernity alienates, gives power to experts and removes it from the community. The social case is to access and reclaim the collective wisdom of the community (including the patient and family), wisdom that exists beyond the functional knowledge of experts. Hospice beds and the building can play a part in the social hospice care model, but a small part and not its totality.

Social hospice care is to reconnect life and death by making the dying process visible and accessible, to reclaim it from the hospice hidden away in nice grounds, to once again make dying an acceptable part of all of our experience.

Social Eco-Leadership

This social application of Eco-leadership expands leadership to the multitude: where the dying patient can take a lead in having greater influence over what they need, where husbands, wives, sons and daughters can take a lead, where hospice neighbours can take a lead, where the faith minister can take a lead, where the doctor and nurse can take a lead, and also where they all can become followers as well as leaders.

The Eco-leadership challenge for the hospice is threefold:

1 *Gain critical mass support:* to clarify and share the vision to gain a critical mass both within the hospice stakeholders (this includes convincing the board, funding bodies and other stakeholders) and in the community at large.

2 *New business model:* to develop a new business model that supports the vision. The existing business model supports the 'patients in hospice beds' delivery of care, and new ways of funding social hospice care will be necessary.

3 *Develop the internal structures and culture, to deliver flexible social care:* to achieve this vision requires a generative leadership, leaders learning from each other and from the community, following and leading in a fluid way. Leading a transformation in hospice care means also to transform professional identities to vocational identities, that will enable a more fluid approach than the traditional roles and hierarchies of power and profession.

The examples we have looked at in this section begin with Eco-leadership as a force for more sustainable approaches to business, and then they transcend this limited view, taking Eco-leadership into the realms of new business models and new social care approaches. What becomes clear is that Eco-leadership in practice demands internal organizational change to deliver external change.

Conclusion

Eco-leadership addresses two interrelated challenges:

1 How to develop successful leadership in post-industrial organizations, recognizing the changes faced in a globalized and networked society.

2 How to respond ethically and creatively to the social and environmental challenges.

The Eco-leadership discourse is growing but uncertainly. When economies go into recession, political and business leaders often hit the Controller leadership button, becoming reactive, and reverting to the very same methods that created the problems in the first place. Crises and constraints also stimulate innovation and change, and this is where hope lies. The challenge is to break into a new paradigm, where functionality and a utilitarian approach no longer determine us, and where we can imagine and create new organizational forms that liberate rather than constrain us. In 1930 Max Weber prophetically warned us of the iron cage that was ensnaring us, and he suggested that carbon fuel was directly implicated in this:

> This order is now so bound to the technical and economic conditions of machine production ... perhaps it will so determine them until the last ton of fossilized coal is burnt ... (Weber, 1930: 123)

Weber was right, the finite resources of carbon fuel and the implications of climate change have awoken us, and for the first time since we ensnared ourselves there is an opportunity to free ourselves from this iron cage of materialism, unending growth and devotion to the market. The primary task of Eco-leadership is to dismantle the modernist hegemony and become reconnected and recognize our interdependence.

The Eco-leadership discourse is now embedded and gaining momentum. Box 36 describes the Eco-leader character. Eco-leadership differs from the other three discourses as it doesn't privilege individual leaders, but focuses on distributed forms of leadership. However, individual characters still internalize and represent the Eco-leadership discourse, whilst leadership evolves in many other forms as well.

Box 36 The Character of the Eco-Leader

The Eco-leader character is a generative leader, who creates organizational spaces for leadership to flourish. Eco-leaders think spatially and connectedly; these leaders think like organizational architects, connecting people and creating networks using processes and technology. Design and aesthetics matter to Eco-leaders; they recognize our working environment is essential to our psychological and spiritual well-being, and to our creativity and productivity.

Eco-leaders are passionate about ethics, humanizing the workplace, developing sustainable business models, engaging positively with local communities, and protecting the natural environment. Eco-leaders are progressive thinkers, interested in current affairs, with some engaged in technological improvements, others not. Some are quietly leading from the sidelines, others are visionaries with a missionary belief in their work drawing also on the

(Continued)

(Continued)

Messiah leadership discourse in order to inspire change. Hopefully they will balance Messiah leadership with a profound belief in ethics, collaboration, diversity and distributing leadership, that counter the hubris, power imbalances and conformist cultures that can arise with Messiah leaders. However, be warned: some environmentalist inspired 'Eco-leaders' become puritanical, missing the connections between beauty and leadership spirit. They can also become domineering and self-righteous, and lose the trust of others. Successful Eco-leaders show openness to diversity, working comfortably with difference; they encourage dialogue and dissent, and delight in autonomist leadership approaches.

   Successful Eco-leaders embody generous and generative leadership. They live by the simple equation that by giving you gain much more. Creating spaces for others to lead, they recognize that leadership is a collective effort. They constantly connect others in the network, allowing mutuality and creativity to blossom.

What is encouraging is that companies like Interface and Unilever are not only winning prizes for their sustainability work, they are also successful businesses, which should help encourage sceptics and shareholders that a longer-term vision and Eco-leadership approach is the future. The challenge is clear: to move from 20th century leadership to 21st century leadership, and to recognize that organizations and the world have irrevocably changed.

I have addressed audiences and consulted in many countries and sectors using Eco-leadership ideas, and the response has been very encouraging, even in unexpected terrain. I have realized that a challenge and gap exist between conceptually and emotionally engaging with the Eco-leadership discourse, and delivering change in practice. There are no magic bullets, but having clearer understandings will help guide us. I have been working with leaders on a practical coaching process I call Analytic-Network Coaching that works to develop Eco-leadership. I use this with individuals and teams, and as an OD (organizational development) intervention. It takes leaders on a five-stage journey, through depth analysis, relational analysis, leadership analysis, network analysis and strategic analysis, essentially connecting the inner-self, the relational self and the leader within, and then identifies where power, resources and change are possible in the wider network, enabling them to develop strategies to influence networked change. At the heart of this process sit systemic ethics and leadership spirit. Box 37 outlines the key points.

Box 37   The Analytic-Network Coaching Process©

The Analytic-Network Coaching Process connects five frames, to create a holistic change process, for those wanting to develop Eco-leadership approaches in practice.

The A-NcP delivers an effective way to connect individual developmental coaching with delivering organizational change. Individuals are coached to become *catalysts of influence* in their organizational networks.

A-NcP is research based and *theoretically robust*. It has been developed from the latest coaching meta-theory (Western, 2012) and successfully tested in diverse organizations with strategic leaders.

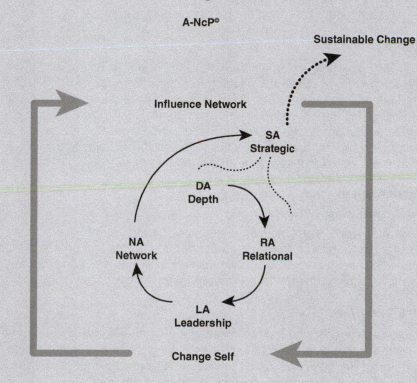

ANc Five Frames

The five *frames* offer an integrated change process, working to help the individual leader make organizational changes.

Depth Analysis

Works on the *Inner-self* to reveal and develop a grounded and confident 'authentic self'. We coach to help clarify values, define what brings meaning,

(Continued)

(Continued)

joy and contentment, coaching the client to develop themselves towards the person they really desire to be.

Relational Analysis

Relational Analysis focuses on the *Relational-self* to improve team and social relationships. Relationships are vital to success; our ability to connect and influence depends on our ability to relate and respond to others with confidence. We examine how individuals get trapped in relational dynamics that prevent them working to the very best of their ability. Improving teamwork and customer relations means improving the quality of relationships.

Leadership Analysis

The aim is to help find the *'leader within'*; to develop their unique and often dormant or unrecognized talent, aligning leadership with an individual's personality, rather than trying to fit them to a specific leadership framework. We believe leadership is everywhere: all have the potential to lead and for contemporary organizations to be successful, leadership needs to flourish! ANc coaching works to improve an individual's leadership capability and in doing so helps the coachee *mobilize leadership* in others.

Network Analysis

Coaching the *Networked-self* is to locate individuals in the networks in which they live and work. 'Thinking Connectedly' is the key to network analysis; to see the bigger picture, and to connect people, power and processes, to produce the outcomes desired. Networked thinking is a vital contemporary leadership capability, one that is often overlooked in coaching.

Strategic Analysis

Strategic Analytic coaching focuses on adapting to change, seeing emergent patterns in the 'big picture' and then acting, taking the leap of faith to make bold strategic decisions. We coach to review the previous four frames and co-create strategies, for the individual to develop themselves and also to deliver organizational success. In frame five, leaders are thinking more creatively and are seeing new developments, new business opportunities, and new ways to link ethics with success. S-A is where leaders become confident and strategic change agents.

This A-Nc process is currently being used to train internal change agents to deliver whole system change in a number of settings, including a complex health eco-system.

For further information on Analytic-Network Coaching see www.simonwestern. com.

Developing support for leaders is essential, and connecting individual talent with network thinking and practices is key to developing success. Chapter 14, Leadership Formation, discusses this further. My experience is that we must refrain from prescriptive solutions, but it is vital to offer structures, containers and processes to help leaders find their way, and to guide them into the wider networks to develop systemic responses, rather than allow them to retreat into the silos of short-termism and individual psychology.

Whilst giving keynote speeches on leadership and coaching in Belarus and central Russia, which are still largely state-influenced, bureaucratic and centralized, I was surprised how much they engaged with ideas of Eco-leadership, in contrast to the Controller leadership discourse that dominates their workplaces. Whichever sector or country I visit, people understand the world is a place of connections and interdependencies, that organizations need to belong, and they are ecosystems that cannot be controlled from the centre any more. More than this, people are increasingly demanding their autonomy, individually and collectively. There is a universal striving for the human spirit to be free, and for leadership spirit to include the multitude, where each of us, independently and together, can work towards a 'good society'.

Eco-leadership is the application of an ecological worldview to organizations, and social and political movements. It describes a way of organizing based on sustainable principles, many of them learned from nature. Yet it doesn't ignore technology and human potential. Eco-leadership is about recognizing the multitude of talent in society, and harnessing the creativity and adaptability in our technical, social and natural ecosystems. The task of Eco-leadership today is to 'Adapt and Belong', to co-create organizations that are adaptive to change, and also 'belong' to the social and natural world. Eco-leadership is to develop 'webs of work' and then connect these to the 'webs of life'.

Suggested Readings

- Capra, F. (1996) *The Web of Life.* New York: Doubleday.

- Jackson, T. (2009) *Prosperity Without Growth? The Transition to a Sustainable Economy.* London: UK Sustainability Commission.

- Maturana, H. and Varela, F. (1987) *The Tree of Knowledge: The Biological Roots of Human Understanding.* Boston, MA: Shambala.

- Redekop, B. W. and Olson, S. (2010) *Leadership for Environmental Sustainability*. New York: Routledge.

- Wheatley, M. (2006) *Leadership and the New Science*. San Francisco, CA: Berrett–Koehler.

Reflection Points

- What does it mean that organizations are ecosystems within ecosystems?

- What are the strengths of distributing leadership throughout an organization?

- Reflect on how eco-leadership works internally to support organizational change and at the same time looks outwards, taking an environmental and social stance. These two positions are traditionally separated, but reflect on how these two activities are complementary and connected.

Sample Assignment Question

At the heart of eco-leadership are the **four qualities**:

1 Connectivity and interdependence

2 Leadership spirit

3 Systemic ethics

4 Organizational belonging

Apply the four qualities of Eco-leadership to an organization you know well. Imagine you are an external evaluator, assessing the success of this organization against these four qualities, and write a report summarizing your findings. Conclude the report by suggesting what initial actions could be taken to improve against each of the four qualities.

13 An Overview of the Leadership Discourses

Introduction

This chapter summarizes the leadership discourses, and describes how they relate to each other and to leadership practice. Figure 13.1 offers a visual overview of how these discourses emerged and dominated over the past century. Each evolved due to different historical, social and economic contexts, and each remains present and informs leadership practice today.

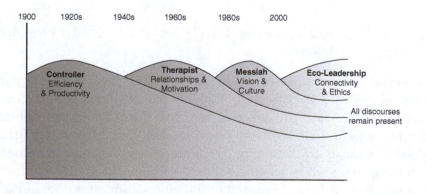

Figure 13.1   The four discourses of leadership

Practitioners don't work consciously within discourses; they follow intuitively what they think 'normative' leadership is. There are no right or wrong discourses, but each has strengths and limitations, and if a single discourse becomes over-zealously used in an organizations, it may become problematic.

A single discourse may clearly dominate different sectors, organizations and departments, but they usually co-exist to different degrees. Individuals usually draw on different leadership approaches in practice, even when they claim and believe they are fixed to one discourse. In leadership practice, the co-existence of discourses usually means one of two things and sometimes both:

1 A leadership synthesis of skills and culture to maximize organizational performance and enhance employee engagement is occurring.

2 Competing and conflicting leadership approaches are creating tensions, often damaging the organization.

I will now offer a brief summary of each discourse, before addressing how they operate together in practice.

Discourse Summary

Table 13.1 summarizes the discourses, followed by a short synopsis on each.

Discourse 1: Controller Leadership Discourse – 'Control resources to maximize efficiency'

The first leadership discourse that emerged at the beginning of the twentieth century, epitomized by Frederick Taylor's scientific management, is the Controller leader. The organization metaphor is the machine, and Controller leadership meant that workers were treated like 'cogs-in-a-machine'. Leadership focuses on controlling resources (including human resources) and making the machine as efficient as possible to maximize production. This discourse is born from scientific rationalism and the industrial revolution, and its ethical stance is utilitarian, with the belief that progress comes through applying science and rationality.

Table 13.1 Summary of the four discourses of leadership

	Controller	Therapist	Messiah	Eco-Leader
Organizational metaphor	**Machine** The organization functions like a machine, requiring inputs and outputs, and maintenance. Employees are functional parts of the machine.	**Clinic** The organization is like a therapeutic clinic, employees requiring psychological support and motivation to perform well. Personal growth is linked to organizational growth and success.	**Community** The Messiah leads a community, giving employees a feeling of belonging (cult-like cultures). The emphasis is on strong cultures, and the brand/company comes before the individual.	**Ecosystem** The organization is an *ecosystem within ecosystems*. The leader looks both ways: internally at the organizational network and externally at the ecosystem of the wider world (social and natural). Making holistic connections enables emergent capacity and adaptivity.
Leader's focus	**Body** Controller leader focuses on the body to maximize efficient production, via transactions, incentives and coercion.	**Psyche** Therapist leader focuses on the psyche and emotions, to motivate and to find the best fit between person and role.	**Soul** Messiah works with the soul. Followers align themselves to the vision, a cause greater than the self (the company). The Messiah is a role model, linking success with personal salvation.	**System** Eco-leaders lead by facilitating the whole system. They make spaces for leadership to flourish, connect people in the network, and develop communication feedback loops enabling systemic self-regulation.
Leadership approach	**Maximize Efficiency** Maximizes efficiency utilizing scientific rationalism to improve productivity.	**People and Profit** Maximizes production though increased motivation, personal growth and team work.	**Clear Vision, Strong Cultures** Leader creates strong cultures, and loyal followers, behind their clear vision for the company's success.	**Connectivity and Interdependence** Leaders recognize their interdependency with and beyond the organization. Connectivity creates an adaptive organization, that addresses social and environmental challenges, and generates business success.

(Continued)

Table 13.1 Continued

	Controller	Therapist	Messiah	Eco-Leader
Perceptions of employees	**Resources** Employees are human resources, 'cogs in the machine', functional and replaceable.	**Clients** Leaders motivate and support staff as if therapeutic clients. Self-actualization takes place through reparation and creativity at work.	**Disciples** Employees are loyal 'disciples'. They admire and identify with the leader. The individual creates an identity within a community of believers, e.g. 'Googlers'.	**Distributed Leaders** Employees are distributed leaders, part of a network, with agency and autonomy, yet also part of an inter-dependent greater whole.
Control	**Bureaucratic** Control via rules, standards, clear tasks, targets and measurement of productivity and performance.	**Humanistic** Control by emotional management and therapeutic governance.	**Culture Control** Workers internalize the cultural norms which become an organizational ideal: 'Apple is a great company'. Policing is via self-surveillance and peer pressure.	**Self-regulating Systems** Control resides in the system itself. The leader facilitates through feedback loops and boundary maintenance. The ecosystem requires resources and nurturing to self regulate.
Ethical stance	**Utilitarian** Scientific neutrality: what matters is efficiency to produce success.	**Humanism** People matter! For company success and for the ethical good of society.	**Leader Dependent** Ethics depend on leader's moral stance, some Messiahs have a clear ethical vision, others are exploitative.	**Sustainability** People, Profit, Planet: sustainable business models, social responsibility and environmental sustainability.

The Controller leader operates as a technocrat leader, focusing only on efficiency, output and productivity. This leadership approach provided huge gains, enabling mass production, cheap access to goods and raised standards of living during the first half of the 20th century. Controller leadership was critiqued from the outset for being inhuman in its mechanistic approach to workers, and for 'instrumental rationalism' where the ends (to make more profit through efficiencies) became more important than the means (how this was achieved). This has led to explicit immorality and less direct forms of systemic violence to people and the natural world.

Leading and Controlling by Numbers

The Controller leadership discourse remains today in manufacturing sectors across the globe, and has undergone a revival in knowledge economies. The rise of an audit culture has meant targets and measurement become the over-riding mechanism of control. Rationalization of public services, national audits by the IMF, and performance management, reflect the rise of Controller leadership through numbers. The audit culture produces a new realm of managers/experts of measurement and data collection, and a new bureaucracy is created. Control by numbers also means reductionism. Quantification doesn't reflect complex economic and social dynamics, and it focuses on what can be measured, rather than to take a systemic and strategic view of the effects of all the parts on the whole. There are however success stories and Controller leadership is an important part of organizational leadership. Low cost airlines and supermarkets are examples of the successful use of Controller leadership, providing cheap and efficient services. The wider questions of the impact on society and the environment, however, are not addressed in this discourse.

Discourse 2: Therapist Leadership Discourse – 'Happy workers are more productive workers'

The Therapist leadership discourse emerged from a 'therapeutic culture' that pervaded Western society. This leadership discourse emerged from the post-war period, reflecting the drive for a more democratic society and the wider social trends of individualism, personal growth and the growing expectations that work should be fulfilling (Furedi, 2003; Lasch, 1979; Rieff, 1966). The Therapist leader emerged from the Human Potential and Human Relations movement. The discourse became dominant in the 1960s, mirroring the counter-culture rebellion against authoritarianism (seen as Controller discourse in the workplace) and the exponential rise in individualism and the personal growth movement. The focus on personal growth and self-actualization was readily translated to the workplace, and used by leaders to motivate individuals and teams, through job redesign and job enhancement to make work more satisfying and to produce team cohesion.

Employers and theorists believed that happier workers would be more motivated and productive than coerced workers. Therapist leadership was more progressive and democratic and aimed to overcome worker alienation under the Controller leadership discourse. Work became a site for personal growth and achievement, a place to create meaning and identity. Under the leader as Therapist, people 'went to work to work on themselves' (Rose, 1990). Personnel departments were established, and management consultants and a huge training and development industry flourished.

Changing work patterns such as the rise of the knowledge worker mean employees bring more of their cognitive and subjective selves to work, which also demands that leaders have the skills to work with subjectivity and encourage creativity and thinking. The recent rise in executive coaching reveals how the Therapist discourse is thriving. Leaders are coached to become more self-aware, to fulfil their human and leadership potential, and to use coaching skills themselves to become more emotionally intelligent and authentic in their leadership roles.

However, this discourse lost its potency in the early 1980s, especially at more senior levels, as it could no longer deliver the economic benefits across global businesses. The Asian Tiger economies were outperforming the West drawing on different leadership approaches. Therapist leadership is about people, motivating individuals and teams, and therefore remains important particularly at middle management and team leadership levels, but it does not equip leaders to be strategic, to work with a culture or lead systemically, creating adaptive organizations.

Discourse 3: Messiah Leadership Discourse – 'Visionary leaders and strong cultures'

Arising in the early 1980s, Messiah leadership discourse provided charismatic leadership and vision in the face of a turbulent and uncertain environment. The Messiah appeals to individuals and society, promising salvation from the chaotic world in which a lack of control is experienced and where traditional community is diminished. As the workplace rises in importance as a site of community, replacing institutions such as the church and family, so the corporate leader replaces the priesthood as a social character of influence (Steve Jobs for example). Companies wanted employees to bring their whole self to work, and therefore the Messiah leaders created strong (conformist) organizational cultures, where workers would be totally committed and loyal to the leader and company (compliant) yet bring their creativity and full energy to work.

The Messiah character (epitomized by the transformational leader) leads by offering visions to which followers can aspire. Their focus is on shaping the culture, as control of employees relies on 'culture control', e.g. using open plan offices and peer surveillance. Leaders hold the power, and claim to transform others and the culture, which is disabling to 'followers'. Brand engagement is not just for customers; employee engagement is vital in company cultures run in this way. Coca-Cola asks its employees to 'Be the Brand', clearly attempting to merge the individual and company identity. The rise in the earnings of leaders graphically represents the increase of expectations on leaders since the Messiah discourse arrived:

> Since 1978, CEO pay at American firms has risen 725 percent, more than 127 times faster than worker pay over the same time period, according to new data from the Economic Policy Institute. (Waldron, 2012)

Visionary leadership is important, as are strong cultures, and Messiah leadership often begins with success, but sustainability is a real problem. These companies aim to create harmony by gaining employees' loyalty and cultural alignment, and in doing so they eliminate difference (nay-sayers are quickly socially disciplined by their peers and will conform or be expelled). Commitment and loyalty and strong cultures are important, as is a clear vision, but there is a tipping point whereby strong cultures become a benign form of totalitarian control. Casey (1995) refers to corporations with 'designer employees' where employees are so over-identified and colonized by the workplace culture that they no longer have the capacity to self-reflect or critique it, and they become 'capitulated selves'.

These corporate cultures produce 'cult-like cultures' that begin by being dynamic but end up producing the 'groupthink' that led to the Enron scandal and financial collapse, in which no-one was willing to question management malpractice, or business models that were clearly less than transparent and highly questionable. Leading with a powerful vision and creating a strong culture offers an nice ideal, but unless the Messiah discourse embraces other discourses in its maturing phase, then these companies produce dangerous cultures.

Discourse 4: Eco-Leadership Discourse – 'Connectivity, sustainability and interdependence'

The Eco-leadership discourse is not just environmentally focused, it's also about leading organizations successfully in the 21st century. Heifetz writes that

'Adaptive challenges require solutions that lie outside the current way of operating' (Heifetz, 1994: 76) and the Eco-leadership discourse has emerged to address the adaptive challenges of our time, taking a systemic and ethical position. Eco-leadership takes a more holistic and networked perspective of organizations in line with the networked society in which we live. Eco-leaders conceptualize organizations as *ecosystems within ecosystems;* a change in one part of the organization affects the whole, like a natural ecosystem. This is very different from conceptualizing an organization using the machine metaphor, as a closed system that makes profits and can be divided into departments and functions.

Eco-leadership is about connectivity, interdependence and sustainability underpinned by an ethical, socially responsible stance. Eco-leaders see organizations as an interconnected living network, with virtual and physical flows between humans, nature and technologies. The task of Eco-leaders is to think spatially, to see patterns and connections, and create a network of leaders distributed throughout the organization, changing the paradigm from hierarchical control to dispersed leadership, which can react more quickly and notice the changes occurring at grassroots levels in the business. Leadership at the outer limits of the organization is as important as leadership at the top.

Ethics and Eco-Leadership: A Paradigm Change

Eco-leadership means renegotiating what is valued and what success means for an organization. It addresses a paradigm change, rather than fixes a problem. Delivering growth and short-term shareholder value is no longer acceptable as the sole measurement of value and success. Eco-leadership is to widen the concept of value beyond financial numbers to include valuing human creativity and dignity, the natural environment, aesthetics, local communities and employees', customers'/clients' well-being. The qualities of Eco-leadership are:

1 Connectivity and interdependence

2 Systemic ethics

3 Leadership spirit

4 Organizational belonging

The Eco-leadership approach doesn't overshadow the other discourses but encompasses them. It acts as a meta-discourse (see Box 38), offering an overview, strategically providing the organization with the right balance of leadership, and encouraging diversity to utilize different people's skills and assumptions to create an adaptive whole.

Box 38   Eco-Leadership as a Meta-Discourse

Eco-leadership acts as a meta-discourse within organizations, influencing how the four discourses work together. Eco-leaders identify the appropriate leadership approaches within each department, and within the whole organization.

As Figure 13.2 shows, Eco-leadership is both inside and outside the boundaries of an organization. Internally Eco-leadership acts as one of the four discourses, and as a meta-discourse guides how the others are utilized. Externally Eco-leadership embraces the wider issues that arise in the ecosystems made up of nature, technology and society.

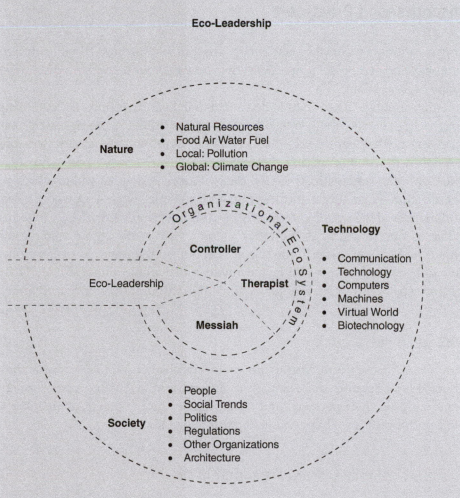

Figure 13.2   'Ecosystems within ecosystems'

(Continued)

(Continued)

The dotted lines indicate how the boundaries between an organization and the wider ecosystems are more open and blurred than our 'normative' constructs of organizations allow for. The 'structural coupling' between organizations and the wider environment cannot be ignored (Maturana and Varela, 1987).

As a meta-discourse, the Eco-leader also guides the organization in a wider context, facilitating emergent strategies to address challenges and grasp new opportunities.

Discourses in Practice

Organizations reveal the leadership discourses through their cultures, language and symbols. Figure 13.3 shows how the four leadership discourses shape organizations.

Rarely are single discourses so dominant that the form is pure. As leadership approaches co-exist, the forms either merge and adapt, or an organizational form exists that contradicts the leadership culture and creates tensions through a transitional period. For example, when Messiah leadership flips into Controller leadership, there is a clash of form, structures and practices, as flat structures and hierarchical pyramids don't mix well. The web of Eco-leadership and the pyramid hierarchy of Controller don't work easily together either, as one undermines the other. Often I work with organizations who pursue an Eco-leadership approach, but cannot get the pyramid of Controller out of their unconscious minds and revert to it without intending to. These tensions speak through the organization, often through resistance to change.

Discourse Preference

Individual leaders and leadership teams rarely consciously choose their preferred leadership discourse, but are drawn to them unconsciously, depending on their personal and social history and contexts, which shape their perceptions of what good leadership looks like.

Personal Valency towards Leadership Discourses

Individuals internalize an 'idealized' leadership stance, which relates to their social location, and their personal experience of leadership, beginning from their parenting. In psychoanalytic terms this process is called 'valency',

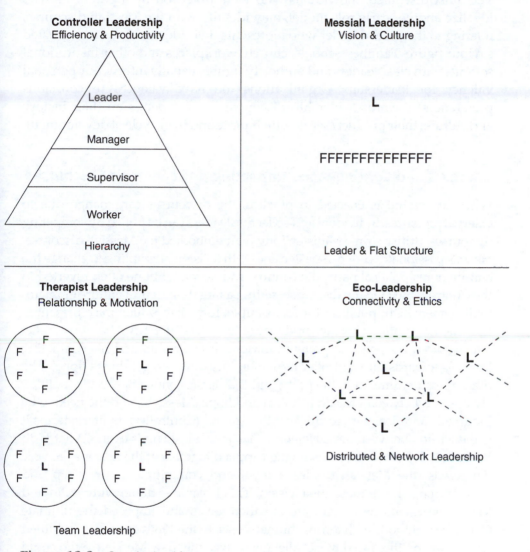

Controller Leadership
Efficiency & Productivity

Leader

Manager

Supervisor

Worker

Hierarchy

Messiah Leadership
Vision & Culture

L

FFFFFFFFFFFFFF

Leader & Flat Structure

Therapist Leadership
Relationship & Motivation

Team Leadership

Eco-Leadership
Connectivity & Ethics

Distributed & Network Leadership

Figure 13.3   Organizational forms

whereby individuals carry within themselves a propensity towards certain group/leadership cultures (Bion, 1961). For example, if a person has a very strict mother or father, or they were brought up in a strict religious culture or a harsh boarding school, this will influence the leader they identify with later in life. They may assume that all leaders should be in the Controller discourse, as this is the norm for them. Alternatively they may internalize a hatred for authoritarian leadership, viewing this early experience as damaging, leading them to seek a reparative leadership model such as the Therapist discourse. Individuals who were doted on by a parent or who idealize another early role model, may identify with the Messiah discourse, relating to the special leader who represents their idealized parent, a trusted saviour figure. Families, schools, church, workplaces and other institutional settings with clear leaders and authority figures usually inform our personal valency for leadership. Organizations too have valences (unconscious preferences) towards leadership discourses; this depends on their history and culture, their product/service, their place and their cycle of development.

Contexts and Contingencies Impacting on Leadership Discourses

When leadership is enacted in practice, the discourses can change due to external pressures. Individual and collective leaders can be pulled by competing discourses. British Prime Minister Tony Blair embodied the Messiah discourse. He was passionate, very persuasive and with a vision attempting to change the culture of his political party, the country and beyond, but he often reverted to the Controller leadership discourse, setting a target-and-audit culture of micro-management in the public sector, for example. Tony Blair's dilemma represented two internal conflicts: his own and that of his 'socialist' party. His own conflict was between his personal preference Messiah leadership and his competing leanings towards the Controller leadership discourse 'to get things done'. The other pressure came from the party, and the classic conflict of socialist politics, always torn between utopian idealism and hope (Messiah), and the need to be pragmatic and deal with realities on the ground (Controller). In literal terms it is the tension between the *Communist Manifesto* and Lenin's essay 'What Is To Be Done?'. These two discourses when applied together at the extreme are very dangerous: the Messiah creates a loyal and committed followership and applies Control to impose their vision. This became extreme with Stalin and Mao, who established a cult around themselves and imposed the ultimate Controller methods with terrible human costs. In the 1980s even Blair's diluted 'third way' politics faced this challenge: he was the 'new Messiah', who could save the public sector after years of decline under Thatcherite politics; yet the pragmatic need to impose change quickly meant a return to the Controller discourse that became dogmatic.

To change discourses is not simply a matter of choice, it firstly requires a recognition of the problems, and that discourses are formed through hidden yet widely accepted assumptions. Blair's Labour party never understood this dynamic, so deep was the party adherence to the underpinning pragmatism of the Controller discourse, that they missed the secondary impacts of forcing change through numbers and targets, such as the rise in bureaucracy, the lowering of morale, and the distortion of clinical care to hit the numbers rather than privilege patient care.

Understanding the leadership discourses makes it easier for leaders to recognize these processes. When they are recognized, leaders can act to ensure that reactivity to short-term pressure doesn't alter their strategic course.

Geographical and Socio-cultural Contexts

Different geographical, historical and socio-cultural contexts also favour different leadership discourses. For example, through my work observations, it appears that in the USA leadership seems more accepted than in Europe, where it is less trusted. The Messiah discourse is therefore more 'at home' in the USA, and the Therapist discourse more likely in Europe as it has less of an overt leadership feel to it. In the Middle East and China, the Controller leader appears to be strong (although I have not researched this in depth and rely on visits and sources I work within from these regions).

Discourses and Levels of Seniority and Functions

Positions within hierarchies, and locations in functions and departments, also impact on the leadership discourse. The Messiah leadership discourse is more favoured, the higher in the organization one climbs. The Therapist leader is favoured in the realms of aspiring middle managers, team leaders, and HR departments. Human Resource departments often fluctuate between the Controller discourse when operating on transactional and contractual concerns, and the Therapist discourse when dealing with leadership/team development. This undermines how HR departments implement developmental policies. Trapped in Controller discourse mindsets from their contractual work, they apply this to developmental work and so often get it badly wrong. Controller discourses are necessary and dominant in finance departments where control by numbers is vital, and Controller leadership is also favoured by project managers, working with limited resources and time constraints.

Working Across the Discourses

Each discourse has its merits and its weaknesses. Discourses are not right or wrong, they exist, representing wider social phenomena. Once aware of the discourse and its meaning we can make some assessment as to how each discourse affects the organization. While we are all captured by a particular dominant discourse, we are not fixed by it. By becoming aware of discourses we are more able to resist those that are not helpful or have oppressive tendencies.

Boxes 39–42 offer examples of how each leadership discourse might impact within different work situations. These boxes are not definitive but examples to promote a dialogue as to which leadership discourses fit different situations and contexts.

Box 39　Controller Leadership in Practice

Strengths	Weaknesses
Focus on output and task Results-driven and improves efficiency Empirical and measurable targets Decisive leadership in a crisis Quantifies what success means Standardizes quality/products Reduces waste (increasingly important for sustainability and cost reduction)	Creates employees' alienation, resentment and resistance Poor use of human resource, does not utilize employee's knowledge, skills and creativity Creates inflexible workforce relations, often leading to employee disputes or lowering morale
Useful settings	**Less useful settings**
Production line, manufacturing Workplaces where efficiency and control is vital, e.g. nuclear industry Accounting and finance departments Construction industry Task-focused project management First-line leadership	Post-industrial workplaces Knowledge-led industries Education sector People-focused services Entrepreneurial business Innovation and creative sector Senior strategic leadership

Box 40   Therapist Leadership in Practice

Strengths	Weaknesses
Motivates and supports individuals	Lacks big picture, strategic focus
Develops team cohesion	Lacks dynamism and energy
Emotionally intelligent leaders, therefore less people problems	Doesn't build strong cultures
Builds trust	Individual and team focus at expense of systems and holistic focus
Empowers others	Organization/teams can become introverted and narcissistic focusing on internal dynamics rather than the task and external focus
Offers personal growth, developing individuals to work smarter and harder	Team leaders become 'good mummies/daddies', creating a childlike dependency in their teams

Useful settings	Less useful settings
Steady state organizations	Fast-changing organizations
People organizations: education, health, public and not-for-profit sectors	Multinationals with complex structures, requiring systemic and culture-led approaches
Value-focused organizations with an ethos of human development	Manufacturing sector and building industry, which require a robust task focus
Middle management-leadership roles, supporting individuals and teams	Senior leadership requiring a strategic focus
Human Resource function	Hi-tech organizations that function on technical expertise
Universities and training organizations	

Box 41   Messiah Leadership in Practice

Strengths	Weaknesses
Builds strong aligned companies	Unsustainable over long periods
Strategic and visionary in aims	Conformist and homogeneous cultures form, that stifle innovation and change
Dynamic energized cultures	Can lead to totalizing fundamentalist cultures
Creates a community that employees identify with and feel they belong in	Leaders can become omnipotent and grandiose
Encourages self-managed 'family' teams within a strong culture	Followership dependency occurs with charismatic leadership: undermining autonomy and creativity
Useful settings	**Less useful settings**
Post-industrial companies	Steady state organizations
Knowledge-based companies	Industrial and manufacturing sector
Global corporations	Organizations requiring continuity and dependency, e.g. healthcare, banking
Senior strategic leadership	Middle management/team leadership
Start-ups and entrepreneurial organizations can benefit from Messiah's vision and drive at outset	Public services

Box 42   Eco-Leadership in Practice

Strengths	Weaknesses
Appropriate to network society	A more difficult concept to grasp and to train leaders, as it refutes reductionist and simplistic solutions
Ethical and sustainable approaches	

Meta-discourse therefore able to integrate other discourses	Requires confidence to follow emergent strategies rather than rely on fixed plans
Engages and retains talent	Takes long-term view rather than short-term, difficult to convince some stakeholders.
Employees' preference for working in progressive companies and distributed leadership always offers opportunities	Leaders need to distribute power and control, and whilst many agree with the principle, letting go takes courage and confidence
Brand loyalty from customers to ethical companies	Creates time to build consensus for this approach
New innovative business models developed due to emergent capability that encourages leadership from the edges	
Reduced costs from energy and waste savings and greater potential for sustainable success	
Useful settings	**Less useful settings**
Most organizations benefit from Eco-leadership	Unethical and exploitative organizations
Senior leaders to establish distributed leadership cultures and lead with emergent strategies	Short-term projects are less likely to use an Eco-leadership approach (although even limited projects should be part of a whole that takes an Eco-leadership approach)
Flat organizations, global organizations	Some organizations demand Eco + other discourses, e.g. the power industry may opt for the Eco-leadership discourse to develop sustainable business in the future, but retain a Controller discourse for safety reasons
Organizations focusing on sustainable futures, complex public sector organizations, e.g. large hospitals and universities, all require Eco-leadership	
Entrepreneurs who see gaps in the market create adaptive companies to respond and develop distributed leadership to maximize strength in a small company	

Layering Discourses

Organizations will have histories, traditions and cultures, and will have been formed under a particular leadership discourse. As social and organizational change occurs new discourses form to adapt, and earlier discourses are diminished but do not disappear. Each new discourse overlays the next, each a progression, developing in accordance to the conditions of its time. Sometimes they clash, sometimes they integrate and merge and sometimes they work in parallel together, in different parts of the organization, and with different leaders.

These discourses are like layers of hidden assumptions that lie beneath the surface of activity and espoused leadership rhetoric. These layered sediments of 'normative' expectations form the foundations, shaping how leaders and managers think and act, and also shaping the organizational culture alongside other factors.

Some organizations begin with a founding leader's vision that establishes a Messiah discourse from which all else emanates. Other organizations begin with a functional idea, believing they can be more efficient and outperform others, setting the Controller discourse as the formative layer. As organizations grow and develop, and the social world changes around them, another set of assumptions to lead and guide the organization evolves. Prior to the Eco-leadership discourse these layers of leadership would often interact in an ad hoc way. The Eco-leader tries to facilitate a balanced ecosystem, getting the balance right between Controller, Therapist and Messiah leadership, providing an adaptive approach that doesn't override the other discourses but embraces them. The layers and the foundations already exist, and are not easily changed, and the task of Eco-leaders is to begin the work of excavation, to expose the layers, see where these basic assumptions came from, and the purpose and meaning they hold for the organization. Unless this is done resistance to change will occur, and wrong changes will be made.

Developing Discourse Awareness

Developing awareness of the leadership discourses helps leaders to be more strategic and to see beyond the rational. So often leaders will try to create change, without paying attention to the unconscious assumptions that create resistance to change, and these assumptions also offer insights that guide us. The leadership discourses provide insights into unconscious assumptions, the expectations that make up an organizational culture.

When I teach in executive education using these discourses I invite participants to undertake a discourse questionnaire[1] that indicates their preference for leadership discourses. The questionnaire reveals personal preferences across all four discourses, rather than selecting a singular discourse, and participants discuss why their preferences are weighted more towards a certain discourse than others, and the balance between them. In companies we invite individuals, teams and whole organizations to undertake a review of the leadership discourses in their departments and the company.

The discourses become immediately recognizable to participants and 'light-bulb' moments often occur, as they realize how the tensions arise between leadership rhetoric and practice. For example, a senior female leader representing the Middle East in a global bank meeting sat through a leadership talk by her boss about the company values and their desire to move towards the Eco-leadership discourse. She spoke to me privately saying her region was dominated by the Controller leadership discourse, it was patriarchal and hierarchical, and this was such a cultural norm that distributed leadership was not yet a reality or feasible. For a long time she had felt trapped between selling the rhetoric of the company whilst knowing the reality on the ground was completely different. She found a way to articulate this to her senior manager using the discourses and we then worked openly with this challenge between global aspirations and regional cultures.

Developing discourse awareness helps leaders to take a critical and strategic stance, and to ask why a certain discourse is favoured, and what implications this has for the employees and the organization.

Conclusion

This chapter has summarized each of the four discourses and has begun to describe how they work together in practice. The future lies in the Eco-leadership discourse taking a meta-position, not to replace the other discourses, but to ensure that each specific organization, and each local part, finds the right emphasis and balance between the discourses.

A lot more research and theorizing is required to develop and support new practices of leadership. But more importantly, leaders can develop a

---

[1] Wild Questionnaire (Indicator of Leadership Discourses) www.simonwestern.com leadership/wild

greater awareness of the layers of leadership that exist in their organization, and reflect on their own and the organization's leadership valency that drives and constricts change. Working with all four discourses, and observing the trends and patterns in the external environment, will enable a more coherent and creative leadership, a leadership fit for the 21st century.

Suggested Readings

- For this chapter the reading required is the four previous chapters in this book.

Reflection Points

The four discourses of leadership are all present today, interacting in our organizations. Usually one is the dominant leadership discourse.

Leaders and organizations have valences (unconscious preferences) for certain discourses.

When discourses operate together tensions can be created if an overview is not taken to facilitate the whole.

The Eco-leadership discourse is a meta-discourse, offering a leadership that oversees how the discourses are enacted, to optimize their strengths and compatibility.

The following reflection points will help you develop 'discourse awareness', to make sense of your own individual leadership practices and the leadership around you:

- What is your personal leadership valency, i.e. your internalized assumptions about leadership? Which leadership discourses do you prefer?

- What is the dominant leadership discourse in your organization?

- Does the leadership discourse you prefer fit with the dominant organizational leadership discourse?

- How does your leadership practice match with your leadership assumptions? Do you practise your preferred leadership discourse, or do pressures pull you into another discourse?

- Observe others and try to identify the leadership discourse/s they inhabit.

- Does the dominant discourse empower or disenfranchise employees?

- What happens to those who resist the dominant leadership discourse?

- Try to identify different leadership discourses in different parts of your organization, e.g. in the finance department and the sales department. If there are differences, why is this and what effect does this have?

- Watch the news and read the newspapers and try to identify the different leadership discourses well-known political and business leaders operate from.

Sample Assignment Question

Reflect on an organization you know well (perhaps your current workplace, or place of study) and discuss the dominant discourses you observe and experience.

Hypothesize why a specific discourse is dominant or weak, referencing the organization's output, its history etc. In conclusion write a one- or two-page 'Consultancy Report' making a recommendation as to which leadership discourse/s would be preferable for this organization to take it into the future and why.

14 Leadership Formation: Creating Spaces for Leadership to Flourish

---

Chapter Structure

- Introduction
- Current Challenges: A Critique of Leadership Development
- Forming Leaders, Leadership Formation
- Leadership Formation in Practice
- Lead2Lead
- Conclusion

Introduction

Leadership education and leadership development have become a huge industry, with university business schools, large and small consultancies and a variety of specialist training companies, all offering training and development for leaders. Within organizations, still more investment is made via human resources, organizational development and leadership development departments, who deliver in-house training (some companies are very active: Hamburger University – McDonald's, and Heineken University for example). This chapter begins with a review of the challenges posed by dominant leadership development approaches, before offering 'leadership formation' as a counter-cultural approach to developing *leadership* rather than leaders.

Leadership formation is a holistic approach that works in multidimensional ways utilizing current best practice such as mentoring and peer learning in communities of practice. It emphasizes self-directed, practice-focused and networked approaches and aligns leadership development with organizational development, utilizing the Eco-leadership discourse to focus on generating and distributing leadership, rather than focusing on behavioural leadership approaches with an elite group of leaders.

Current Challenges: A Critique of Leadership Development

Figure 14.1 shows the dominant premise that underpins most leadership development, i.e. an individualistic and behavioural approach. Whilst there are many other more sophisticated approaches, this format still underpins the majority of leadership development today. The strength of this model is its simplicity and the fit with our individualist society. It enables trainers to sell easily definable products, and HR and OD departments can identify leadership competencies and behaviours, that can be taught, observed, monitored and measured (although the efficacy of measurement is contested by critical theorists). In short it makes rational sense, fits with popular and workplace culture, provides roles and income for experts selling their wares, and it offers answers for companies who need to 'skill up' their workforce, and want deliverable solutions. Leadership formation recognises that individual training is important, however it must not dominate and any individual training should always be part of a more holistic approach. I have worked in executive education for many years and have witnessed very good and very poor individual training. Overall, the efficacy of this approach is problematic as it limits other more generative approaches, and confines leadership to individuals, reinforcing old leadership

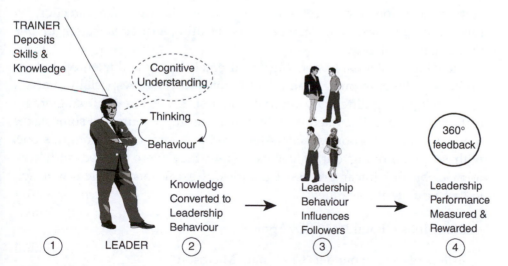

Figure 14.1   Leadership development

stereotypes and cultures, and is reductionist. Mintzberg is critical of dominant models of leadership and management training: 'Business schools have simply enjoyed too much success doing a number of wrong things. So long as society tolerates this – welcomes into positions of leadership people whose education is antithetical to it … why should anything change?' (2004: 415).

Leadership development in large corporations and large public sector organizations usually follows this linear pathway:

1 High-achieving MBAs/graduates are recruited.

2 High-potential leaders are selected within companies for development.

3 They are sent on 'conservative and branded' leadership training programmes, or have in-house training using 'populist' behaviourist and trait methods, e.g. transformational leadership approaches.

4 They are mentored by existing leaders, formally or informally, and acculturated by the organization, following in the footsteps of what has gone before.

This pathway produces leaders who by and large have been 'formed' by a conservative education processes and have conformed to normative practices. Therefore whilst the leadership rhetoric may claim to want innovative, creative leaders who can 'think outside the box', outside the underlying culture, selection and development works in the opposite direction by rewarding familiarity and sameness, and creating a dissonance for anyone thinking innovatively.

These high-potential leaders can be extremely bright and talented, but are unlikely to be entrepreneurial, adaptive or innovative, especially when it comes to thinking differently about the big issues, such as rethinking organizational purpose. It is interesting that many entrepreneurs and some of the most innovative corporate leaders followed a different path from this one, with some dropping out of college before they were formed and 'conformed' by this linear process. Examples of exceptional leaders who followed a different route are:[1]

Steve Jobs – Founder/CEO, Apple

Bill Gates – Co-Founder/Chairman, Microsoft

---

[1] Retrieved December 2012 from www.cnbc.com/id/43974865/Biggest_Businesses_Run_by_College_Dropouts

Paul Allen – Co-Founder, Microsoft

Mark Zuckerberg – Founder/CEO, Facebook

Ralph Lauren – CEO, Polo Ralph Lauren

Richard Branson – Founder/Chairman, Virgin Group

Michael Dell – Founder/CEO, Dell

Anita Roddick – Body Shop

Box 43 summarizes the critique of mainstream leadership development.

Box 43   Critique of Mainstream Leadership Development (LD) Practices

1 **Individualistic:** Develops leaders not leadership. Very few whole-system or OD training interventions to generate leadership across the whole organization.

2 **Conservative:** Old is dressed as new in a risk-averse training industry. Executive education often reflects Messiah and Therapist approaches that are conservative and lack imagination.

3 **Elitist:** LD positions leadership as an elitist, rather than distributed phenomenon. High-potential leaders are selected, trained and groomed for succession. The rest are devalued as 'followers', wasting much of the organization's potential and lowering morale.

4 **Technocratic:** LD often follows reductionist and technocratic thinking instrumentalizing people skills and using motivational psychology to the ends of productivity. Leadership is turned into a set of universal competencies.

5 **Business-focused not leadership-focused:** Business schools focus too much on the functions of business, and not on the complex experience of being a practising leader.

6 **Gap between theory and practice:** Many academics and trainers are too distant from practice. Leaders often express the gaping hole between what they are taught on courses, and its application back in the workplace. Progressive companies are developing new organizational practices that are often ahead of the training rhetoric and methods.

7 **Add-Ons:** When ethics, sustainability, systems thinking, and networked and distributed approaches to leadership are taught, they are often add-ons rather than central concerns, integrated into the company strategy.

Leadership Discourses and Leadership Development

Leadership development is usually prioritized in the following order in relation to the discourses, although the Messiah and Therapist discourses are interchangeable depending on the specific courses/trainings.

1 *Messiah discourse.* Aims: Developing Transformational leadership capability: setting visions, improving skills and competencies, developing influencing skills to inspire followers to achieve their potential.

2 *Therapist discourse.* Aims: Developing leadership 'soft' people skills, and training leaders as coaches, with the goal of improving their ability to lead and motivate individuals and teams. Most leadership development trainers have a preference for this discourse, as they themselves are focused on people development. This often leads to an uncritical bias towards this work in the classroom.

3 *Controller discourse.* Aims: Developing controlling capability to ensure efficiency and performance management, e.g. finance, using data, targets and goals, audit. The Controller discourse is less prominent in specific leadership development, than in management training and MBAs, but as managers are also leaders, they absorb this into their repertoire.

4 *Eco-leadership discourse.* Aims: Ethics, sustainability, distributed leadership, matrix structures, complexity, systems theory and networked approaches. These are all now taught by progressive business schools, yet a huge gap remains between theory and practice. The results are that Eco-leadership theories are taught but often with little experience or know-how to implement the ideas in practice. There is not a simplistic Eco-leadership developmental approach, only plural answers that take place within leadership formation frameworks. Each developmental activity has to be local to address real and specific needs.

The first three discourses evolved from the modernist mindset, reifying the individual and rationalizing leadership into individual traits, competencies, skills and behaviours, that can be learnt. The Eco-leadership discourse takes a post-industrial and postmodern view.

The challenges facing the leadership development industry reflect the same challenges facing organizations. Sadly the overall picture is that leadership development systemically reproduces the existing problems, and the time has come to radically address this. The emergent Eco-leadership discourse is finding its feet within the field of leadership development to address these three factors:

1 A leader does not emerge from training, but from a personal formation process.

2 The organizational task is to generate and distribute leadership, not to limit leadership to an elite group of selected individuals.

3 Leadership goes beyond an individual and is a collective and networked phenomenon. To develop successful leadership in organizations therefore requires collective and networked responses.

This book situates leadership formation as a response to the limitations of the individualistic approach, delivering a more holistic response.

Forming Leaders, Leadership Formation

Figure 14.2 shows a multidimensional and networked approach to leadership learning. Individuals, teams and whole organizations embark on a process of formation that includes all and more of the inputs in Figure 14.2. Leadership formation emphasizes self-directed and informal learning that takes a 'work and learn' approach, rather than splitting training from practice. Leaders are formed through multiple experiences, and the radical task for organizations is to create the contexts that

(a) encourage leadership formation to take place, and

(b) provide the spaces to enable leadership to flourish.

Leadership Formation, Inspired by Monastic Formation

We are formed by our 'habitus' (Bourdieu, 1991) through our social experiences and by the places and spaces we inhabit. Leaders are formed by their personal experiences, the normative practices and the contexts in which they work. Leadership formation, as conceptualized in this chapter, has been inspired by my experiences of working in diverse fields and more recently of a particular experience of staying in a monastery, which reawakened me to the intense reality that our experiences form us, and our environments shape and inspire, or limit us.

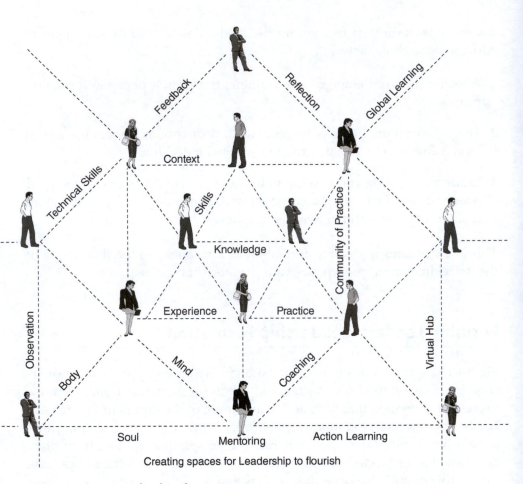

Figure 14.2 Leadership formation

When I wish to be creative, I try to be in creative environments, such as art galleries and museums that surround me with artefacts, images and architectures that free me from the box-like confines of an office. If I want to be inspired, I try to find inspiring environments that mirror my search; often my unconscious leads me to these places. Today, I write on top of a beautiful hill deep in the Polish countryside, sitting with my laptop next to an ancient-looking 'handmade' haystack, overlooking meadows and a wooded valley; a good place to be inspired to write about Eco-leadership and leadership formation. When finishing the first edition of this book, I went to a hermitage high in the California hills of Big Sur, overlooking the Pacific Ocean, where I was inspired by both the beautiful natural setting and by the monks and the monastic institution itself. There I made unexpected connections between monastic formation and leadership formation, as described in Box 44.

Box 44   Leadership Formation Inspired by Monastic Formation

A monk does not learn monk skills, but undergoes a formation process that is both individual and collective. The same principles apply to leadership. When leaders are asked where they learnt leadership, they respond by saying through an inspiring mentor, from an organization that had a great culture, from making mistakes, from their experience, from the university of life.

Radicalism is not always found where it is expected. G.K. Chesterton in his book *Orthodoxy*, a 1908 critique of modernity, observed that, 'I did try to found a heresy of my own; and when I had put the last touches to it, I discovered that it was orthodoxy … I did try to be 10 minutes ahead of the truth. And found I was eighteen hundred years behind it' (Chesterton, [1908] 2004: 4).

Burrell argues for a 'retro-organization', that organizational theory needs rejuvenating by looking not only at modern organizational forms but also at those with longer histories:

> In recognizing the centrality of the Enlightenment to the modern world, this book argues that it is in need of rejuvenation through the medium of dawn-picked extracts of the pre-modern period in European thought and seeks in the pre-scientific era ideas and themes of relevance for today. (Burrell, 1997: 5–6)

In recent years I too have found radical thinking in orthodoxy and turned to a radical tradition that dates back more than 1,700 years.

When on retreat at the Camaldolese (Benedictine) Hermitage in Big Sur, California, I observed how the monks underwent their monastic formation and realized that leaders could learn much from the monastic tradition. The idea of formation challenges our modern idea of learning. The monastic tradition does not emphasize the monks' spiritual vocation being learnt through teaching, training, techniques or personal development. To undergo formation as a monk is not to undergo a series of separate developmental acts, but is a holistic experience that arises from living in the community. Each monk is continually formed by, and also contributes to, the formation of the community.

The monastic communities have mastered and tailored the ability to create sustainable contexts in which the lives of monks are formed, and the monastic community is continually formed too.

A novitiate monk chooses to join a monastic community that has a specific 'charism', the gift of a specific order (the Franciscans or Benedictines, for example), and takes a vow to follow the monastic rule of that order. The monastic setting, the rule and the community, overseen by an abbot, provide the safe containing space that is a prerequisite for developmental activity to take place. Within this physical and spiritual container, the monks are

(Continued)

(Continued)

supported and encouraged to form the 'monk within', where they discern, develop and form their personal and specific charism (their unique gift to serve others) living alongside others undergoing the same formation process.

The monks' life is *formed* through partaking in daily spiritual practices, for example prayer, work, and reading the scriptures and the liturgy (the form of the religious service). It is the whole rather than any of the parts which forms both the novitiate monk and the community. The monks call this holistic experience *'the life'*. In addition to this process, there is spiritual direction. The spiritual director is a guide, a mentor, a 'loving father' in the monastic tradition. Their role is to be receptive and to support the monk in finding his path, not to teach that path, nor to develop the person, but to observe, reflect and guide the new monk through the formation process. Thomas Merton explains:

> Spiritual direction does not consist merely in giving advice. The man who has only an advisor does not really have a director in the fullest sense. Since the spiritual life does not consist in having and thinking, but in being and doing, a director who only gives ideas has not begun to form the one he directs. (1966: 7)

Formation is for the community and the individual. Leaders are not monks, and the settings are very different; however, institutions like monasteries offer us amplified examples of what happens in our own institutions and workplaces. Their continuity that pre-dates modernity also offers us a counter-culture to our modern ways, that privilege knowledge and technique over experience and wisdom, the individual over the community, and self-fulfilment over service to others. These monasteries that have such long and sustainable cultures offer us indications as to how we might think about leadership formation.

1 Leaders are formed by holistic contexts, cultures and practices; by their habitus. Monastic formation is thoughtfully structured with formal processes (e.g. prayer, liturgy, spiritual direction) and the informal 'life', the everyday spaces, practices and patterns that shape and form us. Leadership development can refocus to improve the holistic approach that values both formal training and the informal relationships and mundane rituals that shape our working lives.

2 Leadership formation can mimic monastic formation, simultaneously developing individuals and generating a collective leadership.

Monastic formation aims to generate a living community consisting of monks with diverse gifts and roles. Leadership formation should also try to generate a living community, consisting of distributed leaders with diverse gifts and roles as opposed to a one-size-fits-all leadership competency framework.

Leadership Formation in Practice

Leadership formation mirrors the qualities of Eco-leadership itself, creating spaces, flows and networks that encourage leadership learning and practice. It is difficult to quantify the results of informal leadership formation experiences. However, combined with formal training, the hope is to create a culture of leadership innovation, where leadership development becomes self-generating and self-regulating. Leadership formation also promotes systemic intelligence, where informal feedback systems emerge as distributed leaders communicate in growing networks. Systems knowledge comes through accounting and quantifiable data whereas systemic intelligence includes more subjective data that are found in emotional forms such as resistance and anxiety or positive energy. Distributed leaders are encouraged to share and pay attention to these subjective data, developing a living network that vastly improves organizational information systems. The leadership formation process encourages leaders to harvest the information that comes though informal networks, and to recognize that data and feedback come in diverse forms. For example, systems knowledge comes through accounting and quantifiable data, emotional forms such as resistance and anxiety or positive energy, in technical and virtual forms, written and symbolic data, and through informal meetings in coffee lounges. Distributed leaders encouraged to share and pay attention to this plurality of data then become the hub of organizational information systems.

Resistance to Change

Any big change can seem overwhelming. Ray Anderson, the 'Eco-leader' of Interface, Inc., faced this response when he told Dan Hendrix (the current CEO) of his radical plans for sustainability:

> 'When he first came up with this idea, I have to admit I thought he'd gone around the bend,' Mr Hendrix said … 'But he was right.' (*New York Times*, 2011c)

Distributed leadership is also not without its challenges, as liberating talent means liberating dissent too! When autonomy is encouraged people press for what they believe in; however, a society or organization without conflict is a dangerous totalizing place. Leadership formation creates the spaces to air the conflict and tensions to work through challenges, and to learn to live with difference, not try to negate it.

I have now been working with colleagues using leadership formation processes to develop Eco-leadership in organizations for over six years, and we have been learning together with our clients. We have learnt that leadership formation is an emergent process, it must be applied locally and specifically to context, and integrated into the company's infrastructure, processes and culture. Whilst leadership formation and Eco-leadership are emergent processes, they don't emerge from nowhere! To develop a leadership formation process in an organization requires clarity of purpose, structure, innovation, resilience and emergent capability.

Begin at the Beginning

When faced with the task of developing a leadership formation process within an organization, I follow the dictum to always 'begin at the beginning'. This means exploring where a organization is now, 'excavating the layers' in terms of leadership and culture, and following the actors (Latour, 2005), i.e. to approach the organization without pre-ordained ideas of what leadership should look like. Leadership formation is a co-created and participative process, led by employees alongside organizational leaders and specialist development consultants. Each department, team, and individual shapes their own formation process, and together they shape the organizational leadership formation process as a whole.

I will now give one brief example of a formal leadership formation intervention, designed to ensure that the leadership development was both individual and collective, and that it re-enforced the process of distributing leadership everywhere.

Lead2Lead: A Leadership Formation Case Study

This successful leadership development activity (see www.lead2lead.com) was designed together with my colleague Professor Jonathan Gosling. Leaders undertaking this exchange process would visit another leader, observing their practice, and be visited reciprocally by their exchange partner (Western and Gosling, 2002).

This work developed from a managerial exchange, a five-day work-shadowing programme designed by Jonathan Gosling and Henry Mintzberg, on their innovative International Masters in Practicing Management (IMPM) program (see www.impm.com and Mintzberg, 2004: 322). The course participants were paired up and each spent one week as visitor and one week as host. The visitor would shadow their exchange partner whilst at work. The idea was that each would learn from the manager they were visiting, but more than this also learn from the context. When writing their reflection paper on the experience we asked participants to reflect on: 'What was happening to you? What was happening around you? … Try and deduce patterns in your management style, clues as to how corporate and national culture affect you' (Western in Mintzberg, 2004: 323).

Participants on the IMPM reported the exchanges as profound learning experiences. We researched their learning development and designed a stand-alone leadership exchange programme for individual leaders who would visit another leader from another company/sector, and we offered training and coaching debriefs to leaders to maximize their learning.

Corporate Internal Leadership Exchanges: Building Internal Networks

What emerged from this new leadership exchange process was a secondary form of leadership exchange, designed as an in-house exchange for companies who wanted both to develop individual leaders, create a learning culture and build connections across their organization.

Our double aim was firstly to support individual leadership learning through an exchange process that delivered:

- learning from observing other leaders

- learning from observing work contexts

- learning from reflecting on their personal leadership practice

- learning from being observed

- learning from peer feedback and dialogue

with a secondary organizational development aim to:

- *build networks across the company:* connecting leaders from different functions and geographical sites

- *undertake a cultural audit:* we harvested the information and experiences from the leadership exchanges and these provided the company with exceptional insights into the strengths, challenges and cultural life of the organization.

Box 45 offers a mini-case example of a lead2lead project where we paired 100 senior managers from all parts of a global company that was going through a three-way corporate merger.

Box 45   Lead2Lead: A Leadership Formation Case Study

Building networks and developing leadership, through peer exchanges

'Let 100 Flowers Bloom'

In this lead2lead project we paired 100 senior managers (one level below board) from all parts of this global company to undertake a reciprocal leadership exchange. The company was going through a three-way corporate merger.

Our agreed aims were three-fold:

1 *Organizational alignment.* Creating a common culture. Creating integrated leadership, a common culture and developing shared values. Building communication networks. Sharing best practice.

2 *Undertaking a cultural audit* of the 'new' company to help plan future developmental requirements, to be achieved by utilizing their own leaders as action researchers, creating a true alignment between research and improving practice.

3 *Improving personal leadership capability.* Identifying individual strengths and weaknesses, training in leadership skills, practice in leadership coaching, feedback and communication skills, observation and reflection skills. Learning from each other, sharing best practice, getting feedback when being observed from a knowledgeable leader. Receiving individual coaching to debrief the exchange, and embed and apply the learning.

Planning the exchanges: Matching is the key

Previous experience taught us that the matching process was vital, and working closely with the board and HR team we carefully planned the pairings to ensure best fit for the company and the participants: our criteria were based on three main factors:

1 *Organizational alignment.* Which parts of the organization needed to be better connected and which leaders could utilize the skills from each other's functions/departments?

2 *Personal leadership.* Making the most of matching one leader with another, taking into account strengths and competency gaps in both hard and soft skills and experience.

3 *Maximizing difference.* Our research shows that putting leaders in situations that stretch them makes the exchange learning richer. Difference is based on such things as geography, function and skill sets.

The pre-exchange training

The senior managers were trained in innovative observation techniques to support reflective learning: how best to learn from observing their partner and to learn from self-reflection at the same time. We trained them to 'look awry', that is to see things from a new perspective, and to give feedback to the exchange partner they were going to observe. The skills learnt in training are all transferable and underpin good leadership skills.

The exchange

One hundred managers observing best practice, questioning their own assumptions, reflecting on how they lead their teams, collaborating with a partner to solve topical challenges and dilemmas proved to be a very powerful leadership development programme. Each observed another leader for three days and was observed by that same person for the same amount of time. The reciprocal nature of this approach was important. The leaders gave each other personal feedback, shared stories, recognized developmental needs and identified strengths and best practice across the organization. The energy and buzz of 100 managers visiting and observing each other in the company were tangible!

The debrief

Each leader received one-to-one coaching. Leaders focused on embedding their personal and organizational learning and looking at ways to implement and apply this in practice.

Outcomes

Two things surprised us. Firstly, how little the leaders had recognized their own strengths and capabilities, and how hearing positive feedback from a respected colleague had a widespread motivational impact across the company at a time when it was going through a huge, high-pressure change process. Secondly, how the exchange went beyond the two leaders directly involved and impacted on the whole team behind the leaders. Being visited by a senior manager made the team reflect on their performance and engage in dialogue about generic company issues and local specific challenges and strengths.

Against the original aims the outcomes were as follows.

(Continued)

(Continued)

Organizational alignment: creating a common culture

New networks: The leadership exchange built new networks and promoted better understanding and a positive culture change. These face-to-face human connections which offered real engagement are more powerful, engaging and sustainable than virtual links or business meetings.

Beyond individual learning: Observing a leader in reality meant observing a department or team. Being observed heightens the capacity to reflect on what is normally taken for granted. The whole organization picks up on this process, as most of them are involved in it either directly or indirectly. One hundred leaders exchanging then has an impact on over 1,000 direct employees.

Systemic impact: Creating these exchange networks and normalizing the practice of observation all contributed towards developing an 'Eco-leadership' approach, i.e. developing a systemic awareness of the organization and an ethical and values-based approach to leadership. This type of leadership development shifts the mindsets from functional thinking to a more connected approach. The overall impact from this seemingly simple exchange programme is a culture change process that is greater than the sum of its parts.

Individual leadership performance

Individual leaders improved their performance directly due to learning best practice and gaining feedback and tips on how to lead their teams, run better meetings, and deal with external challenges. It developed communication and feedback skills, and observation training helped build an internal capacity for leaders and their teams to look at themselves, and others, through a different lens.

This brief case study demonstrates the potential to develop leaders at their workplace, drawing on tacit knowledge, developing a greater individual awareness of their local ecology and getting more connected to other parts of their organization, and the whole system.

Cultural audit and exchange news

An additional and powerful aspect of this approach was the feedback we organized through the external coaches we used to debrief the exchanges. The information gathered was fed to a central team who undertook a narrative analysis and collated organizational and leadership themes. This provided a cultural audit of the company from the embedded experience of the company's employees. This is a unique way to gain rich qualitative data about what's really happening in the company. We fed this rich information back to all those who undertook the training and discussed this with the company board where we identified unexpected strengths to build upon and future developmental requirements.

Quotes from the managers reflecting on their learning

'Multiply my learning by 100 leaders and the micro changes that take place with individuals represent a significant change programme within the company.'

Communication

'This exercise has caused both of us to reflect on the critical importance of communication skills among managers, and to consider whether we are making optimum use of communication tools and styles for the most effective and efficient communications within our organization.'

Leadership styles

'I used negative examples to highlight the seriousness of the situation. It was pointed out to me that this sometimes freezes people. I needed to find ways to motivate people, to get them to focus on how they could achieve success and the opportunities for doing this.'

Connectedness and interdependence

'When visiting my partner I asked what does he need to do a good job? This should be the question we ask also of our internal customers. We need to be concerned for their success as well as our own.'

Conclusion

Leadership formation is somewhat counter-intuitive, attempting to create the conditions that enable a future direction and generate future leaders, rather than controlling this process through traditional succession plans and leadership training. The aim is to shape and nurture contexts where dispersed leadership begins to emerge from all parts of the organization. Physical and virtual spaces are created and supported that become 'laboratories of experience', allowing a learning organization to develop, creativity to flourish and leadership to emerge throughout the organization. These spaces also act as containers for anxiety, and as sites for community and cultural audit. They become internalized into the organizational culture. Examples of these spaces can be a simple mentoring network offering traditional mentoring, peer mentoring and reverse mentoring (Western, 2012), communities of practice, networks of learning. Virtual sites, chat rooms, team development sessions, cross-team dialogue sessions, individual and team coaching sessions, anything that creates a reflective and learning space, that enables leadership to emerge and flourish. In one organization I worked with we developed administration staff, encouraging them to take leadership of organizing the annual gathering, a big event that grew to be the most popular event of the year. We saw how leadership when nurtured and supported grows and blossoms.

In the new Scottish Parliament the architect, Enric Miralles, understood this process and designed Contemplation Pods attached to the Scottish MPs' offices, the idea being to create a physical thinking space (Figure 14.3). This physical space is observable on the outside of the building, so they are both practical and symbolic. Hopefully these spaces will become

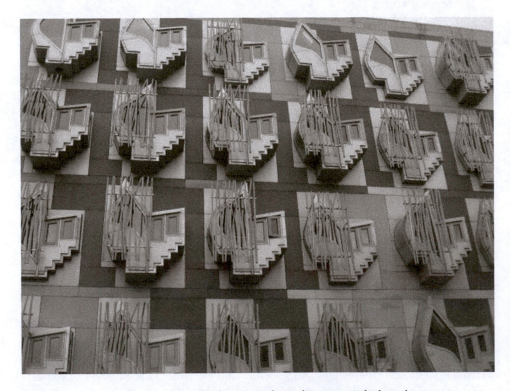

Figure 14.3 Contemplation pods, Scottish Parliament, Edinburgh

internalized and create thinking spaces within us, reminding us of the need to stop, to reflect, to muse, to consider, to drift and to contemplate. They represent a symbolic and secular monastic cell. Leadership is formed in creative spaces like this, through conversations, connections and personal reflection on practice.

Box 46 summarizes the seven principles underpinning leadership formation.

Box 46   Seven Principles of Leadership Formation

1 No personal development without organizational development.

2 Leaders learn more from each other than from trainers.

3 Leaders learn more from work experience than from classrooms.

4 Leaders are formed by personal experience *and* cultural experience.

5 Connecting and networks are as important as learning knowledge and skills.

6 Leadership formation requires a generative and generous culture.

7 Formal and informal development activities and spaces are vital.

Leadership exists all around us, but so much of it goes unnoticed, or is undervalued and uncherished. This is at the expense of greater organizational success, and greater social well-being. It takes the right conditions to nurture the 'leader within', and the task we are faced with is to create and support those conditions. The leader within each individual, and the collective leadership within an organization, both need nurturing and sustaining. Leadership formation will reveal many manifestations of leadership that are currently hidden. Leadership formation is not something that can be prescribed universally or outside of a local context.

A successful leadership formation process means that:

1 Each individual establishes a personal leadership formation process, with a mentor, based on their particular charism and their developmental needs.

2 Each team establishes a team leadership formation process, aligned to their charism and developmental needs.

3 Finally, the whole organization establishes a collective leadership formation process, aligned to the values and vision of the organization.

Leadership formation becomes a part of Eco-leadership across the whole system. It is not an add-on, it does not entail great expense as most of the learning is on the job, and through engagement with others. Leadership formation should not be regarded as a cost centre but as adding value through maximizing the potential of individuals, teams and the collective whole to achieve the strategic goals of the organization.

Suggested Readings

- Freire, P. (2007) *Pedagogy of the Oppressed.* New York: Continuum.

- Scharmer, O. (2009) *Theory U: Leading from the Future as It Emerges.* San Francisco, CA: Berrett-Koehler.

- Senge, P. (1994) *The Fifth Discipline.* London: Century Business.

- Western, S. (2012) *Coaching and Mentoring: A Critical Text.* London: Sage. See esp. chs 9 and 13.

Reflection Points

Leadership formation suggests redirecting attention from developing high-potential individual leaders to generating leadership throughout an organization.

Leaders are formed from multiple experiences, and the task is to focus on spaces rather than individuals, i.e. creating spaces and contexts for leadership formation to take place. Much of this development is self-directed and through peer learning, privileging mentoring, communities of practice and other work-based approaches.

Reflect on these questions that leaders of organizations looking to implement a leadership formation process may ask:

- How can we create the conditions, and contexts, to enable informal leadership formation to occur?

- Where are the spaces in our organization for thinking and creativity?

- Where are the contexts and networks to enable connections and communication to occur across silos?

- How can a cross-disciplinary and cross-fertilization of ideas and sharing of experience and knowledge be encouraged?

- How do individuals and teams support leaders who are not given positional power?

- Are we alert to the potential for leadership to flourish in the most unexpected places?

- Do we have mentors and current leaders available to support new leaders and leadership initiatives?

- How do we value and encourage dispersed leadership?

- How are leadership spirit and ethical leadership behaviour encouraged in our organization?

Sample Assignment Question

Identify the process of leadership formation you have undergone, taking into account that leadership formation begins at an early age. What contexts and people have formed you, and what has shaped your capacity to lead and to follow? In conclusion, write a brief summary of your workplace, or place of study, identifying the formal and informal spaces that enable leadership formation to take place.

15 Epilogue: Leadership in the Aftermath

Figure 15.1 Frank Ghery's 'postmodern' Guggenheim Museum contrasts with the modernist industrial architecture in the city of Bilbao, Spain

> **Chapter Structure**
>
> - Introduction
> - Facing the Aftermath of Modernity
> - Leadership Turns a Blind Eye: The Financial Crisis of 2008
> - Eco-Leadership and the Arab Spring
> - Leadership in the Aftermath

Introduction

Reflecting on how to end this book, I had two main preoccupations. Firstly, that it would be a mistake to try to summarize neatly a critical approach to leadership. It is not possible to end with clear definitions of leadership as they do not exist; it is better for the reader to immerse him- or herself in the text and make their own sense of it. My hope is that ideas will be seeded, and they will bear fruit when the reader is engaged in the practice of leadership in their workplace. In addition, I became preoccupied by two major and 'unexpected' world events that occurred in the short gap between the two editions of this book (2007–2013). I watched both from a leadership perspective, and both events, in very different ways, affirm the core arguments made in this book, particularly about the rise of the Eco-leadership discourse. This short epilogue will briefly reflect on the financial crisis of 2008 and the Arab Spring of 2011, in order to make the case that rethinking leadership and moving towards the Eco-leadership discourse is not an idealized position for academics and dreamers, but an imperative that requires maturity and urgency from us all.

Facing the Aftermath of Modernity

Prior to these two events it was clear to critical theorists that troubled times lay ahead. The first edition of this book warned of the unravelling consequences of social, technological and commercial forces that distorted economic and social conditions towards short-term gain, and directed profits towards a global elite. Political and business leadership ignored the growing pressures on wider society and the environment, turning a blind eye to the mounting problems they faced. Messiah leaders of global corporations and banks exacerbated these problems, chasing visions of unregulated markets producing eternal growth, and prophesying ever-greater profits. These leaders claimed it was their expertise that produced vast profits, and they received excessive remuneration in return. Ethics, good business practices, financial constraint and sustainable success were ignored, with the resulting consequences in 2008. Messiah leaders in business and politics were lost in their own grandiosity and buoyed by success. They were the global winners, and turned a blind eye to the global losers, and to the financial and political tsunami that was about to hit them.

As many argued, a systemic collapse was imminent and predictable; we seemed to be in a state of slow-motion economic, social and environmental crisis. It was the collapse of Lehman Brothers investment bank on 15 September 2008 that triggered a financial, economic, social and political crisis of immense proportions.

Aftermath Time

Manuel Castells and colleagues (2012) claim we live in 'Aftermath time', referencing the post-financial and later economic, social and political crisis:

> Life beyond the crisis requires a transformation of the mindset that led to bankruptcy and despair, and to economies and societies based on a unsustainable model of speculative finance and political irresponsibility.

Yet we live in a time of two aftermaths, one immediate and the other slowly unfolding. The first is the financial crisis and its spreading impact, which is discussed below from a leadership perspective. The second is the aftermath of modernity itself. Modernity's demise has long been discussed, and the postmodern period is with us[1] (Lyotard, 1979/1984). Hypercapitalism in this late-modern period has inflicted a fatal wound on the project of modernity. Key modernist ideas and beliefs have changed in a very short period; our trust in modern institutions and political-civic leadership has diminished, and the modernist idea that nature can be tamed and controlled, yet will remain eternally unharmed, is no longer held. Today we replace the word nature with the concept of the environment, and this is not considered permanent, but a fragile entity that is quickly being destroyed through over-consumption (fossil fuels, food, wood, fish etc.) or through damage by pollution and climate change. In essence, modernity promises progress and this is no longer certain or believed; many fear the future will be worse than today.[2]

---

[1] Whilst acknowledging contested views of the meaning of postmodernity.

[2] These points are well made by Joao Caraca in 'The Seperation of Cultures, page 52 in *Aftermath* (Castells et al., 2012).

Modernity has run its course, having created great gains and many losses. We are now in the aftermath of modernity, and the financial crisis should be read as a symptom of this. We are in a period of transition that requires major adjustments, socially, politically and economically. In terms of leadership, modernity produced three dominant discourses, all emerging from modernity's relentless pursuit of progress and efficiency through specialization, expert intervention and division. The Controller, Therapist and Messiah discourses all emerged from individualistic leaders, specialists applying their expertise to control, motivate and influence others, using different techniques and methods.

Facing the aftermath of modernity requires new leadership that responds to new times. In the first edition I pointed to the beginnings of a new, emergent Eco-leadership discourse that was appearing in the margins of leadership theory and practice. This new form of leadership offered diverse and networked approaches that could not be confined to a rationalized and individualized leadership typology. In Eco-leadership there is no 'modernist' grand narrative of leadership, but a more plural and diverse collection of ideas; leadership is not confined to the top, but is everywhere in multiple forms. In this book the Eco-leadership discourse has a full chapter, having grown and become increasingly recognized and written about since the first edition. The aftermath of modernity requires the development of this 'postmodern' Eco-leadership discourse, and the financial crisis and Arab Spring reiterate why this is imperative.

Leadership Turns a Blind Eye: The Financial Crisis of 2008

When the financial crisis came in 2008, it shocked us not because it happened, but because of the speed of the collapse, and the speed with which it spread. This confirmed the notion that we live in interdependent ecosystems: when one part falls there is an impact on the whole system. Like a virulent strain of virus, financial contamination spread from bank to bank, from the USA to Europe, affecting world trade and global economies. The finance sector quickly infected the whole, creating an economic, political and social crisis that has impacted on millions of lives. Messiah leaders, rewarded in millions to run our financial institutions and global corporations, had completely failed us. Political leaders too had ignored the warnings.

The leadership lessons are clear. Ignoring systemic perspectives, leaders followed blinkered pathways to gain short-term success. Eco-leadership

Figure 15.2 Canary Wharf financial trading centre, London

approaches were not present, and this meant that transparency, autonomous thinking, systemic ethics, organizational belonging, sustainable business models and global interdependencies were ignored in favour of 20th century leadership approaches that exhibited a typical modernist and fundamentalist myopia.

Eco-leadership and the Arab Spring

In 2009 I visited Syria and sat for hours in the peaceful and beautiful Umayyad mosque in Damascus. I wandered the ancient market in Aleppo, walked the green hills with a Kurdish shepherd. In December 2010 protests in Tunisia set off a chain of events that were unplanned and their outcomes unpredictable. Hopefully great gains of liberation will be made, but I feel great sadness too, as the peace and friendship I experienced in Syria have now been smashed. Abrupt transformations carry a huge and tragic cost to humanity.

Figure 15.3 Pilgrim in Umayyad mosque, Damascus, Syria, 2009

The Arab Spring offered the opposite example of leadership to that of the financial crisis. The charade of Messiah leadership was debunked, and Controller leaders were overthrown by disenfranchised peoples. New social movements of resistance swept across the Arab world and Eco-leadership approaches ruled the day. The resistance movements overthrew powerful and seemingly unmoveable authoritarian and controlling leaders like Colonel Gaddaffi, who operated with totalizing control and a Messiah leadership status with self-images in all public spaces. These movements not only overthrew these leaders, but also eschewed traditional forms of leadership and organizational resistance. Trade unions and grass roots Islamic groups such as the Muslim Brotherhood were minor players; they had been visible in the past but were largely repressed and sat on the sidelines as new emergent resistant networks appeared from nowhere. Past experience was that formal organizations could be identified and their leaders arrested and persecuted, preventing a successful revolution. However, this time it was different, as networked leadership took over. No single movement or identifiable leaders meant the resistance was strong, multilevel, adaptive and unstoppable. A small demonstration in Tunisia at the end of 2010 quickly took hold across the Arab world, and regimes fell quickly in Tunisia, Egypt, Libya and Yemen; at the time of writing the challenge to the regime in Syria is still raging, and in other Arab countries the future of oppressive and elitist leaders is under pressure.

Distributed and networked leadership occurred in the virtual realm, and in the physical realm. The social media played an active part in these revolutions. President Mubarak of Egypt recognized this and tried to censor internet and mobile phone communications but to no avail; the cat was out of the bag. Tahrir Square in Egypt became the focal physical site of protest, and news and communications were shared online and through mobile technology. The new forms of leadership that are emerging in new social movements such as the environmental movements, the Zapatistas, Occupy and the Arab Spring, reflect the way technology and communications create new social realities and possibilities on the ground.

In the Arab Spring Eco-leadership approaches resulted in huge changes and the collapse of regimes, yet this is not the end of the story, and there is not a simple happy ending. Questions now arise about post-revolution leadership, and the societies that are being created in the remnants of the upheavals. New social movements can begin revolutions, but new forms of sustainable leadership, governance and organization are required to sustain and continue the progress achieved. These will evolve from old and new forms of leadership and organization.

Leadership in the Aftermath

> If you point your cart North,
>
> When you want to go South,
>
> How will you ever arrive?
>
> (From Ryokan's 'Dew Drops on a Lotus Leaf')

The zen poet Ryokan sums up contemporary mainstream leadership: we know we want to go south, i.e. we are aware of the impending environmental crisis, that unsustainable growth cannot continue, that natural resources are diminishing, that social disparity such as mass unemployment will cause great social unrest, and that new forms of Eco-leadership are required to change direction. Yet we still point our carts north, the EU, USA and everyone else chasing growth, making neo-liberal austerity cuts, leading to the path of self-destruction simply because it's easier, it's what we know, and it offers short-term relief. A crisis is an opportunity to change, and now is the time.

The key lessons are that new environmental, economic and social realities demand new forms of leadership and organization. We cannot live in a 21st century interdependent world, using 20th century thinking and leadership. A major point I make throughout this book is that organizational leaders have to look beyond the world of business and management schools to see what is happening in the wider sphere of life and engage with it. Corporations and organizations can learn from new social movements, not only to try to leverage more success, but also to become more ethically engaged.

New leadership responses must reflect and respond to our times; we live in a networked society and therefore networked leadership is required. We live in a time of environmental crisis and with limited natural resources, and therefore Eco-leadership that attends to ethics and sustainability is necessary. The super-storm that hit New York City in 2012, and swept across the Caribbean, caused the mayor of New York to bring climate change back on the agenda. How many more catastrophes will happen before we act? The key is not to divide up the social, economic, technological and environmental issues, on some pretence they are separate, but to realize they are interdependent, a part of each other, and need an interdependent networked leadership response.

There are no simplistic frameworks saying this is what leadership should look like. There are, however, principles, and many scholars and practitioners are working from diverse theoretical perspectives to develop leadership approaches that address environmental sustainability with the organizational purpose of creating the 'good society'. We must all engage in the process of discovering and developing the spaces that generate emergent leadership.

When I am asked what a good leader is, one answer I give is this: 'A good leader understands that "organizations belong" and that leadership is everywhere.' This answer provokes more questions: 'What does it mean for an organization to belong?' 'How can we realize the leadership potential that is everywhere?' With these two underpinning principles, leaders are at least 'pointing the cart south'; how they make the journey is for them and their fellow travellers to plan, discern and discover en-route.

This book began with a biographical introduction to contextualize my writing and I wish to end it on a personal note. A personal catastrophe occurred in my life during the period between these two editions. A very real existential question arises after such a personal catastrophe: 'How to carry on?' The answer lies in a deep experiential faith, that in spite of tragedy and in despair, grace and beauty remain present in the world. Glimpses of beauty can only be experienced, however, if we remain open to the whole of our experience, to engage with grief, sadness, loss, love, joy and beauty. What has this got to do with leadership? Everything.

References

Ackers, P. and Preston, D. (1992) 'Born again? The ethics and efficacy of the conversion experience in contemporary management development', *Journal of Management Studies*, 34(5): 677–701.

Adler, P. S. (2008) 'CMS: Resist the Three Complacencies!', *Organization*, 15(6): 925–6.

Adler, P. S., Forbes, L. C. and Willmott, H. (2007) '3 critical management studies', *The Academy of Management Annals*, (1)1: 119–79.

Aftermath Project (2012) 'Life beyond the crisis'. www.aftermathproject.com/ (accessed 12 March 2013).

Ali, T. (2002) *The Clash of Fundamentalisms, Crusades, Jihads and Modernity*. London: Verso.

Altman, M. (2001) *Worker Satisfaction and Economic Performance*. Armonk, NY: M.E. Sharpe.

Alvesson, M. (1996) *Communication, Power and Organization*. Berlin: Walter de Gruyter.

Alvesson, M. (2002) *Understanding Organizational Culture*. London/Thousand Oaks, CA: Sage.

Alvesson, M. and Svenginsson, S. (2003) 'Managers doing leadership: the extra-ordinarization of the mundane', *Human Relations*, 56(12): 1435–1459. London: Sage.

Alvesson, M. and Willmott, H. (1992) *Critical Management Studies*. London: Sage.

Alvesson, M. and Willmott, H. (1996) *Making Sense of Management: A Critical Introduction*. London: Sage.

Alvesson, M. and Willmott, H. (2002) 'Identity regulation as organizational control: producing the appropriate individual'. Retrieved from www.jbs.cam.ac.uk/ research/associates/pdfs/willmott_identity_regulation.pdf (accessed 6 February 2013).

Andermahr, S., Lovell, T. and Wolkowitz, C. (2000) *A Glossary of Feminist Theory*. London: Arnold.

Armstrong, K. (2000) *The Battle for God*. London: HarperCollins.

Armstrong, K. (2002) 'Fundamentalism and the modern world: A dialogue with Karen Armstrong, Susannah Heschel, Jim Wallis and Feisal Abdul Rauf', *Sojourners Magazine*, March–April, 31(2): 20–6.

Armstrong, M. (2006) 'Leaders challenge business as usual', *Guardian*, 6 November. Available at www.guardian.co.uk/society/2006/nov/06/12 (accessed 5 February 2013).

Axtel Ray, C. (1986) 'Corporate culture: the last frontier of control', *Journal of Management Studies*, 23(3): 286–95.

Badarraco, J. (2001) 'We don't need another hero', *Harvard Business Review*, 79(8): 120–6.

Bakunin, M. (1871) 'What is authority?', from *Dieu et l'état* (1882). Retrieved from www.panarchy.org/bakunin/authority.1871.html (accessed 4 February 2013).

Bansal, P. and Roth, R. (2000) 'Why companies go green: a model of ecological responsiveness', *The Academy of Management Journal*, 43(4): 717–36.

Barker, R. (1993) '"Tightening the iron cage": concertive control in self-managing teams', *Administrative Science Quarterly*, 38(3): 408–37.

Barker, R. (1997) 'How can we train leaders if we don't know what leadership is?', *Human Relations*, 50(1): 343–62.

Barley, S. and Kunda, G. (1992) 'Design and devotion: surges of rational and normative ideologies of control in managerial discourse', *Administrative Science Quarterly*, 37: 363–99.

Barnard, C. ([1938] 1991) 'The functions of the executive', in M. B. Calas and L. Smircich (1991) 'Voicing seduction to silence leadership', *Organizational Studies*, 12(4): 567–602.

Barr, J. (1981) *Fundamentalism*. London: Xpress.

Bass, B. (1985) *Leadership and Performance Beyond Expectations*. New York: Free Press.

Bass, B. (1990a) 'From transactional to transformational leadership: learning to share the vision', *Organizational Dynamics*, 18: 19–31.

Bass, B. (1990b) *Bass and Stogdills – Handbook of Leadership*. New York: Free Press.

Bass, B. (1998) 'The ethics of transformational leadership', in J. Ciulla (ed.), *Ethics, The Heart of Leadership*. Westport, CT: Praeger.

Bass, B. (1999) 'Two decades of research and development in transformational leadership', *European Journal of Work & Organizational Psychology*, March, 8(1).

Bass, B. and Avolio, B. (1993) 'Transformational leadership and organizational structure', *International Journal of Public Administration Quarterly*, 17: 112–21.

Bass, B. and Avolio, B. (1994) 'Shatter the glass ceiling: women make better managers', *Human Resource Management*, 33(4): 549–60.

Bass, B. and Riggio, R. (2006) *Transformational Leadership*. Mahwah, NJ: Lawrence Erlbaum Associates.

Bass, B. and Steidlmeier, P. (1999) 'Ethics, character and authentic transformational leadership behavior', *Leadership Quarterly*, 10: 181–217.

Bateson, G. (1972) *Steps to an Ecology of Mind: Collected Essays in Anthropology, Psychiatry, Evolution and Epistemology*. Chicago: University of Chicago Press.

Baudrillard, J. (1983) *Simulations*. New York: Semiotext(e).

Baudrillard, J. (1988) *The Ecstasy of Communication*. New York: Semiotext(e).

Bauman, Z. (1989) *Modernity and the Holocaust*. Ithaca, NY: Cornell University Press.

BBC News (2011) 'Does a narrow social elite run the country?', 26 January. Available at www.bbc.co.uk/news/magazine-12282505 (accessed December 2012).

Becker, G. S. (1998) *Accounting for Tastes*. Cambridge, MA: Harvard University Press.

Bell, E. and Taylor, S. (2004) 'From outward bound to inward bound: the prophetic voices and discursive practices of spiritual management development', *Human Relations*, 57(4): 439–66.

Bellah, R. N., Madsen, R., Sullivan, W. H., Swidler, A. and Tipton, S. M. (1996) *Habits of the Heart: Individualism and Commitment in American Life*. Berkeley, CA: University of California Press.

Bennis, W. (1989) *On Becoming a Leader*. New York: Addison Wesley.

Bennis, W. and Nanus, B. (1985) *Leaders: The Strategies For Taking Charge*. New York: Harper & Row.

Bennis, W. and Thomas, R. (2002) 'Crucibles of leadership', *Harvard Business Review*, September, 80(9).

Beradi, F. (2009) *The Soul at Work: From Alienation to Autonomy*. New York: Semiotext(e).

Berggren, C., Adler, P. S. and Cole, R. E. (1994) 'Nummi vs. Uddevalla rejoinder', *Sloan Management Review*, 35(2): 37–9.

Berry, W. (1972) *A Continuous Harmony: Essays Cultural and Agricultural*. San Diego, CA: Harcourt Brace and Company.

Bhaskar, R. (2010) *The Formation of Critical Realism: A Personal Perspective*. Oxford/ New York: Routledge.

Binney, G., Wilke, G. and Williams, C. (2004) *Living Leadership: A Practical Guide for Ordinary Heroes*. London: Pearson Books.

Bion, W. R. (1961) *Experiences in Groups*. London: Tavistock.

Bolden, R. (2011) 'Distributed leadership in organizations: a review of theory and research', *International Journal of Management Reviews*, 13(3).

Bolden, R. and Gosling, J. (2006) 'Leadership Competencies: time to change the tune?', *Leadership*, 2: 147. London: Sage Publications.

Bolden, R., Gosling, J., Hawkins, B. and Taylor, S. (2011) *Exploring Leadership: Individual, Organizational, and Societal Perspectives*. Oxford: Oxford University Press.

Boltanski, L. and Chiapello, S. (2006) *The New Spirit of Capitalism*. London: Verso.

Bond, M. A. and Pyle, J. L. (1998) 'The ecology of diversity in organizational settings: lessons from a case study', *Human Relations*, 51: 589–623.

Bourdieu, P. (1990) *The Logic of Practice*. Stanford, CA: Stanford University Press.

Bourdieu, P. (1991) *Language and Symbolic Power*. Harvard: Harvard University Press.

Bright, A. (2009) 'Here, Now', *The Point*, 1. WORDPRESS. [Online]. Available at: www.thepointmag.com/2009/essays/here-now (accessed 18 April 2013).

Brown, H. (1989) 'Organising activity in the women's movement: an example of distributed leadership', *International Social Movement Research*, 2: 225–40.

Bryman, A. (1986) *Leadership and Organizations*. London: Routledge and Kegan Paul.

Bryman, A. (1993) 'Charismatic leadership in business organisations: some neglected issues', *Leadership Quarterly*, 4: 289–304.

Bryman, A. (1996) 'Leadership in organisations', in S. R. Clegg, C. Hardy and W. R. Nord (eds), *Handbook of Organizational Studies*. London: Sage. pp. 276–92.

Bufe, C. (1988) *A Future Worth Living: Thoughts on Getting There*. Tucson, AZ: Sharp Press.

Bunting, M. (2001) 'Illiberal liberalism', 8 October. Retrieved from http://gospel-culture.org.uk/articles.htm (accessed 5 February 2013).

Burgin, V. (1996) *In/different Space: Place and Memory in Visual Culture*. Berkeley/Los Angeles, CA: University of California Press.

Burgoyne, J. and Pedler, M. (2003) 'A practice–challenge approach to leadership and leadership development'. Paper presented at the Studying Leadership conference, Lancaster University.

Burns, J. (1978) *Leadership*. New York: Harper & Row.

Burrell, G. (1997) *Pandemonium: Towards a Retro-organization Theory*. London: Sage.

Butler, J. (1990) *Gender Trouble: Feminism and the Subversion of Identity*. London: Routledge.

Butler, J. (2004) 'Gender regulations', in J. Butler (ed.), *Undoing Gender*. New York: Routledge.

BYM (1996) 'Britain Yearly Meeting in Quaker Faith and Practice (1995)', *The Book of Christian Discipline of the Yearly Meeting of the Religious Society of Friends (Quakers) in Britain*.

Calas, M. B. and Smircich, L. (1991) 'Voicing seduction to silence leadership', *Organizational Studies*, 12(4): 567–602.

Calas, M. B. and Smircich, L. (1995) 'Dangerous liaisons: the "feminine-in management" meets globalisation', in L. Fulop and S. Linstead (eds), *Management: A Critical Text*. London: Macmillan Press.

Calas, M. B. and Smircich, L. (2003) 'To be done with progress and other heretical thoughts for organization and management studies', in E. Locke (ed.), *Postmodernism and Management: Pros, Cons, and the Alternative: Research in the Sociology of Organizations*, 21. Amsterdam: JAI.

Calhoun, C. (1995) *Critical Social Theory*. London: Blackwell.

Capra, F. (1996) *The Web of Life*. New York: Doubleday.

Caraca, J. (2012) 'The Separation of Cultures and the Decline of Modernity' in M. Castells, J. Caraca and G. Cardosa (eds), *Aftermath*. Oxford: Oxford University Press.

Cardosa, G. and Jacobetty, P. (2012) in M. Castells, J. Caraca and G. Cardosa (eds), *Aftermath*. Oxford: Oxford University Press.

Carrette, J. and King, R. (2005) *Selling Spirituality: The Silent Takeover of Religion*. London: Routledge.

Case, P. and Gosling, J. (2010) 'The spiritual organization: critical reflections on the instrumentality of workplace spirituality', *Journal of Management, Spirituality & Religion*, 7(4): 257–82.

Casey, C. (1995) *Work, Self and Society after Industrialisation*. London: Routledge.

Casey, C. (2000) 'Work, non-work and resacralizing self', *Social Compass*, 47: 571. Retrieved from www.sagepub.com/mcdonaldizationstudy5/articles/Labor%20 and%20Organizations_Articles%20PDFs/Casey_2.pdf (accessed 4 February 2013).

Castells, M. (1997) *The Power of Identity*. London: Blackwell.

Castells, M. (2000) *The Rise of the Network Society, The Information Age: Economy, Society and Culture, I*. Oxford: Blackwell.

Castells, M. (2012) *Networks of Outrage and Hope: Social Movements in the Internet Age*. Cambridge: Polity Press.

Castells, M., Caraca, J. and Cardosa, G. (2012) *Aftermath*. Oxford: Oxford University Press.

Chandler, D. (2010) 'Neither international nor global: rethinking the problematic subject of security', *Journal of Critical Globalisation Studies*, 3: 89–101.

Chesterton, G. K. ([1908] 2004) *Orthodoxy*. Whitefish, MT: Kessinger Publishing.

Churchman, C. W. (1968) *Systems Approach*. New York: Delta.

Churchman, C. W. (1979) *Systems Approaches and Its Enemies*. New York: Basic Books.

Clinton, B. (2012) 'The case for optimism', *Time Magazine*, 1 October. Clinton's Global Initiative.

Cobb, K. (2005) *The Blackwell Guide to Theology and Popular Culture*. Oxford: Blackwell.

Cole, R. (1989) *Strategies for Learning: Small-Group Activities in American, Japanese, and Swedish Industry*. Berkeley, CA: University of California Press.

Collins Dictionary (1992) Third edition. London: HarperCollins.

Collins, J. (2001) 'Level 5 leadership', *Harvard Business Review*, January, pp. 67–76.

Collins, J. and Porras, J. (2000) *Built to Last*. London: Random House Business Books.

Collinson, D. (2003) 'Identities and insecurities: selves at work', *Organization*, 10(3): 527–47.

Collinson, D. L. (2006) 'Rethinking followership: a post-structuralist analysis of follower identities', *The Leadership Quarterly*, 17(2): 172–89.

Conger, J. A. (1994) *The Spirit at Work*. San Francisco, CA: Jossey-Bass.

Conger, J. A. and Kanungo, R. (1987) 'Toward a behavioural theory of charismatic leadership in organisational settings', *The Academy of Management Review*, 12: 637–47.

Conlon, M. (1999) 'Religion in the workplace: the growing presence of spirituality in corporate America', *Business Week*, November.

Constance, R. (2003) 'Designing learning organisations', *Organizational Dynamics*, 32(1): 46–61.

Cooke, B. (2008) 'If critical management is your problem', *Organization*, 15(6): 927–32.

Cooper, A. (1996) 'Bad deeds, naughty words'. Unpublished paper, London: Tavistock.

Cooper, S. (2012) 'Make more money by making your employees happy'. Review. www.forbes.com/sites/stevecooper/2012/07/30/make-more-money-by-making-your-employees-happy/ (accessed February 2013).

Coopey, J. (1995) 'The learning organization: power, politics and ideology', *Management Learning*, 26(2): 193–213.

Corella, D. (2012) 'The politics of sustainability: Wal-Mart and the logic of green capitalism', *La Jajicarita*, 26 March. http://lajicarita.wordpress.com/2012/03/26/the-politics-of-sustainability-wal-mart-and-the-logic-of-green-capitalism/ (accessed 4 February 2013).

Covey S. R. (1989) *The 7 Habits of Highly Effective People.* New York: Free Press.

Covey, S. R.(2004) *The 8th Habit: From Effectiveness to Greatness.* New York: Free Press.

Cuilla, J. (1995) 'Leadership ethics mapping the territory', *Business Ethics Quarterly*, 5: 5–28.

Cullen, J. (2009) 'How to sell your soul and still get into Heaven: Steven Covey's epiphany-inducing technology of effective selfhood', *Human Relations*, 62: 1231–54.

Cunliffe, A. (2008) 'Will you still need me … when I'm 64? The future of CMS', *Organization*, 15(6): 936–8.

Daily Telegraph (Online) (2013) 'Stafford Hospital scandal: deaths force NHS reforms', 5 January 2013. http://www.telegraph.co.uk/health/heal-our-hospitals/9783017/ Stafford-Hospital-scandal-deaths-force-NHS-reforms.html (accessed 11 March 2013).

Dandelion, P. (2008) *The Quakers: A Very Short Introduction.* Oxford: Oxford University Press.

Dartington, T. (2010) *Managing Vulnerability: The Underlying Dynamics of Systems of Care.* London: Karnac.

Deal, T. and Kennedy, A. (1982) *Corporate Cultures.* Reading, MA: Addison–Wesley.

De Beauvoir, S. (1949/1972) *The Second Sex* (translated and edited by H. M. Parshley). Harmondsworth: Penguin Books.

Della Porta, D. (1999) *Social Movements: An Introduction.* London: Blackwell.

Derrida, J. (1982) *Margins of Philosophy* (trans. with additional notes by Alan Bass). Brighton: Harvester Press.

De Rue, D. S. and Ashford, S. J. (2010) 'Who will lead and who will follow? A social process of leadership identity construction in organizations', *Academy of Management Review*, 35: 627–47.

Diana, M. and Eyerman, R. (1992) *Studying Collective Action.* London: Sage.

DiMaggio, P. J. and Powell, W. W. (1983) 'The iron cage revisited: institutional isomorphism and collective rationality in organisational fields', *American Sociological Review*, 48: 147–60.

Dineen, T. (1999) *Manufacturing Victims: What the Psychological Industry is Doing to People.* Toronto: Robert Davies Publishers.

Dor, J. (1997) *Introduction to the Reading of Lacan.* New York: Jason Aronson Inc.

Douglas, T. (1983) *Groups: Understanding People Gathered Together.* London: Tavistock.

Drucker, P. (1973) *Management: Tasks, Responsibilities, Practices.* New York: Harper.

Du Gay, P. (2000) *In Praise of Bureaucracy: Weber Organisation Ethics.* London: Sage.

Dubrin, A. (2000) *Leadership: Research Findings, Practice and Skills*. Boston, MA: Houghton Mifflin.

Dumm, T. L. (1996) *Michel Foucault and the Politics of Freedom*. Thousand Oaks, CA: Sage.

Dvir, T., Eden, D., Avolio, B. J. and Shamir, B. (2002) 'Impact of transformational leadership on follower development and performance: A field experiment', *The Academy of Management Journal*, 45(4): 735–44.

The Economist (2007) 'Snarling all the way to the bank', 23 August. Available at www.economist.com/node/9681074 (accessed 11 March 2013).

Edwards, R. (1979) *Contested Terrain*. New York: Basic Books.

Elmore, R. (2000) *Building a New Structure for School Leadership*. Washington, DC: The Albert Shanker Institute.

Enteman, W. F. (1993) *Managerialism: The Emergence of a New Ideology*. Madison, WI: University of Wisconsin Press.

Etzioni, A. (1961) *Complex Organizations*. New York: Holt, Rinehart and Wilson.

Etzioni, A. (1993) *The Spirit of Human Rights Responsibilities and the Communitarian Agenda*. New York: Crown.

Etzioni, A. (1997) '"Community, yes, but whose?" A debate with Roger Scruton', *City Journal*, Spring: 79–83.

Etzioni, A. (2002) *Next: The Road to the Good Society*. New York: Basic Books.

Eysenck, H. J. and Hans, J. (1953) *The Structure of Human Personality*. London: Methuen.

Fairclough, N. (1995) *Critical Discourse Analysis: The Critical Study of Language*. London: Longman.

Fairclough, N. (2001) *Language and Power*. London/New York: Longman.

Fairhurst, G. (2007) *Discursive Leadership: In Conversation with Leadership Psychology*. London: Sage Publications.

Fanon, F. (1970) *Black Skin, White Masks*. London: Paladin.

Featherstone, M. (1995) *Undoing Culture: Globalization, Postmodernism and Identity*. London: Sage.

Fiedler, F. E. (1967) *A Theory of Leadership Effectiveness*. New York: McGraw–Hill.

Fiedler, F. E. (1974) 'The contingency model – new directions for leadership utilisation', *Journal of Contemporary Business*, 3 (Autumn): 65–79.

Fitzpatrick, M. (2000) *The Tyranny of Health: Doctors and the Regulation of Lifestyle*. London: Routledge.

Fleetwood, S. and Hesketh, A. J. (2006) 'HRM-Performance Research: Under-theorised and lacking explanatory power', *International Journal of Human Resource Management*, 17(12): 1979–95.

Foucault, M. (1972) *The Archaeology of Knowledge*. New York: Pantheon Books.

Foucalt, M. (1978 [French publication, 1976]) *The History of Sexuality, Vol. I: An Introduction* (translated by Robert Hurley). New York: Pantheon.

Foucault, M. ([1977] 1991) *Discipline and Punish: The Birth of the Prison*. London: Penguin.

Foucault, M. (1980) *Power/Knowledge: Selected Interviews and Other Writings, 1972–77* (ed. C. Gordon). London: Harvester.

Fox News (2006) 'Rev. Ted Haggard apologizes for "immoral" act, requests forgiveness', 5 November. Available at www.foxnews.com/story/0,2933,227568,00.html (accessed 4 February 2013)

Freeman, Jo (1972–1973) 'The tyranny of structurelessness', *Berkeley Journal of Sociology*, 17: 151–64.

Freud, S. (1930/2002) *Civilisation and Its Discontents*. London: Penguin.

Friedman, M. (1962) *Capitalism and Freedom*. Chicago: University of Chicago Press.

Friedman, M. (1970) 'The social responsibility of business is to increase its profits', *New York Times Magazine*, 13 September. Retrieved from www.umich.edu/~thecore/doc/Friedman.pdf I (12 March 2013).

Friedman, T. (2009) 'The new Sputnik', *New York Times*, 26 September. Available at www.nytimes.com/2009/09/27/opinion/27friedman.html?_r=1 (accessed 12 March 2013).

Frosh, S. (1997) 'Fundamentalism, gender and family therapy', *Journal of Family Therapy*, 19: 417–30.

Fry, L. W., Keim, G. D. and Meiners, R. E. (1982) 'Corporate contributions: altruistic or for profit?', *The Academy of Management Journal*, 25(1): 94–106.

Fulop, L. and Linstead, S. (1999) *Management: A Critical Text*. London: Macmillan.

Furedi, F. (2003) *Therapy Culture*. London: Routledge.

Gabriel, Y. (1999) *Organisations in Depth*. London: Sage.

Gastil, J. (1997) 'A definition of democratic leadership', in K. Grint (ed.), *Leadership: Classical, Contemporary and Critical Approaches*. Oxford: Oxford University Press.

Gay, P. (1999) 'Sigmund Freud', *Time Magazine*, 29 March. Available at www.time.com/time/time100/scientist/profile/freud03.html (accessed 5 February 2013).

Geertz, C. (1973) 'Thick description: Toward an interpretive theory of culture', in *The Interpretation of Cultures*. New York: Basic Books.

Gemmil, G. and Oakley, J. (1992) 'Leadership – an alienating social myth?', *Human Relations*, 42(1): 13–29.

Gerlach, L. and Hine, V. (1970) *People, Power Change: Movements of Transformation*. Indianapolis, IN: Bobbs–Merrill.

Giacalone, R. A. and Jurkiewicz, C. L. (2003) *Handbook of Workplace Spirituality and Organizational Performance*. Armonk, NY: Sharpe Press.

Giddens, A. (1982) *Profiles and Critiques in Social Theory*. London: Macmillan.

Giddens, A. (1991) *Modernity and Self Identity: Self and Society in the Late Modern Age*. Cambridge: Polity Press.

Giddens, A. (1992) *The Transformation of Intimacy: Sexuality, Love and Eroticism in Modern Societies*. Cambridge: Polity Press.

Goffman, E. (1961) *Asylums: Essays on the Social Situation of Mental Patients and Other Inmates*. New York: Doubleday.

Goleman, D. (1995) *Emotional Intelligence: Why It Can Matter More than IQ*. New York: Bantam Books.

Goleman, D. (2002) *The New Leaders*. London: Little, Brown.

Goodstein, L. (2006) 'Evangelicals fear the loss of their teenagers', *New York Times*, 6 October. Available at www.nytimes.com/2006/10/06/us/06evangelical.html?pagewanted=all&_r=0 (accessed 4 February 2013).

Gray, J. (2003) *Al Qaeda and What It Means to be Modern*. London: W. W. Norton.

Greenleaf, R. (1977) *Servant Leadership*. Mahwah, NJ: Paulist Press.

Grey, C. (2004) 'Reinventing business schools: the contribution of critical management education', *Academy of Management: Learning and Education*, 3(2): 178–86.

Grint, K. (1997) *Leadership: Classical, Contemporary and Critical Approaches*. Oxford: Oxford University Press.

Grint, K. (2005) *Leadership Limits and Possibilities*. London/New York: Palgrave.

Guardian (2012) 'Marine Le Pen scores stunning result in French presidential election', 22 April. Available at www.guardian.co.uk/world/2012/apr/22/marine-le-pen-french-election (accessed November 2012).

Guha, R. (1989) 'Radical American environmentalism and wilderness preservation: a third world critique', *Environmental Ethics*, 11(1): 71–83.

Gwyn, D. (1989) *Unmasking the Idols*. Richmond, IN: Friends United Press.

Gwynne, R., Klak, T. and Shaw, J. (2003) *Alternative Capitalisms: Geographies of Emerging Regions*. London: Arnold Press.

Habermas, J. (1984) *The Theory of Communicative Action, I*. Boston, MA: Beacon Press.

Habermas, J. (1987) *The Theory of Communicative Action, II*. Boston, MA: Beacon Press.

Halperin, D. M. (2002) *How to Do the History of Homosexuality*. London/Chicago: University of Chicago Press.

Handy, C. (1993) *Understanding Organizations*, 4th edn. Oxford: Oxford University Press.

Handy, C. (1996) *Gods of Management: The changing work of organizations*. Oxford: Oxford University Press.

Haraway, D. J. (1991) *Simians, Cyborgs and Women: The Reinvention of Nature*. London: Free Association.

Hardt, M. and Negri, A. (2001) *Empire*. Cambridge, MA: Harvard University Press.

Harvey, D. (2012) 'Restless cities', *ICON magazine*, September.

Hasdell, P. (2008) 'Pnuema', in L. Tilder and B. Blostein (eds), *Design Ecologies*. New York: Princeton Architectural Press.

Heelas, P. (1996) *The New Age Movement: The Celebration of the Self and the Sacralization of Modernity*. Oxford: Blackwell.

Heelas, P. (2002) 'Work, ethics, soft capitalism and the "turn to life"', in P. du Gay and M. Prycke (eds), *Cultural Economy*. London: Sage. pp. 78–96.

Heelas, P. and Woodhead, L. (2005) *The Spiritual Revolution: Why Religion Is Giving Way to Spirituality*. Oxford: Blackwell.

Helgeson, S. (1990) *The Female Advantage*. New York: Doubleday.

Hendricks, G. and Ludeman, K. (1997) *The Corporate Mystic*. New York: Bantam Books.

Hertz, N. (2001) *The Silent Takeover*. London: Heinemann.

Hesketh, A. J. and Fleetwood, S. (2006) 'Beyond measuring the HRM-organizational performance link: applying critical realist meta-theory', *Organization*, 13(5): 677–99.

Hickman, G. R. (2012) 'Concepts of leadership in organizational change', in M. Preedy, N. Bennet and C. Wise (eds), *Educational Leadership*. London: Sage.

Hirschhorn, L. (1988) *The Workplace Within: Psychodynamics of Organisational Life*. London: Cambridge Press.

Hirschhorn, L. (1999) 'Leaders and followers', in Y. Gabriel (ed.), *Organisations in Depth*. London: Sage. pp. 139–66.

Hochschild, A. R. (1983) *The Managed Heart: The Commercialisation of Human Feeling*. Berkeley, CA: University of California Press.

House, R. (1977) 'A theory of charismatic leadership', in J. G. Hunt and L. Larson (eds), *Leadership: The Cutting Edge*. Carbondale, IL: Southern Illinois University Press.

House, R. and Aditya, R. (1997) 'The social scientific study of leadership: quo vadis?', *Journal of Management*, 23: 409–73.

Howard, S. and Welbourn, D. (2004) *The Spirit at Work Phenomenon*. London: Azure.

Huey, J. (1994) 'The leadership industry', *Fortune*, 21 (February): 54–6.

Hughes, R. (2005) *The Shock of the New*. London: Thames & Hudson.

Hughes, T. P. (2004) *American Genesis: A Century of Invention and Technological Enthusiasm, 1870–1970*, 2nd edn. Chicago, IL: University of Chicago Press.

Huy, Q. (2002) 'Emotional balancing of organizational continuity and radical change: The contribution of middle managers', *Administrative Science Quarterly*, 47(1).

Huy, Q. (2001) 'In praise of middle managers', *Harvard Business Review*, September.

Isaacson, W. (2011) *Steve Jobs: A Biography*. New York: Simon & Schuster.

Jackall, R. (1988) *Moral Mazes: The World of Corporate Managers*. New York: Oxford University Press.

Jackson, B. and Parry, K. (2011) *A Very Short, Fairly Interesting and Reasonably Cheap Book about Studying Leadership*. London: Sage.

Jackson, T. (2009) *Prosperity Without Growth? The Transition to a Sustainable Economy*. London: Sustainable Development Commission. Quote retrieved from www.guardian.co.uk/books/2010/jan/23/properity-without-growth-tim-jackson (accessed December 2012).

Janis, I. (1972) *Victims of Groupthink: A Psychological Study of Foreign Policy Decisions and Fiascoes*. Boston, MA: Houghton–Mifflin.

Jaques, E. (1955) 'Social systems as a defence against persecutory and depressive anxiety', in A. D. Colman and M. H. Geller (eds), *Group Relation Reader 2*. Washington, DC: A K Rice Institute.

Jaques, E. (1990) 'In praise of hierarchy', *Harvard Business Review*, January/February.

Johnson, J. (2005) What is an Ecosystem? [Online] Available at: www.stolaf.edu/depts/cis/wp/johnsoja/whatisdiscourse/whatisanecosystem.html (accessed 18 April 2013).

Johnson, P. and Duberley, J. (2000) *Understanding Management Research*. London: Sage.

Joll, J. (1979) *The Anarchists*. London: Methuen.

Jones (1996) *Jesus CEO*. New York: Hyperion.

Kandola, R. and Fullerton, J. (1994) *Managing the Mosaic: Diversity in Action*. London: Institute of Personnel and Development.

Kanter, R. (1979) 'Power failure in management circuits', *Harvard Business Review*, July–August, 57: 65–75.

Kanter, R. (1983) *The Change Masters*. New York: Simon and Schuster.

Kapuscinski, R. (1984) *The Emperor*. New York: First Vintage Books.

Katz, A. (1981) 'Self-help and mutual aid: an emerging social movement?', *Annual Review of Sociology*, 7: 129–55.

Katz, R. F. (2006) 'Studying leadership: knowledge into action'. Paper presented at the 5th annual conference on leadership, Cranfield University School of Management, 14–15 December.

Kellerman, B. (2004) *Bad Leadership: What It Is, How It Happens, Why It Matters*. Cambridge, MA: Harvard Business School Press.

Kengor, P. (2007) *The Crusader: Ronald Reagan and the Fall of Communism*. London: HarperCollins.

Kenny, K., Whittle, A., and Willmott, H. (2012) *Understanding Identity and Organizations*. London: Sage.

Kerr, S. and Jermier, J. M. (1978) 'Substitutes for leadership: their meaning and measurement', *Organisational Behaviour and Human Performance*, 22: 375–403.

Kets De Vries, M. R. F. (1991) 'The leadership mystique', in L. Fulop and S. Linstead (eds), *Management: A Critical Text*. London: Macmillan Press.

Kets de Vries, M. R. F. (1994) 'The leadership mystique', *The Academy of Management Executive*, 8(3): 73–92.

Kets de Vries, M. R. F. (2006) *The Leader on the Couch*. San Francisco, CA: Jossey–Bass.

Kets de Vries, M. R. F. and Miller, D. (1984) *The Neurotic Organization: Diagnosing and Changing Counterproductive Styles of Management*. New Jersey: Jossey-Bass Inc.

Kiely, R. (2005) *Empire in the Age of Globalization: U.S. Hegemony and Neo-Liberal Disorder.* London: Pluto Press.

Klein, M. (1959) 'Our adult world and its roots in infancy', in A. D. Colman and M. H. Geller (eds), *Group Relation Reader 2.* Washington, DC: A. K. Rice Institute.

Klein, N. (2000) *No Logo.* London: HarperCollins.

Klein, N. (2001) 'Reclaiming the commons', *New Left Review*, 9: 81–9.

Klein, E. and Izzo, J. B. (1999) *Awakening Corporate Soul.* Chicago: Fairwinds.

Kotter, J. P. (1990) *A Force for Change: How Leadership Differs from Management.* New York: Free Press/London: Collier Macmillan.

Kunda, G. (1992) *Engineering Culture: Control Commitment in a High Tech Corporation.* Philadelphia, PA: Temple University Press.

Ladd, J. (1970) 'Morality and the ideal of rationality in formal organisations', *The Monist*, 54(4), October.

Ladkin, D. (2006) 'The enchantment of the charismatic leader: charisma reconsidered as an aesthetic encounter', *Leadership*, 2(2): 165–179.

Lasch, C. (1979) *The Culture of Narcissism: American Life in an Age of Diminishing Expectations.* New York: Norton.

Latour, B. (2005) *Reassembling the Social.* Oxford: Oxford University Press.

Law, J. (1992) 'Notes on the Theory of the Actor Network: Ordering, Strategy and heterogeneity,' *Systems Practice*, 5: 379–93. [Online]. Available at: http://files.soc. aegean.gr/sociology/kitrinou/arthra-se-diafores-thematikes-enotites/ACTOR-NETWORKTHEORY/2.PDF

Law, J. (1993) *Organizing Modernity: Social Ordering and Social Theory.* Oxford: Wiley–Blackwell.

Lawrence, W. (1995) 'The presence of totalitarian states-of-mind in institutions'. Retrieved from http://human-nature.com/free-associations/lawren.html (accessed March 2013).

Leitch, A. (1956) 'The primary task of the church', *Christianity Today*, 1(1): 19.

Lessa, I. (2006) 'Discoursive struggles within social welfare: restaging teen motherhood', *British Journal of Social Work*, 36(2): 283–98.

Lewin, K. and Lippett, R. (1938) 'An experimental approach to the study of autocracy and democratic leadership', *Sociometry*, 1: 292–300.

Likert, R. (1961) *New Patterns of Management.* New York: McGraw–Hill.

Lilley, S. and Platt, G. (1997) 'Images of Martin Luther King', in K. Grint (ed.), *Leadership: Classical, Contemporary and Critical Approaches.* Oxford: Oxford University Press.

Lodahl, M. and Powell, S. (1999) *Embodied Holiness.* New York: InterVarsity Press.

LoRusso, J.D. (2011) 'Bringing spirituality into the workplace at the University of Arkansas: saving souls and the world through the freemarket', Religion Nerd, 21 November. http://religionnerd.com/2011/11/21/bringing-spirituality-into-the-workplace-at-the-university-of-arkansas-saving-souls-and-the-world-through-the-free-market/ (accessed December 2012).

Lovelock, J. (1982) *Gaia: A New Look at Life on Earth.* Oxford: Oxford University Press.

Loyrette, H. (1985) *Gustave Eiffel.* New York: Rizzoli.

Lyotard, J-F. (1979) *La condition postmoderne: rapport sur le savoir.* Paris: Minuit.

Lyotard, J-F. (1984) *The Postmodern Condition: A Report on Knowledge.* Minneapolis, MN: University of Minnesota Press.

Maak, T. and Pless, N.M. (eds) (2006) *Responsible Leadership.* London: Routledge.

Maccoby, M. (2000) 'Narcissistic leaders: the incredible pros, the inevitable cons', *Harvard Business Review*, 78(1): 69–77.

MacIntyre, A. (1985) *After Virtue: A Study In Moral Theory*, 2nd edn. London: Duckworth.

Marsh, J. L. (2002) 'The right and the good: a solution to the communicative ethics controversy', in R. A. Cohen and J. L. Marsh (eds), *Ricoeur as Another: The Ethics of Subjectivity*. New York: SUNY Press.

Marx, K. (1845/1978) 'Theses on Feuerbach', in Robert C. Tucker (ed.), *The Marx–Engels Reader*, 2nd edn. New York: W.W. Norton.

Maslow, A. (1968) *Toward a Psychology of Being*. New York: Van Nostrand.

Masson, J. (1990) *Against Therapy*. London: Fontana.

Maturana, H. R. and Varela, F. (1980) *Autopoiesis and Cognition*. Dordrecht: Reidel.

Maturana, H. R. and Varela, F. (1987) *Tree of Knowledge*. Boston, MA: Shambala.

May, A. (2000) 'Leadership and spirit: breathing new vitality and energy into individuals and organizations', *The Academy of Management Executive*, 14(2): 128–30.

Mayer, J. and Salovey, P. (1993) 'The intelligence of emotional intelligence', *Intelligence*, 17(4): 433–42.

Mayer, J. D., Caruso, D. R. and Salovey, P. (2000) 'Models of emotional intelligence', in R. J. Sternberg (ed.), *Handbook of Intelligence*. Cambridge: Cambridge University Press.

McAdam, D. (1982) *Political Process and the Development of Black Insurgency*. Chicago, IL: University of Chicago Press.

McCarthy, J. and Zald, M. (1987) *Social Movements in an Organisational Society*. London: Transaction Books.

McCarthy, T. (1978) *The Critical Theory of Jurgen Habermas*. Cambridge, MA: MIT Press.

McDonald, L. and Robinson, P. (2009) *A Colossal Failure of Common Sense: The Inside Story of the Collapse of Lehman Brothers*. New York: Crown Business.

McGuirk, J. (2012) 'Edge City', *ICON* 111 (September): 76–81.

McIntyre-Mills, J. J. (2008) 'Systemic ethics: expanding the boundaries of rights and responsibilities' *Systems Research and Behavioral Science*, 25(2): 147–50.

McLuhan, M. and Fiore, Q. (1967) *The Medium is the Massage: An Inventory of Effects*. New York: Bantam Books.

Meindl, J. (1995) 'The romance of leadership as a follower-centric theory: A social constructionist approach', *The Leadership Quarterly*, 6(3): 329–41.

Melucci, A. (1989) *Nomads of the Present: Social Movements and Individual Needs in Contemporary Society*. London: Hutchinson.

Menzies Lyth, I. (1960) 'A case study in the functioning of social systems as a defence against anxiety', *Human Relations*, 13: 95–121.

Merton, T. (1966) *A Search for Solitude: The Journals of Thomas Merton, Volume Three 1952–1960*, (ed. Lawrence Cunningham). San Francisco, CA: HarperCollins.

Michels, R. (1915) *Political Parties: A Sociological Study of the Oligarchical Tendencies of Modern Democracy*. Glencoe, IL: The Free Press.

Micklethwait, J. and Wooldridge, A. (1996) *The Witch Doctors: What the Management Gurus are Saying, Why it Matters and How to Make Sense of it*. London: Heinemann.

Miller, E. (1993) *From Dependency to Autonomy*. London: Free Association Books.

Miller, J.-A. (2011) *Lacan's Later Teaching*, Lacanian Ink21 [Online]. Available at: www.lacan.com/frameXXI2.htm (accessed 18 April 2013).

Mintzberg, H. (2004) *Managers Not MBAs: A Hard Look at the Soft Practice of Managing and Management Development*. San Francisco, CA: Berrett–Koehler.

Mintzberg, H. (2012) Cited in 'The Anti-MBA', by D. D. Guttenplan, *New York Times*, 20 May. Available at www.nytimes.com/2012/05/21/world/europe/21iht-educlede21.html?pagewanted=all&_r=0 (accessed 4 February 2013).

Mitroff, I. I. and Denton, E. A. (1999) *A Spiritual Audit of Corporate America*. San Francisco, CA: Jossey–Bass.

Monbiot, G. (2000) *Captive State: The Corporate Take Over of Britain*. London: Macmillan.

Moore, R. (2000) *The Light in their Consciences: Early Quakers in Britain 1646–1666*. University Park, PA: Pennsylvania State University Press.

Morgan, G. (1986) *Images of Organisations*. London: Sage.

Morgan, M. (2011) (ed.) *Classics of Moral and Political Theory*, fifth edition. Indianapolis: Hackett.

Moskowitz, E. (2001) *In Therapy We Trust: America's Obsession with Fulfilment*. Baltimore, MD: Johns Hopkins University Press.

Naess, A. (1989) *Ecology, Community and Lifestyle*. Cambridge: Cambridge University Press.

Naisbitt, J. (1982) *Megatrends: Ten New Directions Transforming our Lives*. New York: Warner Books.

NBC News (2006) 'Branson bets billions to curb global warming', 21 September. www.nbcnews.com/id/14936341/ (accessed 12 March 2013).

Neal, J. (2006) *Edgewalkers: People and Organizations that Take Risks, Build Bridges and Break New Ground*. California: Praeger.

Nelson, N. (2012) *Make More Money by Making Your Employees Happy*. MindLab Publishing. E-book.

Nelson, R. E. and Gopalan, S. (2003) 'Do organisational cultures replicate national cultures?, *Organization Studies*, 24(7): 1115–51.

New Economics Foundation (2010) *Growth Isn't Possible: Why Rich Countries Need a New Economic Direction*. London: nef. Available at www.neweconomics.org/publications/growth-isnt-possible (accessed 4 February 2013).

New York Times (2011a) 'Berlusconi steps down, and Italy pulses with change', 12 November. Available at www.nytimes.com/2011/11/13/world/europe/silvio-berlusconi-resign-italy-austerity-measures.html?_r=0 (accessed February 2013).

New York Times (2011b) 'China leads push to go green', 8 May. Available at www.nytimes.com/2011/05/09/business/energy-environment/09clean.html?_r=0 (accessed February 2013).

New York Times (2011c) 'Ray Anderson, businessman turned environmentalist, dies at 77', 10 August. Available at www.nytimes.com/2011/08/11/business/ray-anderson-a-carpet-innovator-dies-at-77.html?_r=0 (accessed February 2013).

Nietzsche, F. ([1899]1996) *Thus Spake Zarathustra*. London: Unwin, republished Orion Books.

Northouse, P. G. (2004) *Leadership: Theory and Practice*, 3rd edn. Thousand Oaks, CA: Sage.

Oates, S. (1982) *Let the Trumpet Sound: The Life of Martin Luther King, Jr*. New York: Harper & Row.

Obholzer, A. (1994) 'Authority, power and leadership: contributions from group relations training', in A. Obholzer and V. Z. Roberts (eds), *The Unconscious at*

Work: Individual and Organizational Stress in the Human Services. London: Routledge. pp. 39–47.

Obholzer, A. and Roberts, V. Z. (eds) (1994) *The Unconscious At Work.* London: Routledge.

Observer (2010) 'Ryanair must move away from low fares, says O'Leary', 12 September. Available at www.guardian.co.uk/business/2010/sep/12/ryanair-move-away-from-low-fares (accessed 11 March 2013).

Ohmae, K. (1995) *The End of the Nation State: The rise of regional economies.* New York: Free Press.

O'Leary, M. (1994) Quote retrieved from www.telegraph.co.uk/finance/newsbysector/transport/5918074/Ryanair-chief-Michael-OLeary-the-quotes.html (accessed 4 February 2013).

Orwell, G. (1949) *Nineteen Eighty-Four.* London: Secker & Warburg.

Ouchi, W. (1981) *Theory Z: How American Business Can Meet the Japanese Challenge.* Reading, MA: Addison–Wesley.

Ouchi, W. and Price, R. (1978) 'Hierarchies, clans and Theory Z: a new perspective on organization development', *Organizational Dynamics*, 7(2): 24.

Parker, M. (1998) *Ethics and Organisations.* London: Sage.

Parker, M. (2002) *Against Management: Organization in the Age of Managerialism.* Cambridge: Polity Press.

Pearce, C. L. and Conger, J. A. (eds) (2003) *Shared Leadership: Reframing the Hows and Whys of Leadership.* Thousand Oaks, CA: Sage.

Peng, T. (2011) 'The impact of citizenship on labour process: state, capital and labour control in South China', *Work, Employment & Society*, December, 25(4): 726–41.

Peters, T. and Waterman, H. (1982) *In Search of Excellence: Lessons from America's Best Run Companies.* New York: Harper & Row.

Petriglieri, G. and Stein, M. (2012) 'The unwanted self: projective identification in leaders' identity work', *Organization Studies*, 33(9):1217–35.

Pfeiffer, J. (1978) 'The ambiguity of leadership', in M. W. McCall, Jr and M. Lombardo (eds), *Leadership: Where Else Can We Go?* Durham, NC: Duke University Press.

Podolny, J. M., Khurana, R. and Hill-Popper, M. (2005) 'Revisiting the meaning of leadership', *Research in Organizational Behavior*, 26: 1–36.

Polman, P. (2012) 'Unilever's Paul Polman: challenging the corporate status quo', interview with Guardian Sustainable Business, 24 April. Available at www.guardian.co.uk/sustainable-business/paul-polman-unilever-sustainable-living-plan (accessed 12 March 2013).

Power, M. (1997) *Audit Society: Rituals of Verification.* Oxford: Oxford University Press.

Pratley, Nils (2012) Analysis article. *Guardian*, 30 June, p. 5.

Pugh, D. and Hickson, D. (1971) *Writers on Organisations.* London: Penguin Books.

Putnam, R. (2000) *Bowling Alone: The Collapse and Revival of American Community.* New York: Simon & Schuster.

Puwar, N. (2004) *Space Invaders: Race, Gender and Bodies Out of Place.* Oxford: Berg.

Pye, A. (2005) 'Leadership and organising: sensemaking in action', *Leadership*, 1(1): 31–49.

Rachman, G. (2012) 'The backlash against the rich has gone global', *Financial Times*, 7 August, p. 11.

Raelin, J. (2003) *The Leaderful Organization: How To Bring Out Leadership In Everyone.* San Francisco, CA: Berrett-Koehler Publishers.

Redekop, B. (2010) 'Leadership', in *Berkshire Encyclopedia of Sustainability: The Business of Sustainability*. Great Barrington, MA: Berkshire Publishing Group. pp. 303–8.

Redekop, B. and Olson, S. (2010) *Leadership for Environmental Sustainability*. New York: Routledge.

Reicher, S. D., Haslam, S. A. and Hopkins, N. (2005) 'Social identity and the dynamics of leadership: leaders and followers as collaborative agents in the transformation of social reality,' *Leadership Quarterly*, 16: 547–68.

Reynolds, M. and Vince, R. (2004) 'Critical management education and action-based learning: synergies and contradictions', *Academy of Management Learning and Education*, 3: 442–56.

Rice, A. (1965) *Learning for Leadership*. London: Tavistock.

Rich, A. (1980) 'Compulsory heterosexuality and lesbian experience', *Signs: Journal of Women in Culture & Society*, 5(4).

Ricoeur, P. (1990) *Oneself as Another*, trans. Kathleen Blamey. Chicago: University of Chicago Press.

Rieff, P. (1966) *The Triumph of the Therapeutic: Uses of Faith after Freud*. New York: Harper & Row.

Ritzer, G. (1993) *The McDonaldization of Society*. Newbury Park, CA: Pine Forge Press.

Robertson, P. (1982) *The Secret Kingdom*. Nashville, TN: Thomas Nelson.

Robins, N. (2010) 'The ecology of growth', www.neweconomics.org/blog/2010/10/13/the-ecology-of-growth (accessed December 2012).

Roddick, A. (2006) 'About Dame Anita Roddick', 28 September. www.anitaroddick.com/aboutanita.php (accessed 5 February 2013).

Rogers, C. (1961) *On Becoming a Person: A Therapist's View of Psychotherapy*. London: Constable.

Rose, N. (1990) *Governing the Soul: The Shaping of the Private Self*. London: Routledge.

Rose, N. (1991) 'Governing by numbers: figuring out democracy'. *Accounting, Organizations and Society*, 16(7): 673–92.

Rose, N. (1996) *Inventing Our Selves: Psychology, Power and Personhood*. New York: Cambridge University Press.

Rose, N. (1999) *Powers of Freedom: Reframing political thought*. Cambridge: Cambridge University Press.

Roseneil, S. (2006) 'The ambivalences of Angel's "arrangement": a psycho-social lens on the contemporary condition of personal life', *The Sociological Review*, 54(4): 847–69.

Rosener, J. B. (1995) *America's Competitive Secret: Women Managers*. New York: Oxford University Press.

Ruddock, A. (2007) *Michael O'Leary: A Life in Full Flight*. London: Penguin Book.

Ruggiero, G. and Sahulka, S. (eds) (1998) *Zapatistas Encuentro*. New York: Seven Stories Press.

Ryan, R. (2003) 'The writer as freedom fighter, the freedom fighter as writer', *New Formulation*, 2(1).

Sachdev, P. (2011) 'Positive psychology, psychotherapy and the pursuit of happiness', a dissertation for MA Integrative Counselling, Department of Psychology, London Metropolitan University.

Said, E. (1973) *Orientalism*. London: Routledge and Kegan Paul.

Satterwhite, R. (2010) 'Deep systems leadership: a model for the 21st century', in B. W. Redekop and S. Olson (eds), *Leadership for Environmental Sustainability*. New York: Routledge. pp. 230–43.

Saul, J. R. (1992) *Voltaire's Bastards: The Dictatorship of Reason in the West*. Toronto: Penguin.

Schein, E. (1988) *Organizational Culture and Leadership*. San Francisco, CA: Jossey–Bass.

Schwartz, H. S. (1990) *Narcissistic Process and Corporate Decay*. New York: New York University Press

Schwartz, T. (2000) 'How do you feel?', *Fast Company*, June, 35: 296.

Scott, J. (1985) *Weapons of the Weak: Everyday Forms of Peasant Resistance*. New Haven, CT: Yale University Press. pp. 29–36.

Segal, L. (1994) *Straight Sex: Rethinking the Politics of Pleasure*. London: Virago.

Senge, P. (1990) *The Fifth Discipline: The Art and Practice of the Learning Organisation*. New York: Doubleday/Currency.

Senge, P. (1994) *The Fifth Discipline*. London: Century Business.

Senge, P. (2006) *The Fifth Discipline: The Art and Practice of the Learning Organization*. New York: Crown Business.

Sennet, R. (2006) *The Culture of New Capitalism*. Yale: Yale University Press.

Shamir, B., House, R. and Arthur, M. (1993) 'The motivational effects of charismatic leadership: a self-concept based theory', *Organization Science*, 4: 1–17.

Sherman, S. and Freas, A. (2004) 'The wild west of executive coaching', *Harvard Business Review*, 82(11): 82–89.

Sheth, J. (2007) 'Why do good companies go bad?', *FT Press*, 26 October. Available at www.ftpress.com/articles/article.aspx?p=714937 (accessed 4 February 2013).

Sievers, B. (2011) 'Towards a socioanalysis of the current financial crisis', in S. Long and B. Sievers (eds), *Towards a Socioanalysis of Money, Finance and Capitalism: Beneath the Surface of the Financial Industry*. London: Routledge.

Skelton, D. (2011) 'Government of the technocrats, by the technocrats, for the technocrats', *New Statesman*, 16 November. Available at www.newstatesman.com/blogs/the-staggers/2011/11/european-greece-technocrats (accessed February 2013).

Smircich, L. and Morgan, G. (1982) 'Leadership: the management of meaning,' *Journal of Applied Behavioral Science*, 18: 257–73.

Smith, S. and Wilkinson, B. (1996) 'No doors on offices, no secrets: we are our own policemen: capitalism without conflict?', in L. Fulop and S. Linstead (eds), *Management: A Critical Text*. London: Macmillan. pp. 106–7.

Snow, N. (2002) 'Common sense', *Adbusters: Journal of the Mental Environment*, March/April, 40.

Snyder, G. (1990) *The Practice of the Wild*. San Francisco, CA: North Point Press.

Stanford Encyclopedia of Philosophy (2008) 'Michel Foucault'. http://plato.stanford.edu/entries/foucault/ (accessed 11 March 2013).

Starhawk (1986) *Truth or Dare*. New York: Harper & Row.

Steenkamp, J., Batra, R. and Alden, D. (2003) 'How perceived brand globalness creates brand value', *Journal of International Business Studies*, 34 (January): 53–65.

Stein, M. (2003) 'Unbounded irrationality: risk and organizational narcissism at long term capital management', *Human Relations*, 56(5): 523–40.

Stein, M. and Pinto, J. (2011) 'The dark side of groups: a "gang at work" in Enron'. *Group & Organization Management*, 36(6): 697–721.

Stephens, C., D'Intino, R. and Victor, B. (1995) 'The moral quandary of transformational leadership: change for whom?', in R. Woodman and W. Pasmore (eds), *Research in Organizational Change and Development*, 8: 123–43.

Steyrer, J. (1998) 'Charisma and the archetypes of leadership', *Organizational Studies*, 19(5): 807–28.

Stiglitz, J. (2000) 'What I learned at the world economic crisis', *New Republic*, 17 April. Available at www.whirledbank.org/ourwords/stiglitz.html (accessed 4 February 2013).

Stiglitz, J. (2003) 'The Mammon interview: blowing the whistle on Dubyanomics', *Observer*, 12 October. Available at www.guardian.co.uk/business/2003/oct/12/politics.usnews (accessed 4 February 2013).

Stille, A. (2011) 'The paradox of the new elite', *New York Times*, 22 October. Available at www.nytimes.com/2011/10/23/opinion/sunday/social-inequality-and-the-new-elite.html?pagewanted=all (accessed 4 February 2013).

Stookey, S. (2008) 'The future of critical management studies: populism and elitism', *Organization*, 15(6): 992–94.

Strauss, L. (1987) 'Niccolo Machiavelli', in L. Strauss and J. Cropsey (eds), *History of Political Philosophy*, 3rd edn. Chicago, IL: University of Chicago Press. pp. 296–317.

Sullivan, N. (2003) *A Critical Introduction to Queer Theory*. New York: New York University Press.

Svensson, P. (2010) 'The excellent institution'. Editorial. *Ephemera*, 10(1): 1–6.

Swan, E. (2006) *Executive Coaching: Psychobabble or Spaces for Doubt?* Lancaster: Centre for Excellence in Leadership. Working Paper Series CEL.

Taylor, F. ([1911] 1997) *The Principles of Scientific Management*. New York: Dover Publications.

Taylor, K. (2012) 'The new case for women on corporate boards: new perspectives, increased profits', *Forbes*, 26 June. Available at www.forbes.com/sites/katetaylor/2012/06/26/the-new-case-for-women-on-corporate-boards-new-perspectives-increased-profits/?goback=%2Egde_3834048_member_128666923 (accessed 4 February 2013).

Thapan, M. (ed.) (1997) *Embodiment Essays on Gender and Identity*. Mumbai: Oxford University Press.

Thomas, R. Roosevelt Jr (1991) *Beyond Race and Gender: Unleashing the Power of Your Total Workforce by Managing Diversity*. New York: American Management Associates.

Thorsrud, E. and Emery, F. (1969) *Medinflytande och engagemang in arbetet* [Participation and engagement in work]. (Original title, *Mot en ny bedriftsorganisasjon*.) Stockholm: Utvecklingsrådet for Samarbetsfrågor.

Tichy, G. (2001) 'What do we know about success and failure of mergers?', *Journal of Industry, Competition and Trade*, December, 1(4): 347–94.

Tichy, N. and Devanna, M. (1986) *The Transformational Leader*. New York: Wiley.

Tjosvold, D. and Field, R. (1984) 'Managers' structuring cooperative and competitive controversy in group decision making', *International Journal of Management*, 1: 26–32.

Tjosvold, D. and McNeely, L. (1988) 'Innovation through communication in an educational bureaucracy', *Communication Research*, 15: 568–81.

Tolman, D. L. and Diamond, L. M. (2002) 'Desegregating sexuality research: cultural and biological perspectives on gender and desire', *Annual Review of Sex Research*, 12: 33–74.

Tourish, D. and Pinnington, A. (2002) 'Transformational leadership, corporate cultism and the spirituality paradigm: an unholy trinity in the workplace?', *Human Relations*, 55(2): 147–72.

Tourish, D., and Robson, P. (2006) 'Sense making and the distortion of critical upward communication in organizations', *Journal of Management Studies*, 43: 711–30.

Tourish, D. and Tourish, N. (2010) 'Spirituality at work, and its implications for leadership and followership: a post-structuralist perspective', *Leadership*, 6(2): 207–24.

Treacher, A. (2000) 'Ethnicity, psychoanalysis and cultural studies', *Free Associations*, 7(4): 113–26.

Trevett, C. (1995) *Women and Quakerism in the 17th Century*. York: Ebor.

Trist, E. and Bamford, K. (1951) 'Some social and psychological consequences of long wall method of coal-getting', *Human Relations*, 4: 3–38.

Trotsky, L. (1940) *The Class, the Party and the Leadership*. Retrieved from www.marxist.net/trotsky/cpl/index.html (4 February 2013).

Turkle, S. (2011) *Alone Together: Why We Expect More from Technology and Less from Each Other*. New York: Basic Books.

Ulrich, D. (1984) 'Specifying external relations: definition of and actors in an organization's environment', *Human Relations*, 37(3): 245–62.

Vallance, E. (1979) *Women in the House: A Study of Women Members of the House of Commons*. London: Athlone Press.

Von Bertalanffy, L. (1968) *General Systems Theory: Foundations, Development, Application*. London: Allen Lane.

Voronov, M. (2008) 'Towards engaged critical management studies', *Organization*, 15(6): 940–3.

Walby, S. (1997) *Gender Transformations*. London: Routledge.

Waldron, T. (2012) 'Study: CEO pay increased 127 times faster than worker pay over last 30 years', ThinkProgress, 3 May. http://thinkprogress.org/economy/2012/05/03/475952/ceo-pay-faster-worker-pay/ (accessed 1 February 2013).

Walvin, J. (1997) *The Quakers: Money and Morals*. London: John Murray.

Ward, C. (1966) 'Anarchism as a theory of organization', in L. I. Krimerman and L. Perry (eds), *Patterns of Anarchy: A Collection of Writings on the Anarchist Tradition*. New York: Anchor Books.

Washington Post (2011) Obituaries: 'Ray Anderson, "greenest CEO in America", dies at 77', 11 August. Available at www.washingtonpost.com/local/obituaries/ray-anderson-greenest-ceo-in-america-dies-at-77/2011/08/10/gIQAGoTU7I_story.html (accessed August 2012).

Weakland, J., Fisch, R., Watzlawick, P. and Bodin, A. (1974) 'Brief therapy: focused problem resolution', *Family Process*, 13: 141–68.

Weber, M. (1930) *The Protestant Ethic and the Spirit of Capitalism*. London: Allen and Unwin.

Weber, M. (1947) *The Theory of Social and Economic Organisation*. New York: Oxford University Press.

Weick, K. E. (1995) *Sensemaking in Organizations*. London: Sage.

Western, S. (2005) 'A critical analysis of leadership: overcoming fundamentalist tendencies'. Doctoral Dissertation: Lancaster University Management School.

Western, S. (2006) 'Look who's talking', *Coaching at Work*, 1(2): 31–4.

Western, S. (2008) 'Democratising strategy', in D. Campbell and D. Huffington (eds), *Organizations Connected: A Handbook of Systemic Consultation*. London: Karnac. pp. 173–96.

Western, S. (2012) *Coaching and Mentoring: A Critical Text*. London: Sage.

Western, S. and Gosling, J. (2002) *Pairing for Leadership*. Exeter: Exeter University, Centre for Leadership Studies.

Wheatley, M. J. (2006) *Leadership and the New Science*. San Francisco, CA: Berrett–Koehler.

Whitley, R. (1992) *Business Systems in East Asia: Firms, Markets and Societies*. London: Sage.

Whyte, W. H. (1956) *The Organization Man*. New York: Simon & Schuster.

Wilber, K. (2000) *A Theory of Everything*. Boston, MA: Shambala.

Wilkinson, B. (1996) 'Culture, institutions and business in East Asia', *Organizational Studies*, 17(3): 421–47.

Wilkinson, R. and Pickett, K. (2008) *The Spirit Level: Why Equal Societies Almost Always Do Better*. London: Allen Lane (Penguin Edition, 2009).

Wollstonecraft, M. (1982/1792) *Vindication of the Rights of Women*. Harmondsworth: Penguin Books.

Woodhouse, D. and Pengelly, P. (1991) *Anxiety and the Dynamics of Collaboration*. London: Routledge.

World Bank (2002) *Globalisation, Growth and Poverty: Building an Inclusive World Economy*. New York: Oxford University Press.

Yukl, G. (1998) *Leadership in Organizations*, 4th edn. Englewood Cliffs, NJ: Prentice-Hall.

Yukl, G. (1999) 'An evaluative essay on current conceptions of effective leadership', *European Journal of Work & Organizational Psychology*, 8(1): 215.

Yukl, G. (2002) *Leadership in Organisations*, 5th edn. Upper Saddle River, NJ: Prentice Hall.

Zaleznik, A. (1989) *The Managerial Mystique*. New York: Harper & Row.

Zaleznik, A. (1992) 'Managers and leaders: are they different?', *Harvard Business Review*, 70(2): 126.

Zaleznik, A. (1997) 'Real work', *Harvard Business Review*, November.

Žižek, S. (1992) *Looking Awry: An Introduction to Jaques Lacan through Popular Culture*. London: Verso.

Žižek, S. (1999) *The Ticklish Subject*. London: Verso.

Žižek, S. (2002) *Welcome to the Desert of the Real*. London: Verso.

Žižek, S. (2003) *The Puppet and the Dwarf: The Perverse Core of Christianity*. Cambridge, MA: MIT Press.

Žižek, S. (2008) *Violence: Six Sideways Reflections*. London: Profile.

Žižek, S. (2011) 'Marriage between democracy and capitalism is over', *The Raw Story*, 10 October. www.rawstory.com/rs/2011/10/10/slavoj-zizek-marriage-between-democracy-and-capitalism-is-over/ (accessed 1 February 2013).

Žižek, S. (2012) 'Occupy Wall Street: What is to be done next?', *Guardian*, 24 April. Available at www.guardian.co.uk/commentisfree/cifamerica/2012/apr/24/occupy-wall-street-what-is-to-be-done-next (accessed 12 March 2013).

Zohar, D. and Marshall, I. N. (2004) *Spiritual Capital: Wealth We Can Live By*. London: Bloomsbury.

Index

NOTE: page numbers in *italic type* refer to figures and tables, page numbers in **bold type** refer to boxes.